CRITICAL STUDIES
IN THE CYNEWULF GROUP

BY

CLAES SCHAAR

HASKELL HOUSE PUBLISHERS Ltd.
Publishers of Scarce Scholarly Books
NEW YORK. N. Y. 10012
1967

First Published 1949

HASKELL HOUSE PUBLISHERS LTD.
Publishers of Scarce Scholarly Books
280 LAFAYETTE STREET
NEW YORK. N. Y. 10012

Library of Congress Catalog Card Number: 67-30824

Haskell House Catalogue Item # 740

Preface

It is a great pleasure for me to have the opportunity, on finishing this work, to offer my thanks to Professor Olof Arngart, my teacher in English Philology. During the course of my studies I have always enjoyed the benefit of his personal kindness and constant encouragement. And ever since I began to take an interest in the problems of authorship connected with the Cynewulf group — the starting-point of this investigation — I have profited from frequent discussions with him on principles and method, and from his stimulating criticism. I here sincerely thank him for all that he has done for me during the last five years.

I also want to express my thanks to various people who have assisted me during my work. Fil. lic. Casimir Fontaine and Docent Sven Ek have given me valuable help with the interpretation of Greek texts. Mr T. S. B. Hawthorne, M. A., generously placed his time at my disposal when reading my manuscript at the licentiate stage, and Mr F. Y. Thompson, M. A., Mr J. Cross, B. A., and Miss Anne Brereton, B. A., have later kindly read different parts of it. Fil. lic. Bertil Thuresson has rendered me a great service by reading the proofs. The staff of Lund University Library have shown much patience and much kindness to me and greatly facilitated my work, and my thanks are also due to the officials of the British Museum Library, London, and the Bodleian Library, Oxford, for their kind assistance.

I cannot finish this preface without thanking my wife for all her encouragement and help during the time this book has been in the making.

Lund, April, 1949.

Claes Schaar.

Contents

I. Background

Sed modo, qui residui estis, state viriliter, pugnate fortiter, defendite castra Dei. Mementote Iudam Machabeum, quia templum Dei purgavit et populum a servitute liberavit extranea ... Hortamini vosmet ipsos invicem dicentes: 'Revertamur ad dominum Deum nostrum, quia magnus est ad ignoscendum et numquam deserit sperantes in se'.[1] — Alcuin's exhortative words to the monks of Lindisfarne after the disaster in 793, are a manifestation of the same spirit that pervades Anglo-Saxon poetry from beginning to end. Two main motifs are discernible in religious verse, revealing themselves in epic plots and lyrical reflections: the martial theme and the pious theme. The former is not restricted to accounts of struggle between human powers, as in the Cædmon group, or between human and inhuman powers as in Beowulf, but also recurs when the poets devote themselves to the problem of good and evil, as in the Cynewulf canon. Just as Alcuin regarded the Lindisfarne brethren as surrounded by enemies of the soul, waiting for an occasion to take possession of mind and body, so Cynewulf imagined the domination of sin over the mind as a successful siege, the decisive attack of a fiend after the breakdown of the moral fortifications. The pious theme is often logically bound up with the martial theme: the mind engaged in the moral struggle, as well as the military forces fighting the enemies of God, derive the strength to make resistance from an ecstatic devotion to the Lord. Just as the inhabitants of the ravaged monasteries resort to God in their distress, so the persecuted Israelites in Exodus, the tormented and imprisoned saints in Juliana and Andreas, the tempted hermit in Guthlac A, and the lonely seafarer on his perilous voyage, take their refuge with the Lord.

This double attitude to life is, of course, a feature in common with the Christianity of the early Middle Ages. However, it seems as if the insistent emphasis with which the first theme is carried through

---

[1] ed. JAFFÉ, pp. 191, 92.

in Anglo-Saxon poetry is due to special circumstances. There is, first, the Germanic descent, the inherited heroic tradition, which made it natural for Christian poets who were aware of the past to select subjects that came as close as possible to the old sagas about the adventures of the Germanic tribes. Hence the predilection for Old Testament episodes in the earliest poetry; the message of the Gospels as a subject of literary treatment was a stage in a later development. There is, no doubt, a further and more patent reason for the warlike key in the poetry of the Anglo-Saxons. The heroic fashion must have been favoured by the demands of an aristocratic audience (cp. STENTON p. 197), to whose interest contemporary poetry certainly owed much practical support and stimulus. But it is less probable that the heroic style was inspired by contemporary events: the optimism concerning the inner conditions of the country in his own time that is manifest at the end of Bede's History (*qua adridente pace ac serenitate temporum* ... cp. PLUMMER I, 351) must have been comparatively justified also in the days of Alcuin and Cynewulf, and serious violence and disorder things of the past — and of the future.

If, then, the martial theme may be looked upon as rigidly conventional, the pious theme was less probably so. Even if there are numerous signs of dissolution of monastic discipline and of laxity of faith in the 8th century (cp. HUNT, p. 223 ff), a genuine fervour is unmistakable in many of the religious poems, and the expressions of religious ideas did not become petrified to the same extent as the numerous heroic formulas. On the contrary, the frequent reminiscences from the Bible and the Fathers indicate that the Anglo-Saxon poets eagerly searched the Christian Latin literature in their endeavours to find new and more dignified ways of moulding their thoughts and feelings. And probably, from the existence of detailed legends about famous saints, we are entitled to conclude that the tradition about the great hermits and missionaries of the first one hundred and fifty years after the conversion was still fresh in the minds of the age.

It would seem natural if there were only little room for individual modifications in the religious poetry of the Anglo-Saxons, weighed down by the pressure of this double tradition. The situation of the poets in the vernacular was, no doubt, the same as that of the contemporary Latin ones, which has been well defined by MANITIUS (I, 20): "Da die poetische Sprache durch berühmte Vorbilder längst geprägt war, konnte man sich in ihr unter Beachtung der metrischen

Regeln bald zurechtfinden." And yet, it is not to the point when SCHÜCKING remarks (p. 14) that it is difficult "dichterische Persönlichkeiten zu unterscheiden". For we must here make an important distinction. Even if we cannot perceive any conscious endeavours, on the part of the poets, to assert their personalities (except for Cynewulf's successful attempts to hand down his name to posterity), it is nevertheless clear that in fashioning their style the poets have escaped the bonds of anonymity and are exposing their own individualities. As BUTTENWIESER rightly remarks (p. 62): "Die dichterische Individualität ist ein Etwas, das man schwer definieren kann ... So bleibt auch in der alten germanischen Poesie, trotz alles Formelhaften im Ausdruck und des Mangels an Originalität in den Anschauungen, doch dieses Etwas, das die Werke der verschiedenen Verfasser trennt" etc. It is this mysterious 'Etwas' that we shall try to examine a little more closely in our chapter on the style of the poems analysed. It will be seen that we can learn a great deal about an author's poetic individuality, i. e. about his mind, taste, and schooling, from his style and from his attitude to the traditions referred to, above all the vernacular tradition, and this mental physiognomy of his is perhaps more interesting than his name and birthplace. SCHÜCKING's opinion about the uniformity of Old English poetry must be said to be characteristic of scholars in general; very few critics who maintain that there are differences of style between the poems, have really demonstrated differences of a psychologically important character.

We have chosen, as the object of our analysis, a group of poems which will be termed "the Cynewulf group" and which comprises the four poems signed by this author (Elene, Juliana, Christ II, and the Fata Apostolorum); further Andreas, The Dream of the Rood, Christ I and III, Guthlac A and B, and the Phoenix. These texts occupy an intermediate position in time between the earliest poetry (the Cædmon group, Beowulf cp. p. 117), and late texts such as the Metres of Boethius and the Psalms; the Cynewulf canon is generally held to date from the end of the eight or the beginning of the ninth centuries. The search for individual characteristics is of special interest in these poems since a discussion of priority and attribution relevant to them has been going on for a long time. But this is not the only sort of criticism to which these poems give rise. They offer numerous problems of textual criticism which have not yet been satisfactorily dealt with, and an examination of some obscure passages tends to reveal the poets' original intentions. Now critical work on the Cynewulf group has been marked, hitherto, by a certain particularism. Those who have dealt with textual criticism, generally, are not those who have worked on the problems of style, and those who have gone into the question of sources have had little or nothing to do with the other two fields. Such as distribution of the problems is natural in cases when the texts are large and difficult to survey. But when it comes to such comparatively short texts as those of the Cynewulf group, this disintegration of the philological work is unnecessary and delays the emergence of a uniform critical conception. The opinions of different scholars on a certain complex of philological problems are more likely to coincide if they all have the same comprehensive view of their material than if they have not. Again, the solution of one problem is not seldom closely linked up with the solution of another. Points of textual criticism go a long way to facilitate work on stylistic questions. And the inherent difference of style and technique between the poems of the Cynewulf group would be exaggerated and the relations between them distorted unless this difference is seen in the light of a revision of the texts which will, I hope, exhibit their more normal and more authentic qualities. However, such a critical revision is not possible without an investigation of the relations of our texts to other versions of the same stories, as is further explained on p. 46. It is, further, of considerable importance for an examination of stylistic and literary qualities to see how far the Old English poets are dependent on their Latin sources, on the one hand, and on the other, to what extent the vernacular narrative manner is employed in their work.

In the respects here referred to it will be apparent, I hope, that the following three main chapters, while they may be read independently, are intended to supplement one another and to make up a single whole.

II. The Subject-matter

We shall here give an account of the Christian Latin subject-matter of our texts and briefly sketch the hagiographic or homiletic tradition underlying the poems. We shall also pay attention to the poets' independence of this tradition by examining how far events and episodes are described in terms of Anglo-Saxon civilization and ideology. This is the case with descriptions of battles and warriors; of sea, voyages, and ships; sometimes of various natural phenomena, of the beauty or the horrors of nature and scenery. References to Anglo-Saxon life and customs are also mingled with the foreign material. Passages of this kind (but not isolated words or phrases), which are generally elaborations of brief hints or short sections in the original, will be called Anglosaxonisms. We shall not, in this chapter, examine to what extent these Anglosaxonisms are due to borrowing from other poems. Such passages in Cynewulf's poetry have been analysed by DUBOIS (p. 133 ff), who, however, does not always make convincing distinctions between the Latin and the vernacular elements. Neither does KRAPP A (p. LI ff) quite clearly determine to what degree Andreas "follows the traditions of native heroic verse". The Anglosaxonisms are part of the Germanic narrative tradition, which has been thoroughly analysed by MEYER, HEUSLER, LAWRENCE, PONS, and others, whose work helps us to recognize and single out these conventional "Germanic" sections in a context imitated from a Latin original. The frequency of Anglosaxonisms is different in the different poems.

When considering the subject-matter and the tradition that lay before an Anglo-Saxon poet, we have, of course, to compare the Old English poem with the Latin version that comes closest to it. But, as a rule, this is not enough. There are nearly always divergencies in the Old English poem from the Latin version, and these divergencies may be accounted for if we extend the comparison to other versions of the same story. Thus, if a certain episode in the Old English poem should be missing in an otherwise similar Latin version, but is to be found in some other version, it is more probable that it existed in some other original than the Latin text previously compared than that the Old English poet should have drawn from this version, though with a certain freedom. Similarly most omissions may be accounted for. On the whole, one does well not to draw rash conclusions as to the independence of an Old English poet from the fact that there are some divergencies, in his work, from other versions of the same legend. Hagiographic literature was widely spread in the early Middle Ages, and we do not know how many such versions may have contained the same divergencies and are now lost. Sometimes a new version of a legend is discovered, and not rarely do we find that such a text contains some episode that is also met with in an Old English poetical version and was considered, earlier on, an innovation of the Old English poet's (cp. pp. 24, 29). In this way the range of the poet's supposed originality narrows in proportion, as more versions of his legend get known. Only the Anglosaxonisms, in fact, are certain instances of the poet's independence of the Latin original.

It is when we examine hagiographic poetry that a comparison with many other versions is of special importance. Some of our poems, however, are composed of homiletic material, and in these cases we have mostly to do with some specific source in the patristic literature.

When opinions are divided on the question of sources, I concentrate on the suggestions which seem to be the most important.

Andreas

We have first to consider the question concerning the provenance of Andreas. Behind the various difficulties of tradition there is a problem of more general importance: how widely spread was the knowledge of Greek during the eighth and ninth centuries in England and what is the contribution of the Andreas poem to the solution of this question?

The legend about the adventures of St. Andrew in the city of the cannibal Mermedonians, where he is sent by God in order to rescue St. Matthew, was extremely popular among the Christians of the first centuries. It is one of the Christian legends which have been built around a heathen framework: its strange woof of adventure story,

mixed with the studied brutality of the type found in many Old
Christian legends about saints, is explained by the narrative having
its origin, according to BLATT (p. 17), in the Greek novellistic
literature on fantastic voyages. A less probable suggestion (REINACH
p. 405 ff) takes it as far back as some Egyptian tale spread all over
the Mediterranean and the Black Sea. Anyhow, after the Christian
elements had been worked into it it must have been known in a
much wider sphere: apart from a great many Oriental versions in
Syrian, Armenian etc., Occidental translations into Greek and Latin
are preserved, though much more sparingly. The reason for their
relative rarity, as well as for the fact that they have been only lately
discovered, is probably, according to BLATT (p. 1), "dass der zum
Teil abstossende Inhalt dem kirchlichen Empfinden des Abendlandes
nicht entsprach".

When it comes to considering the affinity of the Western
translations of the legend and notably their relations to the Old
English poetic version, one has to take the following texts into
account: first the Greek Πράξεις 'Ανδρέου καὶ Ματθεία εἰς τὴν πόλιν
τῶν ἀνθρωποφάγων (P) "The acts of Andrew and Matthew in the city
of the maneaters". This prose-text, probably representing the oldest
tradition, must be taken as a starting-point. The edition used is the
one by LIPSIUS-BONNET (Acta Apostolorum Apocrypha II, 1, p. 65 ff),
reprinted by BLATT. (An earlier edition, TISCHENDORF 1851, has been
translated into English by ALEXANDER WALKER, Ante-Nicene Christian
Library, XVI, 348 ff.)

As for Latin versions of the tale, we must concentrate mainly on
the so called Casanatensis (C), which is important, getting closest
to the Greek, and on the Vaticanus (V), a rhythmic version, in many
respects differing from the Greek and a good deal shorter than the
Casanatensis. Both these texts probably go back to some date between
the 6th and the 9th centuries and are preserved, the Casanatensis in
a MS from the 12th century, the Vaticanus in one from the 11th
(BLATT p. 4). The two versions were edited with an exhaustive philological commentary by BLATT in 1930. With this group of texts one
must also compare the Old English prose legend of St. Andrew
printed by BRIGHT (B). Apart from the two long Latin versions there
is also a Latin fragment, closely corresponding to parts of chapters
17 and 18 in the Greek text and the Casanatensis, and quoted in full
in KRAPP A, p. XXIII ff. The editor points out that this fragment and
the Old English prose version form a special group that differs from

the Greek; however, the fragment is too short to be of any value in a comparison. HOLTHAUSEN (Anglia LXII, pp. 190—192) mentions the existence of a further Latin version of the legend in Bologna but only gives the opening section of this version, which, according to him, is closely related to the Casanatensis text.

Since the long Latin versions were not known earlier, the discussion concerning the original of the Old English poetic narrative (A) turned on the question whether or not the Greek legend was the source of Andreas. GRIMM's assumption that this was the case was supported by FRITZSCHE (p. 23 ff), who stresses the apparent correspondences between the Greek and the Old English texts and explains the deviations of the latter version by supposing that the poet skipped or overlooked passages in the former. LIPSIUS (I, 547 ff) thought that the source of Andreas was some unknown Latin text. The existence of such a text, he believed, was proved by a brief summary of the Andreas legend, made by Gregory of Tours, which has been worked out from a Latin text, too circumstantial, according to Gregory, to be quoted at length.

In 1886 ZUPITZA (ZfdA XXX, 175 ff) introduced the Old English prose version into the discussion: pointing out the similarity of a Latin sentence that has crept into the Old English prose text to the corresponding Greek passage, and some other parallels between the two versions, he concludes that the source of the prose text was a summary of a Latin text very similar to the Greek legend. Some details common to the two Old English versions but absent from the Greek are the names Achaia, the country from which Andrew started his expedition to the man-eaters, and Mermedonia, their city. These details, according to ZUPITZA, existed in the Latin text which in its unabridged condition lay before the Old English poet, and, summarized, was used by the prose homilist.

Among the studies on the relationship of the Old English Andreas to P it remains to mention BOURAUEL's essay, in which the author after a thorough collation of the Greek MSS and the Old English texts somewhat obscurely declares (p. 117), on the one hand that the Andreas poet did not draw from Greek material only, on the other that it is not proved that he worked exclusively with Latin sources. He thinks many texts were used by the author.

After the appearance of BLATT's edition HOLTHAUSEN (Angl. Beibl. XLIV, p. 90—91) made a brief comment, pointing out the great importance of the Casanatensis and the Vaticanus texts to future editors of Andreas. Apart from a few remarks by BLATT, no comparison of these texts with the Old English poetic and prose versions and of the whole group with the Greek original text has as yet appeared. BLATT, however, compares the Greek version with the Casanatensis and the Vaticanus texts (p. 5 ff).

Taking the five texts mentioned above into account, it is clear, first, that they divide up into two main groups according to their completeness and their general character. To the first group belong the detailed and fantastic P, C, and A; to the second the shorter and less miraculous V and B. A comparison will show the similarities and the differences.

1. Events before Andrew's departure: in all versions the apostles cast lots to decide the province to which each will carry his mission. Mattheus (C, A, B) Matthias (P, V) has the land of the maneaters assigned to him. The terrible qualities of this tribe is most fancifully described in C (the human sacrifices set forth in detail). Their city is called Mermedonia in C and twice in A, Myrmidonia in V, Marmadonia in B, Marmedonia three times in A; P has no name for it. Matthew, after his arrival in the city, is blinded by the inhabitants. He is then given a poisonous drink but although he swallows it in P, C, V, and A, he is psychically unharmed, unlike his fellow-prisoners, who turn brutish. In B, however, Matthew more realistically escapes transformation because he refuses to drink. In all texts Christ then visits Matthew in prison and promises that in 27 days Andrew will release him. In P, C, V, B Matthew now recovers his sight, but in A nothing more is said about this than that he prays to get it back. The Mermedonians enter the prison and agree that they will eat Matthew in three days. Meanwhile the Lord appears to Andrew who is preaching in Achaia (the name not in P) and commands him to go to Mermedonia and rescue Matthew. This he does after certain protests. With his attendants he walks to the coast where he sees a boat on the sea (C), at the shore (A, V, B), without further localization (P).

2. Events at the time of embarkation and during the voyage: in the vessel are Christ and two angels (P, C, A, B) in human shape; according to V all three appear as angels. Andrew, who does not recognize the men in the boat, asks where they are going (P, C, V, B); from where they come (A) (cp. p. 277). Although Andrew admits that he has no money with which to pay for a voyage, obeying the commands of Christ his Lord, he is taken into the boat after having

heard that the vessel is bound for Mermedonia (P, C, V, B); that it comes from there (A). In P, C, A Christ orders one of his angels to fetch loaves that the passengers might fortify themselves. This episode is not mentioned in V and B. A storm arises and the helmsman tempts Andrew's attendants by proposing to set them ashore so that they may safely abide the apostle's return from his dangerous expedition (P, C, A, B), but they resist this temptation. The voyage is then described differently in the two groups of texts. In P, C, A Christ asks Andrew to tell something about his Lord in order to allay the fear of his attendants. The apostle tells them the Genezareth episode, and they finally fall asleep. Andrew praises the helmsman's skill, but the latter attributes the smooth running of his boat to the presence of a servant of God. A lengthy conversation now ensues: the Lord first asks Andrew why the Jews did not believe in Jesus and insinuates that the reason was His inability to work miracles. Andrew indignantly answers by enumerating a list of wonders (the curing of sick people, the changing of water into wine, the feeding of the multitude). Christ asks whether He really worked these miracles in the presence of the leaders and the scribes and not only before the people (cp. p. 55). Andrew asserts that the chiefs also saw and heard the power of the Lord and then relates a long tale about the unbelief of the priests and about one of two sphinxes Cherubim and Seraphim, who by the orders of the Saviour begins to speak and praise the power of Christ and His divine origin in the presence of the incredulous priests. The priests, however, persist in their scepticism. In P and A another miracle is now related about Christ and the sphinx: In a last attempt to convince the unbelievers the image is told to go to the tombs of Abraham, Isaac and Jacob, to rouse the patriarchs out of their sleep and command them to come and extol the divinity of Jesus. They all do as they are told. All these fantastic occurrences are more lengthily related in A than in P and C.

Andrew now falls asleep and is carried, together with his likewise sleeping disciples, by the two angels through the air as far as the city of the Mermedonians, where they are placed on the ground before the gates. The angels then ascend into Heaven. When the three men wake up, Andrew realizes that the man in the boat was Christ himself. His disciples tell their master about a dream: it seemed to them that they were transported to Heaven by two angels in the shape of eagles and saw Christ in all His glory surrounded by angels, patriarchs, and apostles. Andrew makes an apology for not having recognized the Lord. Christ appears as a young man, orders the apostle to go into the city and release Matthew, prophesies the cruel treatment of Andrew but tells the apostle not to fear for his life. Andrew enters the city without being seen by anyone, accompanied by his disciples (P, C; in A nothing is said about them).

V and B differ from this version inasmuch as they dispense with most of these fabulous episodes. All that occurs in B before Andrew's arrival in the city of the man-eaters is a brief description of the Genezareth episode by Andrew after Christ has asked him to comfort his disciples; further the transport through the air, Andrew's apology, the revelation of the Lord before the apostle, and His command and prophecy. Then Andrew and his two disciples invisibly enter the city.

In V there is no question of a storm. The angel steering the vessel asks Andrew to tell him about the native country, the family, and the miracles of his Lord, and the apostle gives a short biography of Christ. The angel says he wishes God to protect the three men during their stay in the dangerous country. They have now reached the shore and Andrew asks for the sailor's name. The angel reveals his identity and Andrew suddenly finds himself alone with his attendants. He praises God and a divine voice is heard from above commanding and prophesying as in the other versions. Andrew then goes into the city.

3. Andrew among the Mermedonians: the events in the city are in the main different in the two text-groups but between V and B there are also certain divergencies. In P, C, A and B Andrew walks through the city to the dungeon where Matthew is imprisoned. When he approaches the door seven guards, standing in front of it, fall dead to the ground (not in V). The doors open automatically, Andrew enters and discovers Matthew and his fellow-prisoners. He then rebukes the devil in a speech missing in A, where there is a gap in the text, and in B, where the text is intact. The release of the prisoners is related more in detail in P, C, and B than in A; in the former texts Matthew and Andrew (only Andrew in P and B) put their hands on the prisoners' eyes and hearts, and they recover their sight and wits. They are then told to go with Matthew out of the town, sit down under a fig-tree and eat of its fruit: in P and C it is added that the more they eat, the more fruit the tree will bear. Matthew and the others leave the town (in P and B eastwards) and are carried, at Andrew's entreaty, by a cloud on to the top of a mountain where St. Peter is standing. In B they get to the hilltop without the help of

a cloud. The number of people thus released is 270 men and 49 women in some of the MSS of P, 248 men and 49 women in one MS and in C and B, 249 men in two MSS; cp. BLATT p. 10.

In A the liberation is quickly achieved: the crowd is just delivered and led by Matthew out of town, swept in a cloud; no curing of blindness, no fig-tree, no mountain with St. Peter standing on the top. The number is here 240 men and 49 women, but two half-lines (1036 b and 1040 b) are missing.

In V we get yet another version of the episode in the prison; before the prisoners get their sight and their freedom back they are baptized, and then without further ado they leave the town as in A, though without the cloud as in B. In V we hear of 297 converted people.

In all the texts Andrew now goes to the centre of the city and sits down under a pillar. When the man-eaters discover the escape of the prisoners they are seized with anger and bewilderment, death by starvation being imminent. In P and C the hungry people take the bodies of the seven guards in order to eat them; in both versions the hands of the men, at the point of cutting up the carcasses, petrify as the result of a prayer said by the invisible Andrew. In A we are only told, laconically, that the cannibals ate the dead bodies — *nyston beteran ræd*. In V and B the more or less successful feeding on the guards is avoided.

P, C, and A go on revelling in the atrocities of the Mermedonians. In P and C, after the failure with the cannibal meal, a crowd is summoned and seven old men are picked out by lots to make up for the lost food. One of them offers his son instead and later also his daughter. This is not enough for C: here the two children have to be weighed up and are accepted by the cannibals only when they turn out to weigh as much as their father. The swords of the Mermedonians, about to slaughter the children, melt away after another prayer of the apostle. In A the same things happen, though we only hear of one old man and his son. V and B exclude the whole scene. In all the versions the devil now appears in human shape and points out to the terrified bystanders the presence of Andrew. In V and B, then, this happens immediately after the cannibals have discovered that their prison is empty.

In P, A, and B Andrew is still invisible and has a dialogue with the devil till the Lord tells him to appear and he is caught. In the two Latin texts the Mermedonians rush at Andrew as soon as they hear that he is among them. In P they discuss what to do with him and agree on putting a rope round his neck and dragging him through the streets each day till he dies. In C, before this method is decided on, the men attacking Andrew shrink from him seeing the sign of a Cross on his forehead. This text also has a different dialogue between Andrew and the tempting devil. In V it is only when Andrew remains alive after ill-treatment that the torture is decided upon; in B it is carried out on the devil's advice, in A he has nothing to do with the decision.

Andrew is now dragged through the streets of the city each day for three days; the nights he spends in the dungeon. All versions except C describe the torture of each day; in this text we learn that it has gone on for so long only when Andrew finally complains of his sufferings. In P, A, and B the devil with seven attendants (in A with six) appears in the prison, during the night before the third day, scorning and tempting the apostle; here the episode about the sign on his forehead is put in. On the third day Andrew is worn out and bemoans his torments (P, C, A, B); Christ shows him that trees are flowering on the ground where his flesh and hair were recently spread out (P, C, A, B); gives him to know that his torments are now finished (all versions), and says that on Andrew's command a certain image of stone will let forth a torrent which will punish the heathen tribe (all versions). Andrew speaks to the image, and water gushes forth from its mouth and floods the city, rising till it reaches the necks of the inhabitants. They flee in all directions, and the terror and bewilderment is increased by the water being so briny as to corrode the flesh of the men (P, C, B). On top of it all the city is encircled by a girdle of fire preventing the Mermedonians from getting out. The inhabitants of the chastized city now begin to cry and ask for mercy. Andrew orders the fire and water to recede; the fire disappears and into an abyss in the earth the flood goes down, carrying with it þa wyrrestan of the inhabitants (P, C, A).

The end is similar in P, C, A, and B: Andrew bids the people who were drowned by the water to arise, the converted heathens are baptized, a church is built and a bishop (called Platan in A, Plato in V) ordained; Andrew leaves the Mermedonians after his departure has been put off for seven days.

V, however, takes a course of its own: the man-eaters, overcome by water, fire, and the spiritual power of Andrew, kneel to him and ask from where he gets his strength. There follows a summary of parts of the Old and New Testaments: Andrew's first sermon addressed to the converted people. The drowned men are recalled to life, all are converted, Plato is ordained as the bishop among many priests, Andrew finally returns triumphantly to Achaia where he is pompously received by the people.

*

Considering first the relation of A to C and P, it is obvious that its affinities to both of them are very close. But as the text most similar to A we have still to put up with P: the divergencies in C are too many to allow it to occupy the position of the Greek text. Thus in C the episode with the sphinx and the three patriarchs is missing, further this version condenses the capture of Andrew to a single fairly short sentence; the devils of P, A, and B do not visit him in prison; each day of torture is not described as in the other versions. Still, the Casanatensis goes a long way to fill up the tradition of the legend represented by P and A. The form Mermedonia in A is supported by C. Again, C and A differ from P on the following points:

1. C 1, 18 ... *menteque iam non habentes, ... fenum ut boves vel pecora conmedebant*; A 38 ff *ac hie hig ond gærs ... gedrehte* (speaking of the fatal effect of the poisonous drink; P, V, B only say that the prisoners' minds change).

2. Further the speech of the Lord intended to induce Andrew to go and rescue Matthew is more elaborate in C and A than in the other versions; to C 4, 3 ff *descende in civitatem que dicitur mermedonia, et proficiscere in ea, quia ibi sunt conmorantes iniqui et pessimi viri, et eorum sanguinem bibunt. Ibique mittam te ad eos, ... et eruas de carcere matheum quem ante te ibi missum habui ... Quoniam ecce tantum tres dies restant, ad producendum eum ad interficiendum, et conmedendum* answers, with small divagations, A 174 ff *Đu scealt feran ond frið lædan, siðe gesecan, þær sylfœtan eard weardigað, eðel healdaþ morðorcræftum ... Đær ic seomian wat þinne sigebroðor mid þam burgwarum bendum fæstne. Nu bið fore þreo niht þæt he on þære þeode sceal fore hæðenra handgewinne þurh gares gripe gast onsendan, ellorfusne, butan ðu ær cyme*. The comments on the man-eaters are not met with in the other versions, nor are the laboured passages comparable to the short commands of the other texts.

3. When Andrew and his disciples are about to embark for Mermedonia C and A give the logical sequence 1) the temptation of the
Lord 2) Andrew's resisting it; C 6, 10 ff: *dominus ... dixit, quid enim
daturi estis nobis, naulum naviculationis? Et respondens sanctus
andreas ... Crede mihi frater, quia nec aurum habeo, neque argen-
tum* etc. A 292 ff *We ðe ... mid us willað ferigan ... syððan ge
eowre gafulrædenne agifen habbað ...; Andreas ... mælde: næbbe ic
fæted gold ne feohgestreon* etc. It should be observed that Andrew's
remark l. 271 (*þeh ic beaga lyt ...*) is occasional and does not form
part of the conversation about payment, which does not start till
l. 295. The untimely mention of Andrew's poverty in A must be
regarded as one of the instances of the inferior narrative technique
in this poem, cp. further p. 318 ff. Anyway, this little slip is by
no means comparable to the different structure of the episode in P.
This text misses the point by letting Andrew start the discussion
about the ναῦλον. The A and C tradition here agrees with the V and
B ones in supporting a better reading, but the wording, especially
that of Andrew's reply, is peculiar to V and B: V has *respondit
nauta nobis vos dignum prebete naulum ... Tunc ... apostolus: Hoc
namque preceptum noster nobis donavit didascalus ne virgam quidem
peramque in via ... feramus*; and B ... *sellað us eowerne færsceat.
Se haliga Andreas him andswarode, Gehyrað gebroþor, nabbað we
færsceat ...* (Christ says:) *nabbe ge mid eow hlaf, ne feoh* etc.

4. In P, ch. 12, the Lord goes with His disciples into the desert
and works miracles in their presence in order to strengthen their
faith which has been shaken by the incredulous words of the chief
priests. In C and A, however, this motivation is lost (A ll. 696 ff);
and P is here the more consistent version: if the apostles, as in C
and A, had not become sceptical after the priests' speech, there was
no need to take them apart to regain their confidence by a demonstra-
tion of miracles (cp. BLATT p. 55). There is, however, this difference
between C and A that whereas C expressly says: *Nos autem audientes
hec verba incredulitatis, nichil eorum respondentibus, set cor nostrum
perseveravit in verbo veritatis eius*, such a positive declaration of
faith is not made in A, which only tells us that the priests tried to
entice the apostles to desert the Lord. But we clearly understand from
the passage that the priests did so unsuccessfully.

5. After Andrew and his disciples have woken up after the flight
with the angels the apostle tells the others the truth about the helmsman of the boat. This passage is strikingly shorter in C and A than

in P. C has (17, 6) *quia in illa nave in qua veniebamus, ipse nauclerius cum quo loquebamus dominus erat iesus christus, ipse enim tenebat oculos nostros ne eum agnosceret, propterea non agnovimus eum,* corresponding to A 854 ff *In þam ceole wæs cyninga wuldor, waldend werðeode. Ic his word oncneow, þeh he his mægwlite bemiðen hæfde.* Then the disciples tell him of their dream. P has a fuller speech, beginning with the favour shown to them by the presence of Christ in the boat; then comes the explanation why they could not recognize him: "He had made Himself similar to the helmsman of a boat, and humbled Himself, and He appeared to us as a human being, for He wanted to tempt us." Andrew then in a prayer apologizes for his ignorance. It is only here that the disciples' dream comes in.

6. Andrew has finally been caught by the Mermedonians, and in P the people engage in a discussion on what to do with the intruder: beheading and burning are looked upon as not sufficiently drastic modes of death, and finally a man, possessed with the devil, suggests in detail the torture which is then used to punish the apostle. This preliminary part is not found in A and C: after the respective dialogues of these versions between Andrew and the devil, and after God's command in A that the apostle shall appear to the cannibals, the torture begins at once: C 28, 6 *mittentes funiculas in collo eius, trahentes eum per omnes vicos*; A 1229 ff *Heton þa lædan ofer landsceare ... Drogon deormodne æfter dunscræfum* etc.

Consequently one might say, in view of our comparisons, that even if in the main A comes closer to P than to C, the C text is more akin to it as regards the shaping of certain details.

Now for the earlier much debated question whether the source of Andreas was a Latin or a Greek text. Any definite proof for the one or the other alternative has as yet not been found, but nowadays scholars generally agree in assuming some Latin text not preserved. Apriori evidence alone, it must be admitted, very strongly supports this view. One might observe that in Alfred's time, according to his complaints in the Preface of the Pastoral Care, the knowledge of Latin was in a sad state not only in the South but probably also *begiondan Humbre.* Greek is not even mentioned. Even earlier, when classical learning flourished in England, knowledge of Greek must have been considered an utter rarity. The influence exerted by the Canterbury School, where no doubt Greek was taught since Theodore's and Hadrian's days (STENTON p. 181), was strongly felt in the monastic civilization of Northumbria (HODGKIN I, p. 309), but the number of people thoroughly understanding a Greek text was probably very small, according to such a reliable authority as LAISTNER. Bede must be counted among them (LAISTNER p. 125); cp. also PLUMMER p. LIV. But Alcuin, in whose writings many Greek words and phrases occur, is proved by LAISTNER to have taken this Greek matter over bodily from Jerome and other writers (p. 192).

In fact, it seems as if Greek erudition in Western Europe during the early Middle Ages, apart from Ireland where it was evidently more widely spread, was met with only in men whose culture was at the height of what was possible in this period. There was another group of people "knowing Greek", as LAISTNER points out, those who were acquainted with its alphabet, a few passages, or a few words, but this category we need not take into account here.

That a Latin text was used by the author of Andreas seems thus, a priori, to be fairly certain. It must have been very similar to P and the treatment of some details it had in common with C.

Before we leave the questions connected with the Andreas texts, it remains to consider the relation of the Old English prose version to the other versions and notably to the Anglo-Saxon poem. The prose version B seems to be an abridgement of the longer narrative in P, C, and A, but is not very closely related to V. Thus we can distinguish a popular tradition (P, C, A), which has been provided with fantastic and fabulous elements: as many miracles and supernatural tales as possible have been crammed into it, and so the lengthy dialogical digressions during the voyage have been produced, unnecessary to the plot of the poem. Another tradition is represented by V, which dispenses with nearly all the thaumaturgical elements but contains a great deal of edifying and moralizing matter. B may be said to form an intermediate link between these traditions: some of the marvellous details have been omitted (various miracles related during the voyage); others are retained (the flight through the air with the angels, the miracle of the flowering trees growing out of the blood-stained ground).

As a deviation from the text of the source, we have apparently to consider the curious autobiographical passage at ll. 1478—1489 a in which the poet expresses his doubts as to his capacity to tell the story about Andrew. After some hesitation he nevertheless decides to relate a bit further *lytlum sticcum*. This section is interesting since it may contain a personal confession on the part of the author, even if we must not overlook the possibility that the diffidence of these lines may be conventional. Personally I am inclined to think that the poet, in this passage, regrets that he does not know more about the saint and his life: *Ðæt scell æglæwra mann on moldan þonne ic me tælige findan on ferðe, þæt fram fruman cunne eall þa earfeðo þe he mid elne adreah.* The poem is very rich in details which are not to be found in the other versions but must be explained as parts of the heroic poetical tradition. Apart from borrowings and imitations from earlier poetry, which will be dealt with in ch. IV, 7, we have, first, the representation of the apostles ll. 7 ff as a band of brave and famous warriors. Ll. 45 ff the Mermedonians meet Matthew as an army meets the enemy. Ll. 125 b ff the Mermedonians, preparing themselves to see that their prisoners are alive, are portrayed as an army ready for the field. 230 ff Andrew, prepared for his mission to the man-eaters, appears as a warrior, bold, resolute, brave: *gearo to campe.* (The passage does not fit in with the context, cp. p. 320). 405 ff Andrew's disciples, refusing to abandon their master, express themselves like the retainers of a Germanic chieftain. KRAPP (A, note) rightly compares Tacitus, Germania 14, Wiglaf's speech Beow. 2884 ff, and Mald. 220 ff. Also the final section of the poem, ll. 1706— 1722, is much elaborated as compared with the other versions, as KRAPP (A, note) points out. The departure by water is no invention of the poet's, as KRAPP thinks (ibid.); such an episode is also found in the Vaticanus. KRAPP finds a reminiscence from the close of Beowulf ll. 3179—3183 in the account of the Mermedonians' farewell to the apostle. But there is only a general similarity and we have hardly an instance of imitation here. To these Anglosaxonisms we may also add the frequent descriptions of natural phenomena: dawn (123 ff, 241 b ff, 836 b ff), night (1247 b ff, 1304 ff, 1456 b ff), winter weather (1255 ff), storm (369 b ff) etc.

Elene

Among the numerous versions of the legend about the finding of the Cross the one most similar to the Old English epic is, no doubt, as is generally held, the Vita Quiriaci of the Acta Sanctorum (Mai I, 450 ff). There are also, however, other Latin versions that come close to Elene: the Inventio Sanctæ Crucis, edited by HOLDER, and the legend in the Vitæ Sanctorum (MOMBRITIUS). As HOLTHAUSEN remarks (p. XII), Cynewulf's source must have been closely related to these three Latin legends. A certain stability of transmission, however, must have existed in the tradition about the finding of the Cross such as we have it in Cynewulf's poem. The legend seems to have originated in Syria, and a comparison of two Syrian versions with the Old English one (RYSSEL p. 8ff, NESTLE p. 43 ff), reveals fairly close correspondences. After HOLTHAUSEN's collations of Elene with other versions of the Cross legend (ZfdPh XXXVII, 1 ff, Archiv CXXV, 83 ff), we are in a position to single out those portions of Elene which are not elsewhere to be found (cp. HOLTHAUSEN p. XIII). The poet follows his original in the broad outline of the narrative and in certain details. The advance of the heathen army, the preparations of the Romans, Constantine's fears, his dream, the sign of the Cross, the successful fight, Constantine's queries about the Cross, the answer of the wise men, the revelation of the Christian truth, Constantine's baptism, Elene's expedition, her arguments with the Jews, Judas's speech, his argument with the queen, the torture and the result, Judas's prayer, the finding of the crosses, the miracle of the Cross of Christ, Judas's dispute with the devil, Elene's admiration of Judas's faith, the adornment of the Cross and the erection of a church, Judas's baptism and ordination as a bishop, Elene's demand for the nails of the Cross, the finding of the nails, the joy of all, the prophecy, the queen's doings before the departure; all these episodes belong to the traditional legend. A detail peculiar to Elene is the episode about the message to Constantine after the finding of the Cross, the joy of the emperor and his subjects, and his despatch in return ordering Elene to build a church (ll. 967—1016). The close of Cynewulf's poem (1236—1321), with religious and elegiac meditations and the account of Judgment Day, is Cynewulf's addition and not found in the other versions. Obvious Anglosaxonisms are the detailed descriptions of the approach of the heathens, the battle and the overthrow of the enemies (ll. 18 b—53, 105—143); further Elene's voyage to the land of the Jews (225—275), which is apparently inspired by similar passages in Beowulf (cp. p. 240 ff). Among the details in the Vita missing in Elene one may mention Elene's interest in the tradition about the Crucifixion and the queen's destruction of the temple of Venus (cp. GLÖDE, Anglia IX, p. 309). The style of Cynewulf's poem is much fuller than that of the Latin legends.

In a few cases critics have raised doubts as to the originality of some of the episodes here referred to. Thus Brown (Engl. Stud. XL, 1 ff), pointing out some interesting (though sometimes doubtful) correspondences between Elene and a Middle Irish version, the Leabhar Breac from the 14th century, remarks that a description of the voyage, missing in other versions of the legend, links Elene up with this Irish version (p. 17). This link, according to Brown, is Leabhar Breac l. 112: ... "über das tyrrhenische Meer ostwärts nach Asien". The author, however, omits the context of the Irish version, which, in Schirmer's translation, is to the following effect (p. 33): "so schickt er (Konstantin) Boten mit einem Schreiben über das tyrrhenische Meer ostwärts nach Asien an den Ort, wo seine Mutter, nämlich die selige, gerechte Helena weilte ...". Helena, then, was already in Asia when she received the emperor's message, and we do not, in the Irish version, hear of a voyage that she makes herself in order to arrive in the land of the Jews. On the contrary, the Leabhar Breac, like the Vita Quiriaci, only states: "sie ging daher nach der Stadt, nämlich Jerusalem". Moreover, the detailed description of the voyage in Elene is not at all comparable to the brief line in the Leabhar Breac. The difference, consequently, between the episodes in Elene and in the Irish text is greater than the similarity.

As a matter of fact, too much loose criticism is often indulged in by critics pointing to some new version of a legend or an episode, such scholars being easily apt to exaggerate the importance of their discovery. Thus Grau, comparing Elene ll. 1236 ff with passages taken from a sermon by St. Ephrem the Syrian (*Lamentatio ex ipsius doctrina*), categorically asserts: "Dass der Dichter die Lamentatio als getrenntes Stück gekannt hat, ist nicht zu bezweifeln" (p. 25). But Grau's parallels are more than doubtful; to quote only some examples: El. 1242 b ff *Ic wæs weorcum fah, synnum asæled, sorgum gewæled, bitrum gebunden, bisgum beþrungen* is said to correspond with *Hei mihi, defecerunt dies mihi, et iniquitates meæ multiplicatae sunt*; 1245 ff *ær me lare onlag þurh leohtne had gamelum to geoce* etc. with *qui me in hoc religionis habitu beatum censebant ac prædicabant*; 1249 a *bancofan onband, breostlocan onwand* with *qui renes scrutatur et corda*(!); 1256 b ff *A wæs secg oð ðæt cnyssed cearwelmum, ꝸ drusende* with ... *cum interim essem intus immunditia et iniquitate plenus*(!) etc. It is obvious that nothing can be concluded from such "parallels", which hardly deserve that name even when judged by the most modest philological standards. In all probability the "autobiographical" section and the acrostic passage in Elene are the poet's own original invention. On the other hand, it seems likely that the last section, ll. 1277—1321, was inspired by some theological treatise on the Judgment Day, but, as far as I know, there is nothing to indicate that Cynewulf borrowed the phrasing of his version from such a source. That he may have taken over the general idea is another matter, and the description of the events after the Judgment Day which most closely resembles his concluding lines is, as DUBOIS has shown (p. 78), the *Sermo* CIV, 8, by St. Augustine (*Sors triplex hominum in judicio*, MIGNE P. L. 39, 1949), which contains the same division of humanity into three groups as we find in Elene: one group, the righteous, are not injured by Purgatory; another, the morally tepid, must remain there for a long time; a third, the sinners, must stay there for ever. Cynewulf, then, seems indebted to St. Augustine for the matter, though not for the form, of part of his final section ll. 1236 ff.

Juliana

The legend of St. Juliana has come down to us in several versions. The oldest is the legend of Acta Sanctorum (Feb. II, 875 ff); and later Latin versions are the Alia Vita (Petrus Subdiaconus) three Munich texts published by BRUNÖHLER, the version of the Legenda Aurea, and the text of the Bodley MS 285, printed by D'ARDENNE in her edition of the ME life of St. Juliana, contained in Royal MS 17 A 27 and Bodley MS 34. A ME poetic version is preserved in the Ashmole MS 43. There is also a Scottish legend, and other versions are preserved in Greek, in Middle High German, in Old French, in Italian, and in Old Swedish. Cynewulf's version and the Acta have the main events of the story and many details in common.

In both versions we hear of a Christian maiden Juliana, living in Nicomedia (Cynewulf Commedia) during the reign of Maximianus, the persecutor of the Christians; of her heathen father and of the rich Eleusius (Cynewulf Heliseus), her heathen wooer. We learn of her refusal to marry Heliseus unless he renounces idolatry and turns to the Christian God. In both versions Juliana has a controversy with her father who, after unsuccessful attempts to persuade her and to break her resistance forcibly, hands her over to Heliseus. He tries in vain to entice her to give up her faith, and Juliana is then scourged twice. Both versions have dialogues between the wrathful heathen and the indomitable saint. Juliana is then imprisoned, still a staunch Christian; a demon appears in the shape of an angel; his identity is soon revealed with the help of God, and Juliana compels him to tell all the crimes he has comitted from the beginning of the world. Large portions of both versions are devoted to the detailed description of these evil deeds. Juliana is then taken out of the prison and tortured with fire and molten lead, neither of which can harm her since she is preserved by an angel. Heliseus then orders her execution, the saint says a prayer and is beheaded; her body is solemnly buried, but Heliseus and his men perish miserably on the sea.

Before we consider the most important differences between the Acta and Cynewulf's poem it is necessary to make an important reservation: Cynewulf's Juliana is a mutilated poem. After l. 288 a folio has been lost, and similarly after l. 558. For this reason part of the conversation between the demon and Juliana is missing, and the second gap corresponds to the first half of the third chapter in the Acta, which contains a dialogue between Juliana and Heliseus, a description of torture with a knifestudded wheel and fire, and a prayer in which the saint evokes scenes from biblical history. The Acta then tells us that a large number of the Nicomedians were converted, that they prayed to God, and that they were executed by order of their heathen lord. Cynewulf no doubt took over the conversion of the people since the lines immediately after the gap contain the end of a passage describing their praise of the Christian God, but he, or his source, excluded the wholesale execution of the converts (cp. p. 95).

The most important comparisons of Cynewulf's poem with the Acta have been made by BACKHAUS, GLÖDE (Anglia XI, 146 ff), and GARNETT (less thoroughly). According to BACKHAUS (p. 53) the author of the Liflade did not know Cynewulf's poem. GLÖDE (p. 158) says that the Acta cannot have been Cynewulf's source, and GARNETT (p. 288) holds that the source was a text similar to the Acta and that Cynewulf was not a slavish follower of the text but worked independently. BRUNÖHLER (p. 41) thinks that all the non-Latin versions are based on some unknown Latin original. According to KENNEDY (p. 209) "there is nothing in *Juliana* so alien to the Latin of the *Acta* as to indicate that the poet *must* have been using a different text. Cynewulf would naturally have used his source material with a poet's freedom".

Several divergencies from the text of the Acta, however, are supported by other versions of the legend. We shall compare Cynewulf's poem with the ME texts, the MHG Priester Arnolts Legende von St. Juliane, the Scottish fourteenth century legend, and the OF La Vie sainte Juliane:

1. The Acta says that Juliana's mother detested the pagan rites (cp. GLÖDE p. 154). Cynewulf omits the passage, and so do the authors of the ME, the Scottish, and the OF versions.

2. Unlike the version of the Acta, Juliana intends to preserve her maidenhood for the love of Christ (ll. 28—31) although, a few lines further down, she offers to marry Heliseus on condition that he is converted to Christianity. For this inconsistency Cynewulf, however, can hardly be blamed, as STRUNK believes (p. XXXIV), the same version being met with in The Liflade and in the OF version (cp. D'ARDENNE p. XXIII).

3. In the Acta Juliana, after Heliseus has asked her to marry him, tries to delay her decision by telling the suitor that he must become a prefect before she can accept him. Then, after he has fulfilled this condition, she invents a new pretext for escaping him: unless he converts himself to Christianity it is impossible for her to comply with his wishes. This deceitful attitude of the saint is also met with in the Liflade, the Ashmolean poem, and the OF version. In Cynewulf the demand that Heliseus shall become a prefect is duly left out, but the Old English poet is not alone in omitting this morally doubtful incident: it is also missing in Arnolt's poem and the Scottish Juliana. It seems therefore probable that this omission belonged to some other tradition than that of the Acta. BRUNÖHLER's remark (p. 38) that this omission is only "zufällig" is doubtful; he shows that it occurs also in one of the Munich texts, in a MHG short version and in the Legenda Aurea, and it seems probable that an omission in the original of these versions was also characteristic of Cynewulf's source. Anyhow we need not assume, with KENNEDY (p. 210), that "Cynewulf, undoubtedly finding a blemish of characterization in this duplicity, and in subordination of a prenuptial proviso so important in the eyes of the Church, omits all reference to the prefecture" etc.

4. In Cynewulf ll. 227 ff Juliana is scourged a third time, which detail the Old English version has in common with the Liflade — but not the Ashmolean and the OF versions, as D'ARDENNE says (p. XXIII). It is one of the few instances where an addition is made to what occurs in the oldest Latin text.

5. In the Acta, when Juliana has been imprisoned, before the appearance of the devil, she says a prayer in which God is asked to preserve her as He preserved Daniel in the lion's den, the three men in the fiery furnace, the sons of Israel in the desert, etc. In Arnolt there is only a small remnant of this prayer ll. 249 ff; and in the other versions only the Liflade preserves it in full. In Cynewulf it is shortened into a few lines of indirect speech ll. 238 ff.

6. Another prayer in the Acta said by Juliana in a moment of weakness, after the prayer and the execution of the converts and before the intervention of the angel, is avoided by the Old English poet as well as by Arnolt and the Ashmole and Scottish poets.

7. The end of the legend is rendered in different ways in the different versions. In the Acta the saint's body is buried by *mulier Sephonia senatrix* in Puteoli; Arnolt has no mention at all of a removal of Juliana's body. The OF version makes the body rest *En Esturges en la montangnie*; the Liflade comes closest to the Acta, bringing the body with *a seli wummon sophie inempnet* to Campania, but Puteoli is not mentioned. So also Ashmole. The Scottish Juliana, like Arnolt, avoids the detail. In Cynewulf's Juliana the people of Nicomedia bury the saint in their city.

8. All versions, except Cynewulf's, contain names of heathen gods such as Apollo, Diana, etc.; or the names of Satan, Beelzebub, Belial. The avoidance of these terms in Cynewulf corresponds to his omitting the name of Venus in Elene.

We see, then, that the most striking divergencies from the Acta, instead of pointing to Cynewulf's free treatment, seem rather to indicate dependence on a different tradition.

An interesting problem is the source of ll. 382—413, in which the devil's temptations and deceptions are described as a regular siege carried out according to a definite strategical scheme. STRUNK (p. 56) thinks that there is an echo of Ephes. VI, 10—19, and DUBOIS (p. 139) and KENNEDY (p. 211) have similar views. However, I think we may come closer to the original of the passage, whose imagery is not of an Anglo-Saxon character. I suggest that the poet in his description of the righteous man armed by God, and of the soul as a fortified city, may have been inspired by Jerome's eloquent *Comment. in Ep. ad Ephesios*, Lib. III, ch. VI (MIGNE, P. L. 26, 543 ff): *Ad extremum quasi vir bellator et fortis, omnes sectas contrarias veritati concidet, interficiet, jugulabit, gladium spiritus, id est, verbum Dei, manu tenens ... Si enim abstinuerimus nos a corporum voluptate, parum*

*cautos in avaritia (diabolus) capit. Quod si et avaritiam cum voluptate
contemnimus, per luxuriam irrepit, et facit nobis ventrem esse deum,
et per hanc etiam illa quæ fortia esse videbantur, expugnat. Et
quomodo solent sapientes exercituum principes, ea vel
maxime oppugnare urbium loca quæ parum munita
sunt, ut cum per illa irruperint, facile munita capi-
antur; ita et diabolus per ea quæ patere videt, aut
certe non firmiter clausa, quærit irrumpere, et ad
ipsam arcem cordis et animæ pervenire.* Here we have not
only the idea underlying ll. 393—413 a in Cynewulf, but also closely
corresponding metaphors. I fail to see that "l'élément germanique
l'emporte sur l'élément latin, et Bélial, décochant à son adversaire
les flèches de la tentation, ressemble fort à l'archer des armées anglo-
saxonnes dont les traits empoisonnés se fichent au cœur de l'ennemi"
(DUBOIS, p. 140); cp. Ephes. VI, 16 *scutum fidei, in quo possitis omnia
tela nequissimi ignea extinguere.*

But on some points Juliana is obviously independent of the
Christian Latin tradition. Anglosaxonisms are to be found in the
account of the destruction of the heathens, ll. 671 b ff, who perish
in the waves as a band of Vikings; this conventional description is
continued ll. 683 ff, where the heathens' stay in hell is depicted as
the melancholy situation of retainers who are deprived of the
customary joy at receiving precious gifts from their leader in the hall
(cp. DUBOIS pp. 139, 147). Heliseus, ll. 18 ff, is further portrayed as
a powerful chieftain, and we notice the striking and highly conventional lines with the two warriors ll. 62 ff (also noticed by KENNEDY
p. 213), a small detail standing out distinctly in the context.

The subject-matter of the poem, of course, sets certain limits to
possible Anglosaxonisms in Juliana: the female hero does not give
rise to comments on all the qualities and virtues generally eulogized
in Old English poetry and reserved for men. (It will be observed that
even the author of Judith is none too ingenious when it comes to
elaborating the excellent qualities of his heroine.)

Christ II and the Fata Apostolorum

The second part of the Christ trilogy raises problems of quite
another character than Elene and Juliana. In Christ we have not to
do with a legend extant in many versions dating from different

epochs. The poem is a homiletic one and contains far more lyrical and invocatory matter than we find in the epics. The poem also, unlike the two other works, points to a special text as its chief source: to DIETRICH (short remark p. 204) and COOK (C XLIII, 115 ff) belongs the honour of having designated the end of the 29th Homily of Gregory the Great, the Homily on the Ascension (MIGNE P. L. 76, 1218 ff), as the model of Cynewulf's poem. An additional source, according to COOK C (p. 116 ff), is a hymn by Bede (*Hymnum canamus gloriæ*). All the sections in Gregory's homily are to be found in Cynewulf's poem, interpolated with scriptural passages and lyrical comments in the following way, according to COOK C (p. 114 ff).

Into the middle of Gregory's introductory explanation of the robes of the angels appearing at the Ascension Cynewulf inserts a description of the Ascension according to the Gospel and of the return of the apostles to Jerusalem (ll. 456—545). Then Gregory's explanation is continued till l. 557. The Harrowing of Hell follows and some meditations on the subject, and the remaining lines before 612 are taken up by a lyrical passage on the Grace of God. Then, up to l. 755, we get Gregory almost uninterrupted: the Ascension of Christ incarnate, symbolized by Job as the flight of a bird; human achievements are the gifts of the Lord; the Church is fortified by the Ascension; Christ's work of salvation is symbolized in six leaps: the descent to the Virgin, into the manger, to the Cross, into the tomb, into hell (not Gregory), up to Heaven. An admonition to mankind to follow Christ into Heaven. 756—782 Another interpolation: angels and our own prayers protect us against the arrows of the devil, cp. above p. 30. 782—796 Gregory: the terror of the Judgment; 797—807 Cynewulf's rune passage; 807—849 the Judgment continued, and finally Gregory's hope for salvation from the sin and inconstancy of the world.

An interesting thing about the style of the beginning of Christ II is that its repetitions seem to be inspired by corresponding mannerisms in Gregory and that thus a tendency in Anglo-Saxon poetical style is supported by his rhetoric. Instances are:

Hoc autem nobis primum quæ-rendum est, quidnam sit quod nato Domino apparuerunt angeli, et tamen non leguntur in albis vestibus apparuisse …	443 ff. … *hu þæt geeode … þæt þær in hwitum hræglum gewerede englas ne oðeowdun, þa se æþe-ling cwom, beorn in Betlem.* …

Quid est ergo quod nato Domino,   453 b ff. *Hwæþre in bocum ne*
non in albis vestibus ... angeli   *cwið þæt hy in hwitum þær*
apparent ...   *hræglum oðywden in þa æþelan*
    tid etc.

Albæ etenim vestes ...   545 b ff. *Hwite cwoman eorla*
    eadgiefan englas togeanes.

In assumptione ergo ejus angeli   547 ff. *Ðæt is wel cweden, swa*
in albis vestibus videri debuerunt   *gewritu secgað, þæt him albeorhte*
...   *englas togeanes in þa halgan tid*
    heapum cwoman etc.

There are some Anglosaxonisms in Christ II, although the theme
of the poem might seem difficult to bring into harmony with the
Germanic poetical tradition. But in the enumeration of the different
faculties with which the Lord endows humanity, ll. 664 ff, we have
a formulary *sum*-series of unmistakably vernacular origin. Similar
series occur in the Gifts of Men ll. 30 ff, 106 ff; the Fortunes of Men
ll. 10 ff, Wanderer 80 ff, etc.; cp. further GREIN-KÖHLER, p. 645. "Si
anglo-saxonne que paraisse cette description, le point de départ en
est scripturaire et patristique", remarks DUBOIS, p. 150, and quotes
the original passage in St. Paul (I Cor., XII, 8, 10): *Alii quidem per*
spiritum datur sermo sapientiae, alii autem sermo scientiae secun-
dum eundem spiritum. Alteri fides in eodem spiritu; alii gratia sani-
tatum in uno spiritu. Alii operatio virtutum, alii prophetia, alii discretio
spirituum, alii genera linguarum, alii interpretatio sermonum. But
the point is, first, that in rendering this the poet was able to resort
to the Anglo-Saxon poetical tradition; secondly, that the brief
scriptural paragraph has been elaborated into a description of
different kinds of occupation which gives us an insight into contemporary Anglo-Saxon life. *Sum mæg fingrum wel ... hearpan*
stirgan; sum mæg ryne tungla secgan; sumum wiges sped giefeð æt
guþe; sum mæg fromlice ... sundwudu drifan; sum mæg heanne
beam stælgne gestigan (which was unnecessarily questioned by
GEROULD MLN XXXI, 403 f); *sum mæg styled sweord ... gewyrcan;*
sum con wonga bigong; all these qualities are original and have
nothing to do with those referred to in the Bible. Cp. also KENNEDY
p. 227. We have further, in the account of the Ascension ll. 512 and
571 ff, an interesting example of a patristic passage moulded and
modified to suit the Anglo-Saxon's ideas and attitude to Christian
conceptions. As DIETRICH remarks, with a fine sense of the difference

between Gregory's and Cynewulf's ways of rendering the episode: "Die himmelfahrt steht nicht vor uns als abschied und rückkehr, sondern als der einzug des siegeshelden in des vaters land und burg, als ein ankommen in herrlichkeit" ... "der sohn des königs nimmt den gabenstuhl der halle ein" etc. (ibid., p. 209). The final lines of the poem, 850—66, are undoubtedly Cynewulf's own addition, and the symbolic representation of human life as a perilous voyage is in the traditional style. A similar symbolism is probably used in the Seafarer.

The Fata Apostolorum would hardly have attracted attention if Cynewulf's acrostic had not been attached to it. Of this enumeration of the fates of the apostles some unknown martyrology may have been the basis, and our chief concern is to look for correspondence with the order in which the fates are told. The sequence comes closest to the *Notitia de locis Apostolorum* by Jerome, but there are also correspondences with *De Vita et obitu utriusque Testamenti Sanctorum* by Isidore, and the *Martyrologium* by Bede (cp. BOURAUEL p. 101 ff). HAMILTON is convinced that the source of the poem was of Anglo-Irish origin. SISAM remarks (p. 327) that "Cynewulf's order is not found in Insular documents before 800 and is found in several late Old English manuscripts". The Fata Apostolorum, it need hardly be pointed out, is almost wholly written in the heroic Anglo-Saxon tradition. The mission of the apostles is set forth as the fight between bold and steadfast warriors and dark and evil powers, the final death and martyrdom of God's servants is looked upon as the tragic but glorious overthrow of faithful retainers. This spirit of the poem is suggestive of Andreas and goes a long way to explain why the Fates has so frequently been attributed to the author of the longer epic. For borrowings which add to the heroic colouring of the poem cp. p. 250 f. The final section, ll. 88—122, which contains Cynewulf's acrostic and in which the reader is asked to pray for the poet's soul, is no doubt the author's own addition. It reveals, however, a certain barrenness and lack of inspiration which is markedly different from the creative and vivid imagination of the closing sections in the other poems signed by Cynewulf. This difference will be analysed in ch. IV, 7 (p. 259 ff).

The Dream of the Rood

The Dream of the Rood may have been modelled on some earlier version of the same theme or it may be the poet's original work; it is difficult to say which. In a discussion of this problem it is natural to raise the question as to the relation between the Dream and the inscription on the Ruthwell Cross and the Brussels Cross, which present some striking parallels. KRAPP (p. XL) is of opinion that the short Ruthwell and Brussels inscriptions were extracted from the poem, and DOBBIE also thinks that the Dream is earlier than the Ruthwell inscription (p. CXXII). On the other hand SCHÜCKING (p. 28), and DICKINS-ROSS (p. 18), are inclined to believe that the Dream and the Ruthwell version are both derived from an original poem. It is hard to know which alternative is the more probable, but it cannot be doubted that a very close relationship must exist between the three texts. It is important that all three of them stress the fact that the Cross was wet with the blood of Christ: *miþ blodæ (b)istemi(d)* (R), *blode bestemed* (B), *mid wœtan bestemed, beswyled mid swates gange* (D. R.); this detail recurs in Christ III (*blode bistemed*, 1085) and is not to be found in the possible source of that poem (cp. p. 39). This feature seems to point to a vernacular Cross tradition. In the second half of the Dream, containing the poet's personal reflexions, an elegiac strain is unmistakable at l. 131 b ff, where the poet laments the death of his friends in a manner suggestive of the Seafarer l. 80 b ff, the Wanderer 37 ff, 78 ff.

Christ I

The source of Christ I, as COOK C (XLI ff), MOORE (MLN XXIX, 226—27) and BURGERT have demonstrated, is a series of liturgical hymns, the so-called Greater Antiphons of Advent or the O-Antiphons; further two Antiphons for Lauds on Trinity Sunday, and, as MOORE discovered, the Antiphon *O admirabile commercium*, which is the source of the last section of the poem. These hymns serve as models for different paragraphs in Christ I in the following manners (cp. BURGERT, pp. 23 ff):

ll. 1—17 — *O Rex Gentium* (the King of nations, the cornerstone, is implored to rescue mankind).

ll. 18—49 — *O Clavis David* (the Key of David, which opens and shuts, is besought to deliver the prisoners from death and darkness).

ll. 50—70 — *O Hierusalem* (the city of God is asked to lift up her eyes and see her rescuer, the Lord).

ll. 71—103 — *O Virgo virginum* (dialogue: wonder at the secret of the Virgin, who answers that there is no need for wonder; a divine mystery has happened).

ll. 104—129 — *O Oriens* (prayer to the Light Eternal to come to those sitting in darkness).

ll. 130—163 — *O Emmanuel* (prayer to the giver of law to save us).

ll. 164—213 contain the so-called *Passus*, a dialogue between Mary and Joseph. No source is known for this section.

ll. 214—274 — *O Rex Pacifice* (prayer to the King of peace to come by the golden gate and deliver the sinners).

ll. 275—347 — *O mundi Domina* (Christ, like a bridegroom from his chamber, came from the Virgin's womb; the ruler of stars rests in the manger).

ll. 348—377 — *O Radix Jesse* (prayer to the Root of Jesse, whom kings and Gentiles worship, to save us soon). Further source: the Preface for the Mass *In Vigilia Domini in Nocte*, from the *Liber Sacramentorum Si. Gregorii Magni*, cp. MIGNE P. L., 78, 30.

ll. 378—415 — *O Beata et Benedicta et Gloriosa Trinitas, Pater et Filius et Spiritus Sanctus. Te jure laudant, Te adorant, Te glorificant omnes creaturæ tuæ, O Beata Trinitas.* (The two Antiphons for Lauds on Trinity Sunday.)

ll. 416—439 — *O admirabile commercium* (the Creater of man, born by the Virgin, deigned to descend as a man among men).

The whole poem, then, can be said to have been modelled on known liturgical texts except for the *Passus* ll. 164—213. However, it is more than probable that some homiletic text, now unknown, served as the original of the *Passus* since COOK (JEG Ph IV, 421—451) is able to compare this passage with one Latin and four Greek dramatic dialogues of a similar kind. Such a dialogue, then, must have found its way to the author of the *Passus*. It is quite possible, as DUBOIS suggests (p. 71), that the 13th chapter of the so-called *Proto-Evangelium Jacobi* is the source of the dialogue. A second question is whether this *Passus* should be regarded as the work of the poet or of a later interpolator. BURGERT, pointing out that the *Passus* "mars the symmetrical proportions otherwise maintained in the grouping of the smaller divisions of Christ I" (p. 21) seems inclined to consider the *Passus* an interpolation "by a later writer". However, granted that the poem, if this is so, "receives a better form of construction" (p. 22), we should not permit ourselves to be too much biassed by considerations of architectonical symmetry. Anglo-Saxon poets, as everybody knows, had their own ideas about symmetry, and I can see no vital objection to the natural assumption that the *Passus* was part of the poet's original plan of composition. BURGERT's further theory, that the final section 416—439 (*O admirabile commercium*) should be "a later addition", not necessarily made by "a later writer" (p. 22) is no more likely than his doubts concerning the authenticity of the *Passus*.

If we are entitled to conclude anything from what to us appears as a lack of symmetry, it can only be, it seems, that it is in the plan of composition that the poet's personality asserts itself. He is bound by his sources, but in the arrangement of the material derived from them he is, to some extent, free. There does not seem to be any Anglo-saxonisms in this poem.

Christ III

The question as to the source of Christ III is more complicated because the poem, to all appearances, has been put together by fragments from different sources. DEERING, speaking about the motive of the Judgment fire, mentions that Augustine (*De Civitate Dei 20, Sermo CIV*) and Bede (*De Temporum Ratione 70*) teach the purifying power of the Judgment fire (pp. 27, 28). COOK (C, 171 ff) suggested that the main material of the poem was derived from the alphabetic hymn included in Bede's *De Arte Metrica*. This hymn is made up of one couplet for each letter, and according to COOK, each couplet corresponds to an episode or a motif in the Old English poem. The correspondences, however, are in many cases slight and insignificant. Yet the order of the motifs in Christ III is, in the main, the same as that in the alphabetic hymn, so it seems highly probable, in spite of GRAU's objections (p. 49), that the structure of the poem is taken from Bede's hymn. As possible sources for the passage 1379—1498 (Christ reproaches the sinners for their obstinacy and indifference towards the Lord, his sacrifice and sufferings) COOK regarded St. Ephrem the Syrian, *De Judicio et Compunctione* (Opera 5, 51) or, more probably, *De Extremo Judicio* (*Ego te, o homo*) by Cæsarius of Arles (MIGNE, P. L. 39, 2207, ascribed to St. Augustine). This latter sermon, in fact, comes very close to the section in Chr. III and may without difficulty be considered the original. GRAU (p. 42 ff) makes a detailed study of foreign influence on our poem, and, though many of his parallels seem doubtful, he points out some interesting correspondences. His contention that a Homily by Pseudo-Chrysostomos (MIGNE, P. G. 61, 775 ff) was the main source of the poet must probably be rejected (cp. the problem of the Andreas source p. 22 f). But it is possible that some Latin translation of the Greek text was the original. Apart from this Greek text, GRAU holds (p. 52) that the poet drew copiously from the Apocalypse, ch. 14, the *Carmen de Resurrectione Mortuorum*, the Sermons of St. Ephrem the Syrian (*De Judicio et Compunctione*), the 4th Book of Esra, and the last chapter of the *Divinæ Institutiones* by Lactantius. GRAU's comparisons, whatever the exact value of his analysis may be, make it very probable that the author of Christ III had before him various versions treating of the Day of Judgment and derived the different ideas and motifs in his poem from different parts of them; if the versions were not exactly those quoted by GRAU, they were at least closely related to them.

WILLARD, in a detailed essay, compares Christ III with the hymn *De Extremo Judicio* by Cæsarius of Arles (cp. COOK above) and the Homily VIII of the Vercelli Book. He comes to the result that the two Old English texts are independently derived from Cæsarius, and thus confirms COOK's theory. DUBOIS suggests other parallels to Christ III, such as various apocryphal writings and Gregory's Moralia XXI. ch. 22 (MIGNE, P. L. 76, 210); p. 58. KENNEDY, pp. 246, 48, draws attention to parallels in Gregory, *Hom. in Evang.* 1, 10. for 1151, 1143, 1132, 1141—42, 1161; and in Gregory's *In Septem Psalm. Poenit. Expositio* (MIGNE, P. L. 79, 657—58) for the last section of the poem, 1634—64. The whole poem, in fact, seems to have been modelled wholly on foreign material, and it is difficult to distinguish parts of a more original character. As KENNEDY points out, p. 245, certain sections seem to have no specific correspondences in the Latin texts and hymns referred to, for instance the description of the giant Cross that shall shine instead of the sun on Judgment Day (1181 ff) and is wet with the blood of Christ (cp. GRAU p. 66). It may be that the poet is more independent in this section, but the idea was certainly not his own. It seems, on the whole, hardly possible to find any passage in the poem where vernacular Anglo-Saxon tradition unmistakably asserts itself. There was not room in the poet's mind, apparently, except for phrases, ideas, and echoes from the works of the leading spirits of continental Christian tradition.

Guthlac A

The question as to the source of Guthlac A is also rather a difficult problem. The discussion deals mainly with two alternatives: Felix's Latin life of St. Guthlac of Croyland (Acta Sanctorum XI. 37 ff) is the source of Guthlac A; or the Old English poem was written independently of Felix's biography. The latter theory is defended by CHARITIUS (p. 307), TEN BRINK (p. 73), FORSTMANN, and also by BRANDL (p. 1039); the former by FRITZSCHE (p. 23), LEFÈVRE (thoroughly, p. 227), KÖRTING (p. 51), WÜLKER (Geschichte der engl. Litt., 1906, p. 45), LIEBERMANN, and GEROULD (MLN, XXXII, 77 ff). Now apart from the portions of the Vita that have no parallels in Guthlac A, such as Guthlac's life before the conversion and various events after the return from hell, it is obvious that the Old English poem contains large sections which cannot be accounted for by a comparison with Felix's version. Thus Gu. 1—92 (the bliss of Paradise and the vanity of the world, the lovers of earthly wealth and those who hope for eternal reward) has no parallel in Felix. (As for the source of some of these lines and as for the problem connected with them cp. below pp. 41, 107.) 93—140 a (Guthlac is steadfast; an angel and a devil fight about his soul, the latter flies): in the Vita (ch. II, 17, p. 41) the hermit is tempted by a devil for three days (a poisoned arrow penetrates into his soul); then St. Bartholomew descends from Heaven, *pollicens ei in omnibus tribulationibus adjutorem sui venturum esse.*

The accounts of the various torments and temptations that Guthlac has to suffer are highly different in the two versions. In the Old English poem he is tempted and remains steadfast (153 b—167 a,

184—189 a), he is threatened with fire but does not flinch, never did the devils meet such a bold adversary (191 b—214). The devils further threaten to attack him in larger crowds, the saint defies them; the devils again threaten him with hunger and death; Guthlac is undaunted (233—322). The demons come to tempt him; he is staunch, speaks resolutely to them; they take him with them in a flight through the air and show him monastic corruption; they must land him safely on his hill (348—429 a). The devils speak to Guthlac about false holiness, he answers that they have only shown him the life of sinners and that maturity is not found in youth (451—512). Guthlac is now led by the devils to the door of hell, they threathen him with destruction there because he is not truly righteous (557—589). Guthlac answers (590—684 a) that no one can harm him against God's will, that he himself is holy but the devils eternally damned. 684 b—751: a messenger from God now orders the devils to bring Guthlac unharmed back to his hill; they do so, the plain blossoms, all creatures welcome him there. The Latin text has only few features in common with this version. Guthlac is first visited by two devils (ch. II, 18, pp. 41, 42), who blame him for slackness in his fasting; Moses, Elias, the Saviour, and the monks of Egypt fasted much more assiduously. But Guthlac prays to God and the devils disappear in the air. Ch. II, 19, p. 42: devils *aspectu truces* swarm into Guthlac's hut, take him prisoner and drag him through marshes and brushwood. When he remains steadfast, they fly with him through the cold air where they meet another host of devils, and Guthlac is now brought down into hell. There he sees the torments of damned souls and evil spirits and forgets his own agonies. When the devils are prepared to throw him into the fire he curses them as the race of Cain; St. Bartholomew descends from Heaven and orders the devils to bring Guthlac back; on their way upwards they meet a choir of angels.

It will be seen that except for the message of St. Bartholomew these central episodes in the two versions are wholly different, and it is therefore meaningless to maintain, with GEROULD, that the Old English poem is a free treatment of Felix's Vita, or, with LIEBERMANN, that the poet "bloss seiner Phantasie gefolgt sein kann" (p. 247) in the independent sections. If comparisons with an earlier text are to have any value at all, obvious deviations from the version of such a text must be a strong objection to the theory that the poem was derived from it. Apparently the source of Guthlac A was some other biography than Felix's; FORSTMANN (p. 35 ff) has given ample proof of the popularity of the Guthlac legend in the Middle Ages. As for the source of the first section of the poem, ll. 30—62, GEROULD has shown, p. 79, that the poet is indebted to a text similar to some meditations by Gregory of Tours (*Multi variique sunt gradus*, MIGNE P. L. 71, 1055) and to Lactantius' *de Ira Dei*. GRAU thinks (p. 90, 91) that they are derived from some sermons by St. Ephrem the Syrian, but his parallels are far from convincing. Guthlac A contains no clear Anglosaxonisms (cp. further p. 299); perhaps the portrayal of the blossoming plain and the song of birds and cuckoos ll. 742—48 a, is a specimen of vernacular landscape poetry.

Guthlac B

If the source of Guthlac A must be considered unknown, the same cannot be said of Guthlac B, the account of Guthlac's illness and death. Undoubtedly we have here an Old English adaptation of Felix's *Vita S. Guthlaci V*, 35 and 36. All the stages and the different details of the illness and death of the saint are met with in this sections of the Latin text: the onset of the illness, a sign from the Lord; the sorrow of the faithful servant and his anxious questions; Guthlac's comforting speeches and his wonderful sermon; the servant finds him in the chapel and is ordered to inform his sister about his death; the servant's question about the mysterious messenger and Guthlac's reply; the sweet odour and the celestial light in the dark; Guthlac's death, the light and the angelic song; the servant's flight, his expedition and visit to Guthlac's sister.

This narrative is intermingled, however, with certain details which may point to a specific source. Ch. V in Felix's narrative begins with some short remarks about death, which is in Adam and comes to all, and these remarks have been expanded, in Guthlac B 819—878 a, to a survey of human destiny: the bliss in Paradise, the fall of man, and the relentless sway of death ever since that fateful hour. GRAU (p. 94 ff) has pointed to parts of the *Carmen de Resurrectione Mortuorum* as possible sources of this section; it is of interest that the Phoenix, 393—423, contains a similar passage.

Guthlac B contains several portions which seem to have been composed independently of the Latin original and in the Anglo-Saxon poetical tradition. To them belong the various natural phenomena, on which the author dwells with obvious interest, quite different from Felix's brief and dry manner: the succession of night and day 1096 b ff, 1278 b ff, 1330 b ff; further the sweet odour, which calls to the poet's memory the aromatic fragrance of a summer's day 1271 b ff; the combined fairness of celestial light and heavenly music 1308 b ff. And we may agree with KENNEDY (p. 258) that the final lines, the servant's lament of his dead master, is written in the elegiac strain, though it is very doubtful whether the poet had the Wanderer in mind, as KENNEDY thinks. Yet the section reminds us strongly of this poem as also of the Seafarer and parts of Beowulf. Anyhow, it seems clear that in Guthlac B the vernacular tradition is a much stronger element than in Guthlac A. This also appears from an analysis of parallels in the poem (cp. p. 300 ff).

The Phoenix

Critics have always agreed on the main source of the Phoenix: *De Ave Phoenice* attributed to Lactantius. Here we find, in broad outline, the same legend about the marvellous bird: his paradisic home, his worship of the sun, the building of his nest, his death in the flame, his resurrection, the beauty of his body, the wonder of the people and the adoration of the birds, final reflections on the nature of the bird. To some extent, however, the poet seems to be independent of Lactantius' version, as EMERSON has pointed out. Thus references to classical mythology such as Phaeton, Deucalion, Aurora, Phoebus, have been omitted; the description of the birds crowding around the Phoenix, ll. 335 b—55 a, is much longer and more detailed than the short lines (155 ff) in Lactantius; and the frequent references to God in the Old English poem (9 b—10, 36 b, 46 b, 48 a, etc.) are not to be found in the Latin original. Yet EMERSON no doubt exaggerates the originality of the poet: his hypothesis that the Phoenix is nowhere mentioned as the servant of God, is based on a very doubtful old conjecture (cp. p. 86); his opinion that the description of the Phoenix ll. 291 ff is a "distinctly individual picture" is no objection to the obvious fact that it is closely copied from the Latin; and we cannot claim any originality for the author merely because he continues his poem beyond the limits drawn by Lactantius. It is not easy to say where the poet got the ideas and motifs in the expository part ll. 381 —677, in which the Phoenix symbolism is explained and expounded.

Commodianus, Claudian, Tertullian, Ambrose, Dracontius, Eusebius, Bede, Rabanus Maurus, all have something to say about the similarity of the fate of the Phoenix to the Resurrection of Christ and the dead (cp. Schöll, p. 12 ff), but their brief comparisons have nothing suggestive of the elaborate and intricate symbolism in the Old English poem. Grau, p. 114 ff, has pointed out parallels in parts of the *Carmen de Resurrectione Mortuorum* (cp. p. 302 f), and some of them may quite possibly have been in the poet's mind, but probably the main source must be sought elsewhere. Certain facts seem to point to a connexion between the symbolic interpretation of the Phoenix legend on the one hand, and the Greek Physiologus on the other; but this is a matter of textual criticism and will, accordingly, be dealt with in the next chapter.

The poem does not seem to be clearly influenced by Anglo-Saxon poetical tradition. The picture of the landscape in the first section is highly conventionalized and in close correspondence to Lactantius. The harvest metaphor 240 b ff may be the poet's own invention but is not of a kind that we are used to in Old English poetry.

We have found, then, that only the sources of Christ I, Christ II, Guthlac B, and the first half of the Phoenix can be determined with some certainty. The sources of the other poems have not come down to us, though they must be very similar to other versions extant. All the poems are fundamentally dependent on hagiographic or homiletic tradition although this foreign element, in some of them, is less dominant than in others: Andreas, the Cynewulf canon, Guthlac B, and, to some extent, the Dream of the Rood, are composed in the vernacular tradition, with more or less obvious and frequent Anglosaxonisms, in a way that is not to be found in the other poems. There is, then, an obvious difference between Christ I and III, Guthlac A and the Phoenix on the one hand, and the other poems on the other. The authors of the former group are inspired by foreign models only; they seem to belong, if we may say so, to a new age, when motifs and ideas were taken exclusively from Christian ideology, whereas the authors of the rest of the poems are still aware of Germanic tradition and permit ideas and themes, derived from it, to blend with the Christian matter. This fusion of vernacular and foreign matter has been most successfully completed in the Cynewulf canon, Guthlac B, and the Dream; in Andreas the Anglosaxonisms sometimes clash rather violently with the Christian colouring and ideology of the subject-matter, as will be further demonstrated in chapters IV, 7 and 8.

III. Texts, Textual Criticism, and Interpretation

Andreas, the Fata Apostolorum, The Dream of the Rood, and Elene are preserved in the Vercelli Book, dating probably from the end of the tenth century, the rest of the poems have come down to us in the Exeter Book from about the same time. The oldest editions date from the early eighteen-forties. GRIMM's edition of Andreas and Elene was published in 1840, and so was GRUNDTVIG's text, with translation, of the Phoenix. THORPE's version of the Exeter Book appeared in 1842, and KEMBLE's "The Poetry of the Codex Vercellensis, with an English Translation", in 1843—46.

In the following years KLIPSTEIN's and ETTMÜLLER's great selections from the Exeter Book were published (1849 and 1850), but these editors did not do much to improve the condition of the texts. The real foundation of the scholarly study of Old English poetry was laid in 1857 and —58, when GREIN published his "Bibliothek der angelsächsischen Poesie". In this work he presented an almost complete edition of the Anglo-Saxon poems (with the omission of some of the Riddles), with a thorough critical treatment of the texts. The importance of the work can hardly be overestimated — there are few corrupt or difficult passages for the improvement or interpretation of which GREIN did not at least make some suggestion which might stimulate other attempts at a solution. GREIN became the authority on Anglo-Saxon poetry, especially so after the publication of his valuable "Sprachschatz" in 1864. Sometimes, however, the weight of his authority is somewhat oppressive, and modern editors are often inclined to rely on his conjectures although they may not be superior to other solutions suggested. Thus it is to GREIN that we ówe the strange omission of *ne* in El. 924 ff *Gen ic findan ne can þurh wrohtstafas wiðercyr siððan* (cp. p. 66) and the doubtful emendation El. 1239 ff *Nysse ic gearwe be ðære rode riht* etc., which has been adopted by most critics and editors (cp. p. 69). Another instance of excessive loyalty to GREIN is Chr. I 59 *Sioh nu sylfa þe geond | þas sidan gesceaft*, which placing of the caesura obscures the meaning but has nevertheless found favour with a number of critics (cp. p. 72).

An important edition of Elene was published in 1877 by ZUPITZA, whose concentrated work, text + glossary, contains a series of good readings, conjectural or conservative (such as *þryðbord stenan* 151 (cp. p. 61), *ge he ða rode tæhte* 631b (cp. p. 65), *Gen ic findan ne can* 924b (cp. p. 66), *þurh wigan snyttro* 937 (cp. p. 68), and others). In his second and third editions, 1883, 1888, other changes have been made, but these have not improved the text. ZUPITZA's work was the basis of KENT's edition in 1889, which contains nearly all of ZUPITZA's readings and, in addition to the older scholar's laconic version, provides a section of notes, some of which, however, are rather obscure. During the years 1883—98 GREIN's Bibliothek was reedited by WÜLKER and ASSMANN (third volume, containing the Exeter Book and the late poems). The critical notes of this edition are very detailed on certain textual points, and otherwise it contains a great many improvements, especially as regards punctuation (cp. Andr. 138 ff, 1222 ff pp. 50, 58, and others).

In 1892 GOLLANCZ published his "Cynewulf's Christ". In this work, as well as in his edition of the first eight poems of the Exeter Book (1895), a whole series of good readings has been suggested. Instances are Christ 310b ff (cp. p. 75), 537 ff (p. 76), Ph. 64 (p. 86), Ph. 646b ff (cp. p. 89), Jul. 149 ff (cp. p. 91), Jul. 490b ff (p. 94), etc. As for Ph. 646 b ff GOLLANCZ's version is not entirely satisfactory, but he indicates where a solution is likely to be found. BRIGHT's Anglo-Saxon Reader was also published in 1892, containing an edition of the Phoenix. In 1900 appeared COOK's "The Christ of Cynewulf", which contains a considerable amount of information on the possible sources and the general religious background of the poems, but which does less justice to the philological aspect of the problems. This may also be said about COOK's edition of Elene, Phoenix, and Physiologus 1919. KRAPP's "Andreas and the Fates of the Apostles" was issued in 1906. It contains a full discussion of problems connected with these poems and detailed textual notes. Although KRAPP's handling of textual points is not quite reliable (117 *hweorfan* for *hweorfest*, cp. p. 49, 198 *wēgas ofer widland*, cp. p. 50, 260 ff *swa þæt ne wiste* etc., cp. p. 51, and others), the edition is an important contribution to our knowledge of the Andreas legend, which had been edited separately only in BASKERVILL's small volume of 1885 (2d ed. 1891).

STRUNK's version of Juliana in 1904 is valuable chiefly for comparisons with non-Old English versions of the legend, notably the Acta Sanctorum. In 1934, The Dream of the Rood was published by DICKINS and ROSS, in 1935 by BÜTOW, with detailed notes. This poem was, up till then, available in the editions of BOUTERWEK 1854, STEPHENS 1867, PACIUS 1873, KLUGE 1888, COOK 1905, and further RICCI 1926. In his four successive editions of Elene (1905, —10, —14, —36), HOLTHAUSEN often revises his earlier opinions of difficult passages, thus giving a great many suggestions for the solution of such problems. SCHLOTTEROSE's "Die altenglische Dichtung Phoenix" (1908) is a product of radical criticism and contains a great many violent and needless alterations. CRAIGIE's "Specimens of Anglo-Saxon poetry" (1923—31), with large sections from Andreas, Elene, Juliana, Guthlac, and with the whole of the Dream of the Rood, does not present many innovations in the arrangement of the text, and KRAPP's and KRAPP-DOBBIE's editions of the Vercelli Book (1932) and the Exeter Book (1936) are important chiefly because of the exhaustive critical apparatus. The text in these editions often leaves a great deal to be desired (as for instance the strange treatment of Jul. 556 ff, cp. p. 95), not least as regards punctuation, but the works are useful as a summing up of what we know about the poems concerned.

Only the most important partial texts have been included in this survey of the editions. Around these editions a considerable amount of critical work has grown up. Among the most important contributions to the discussion are the different articles and notes by SIEVERS, COSIJN, KOCK and KLAEBER, thanks to whom a great many textual puzzles have been finally solved.

With the exception of some gaps in Andreas and Juliana and the damage to the opening section of Christ I, the state of our texts is fairly good. The corruptions that have crept in must be restored either by comparison with other versions than the Old English poems or, if this is not conclusive, with the help of conjectural criticism since the poems have come down to us in one shape only. However, in the discussion of textual problems, as a general principle, we should let the readings stand wherever we can. A MS reading may occasion doubt and yet be flawless, being an instance of a not very frequent usage (as for instance Ph. 287 ff *bið him edniwe þære sunnan þegn*, cp. p. 86). There are ἅπαξ λεγόμενα enough in Old English poetry to warn us against discarding strange words and rare constructions too hastily. It is also necessary to make allowance for the special poetical style with its repetitions, digressions, vagueness, and frequent inconsistencies, which makes the application of cut and dried logical standards inadvisable. Still, we should not give up every hope for logic and consistency in the texts. Whether we are entitled to look for such consistency or not, depends entirely on the nature of the style of the poem. Thus it would be uncritical to try and polish and rationalize passages written by an author like the Andreas poet, for the very good reason that his style is often abrupt and extravagant. A passage, for instance, such as 954 (*scel þin hra dæled ... weorðan, wættre geliccost*), *faran flode blod*, in spite of the exaggeration and the forced syntax, gains nothing by a smoothing down to *faran on foldan blod* or the like. Such a "Verschlimmbesserung" is nothing but a needless normalization, for the MS reading is what we expect of such a poet. If, on the other hand, a poem characterized by its coherent style, contains some quite unexpected inconsistency, we may be justified in suspecting some corruption. This is probably the case in El. 56 ff, which passage, after the description of the emperor's dismay at the sight of the barbarians armies, reads ... *ðæt he on Romwara rices ende ... werod samnode, mægen unrime*, but then continues: *hæfde wigena to lyt* etc. (cp. p. 60). Very frequently, however, inconsistencies in the texts of the editions are due to wrong punctuation and have nothing to do with the poets' original intentions; illustrations of this are Andr. 474 b ff (cp. p. 54), 603 ff (p. 55), 1222 ff (p. 58); Chr III 1312 ff (p. 77), Ph. 646 b ff (p. 90).

On the whole, comparisons of a passage discussed with the poet's own usage prove more fruitful than extensive collations with the poetry of other Germanic languages. This practice was common in the earlier stages and was advocated especially by Kock (cp. NN I, 69). We must proceed by degrees and begin by comparing a debated point with similar ones in the same poem or in poems by the same author or belonging to the same category. In case this kind of material should prove too scanty, we may take the body of Old English poetry into account. Then if this is unproductive we can review the passage in question in the light of similar cases in non-Old English Germanic poetry.

It is implicit in the conservative critical method that the assumption of gaps in the text should, if possible, be avoided. If we suppose a gap, we no longer trust the actual reading and give up the attempt to derive any meaning from the material extant. Instead we yield to the temptation to fill in the supposed lacunas, which can sometimes be repaired without any alterations (as for instance El. 436 ff; cp. p. 62), sometimes, it seems, with a slight emendation (as in Gu. 541 ff, cp. p. 83). Apart from obvious cases when a MS leaf is missing or when words in the text have been blotted out, gaps may be assumed with the greatest certainty when an alliterative word is missing, since we do not readily admit that the poet consciously left out such an essential part of the verse. Sometimes it may be difficult enough to restore such passages although the possibilities of emendation are limited by the alliterative pattern; sometimes we need only supply a missing part of a common alliterative formula, such as Andr. 194 ff

> Ðæt mæg engel þin   eað geferan,
> ⟨halig⟩ of heofenum   con him holma begang.

The discussion of these principles leads us to the important question as to how far criticism should be dominated by metrical demands. It is obvious that emendations must conform to the metrical usage, though they need not cautiously be limited to forming only the commonest types of verse. But the countless alterations made, not least by SIEVERS, so as to render the lines pretty and flawless illustrations of metrical theories are needless and have nothing to do with sound criticism. The Anglo-Saxon poets were no metrical fanatics, as so many modern critics seem to think, notably v. D. WARTH, whose treatment of the texts is determined by a rigorous adherence to certain metrical dogmas. The best way, it seems, to decide whether a metrically deficient passage needs some alteration or not is to analyse the meaning: if the passage is obscure there may be reason for emendation, if the meaning is clear the passage is only an instance of the metrical licence so frequent in Old English poetry, and we had better let it stand as it is. Thus Andr. 669 ... wuldre gewlitegod. Huscworde ongan ... does not provide good alliteration, but huscworde is exactly the word demanded by the situation, and KRAPP is well justified in preferring it to SIMONS' usic worde or KOCK's wordhusce.

The importance of palæography has been too often neglected by textual critics. If a MS reading seems to be a copyist's error, we must examine the context of the suspected word or letter in order to discover, if possible, what may have distracted the scribe's attention and caused the slip. In this way we limit the range of possible suggestions for the restoration of the corrupt material.

In dealing with the texts for critical purposes I take, as starting-points, KRAPP's edition of the Vercelli-Book for Andreas and Elene, and KRAPP-DOBBIE's Exeter Book for the rest of the poems. HOLT-HAUSEN's Elene, it is true, is more recent, but his text is inferior to KRAPP's. For collation with the manuscripts we have at our disposal the useful facsimiles by WÜLKER and FOERSTER (the Vercelli Book, 1894 and 1913), and CHAMBERS (the Exeter Book, 1933). It is often convenient to take the reading of the MS as a basis in the critical discussion, notably when opinions are sharply divided as to the authentic version of a passage.

In the following paragraphs I concentrate on points previously overlooked or cases when, in my opinion, old suggestions ought to be preferred to generally accepted recent ones; or textual problems which are still supposed to be unsettled although the right solution seems to have been given earlier on. In this later case some further explanation is afforded in support of the earlier suggestion. On the whole the passages discussed will illustrate the principal points dealt with above.

Andreas

113 ff
> Is to þære tide   tælmet hwile
> emne mid soðe   seofon ond twentig
> nihtgerimes,   þæt ðu of nede most,
> sorgum geswenced,   sigore gewyrðod,
> hweorfest of hendum   in gehyld godes.

Thus the MS. COSIJN Btr. XXI, 8, KRAPP, TRAUTMANN BEV, p. 109 change to hweorf⟨an⟩, possibly under the influence of most-brucan 105 ff. But the alteration is probably wrong: as in many other verbs, the additional meaning of a verb of motion is not infrequent in mot, as Riddle 39,20 Næfre hio ... to helle mot, Jul. 457 ær þu heonan mote, Seef. 119 ... þæt we to moten in þa ecan eadignesse; and hweorfest here is apparently a variation of most l. 115 stressing the element of motion implied in that verb: "(when) you will go" ... Of nede is then parallel to of hendum.

138 ff   *Cirmdon caldheorte,*   (*corðor oðrum getang*),
       reðe ræsboran.   *Rihtes ne gimdon,*
       meotudes mildse.

The passage is chopped to pieces by KRAPP. Why the parenthesis is there is hard to understand as *corðor oðrum getang* is in no wise implied by *cirmdon caldheorte* or subordinate to it, neither is there any reason for separating *gimdon* from its natural preceding subject. As moreover the passage should apparently be regarded in connexion with Chr. 706: *Ðær ða synsceaðan soþes ne giemdon, gæstes þearfe,* we get the simple reading (WÜLKER'S):

       Cirmdon caldheorte,   *corðor oðrum getang,*
       reðe ræsboran   *rihtes ne gimdon,*
       meotudes mildse.

194 ff   *Ðæt mæg engel þin*   *eað geferan,*
       halig of heofenum   *con him holma begang,*
       sealte sæstreamas   *ond swanrade,*
       waroðfaruða gewinn   *ond wæterbrogan,*
       wegas ofer widland.

A debate on the meaning of *wegas* was started in KRAPP A, in which edition the author considered the interpretation *wĕgas*, 'ways, paths over the wide land' (GREIN, KEMBLE) out of keeping with ll. 195 b— 197. KRAPP reads *wēgas*, 'waves over the earth', as a variation of *holma begang* etc. This reading, according to him, is also supported by the end of Andrew's speech, ll. 200 b—201: *ne me herestræta ofer cald wæter cuðe sindon.* "The whole passage", concludes the editor, "is consequently descriptive of journeyings by water". But *wēgas ofer widland* is hardly a natural Old English expression for 'sea', and the word for 'wave' is spelt *wæg* eight times, *wēg* three times in the poem. Further, as KLAEBER rightly observes (Archiv CXX, 154), the parallelism of meaning need not be complete, so that instead of varying 'sea', the expression *wegas ofer widland* may carry a meaning of its own. But I do not follow his suggestion that it may denote "ways in general", and that it can be applied "both to sea and land". *Widland* admits of only the second interpretation. Now, no serious objection can be raised to the reading *wĕgas ofer widland*, 'paths over the earth'. It is natural that the apostle, reluctant to make the perilous expedition himself, should recommend the powerful angel with his knowledge of all ways on sea and land. In view of the mass of Old English kennings for sea and the Andreas poet's fondness for them (cp. p. 316) it is not surprising that this word was made the object of excessive variation in the sentence and not the far less poetical 'ways over the land'. The *herestræta ofer cald wæter* 200 b—201 a is apparently another instance of the same poetical predilection.

260 ff   *Him ða ondswarode*   *ælmihti god,*
           swa þæt ne wiste,   *se ðe þæs wordes bad,*
           hwæt se manna wæs   *meðelhegendra,*
           þe he þær on waroðe   *wiðþingode* etc.

Andrew and his attendants have just asked from where God and His two angels, disguised as sailors, have come in their ship. In ll. 264 ff God answers that they come from Mermedonia. Now KRAPP thinks that *swa þæt ne wiste se ðe þæs wordes bad* means "As though God did not know", and rejects KOCK's translation (Anglia XLVI, 68) "without Andrew knowing", which he thinks does not fit in with *hwæt se manna wæs* l. 262. But it is difficult to see how God, saying that He comes from Mermedonia, can give this piece of information "as though He does not know" who Andrew is. This gives no sense unless there is something in God's answer denoting that He takes Andrew to be someone else. Contrary to KRAPP's opinion the interpretation "without Andrew knowing" fits the context very well: asking, l. 257, from where the *macræftige menn* come, the apostle reveals his ignorance of God's and the angels' identity, and *hwæt se manna wæs* gives the reason why Andrew could not recognize the Lord. *Bad* in l. 261 also accords better with this interpretation: Andrew is awaiting the reply to come. For instances of *swa* = without cp. Andr. 813, 986. The passage consequently means: "Then the Almighty God answered him (A) without the one (A) waiting for his reply knowing who the speaking man (G) was whom he (A) was talking to on the shore".

267   *Snellic sæmearh*   *snude bewunden*

This MS reading defended by KRAPP cannot be accepted. *Bewunden* demands an instrumental, and *sunde* (COSIJN Btr XXI, 9; SIMONS

p. 130, TRAUTMANN BEV, p. 110) is the only possible alternative. Cp.
l. 269 *wære bewrecene* and El. 251 *sunde bewrecene*, an almost certain
emendation of the MS *sande bewrecene*. The confusion in Elene was
apparently due to *sund* being a rarer word than *sand* at the time when
the MS was written.

337 ff   *Ne ðurfan ge on þa fore*   *frætwe lædan,*
         gold ne seolfor.   *Ic eow goda gehwæs*
         on eowerne agenne dom   *est a h w e t t e.*

GREIN-KÖHLER's translation of *ahwettan* (p. 370), 'subministrare',
and BOSWORTH-TOLLER's, 'provide' (p. 32), seem wrong. Neither is it
necessary to take, with SIMONS, the passage to be corrupt (p. 35).
Ahwettan here, with a shade of the usual significance of (*a*)*hwettan*,
means, I think, 'increase', and the passage should be translated: You
need not take with you gold and silver etc. because I will i n c r e a s e
the favour (liberal supply) of every good etc. (i. e. in proportion as
you yourself cease to take notice of it).

359 ff   *Gesæt him þa se halga*   *h o l m w e a r d e neah,*
         æðele be æðelum.

Following a suggestion by COSIJN (Btr XXI, 9), KRAPP changes to
helmwearde, whereas the other edd. retain the MS reading. He refers
to the Greek, which reads "he sat down at the sail of the ship"
(παρὰ τὸ ἱστίον τοῦ πλοίου BLATT, p. 44), and to the OE prose legend,
which has *and he gesæt beforan þam steorreþran þæs scipes, þæt
wæs Drihten Hælend Crist* (BRIGHT p. 117). But *holmwearde*, besides
being the more poetical word, is supported by *weges weard* 601,
wæges weard 632, and is hardly disputed by the readings of the other
versions. A somewhat more complicated point is 396 *Him of holme
oncwæð hæleða scyppend.* COOK (First Book, p. 221) first suggested
helman, which was accepted by TRAUTMANN BEV, p. 111, and KRAPP.
But *helman* is not a good alteration, being a prose word, and *of holme*
is not an impossible instance of the vague poetical usage in Andreas.

369 b ff   *Ða gedrefed wearð,*
         onhrered hwælmere.   *H o r n f i s c plegode,*
         glad geond garsecg,   *ond se græga mæw*
         wælgifre wand.

Schücking, Dichtersprache, compares the passage with Beow. 540 ff *wit unc wið hronfixas werian þohton*, which was the reason why Beowulf and Breca carried swords during the swimming-match. Schücking questions the authenticity of *hronfixas* in the Beowulf passage: "Trotz des durchaus unrealistischen Charakters der altengl. Poesie fragt man sich: sollte es sich hier in der Tat um Walfische handeln? Gegen die sich ein Einzelner mit dem Schwert wehren will?" (p. 55). His second objection, that *hronfisc* is nowhere else used for 'whale', is of minor importance since it occurs also in the Epist. Alex. 510. However, Schücking recommends an alteration to *hornfisc* as in Andreas, the vocabulary and style of which being so close to that of Beowulf. As for the meaning of *hornfisc* he makes no suggestion.

The correspondence between Andreas and Beowulf is an important point, but it seems to lend weight to the view contrary to Schücking's. He has himself very strongly emphasized the strange vagueness and unreality of the Old English poetical world, and it is in conformity with the tenor of his own statements that we may attempt another interpretation than his of the passages involved.

The scene in Beowulf is highly fantastic and the proportions enormous: the fight with whales is in perfect accord with the superfluity of strength displayed in the seven day swimming-match. And to increase the atmosphere of horror on the raging sea in Andreas, whales may be more appropriately added to the darkened sun, the violent breakers, and the rapacious gull than *hornfisc*, a stroke of naturalism stylistically as well as zoologically dubious, whether it may mean garpike, swordfish, narwal, or sawfish. The reading *hronfisc* in Andreas is suggested as a possibility in Krapp A; it is even highly probable, and it seems as if the poet was inspired by its use in a similar situation in Beowulf and then a simple copyist's error was responsible for the MS reading.

474 b ff

	Ic wille þe,
eorl unforcuð,	*anre nu gena*
bene biddan,	*þeah ic þe beaga lyt,*
sincweorðunga,	*syllan mihte,*
fœtedsinces.	*Wolde ic freondscipe,*
þeoden þrymfœst,	*þinne, gif ic mehte,*
begitan godne.	

KRAPP adopts this bad reading from BASKERVILL, who seems to have picked it up from GRIMM. It is obvious that the *þeah*-clause must be subordinate to the *wolde*-clause since it is to the friendship with the helmsman that Andrew's poverty is an objection, not to the request to obtain this friendship. GREIN and WÜLKER have the only possible punctuation:

> Ic wille þe,
>
> eorl unforcuð,   anre nu gena
> bene biddan: þeah ic þe beaga lyt,
> sincweorðunga,   syllan mihte,
> fœtedsinces,   wolde ic freondscipe
> þeoden þrymfœst,   ... þinne ... begitan godne.

489   Ic wœs on gifeðe   iu ond nu
> syxtyne siðum   on sœbate.

I cannot see that *on gifeðe* of the MS, defended by WÜLKER and KRAPP, gives much sense; how does it fit in with *syxtyne siðum*? Following GREIN's old and sound suggestion we had better read *geofon*, palæographically and grammatically smoothed of by TRAUT-MANN, BEV, p. 113, into *gifene*. With this reading agree the τὴν θάλασσαν of P (BLATT p. 50) and the *in mare* of C ibid. p. 51. The destruction of the correct reading *on gifene* may be due to *geofon* being a rare and difficult word for the scribe.

568 b ff   Æþelinge weox
> word ond wisdom,   ah he þara wundra a,
> domagende,   dœl œnigne
> frœtre þeode   beforan cyðde.[1]

In this passage Christ, disguised as a sailor during His voyage with Andrew, makes the insinuation that perhaps, during His time on earth, He did not perform any miracles and that the Jews therefore did not believe in Him. But Andrew protests in surprise: "How is it possible that you have not heard about His power?" etc. (ll. 573 ff). KOCK, JJJ p. 3, thinking that Christ denies having worked miracles, reads *ne* for *he* or *ne he* l. 569. The same idea induces HOLTHAUSEN

---

[1] The note on this passage and the notes on Andr. 603 ff, 1547 ff; El. 56 ff, 924 ff were published, in a shorter form, in Stud. Neophil. xix, No 3.

(Anglia Beibl. XXXI, 27) to read *na* for *a* in the same line and KRAPP, who says that the Greek text and Andrew's answer demand a negative, to choose *nænigne*.

Now a negative here does not agree with l. 564: (*Hæleð no gelyfdon*) *þeah ðe he wundra feala weorodum gecyðde*. Further the Greek has not a negative but a question: "Perchance he did not work any miracles before them?" (τάχα οὐκ ἐποίησεν σημεῖα ἐνώπιον αὐτῶν;) (BLATT p. 52). And the Casanatensis reads *forsitan signa et mirabilia non fecit coram eis* ibid. p. 53. The Lord wants to put Andrew's belief in Him to the test by pretending to doubt the miracles. In order to preserve the coherence of the text and follow the Greek and Latin readings, one may therefore read *ah*, the interrogative particle, for *ah* 'but':

> Æþelinge weox
> word ond wisdom;   ah he þara wundra a,
> domagende,   dæl ænigne
> frætre þeode   beforan cyðde?

Even if it has already been said that Christ worked the miracles, there may still be room enough for doubt: Did He really show them any wonders?

603 ff Andrew has just enumerated the most important miracles. But Christ continues His sceptical questions:

> Miht ðu me gesecgan,   þæt ic soð wite,
> hwæðer wealdend þin   wundor on eorðan,
> þa he gefremede   nalas feam siðum,
> folcum to frofre   beforan cyðde,
> þær bisceopas   ond boceras
> ond ealdormenn   æht besæton etc.

So all editions. In the Greek text and the Latin Casanatensis version the Lord asks whether the reason for the incredulity of the Jews, in spite of the miracles, might be that they were performed only before the people and not before the high priests. The reading here quoted, in which *cyðde* goes with both *folcum to frofre* and *þær bisceopas — æht besæton* so that the people and the high priests are put on the same level, is then not only an unnecessary deviation from the Greek and the Latin texts but also violates the consistency of the Old English poem since immediately before these lines the feeding of the multide has been related and a few lines further down Andrew answers: *"he swiðe oft beforan fremede folces ræswum wundor æfter wundre"*, etc. Changing the punctuation, we can restore the original context, combining *gefremede* with *folcum to frofre:*

> ... *hwæðer wealdend þin   wundor on eorðan,*
> *þa he gefremede   nalas feam siðum*
> *folcum to frofre,   beforan cyðde*
> *þær bisceopas   ond boceras*
> *ond ealdormenn   æht besæton.*

996 b ff
>   *Ða se halga gebæd*
> *bilwytne fæder,   breostgehygdum*
> *herede on hehðo   heofoncyninges*
> *god dryhten dom.*

Several suggestions have been made in order to emend the last two halflines. Cosijn (Btr XXI, 13) proposed *heofoncyninges⟨þrym⟩ | dryhtendom gŏdes;* or *heofonrices gŏd | dryhtnes⟨ecne⟩ dom.* His first conjecture was accepted by Craigie, who however changed the order of l. 999 to *gŏdes dryhtendom.* In this condition Cosijn's suggestion has also been accepted by Krapp. Trautmann (BEV, 120), v. d. Warth, p. 24 and Kock (JJJ, 4) have readings which violate the lines too much to be of any critical interest. Earlier scholars were more considerate of the text: Grein read *heofoncyninges |, gŏdes dryhtendom,* taking *gŏdes* as a parallel to *heofoncyninges.* But two or more parallel genitives immediately preceding a noun are so rare that the possibility of such a construction here can practically be excluded. Baskervill and Wülker, taking *gŏd* to mean "munificentia", read *heofoncyninges | gŏd, dryhtendom;* but this is hardly possible as one expects a repetition of the genitive before the second noun; besides, the verse becomes unacceptable. Simons pp. 27, 68, gives a reading which has been overlooked but which I think must be accepted:

> ... *herede on hehðo   heofoncyninges gōd,*
> *dryhtnes domas.*

This reading fits the context perfectly well and involves only a slight change. The Andreas scribe sometimes forgets inflexional endings; cp. 43 *þegn* for *þegnas,* 843 *wis* for *wisa,* 1404 *leoð* for *leoðu.*

1080 ff   The Mermedonians send men to fetch their prisoners, whom they intend to eat. A ghastly surprise is in store for the messengers: the prisoners have disappeared, the guards lie dead. They return and report to their people:

> *sægdon þam folce   þæt ðær feorrcundra,*
> *ellreordigra,   ænig n e to lafe*
> *in carcerne   c w i c n e gemette,*
> *ah þær heorodreorige   hyrdas lagan,*
> *gæsne on greote,   gaste berofene* etc.

The passage has met with almost general disapproval. THORPE changes to *cwicne ne metton,* GRIMM to *cwicne ne gemetton,* which was adopted by KRAPP; GREIN to *cwic ne gemetton.* KRAPP explains his alteration by saying that *cwicne gemette* does not fit the context; TRAUTMANN, BEV, p. 121, and v. D. WARTH, p. 26, suggest other emendations of little interest. What troubles these critics is the absence of a subject of *gemette*; this subject WÜLKER takes to be *ænig,* reading *ænig ne to lafe* and *cwic ne gemette,* and translating "dass der fremden nicht einer übrig geblieben im gefängnisse (ihnen) lebendig begegnet sei". SIEVERS remarks on this (Btr. XVI, 551) that *gemette* requires an object, and, in fact, a use of *gemetan* such as WÜLKER suggests is hardly possible. However, there is nothing to prevent us from taking *ænig* as the subject and *cwicne* as the object required, reading:

> *sægdon þam folce   þæt ðær feorrcundra,*
> *ellreordigra,   ænig ne to lafe*
> *in carcerne   cwicne gemette* etc.

In that case *to lafe* goes with *cwicne*: "that nobody had met any one of the strangers left alive". The separation of *ænig* and *ne* is hardly a real alteration. Strictly speaking, this version and all the other versions suggested are inaccurate since those who are not left alive are really the guards, but the poet seems to have mixed up the two ideas: the prisoners were no longer there; the guards were no longer alive.

1116 b ff   *Ða wæs rinc manig,*
> *guðfrec guma,   ymb þæs geongan feorh*
> *breostum onbryrded.   To þam beadulace*
> *wæs þæt weatacen   wide gefrege ...*

Punctuation according to KRAPP, following CRAIGIE. But *to þam beadulace* has nothing to do with *wide gefrege* but belongs to *breostum onbryrded*, constructed ἀπὸ κοινοῦ. After *beadulace* a new sentence must begin. With WÜLKER and BASKERVILL we must read:

> ... *breostum onbryrded*   *to þam beadulace.*
> *Wæs þæt weatacen ...*

1222 ff (*com werod unmæte ...*)
> *ond þam halgan þær*   *handa gebundon.*
> *Sippan geypped wæs*   *æðelinga wynn,*
> *ond hie andweardne*   *eagum meahton* (*gesion.*)

It is true that the style of Andreas is sometimes crude, but such a monstrous hysteron proteron as KRAPP, following BASKERVILL and KOCK (Anglia XLIII, 302), here lays to the poet's charge, the latter could never have comitted. Of course *sippan* is a conjunction, not an adverb; with WÜLKER and CRAIGIE:

> *ond þam halgan þær*   *handa gebundon,*
> *sippan geypped wæs*   *æðelinga wynn ...*

1317 b ff   *Hwæt is wuldor þin,*
> *þe ðu oferhigdum*   *upp arærdest ...*

So nearly all editions. With GREIN we had better read *Hwær ...*, which gives a better meaning and fits the Greek ποῦ ἐστιν ἡ δύναμις; (BLATT p. 82) which, by the way, may be a reminiscence from Jes. 63, 15: *Ubi est zelus tua, et fortitudo tua ...?*

1509 b ff (*On ðe sylf cyning wrat ...*)   *wordum cyðde*
> *recene geryno,*   *ond ryhte æ*
> *getacnode*   *on tyn wordum,*
> *meotud mihtum swið.*   *Moyse sealde,*
> *swa hit soðfæste*   *syðþan heoldon,*
> *modige magoþegnas,*   *magas sine,*
> *godfyrhte guman,*   *Iosua ond Tobias.*

The passage must be read otherwise: KRAPP's full stop after *swið* gives no meaning. *Sealde* goes with *Moyse*, *swa*, probably, is an adverb = "in like manner":

> Meotud mihtum swið,   Moyse sealde;
> swa hit soðfæste   syðþan heoldon ...

"and, like Moses, the pious ones held it sacred ..." That God wrote His commandments on the pillar in the prison seems odd, but a comparison with P reveals that the Old English epic here cuts out Andrew's exhortation to the pillar telling it not to feel unworthy, being only a stone, to carry out God's command about the water since it was on tables of stone that He wrote the ten commandments. Joshua and Tobias is also a strange combination mentioned neither in P nor in C, and KRAPP thinks Tobias might stand for Caleb in the Numbers. I believe Joshua and Tobias are only mentioned as pious people respecting divine law: Joshua as Moses' successor, Tobias as the one who *viam veritatis non deseruit* (Tob. 1, 2).

1547   Ðær wæs yðfynde   innan burgum
         geomorgidd wrecen,   gehðo mænan,
         forhtferð manig,   fusleoð galen.

So the MS and nearly all editions. Apparently such a mixture of constructions is not what we expect here, and KRAPP reads

> ... geomorgidd wrecen.   Gehðo mændan
> forhtferð manig,   fusleoð golon.

GRIMM reads *mæned*, thus making it parallel with *galen*, ETTMÜLLER takes his bearings from *mænan* and reads *wrecan* and *galan*. TRAUTMANN (BEV, 131) believes in some omission between ll. 1548 and 1549. There is no need whatever for the latter assumption, and as for ETTMÜLLER's reading, it would only intensify the un-Germanic construction. Of course KRAPP's reading might be accepted, but there is nothing to make it evident and I think it would only be a trite normalization. Probably the words as they stand are what the poet wrote and then we have to do, probably, with a Latinism since in Latin an accusative with infinitive as the subject of an impersonal expression is common, even if it is not in Germanic languages. I think, then, that *gehðo mænan forhtferð manig* go together as the subject of *Ðær wæs yðfynde*, and that *geomorgidd wrecen* and *fusleoð galen* correspond:

> *Ðær wæs yðfynde*   *innan burgum*
> *geomorgidd wrecen,*   *gehðo mænan*
> *forhtferð manig,*   *fusleoð galen.*

Elene

56 b ff

>   *Cyning wæs afyrhted,*
> *egsan geaclad,*   *siððan elþeodige,*
> *Huna ond Hreða*   *here sceawedon,*
> *ðæt he on Romwara*   *rices ende*
> *ymb þæs wæteres stæð*   *werod samnode,*
> *mægen unrime.*

The passage has been the object of a lively discussion. For one thing the form *sceawedon* has been considered incongruous with *cyning*, and TEN BRINK (Anz. f. d. A. V., 58), WÜLKER, and further COOK EPh., and KRAPP alter to *sceawede*, whereas EKWALL (Anglia Beibl. XXXIII, 65) seems inclined to follow the MS reading. Secondly *ðæt he* in l. 59 has been attacked in various ways. ZUPITZA, GREIN, HOLTHAUSEN, change to *þæt þe*, though the latter two later return to the MS reading; TEN BRINK (ibid.) reads *ðæt hie*, which implies the reading *samnodon* in l. 60. KOCK, Engl. Stud. XLIV, 394, thinks that *he* refers to *here*, and KRAPP asks himself whether *ðæt* stands for *oððæt*, or, if we keep *ðæt*, whether it introduces a result clause.

The real error in this passage is not a formal one, as these critics seem to think: how can *he*, referring to *cyning*, collect a *mægen unrime*, when it has just before been mentioned that Constantinus' army was too small (*þeah hie werod læsse / hæfdon to hilde þonne Huna cining*), l. 48, 49; a statement repeated also in l. 63 (*hæfde wigena to lyt*)? Such an inconsistency is quite out of harmony with Cynewulf's manner, the more so as the contradictions immediately follow one another (cp. p. 319). Besides, Cynewulf seldom introduces a new action, even in a repetition, in a result clause (cp. pp. 156, 57), as KRAPP suggests. Now as for the solutions I think the alteration to *sceawede* is correct: *sceawedon* is an easy error after *Huna ond Hreða here* and implies too harsh a change of subject; besides, the Latin has *videns ... contristatus est.* The suggested alterations of *ðæt he* seem to me to be wrong. *Pæt þe* is not elsewhere found in Elene. *Ðæt hie* involves a second alteration: *samnodon. He* referring to *here* is far-fetched and illogical (*he samnode, werod*). From a palæographic point of view *oððæt* is bold and does not solve the difficulty with *mægen unrime.*

I think one may arrive at a simpler explanation by tracing what happened when the scribe wrote the passage down. Just as *Huna ond Hreða here* influenced *sceawede*, so these same words had an effect on line 59 as well, in so far as *he* probably came into that line as a perseveration from the initial h-series in l. 58. I omit *he* and take *samnode* as an intransitive with *werod* as its subject, the clause ll. 59—61 being an epexegetic enlargement of *here*, depending on *sceawede* constructed ἀπὸ κοινοῦ:

> Cyning wæs afyrhted,
> egsan geaclad, siððan elþeodige,
> Huna ond Hreða here sceawede,
> ðæt on Romwara rices ende
> ymb þæs wæteres stæð werod samnode,
> mægen unrime.

150 b ff   Com þa wigena hleo
> þegna þreate þrýðbord stenan,
> beadurof cyning burga neosan.

The passage has met with many objections. GRIMM altered to *þrýð-bord scenan* (to make to shine), and was followed by KEMBLE and ETTMÜLLER. KÖRNER (Engl. Stud. II, 254) changed to *stunian* (resound), and TRAUTMANN (BEV, 99) to *stellan*, "lay down the shield". SARRAZIN (ZfdPh XXXII, 548) emended to *þrýðbold secan* and HOLTHAUSEN, COOK ibid., GREIN-KÖHLER pp. 631, 726), and KRAPP approve. I cannot see why the words are objectionable and why we cannot follow GREIN, ZUPITZA, and WÜLKER in retaining them. *Ðrýðbord stenan* would mean 'adorn the shield with gems', an action not surprising after a victory when rich spoils have been taken, as *huðe hremig* l. 149 indicates. The distribution of the spoils may have taken place after the army's return home, and in poetical language *þrýðbord stenan* and *burga neosan* can therefore mean the same thing and be parallels (cp. p. 195).

436 ff   *swa þa þæt ilce gio   min yldra fæder*
sigerof sægde,   (þam wæs Sachius nama),
frod fyrnwiota,   fæder minum,
. . . . eaferan,
wende hine of worulde   ond þæt word gecwæð:

Ever since Grein a gap in the text between *minum* and *eaferan* has been assumed. Zacheus has told his son Simon, Judas's father, what will befall the Jews if the hiding-place of the Cross is revealed, and Simon repeats the same thing to his son in the speech following *gecwæð*. The suggestions as to how the supposed gap should be filled differ according to the critics' opinions about the identity of *eaferan*. Grein, thinking it applies to Judas, emends elaborately ⟨þe hit siððan cyðde sylfa his⟩ *eaferan*. Holthausen apparently holds *eaferan* to be Simon and prefers ⟨Symon wæs haten, sinum⟩ *eaferan* and Craigie's ⟨þam wæs Simon nama, swæsum⟩ *eaferan* testifies to the same opinion. Krapp, although like Zupitza and Wülker he supplies nothing but only indicates the gap, seems inclined to accept any proposition implying Simon to be the subject of *wende*, which goes without saying. Now all these suggestions are highly uncertain and except for Grein's emendation, which constructs a pronominal subject of *wende*, they seem strangely unnecessary and do nothing to make the passage clearer.

In the MS there is no visible omission between *minum* and *eaferan*. Further the reading *fæder minum eaferan* is metrically more acceptable than *fæder minum*, which has been improved by Sievers, Btr X, 483, Cook ibid., and Holthausen into *fædere minum*. From a formal point of view, then, there is no need to shove *eaferan* down like a fragment of the next line. As for the context I agree with those who consider *eaferan* to be Simon. But I do not see why there should be a gap and why emendations should be necessary. *Eaferan* is parallel to *fæder* and expresses a notion implied in that word: "my grandfather told my father, his son". The inverted order of the two words is apparently due to alliterative demands. The subject of *wende* must then be supplied from *fæder*, an operation which is also necessary if one accepts Holthausen's or Craigie's emendations. The construction might seem harsh, but the implying of a subject from a noun in an oblique case is not without parallel in Cynewulf; cp. Juliana 382 ff: *Gif ic ænigne ellenrofne gemete modigne metodes cempan wið flanþræce, nele feor þonan bugan*

from beaduwe, ac he ... (and if h e will not fly away). The reading
would then be:

> *swa þa þæt ilce gio   min yldra fœder*
> *sigerof sægde,   (þam wœs Sachius nama),*
> *frod fyrnwiota,   fœder minum, eaferan;*
> *wende hine of worulde   ond þæt word gecwœð* ...

522 ff   *Forðan ic þe lœre   þurh leoðorune,*
            hyse leofesta,   þæt ðu hospcwide,
            œfst ne eofulsœc   œfre ne fremme,
            grimme geagncwide,   wið godes bearne.

This is the moral sense of Simon's long speech about the evil of
man and the Grace of Christ. The form *leoðorune* has caused great
trouble. SIEVERS (Btr. X, 504) prefers *lēoðrune* or alternatively
lĕoðurune, and is followed by ZUPITZA in his third and fourth editions.
COOK ibid., followed by CRAIGIE; and GREIN-KÖHLER (p. 415) also have
leoðrune. SWEET, in Student's Dictionary p. 107, reads *leoðo-run*,
translated as 'advice'. TRAUTMANN, BEV. p. 100, emends, with little
palæographic probability, to *leornunge*. KRAPP retains the MS reading
but leaves the translation an open question. He rightly remarks that
leoðrune, 'advice in song' gives no appropriate meaning and that
what one would expect as the first element of the compound is "some
meaning like 'kindly', 'friendly', 'gentle', as in *leofspell* l. 1016".

I wonder if we cannot draw the practical conclusions of this last
observation by emending to *þurh liðe rune*, which, as far as I can
see, is the only possibility of getting a tolerable meaning here.
Palæographically, *leoðorune* may be explained by an anticipation of
eo .in the following *leofesta* with *eo* influencing also the second
syllable in *liðe*. As for possible metrical objections, a second half-line
like *þurh liðe rune* is no more out of keeping than 495 b *to wrœce
ne sette*, 581 b *to woruldgedale* (if we follow KRAPP's arrangement),
631 b *ge he ða rode ne tœhte*, or 1251 b *ic þæs wuldres treowes*. With
liðe rune we may compare *liþum wordum* Gu. 363.

613 b ff   *ond him hlaf ond stan*
            on gesihðe bu   geweorðað ...

Various suggestions have been made to supply the missing
alliterative word. ZUPITZA, HOLTHAUSEN in his first edition, COOK ibid.,

and KRAPP read *samod geweorðað*, but I think *geseted weorðað*, the emendation in HOLTHAUSEN's fourth edition, apparently inspired by TEN BRINK's *gesette weorðað* (Anz. f. d. A, V, 60), is the most natural. Cp. the Vita Quiriaci: *Et quis panibus et lapidibus sibi appositis lapides manducat.*

627 ff   *Iudas maðelade,   him wæs geomor sefa,*
            hat æt heortan,   ond gehwæðres wa,
            ge he heofonrices   ... swamode
            ond þis ondwearde   anforlete
            rice under roderum ...

This passage has become classic in textual criticism of Cynewulf. The omission in the MS of the alliterative word in the second half of line 629 and the odd *swamode* in the same line have given rise to a great many conjectures. Commentators generally agree that *hyht* is the word to alliterate with *heofonrices*, but opinions differ about *swamode*. GREIN (Germ. X, 424) changed *mode* to *niode*, which would mean "that he should be forced to give up the joy of heaven". Some critics, such as ZUPITZA and KRAPP, read *swa mode*. But "in such a way" does not fit the context very well. COOK ibid. proposes *swa mærne*, which is a somewhat arbitrary alteration. HOLTHAUSEN has the reading *heofonrices ⟨hyht⟩ swa snūde | ond þis andwearde ...*; in Anglia Beibl. XLIX, 348 he suggests *swa moðe*, related to *meðe*. Such a word is however unprecedented. KLAEBER (Anglia XXIX, 272) reads *hyhtwynne samod*, another variation of the possibilities. TRAUTMANN (BEV, 102), and also CRAIGIE and KOCK keep *swamode* as a verb, and the latter critic (JJJ p. 22) defends it in the sense "forego, move or stray away from". The word is generally held to mean "grow dark" (thus BOSWORTH-TOLLER, p. 943, HOLTHAUSEN, Et. W. p. 332), but it seems as if more attention ought to be paid to KOCK's doubts concerning this meaning. KOCK, commenting on Guthlac 1069—71 where *rodor swamode* occurs, says: "The Teut. *$swaim$-, as far as I can see, means 'move (in a vague manner, not in a straight direction, not with a fixed goal)'. ... ONo *sweima* means 'wander', 'stray', OE *aswæman* 'move on', 'wander about', *aswamian* 'pass on' (disappear)." Still, by change of meaning, *swamian* in the Guthlac passage probably means 'grow dark', but in the Cynewulf poem it really seems to be a verb of motion and should be retained

as the lectio difficilior, superior to other suggestions. Kindred words
are Norw. *svima* "languish", "cease"; Icel. *svia*; and MHG *sweimen*
"soar", "tumble"; OFris. subst. *swima* "swoon". To move "in a vague
manner" or "to go away", "retire", seem then to be the two chief
meanings of words of this group. In Elene *swamian*, parallel with
anforlete, has the sense "to move away from, to leave". A genitive
with *swamian* would then be an instance of the common genitivus
separationis, found with such verbs as *lysan*, *ageotan*, *asceadan*,
awerian etc. KOCK compares (*wuldres*) *blunne*, Andr. 1380, which is
close in meaning to a form of *swamian* with the genitive. I think
then that one has every reason to keep *swamode* and to read,
supplying a genitive:

> *ge he heofonrices* *⟨hyhtes⟩ swamode*
> *ond þis ondwearde* *anforlete ...*

translated: "that he should go away from the joy of heaven, leave
this present world".

628 b ff   *... ond gehwæðres wa,*
> *ge he heofonrices* *⟨hyhtes⟩ swamode,*
> *ond þis ondwearde* *anforlete,*
> *rice under roderum,* *ge he ða rode ne tæhte.*

The problem is whether *ne* should be omitted or not. ZUPITZA was the
first to recommend dropping it, taking l. 631 b as Judas's second
alternative. HOLTHAUSEN wavers: in the first and second edition he
omits the *ne*, in his third he reads *ðæt reht* for *ða rode ne*, and in his
fourth *gif he ða rode ne tæhte*, inspired by TRAUTMANN, BEV p. 102.
KLAEBER likewise omits *ne* (Anglia XXIX, 272), but KRAPP keeps it,
thinking that *gehwæðres wa* refers to "the heavenly and the earthly
life".

But there can hardly be any doubt that *ge-ge* really introduce
the two alternatives: if Judas does not reveal the secret about the
Cross he will die and his soul will not be redeemed after death; if
he does, the power of the Jews, according to his grandfather, will be
for ever broken. Thus both things are equally odious to him, hence
his dilemma. *Gehwæðres wa*, then, cannot refer to the loss of heavenly
and earthly life: that is only the one alternative, the other is implied
in the revelation of the Mystery of the Cross. It seems clear, therefore,

that *ne* should be left out. But the second question is, was *ne* mis-written for something else, or did the MS originally contain nothing in its place? It seems scarcely probable that the scribe should have introduced a negation from nowhere. I suggest that *ne tœhte* was mis-written for *getœhte*: the pattern *gehwœðres — ge — ge — getœhte* would be quite in keeping with Cynewulf's inclination for stylistic devices (cp. pp. 188—193). Cp. also 601 *þœt he be ðœre rode riht getœhte*, 1074 ff *Ðu me ... þone œðelan beam ... ryhte getœhtesð.*

924 b ff

                                        Gen ic findan ne can
   þurh wrohtstafas   wiðercyr wiððan
   of ðam wearhtreafum,   ic awecce wið ðe
   oðerne cyning,   se ehteð þin,
   ond he forlœteð   lare þine ...

So the MS. ZUPITZA in his first edition keeps the *ne* of the MS, but all other editors after GREIN omit it. *Wiððan* was altered by GREIN to *siððan*, and HOLTHAUSEN, ZUPITZA, COOK ibid., and KRAPP follow him. WÜLKER retains *wiððan*, translating *wiðercyr* 'abfall in religiöser be-ziehung, hæresie', i. e. the devil admits that he has been defeated, but he can find revenge upon the victorious powers in 'another king': Julian the Apostate, according to GREIN. WÜLKER'S *wiððan* seems doubtful, *wiðercyr* in the sense "apostasy" not very convincing and his instance of *wiðercora* = "sinner", "apostate" too distant (Ælfric, Hom. I, 332) to be of any interest to a *wiðercyr* in Cynewulf. Further *wiðercyr ... of* can scarcely mean anything but "return from" as the other editors think. The alteration to *siððan* I think is correct, as also GREIN's identification of *oðerne cyning* with Julian the Apostate. KRAPP thinks this is "remote" — but which other *"cyning"*, after Constantine, can be meant by one who *ehteð þin, ond he forlœteð lare þine, ond manþeawum minum folgaþ?*

Still I cannot help thinking that the passage has not received full justice. The reading *Gen ic findan can*, on which all editors agree, obscures the context. The devil in the lines preceding the passage in question laments his failure, deplores his inability to keep the souls in his prison, bemoans the misery of his own realm compared to the splendour of the kingdom of God. He also states that he was often confined in his hell by the Saviour. Then, after having declared that Judas adds to his misery, he proceeds, according to the editors, by saying "I can find again a return by foul deeds from hell, I will stir up another king against you ..."? I can see no coherence between these statements: the devil has no reason to complain of his broken power if he is still able to visit the earth plotting against humanity as before. Further, what would *oðerne cyning* mean? If the devil could himself find a means of return from hell, why should he send another king? I prefer to keep the *ne* of the MS:

> *Gen ic findan ne can*
> *þurh wrohtstafas*   *wiðercyr siððan*
> *of ðam wearhtreafum;*   *ic awecce wið ðe*
> *oðerne cyning ...*

taking the sentence beginning by *ic awecce* as adversatively asyndetic: "I myself cannot again find my return etc.; but I will rouse another king" ... The devil means that now as often before he will be shut up in his hell (*se hælend me in þam engan ham oft getynde*, l. 919 ff), being vanquished by the good powers, and will not be able to make his way out by a crime (like the one told of in Genesis), but he will revenge himself by sending "another king", an evil persecutor who will obey his commands. The Leabhar Breac reads: "... dass ich fortgetrieben werde von dir. Ich werde einen Plan gegen dich finden ... der einen gegen dich erwecken wird" etc. (375 ff). It should be observed how often the devil's confinement in hell as a punishment is referred to in this poetry; cp. Andr. 1190 "*Ðe se ælmihtiga heanne gehnægde, ond on heolstor besceaf, þær þe cyninga cining clamme belegde*", and El. ll. 941 ff where Judas replies to the devil: "*þec se mihtiga cyning in neolnesse nyðer bescufeð ... on fyrbæðe suslum ... wunodest ... ond þær awa scealt ... wergðu dreogan*". These remarks seem to refer to the fall of the devil after the revolt against God, but the same relegation of the devil or his followers to hell apparently takes place every time they fail in their seductions among humanity, cp. Juliana 382 ff: "*Gif ic ænigne ellenrofne· gemete modigne metodes cempan ... ic sceal feor þonan heanmod hweorfan, hroþra bidæled, in gleda gripe gehðu mænan,*"

934 ff   *Him ða gleawhydig*   *Iudas oncwæð,*
         hæleð hildedeor,   (*him wæs halig gast*
         befolen fæste,   *fyrhat lufu,*
         weallende gewitt   *þurh wigan snyttro*).

Following a suggestion by GREIN (Germania X, 424) the editors change to *witgan* except ZUPITZA and WÜLKER, who read as in the MS. The conservative reading is much superior to the alteration: *witga* means 'prophet' and is used by Cynewulf either about the prophets of Israel or about Judas's father Simon (El. 592), who was looked upon as a predictor by the Jews. *Wiga* here is as appropriate as possible since the converted Judas is fighting his oral duel with the devil and has just been called a *hæleð hildedeor*.

939 ff   "*Ne þearft ðu swa swiðe,*   *synna gemyndig,*
           sar niwigan   *ond sæce rœran,*
           morðres manfrea,   *þæt se mihtiga cyning*
           in neolnesse   *nyðer bescufeð ...*"

ZUPITZA reads *þæt þe se mihtiga* ... to get an object for *bescufeð*, and SIEVERS (Anglia I, 579), KRAPP, and HOLTHAUSEN agree with him. WÜLKER finds the addition unnecessary and reads as in the MS, but COSIJN, Anteekeningen p. 32, emends *þæt* to *þec* and is followed by TRAUTMANN, BEV p. 105, and COOK ibid. COSIJN's criticism of ZUPITZA, in my opinion, hits the mark: "De bewering dat de Duivel niet zoo ver mocht gaan dat God hem in de hel terugstoot (is) juist het tegendeel ... van wat Judas wenschte: immers des Duivels aanwezigheid was volstrekt ongewenscht". As a defence for COSIJN's conjecture it should be pointed out that its syntactical advantage is great: *þec* introduces an asyndetic causal clause containing the reason why the devil's evil designs are henceforth thwarted. Palæographically, the emendation is very easy owing to the similarity between *t* and *c*.

1239 b ff   *Nysse ic gearwe*
     be ðære riht   *ær me rumran geþeaht*
     þurh ða mæran miht   *on modes þeaht*
     wisdom onwreah.   *Ic wæs weorcum fah,*
     synnum asæled,   *sorgum gewæled,*
     bitrum gebunden,   *bisgum beþrungen,*
     ær me lare onlag   *þurh leohtne had*
     gamelum to geoce,   *gife unscynde*
     mægencyning amæt   *ond on gemynd begeat,*
     torht ontynde,   *tidum gerymde,*

bancofan onband,   *breostlocan onwand,*
leoðucræft onleac.   *Ðæs ic lustum breac,*
willum in worlde.

This "autobiographical" passage offers one of the most discussed and interesting problems of Cynewulf criticism and the suggested solutions of the difficulty in l. 1240 a are numerous. Ever since GRIMM's days different attempts to elucidate the passage have been made, but neither his nor ETTMÜLLER's and LEO's suggestions are of very much interest nowadays. GREIN, thinking that a word had been left out, read *be ðære r o d e riht*, which has been accepted by a number of scholars (RIEGER, ZfdPh I, 316, ZUPITZA, HOLTHAUSEN, COOK ibid., and KRAPP). HOLTHAUSEN, with SIEVERS Btr. IX, 236, unnecessarily modified the reading into *reht* and *gepæht* 1240 b for the sake of rhyme. KOCK (Anglia XLIV, 107) creates a new Old English word, reading *be ðære rehtan ræhð*, explaining *ræhð* as "exposition". WÜLKER questions GREIN's reading: "Warum hier auf einmal das kreuz erwähnt sein soll inmitten der allgemeinen betrachtungen sieht man nicht ein". He suggests himelf the emendation *be pære rihtan æ, ær me* etc. to get a more appropriate expression for the general reflections of the passage and one that differs less from the version of the MS. SEDGEFIELD, finally, prefers *be ðære rihtan eaht, eaht* meaning 'deliberating' (Verse Book).

The readings of SEDGEFIELD and KOCK imply no improvement of the text from the point of view of meaning, and palæographically they are equally doubtful. GREIN's suggestion is more possible, but I must agree with WÜLKER that it suffers from an obvious lack of conclusiveness, having no organic connection with the rest of the passage. Further it does not go very well with 1251 b ff *ic pæs wuldres treowes oft, nales æne, hæfde ingemynd* etc., and probably GREIN emended mechanically on the analogy of passages like 601 *pæt he be ðære rode riht getæhte.* KENT, in a note on the passage, explains this emendation: ... "that is, that the extended knowledge derived from his reading and aided by his reflection, had given him a clearer insight into the real significance of the cross"; all this is in itself quite possible, but there is nothing in the passage that really supports this somewhat fanciful piece of exegesis. Even if WÜLKER's reading is far better, still it provides the text with an unnecessary truism and does not conform with the line of thought of the passage.

In the paragraph in question, which has an unmistakably introspective character as distinguished from the impersonal tenor of the following rune passage, we find that the poet is speaking of his condition before and after a spiritual gift has been bestowed on him (*rumran geþeaht ... wisdom onwreah ...; lare onlag ... gife unscynde mægencyning amæt ond on gemynd begeat*). This gift is obviously the insight into the Christian truth, and the author's feelings a f t e r receiving it (*þæs ic lustum breac, willum in worlde*) forms a characteristic contrast to his situation b e f o r e receiving it: *Ic wæs weorcum fah, synnum asæled, sorgum gewæled, bitrum gebunden, bisgum beþrungen.* Now 1. 1239 b—40 a also tells us something about the poet before Grace was granted him, and it would fit in quite naturally with the already mentioned lines which follow if we read, taking *ðære* to be a contraction of *ðā ræ* [2] —:

> *Nysse ic gearwe*
> be ð a m r æ d e riht   *ær me rumran geþeaht* etc.,

translating: 'I did not know at all the truth about welfare' ...

For *ræd* in this sense cp. Hy 4, 17 *þeah þe ic wuldorcyninge waccor hyrde, þonne min ræd wære*; Met 2, 12 *me þa berypton rædes and frofre*; 21, 9 *to þæm gesælðum saula rædes*; Dan. 30 *oð þæt hie langung beswac eorðan dreamas eces rædes*; Beow. 1201 *geceas ecne ræd*; for *riht* El. 601 *þæt he be ðære rode riht getæhte*, Order of the World 13 *cuþon ryht sprecan*, cp. GREIN-KÖHLER, pp. 542, 555. Thus we get a coherent description of the poet's spiritual experience from 1236 (*Ðus ic frod ond fus ...*) down to 1251, the passage in all the Cynewulf poems in which the poet speaks most intimately about himself.

The textual criticism of the Exeter Book offers some attractive problems owing to the sometimes fairly complicated ideas and beliefs which underlie the text and to which due attention must be paid. The following suggested solutions of the problems that differ from those of earlier critics often prove to be points of interpretation rather than emendations — there is then nothing wrong with the readings of the MS, but the original meaning has been lost during the critical treatment of the text. In such cases a change of punctuation, at most, is

---

[2] For the palæographic explanation I am indebted to a suggestion by Professor Arngart.

the only operation necessary. Most of our texts, like the main part of the Exeter Book, is in very good condition with neat and clear writing; but the opening section of Christ I has been for ever obscured for us by the severe damage inflicted on the first folio. This damage extends to a few places in the otherwise legible text of the first 155 lines, but there the injury is no worse than that emendations can be ventured upon although, of course, not without the uncertainty that always attends the filling in of textual gaps. Some of the puzzles have already been cleared up by using ultra-violet rays and the original readings are used in KRAPP-DOBBIE's edition.

Christ I

22 ff
Huru we for þearfe þas word sprecað,
ond m⟨one⟩ giað þone þe mon gescop
þæt he ne . ete ... ceose weorðan
cearfulra þing, þe we in carcerne
sittað sorgende, sunnan wenað,
hwonne us liffrea leoht ontyne etc.

The source of these lines is a part of the Great Antiphon of Advent (BURGERT p. 24): (*O Clavis David*) *veni, et educ vinctum de domo carceris, sedentem in tenebris et umbra mortis.* Man is compared to a prisoner, waiting for the Saviour to release him. The remaining letters around the gap on line 24 are only faintly legible and can be accepted with certainty only with the help of the ultra-violet ray. CHAMBERS reads *hete* in 24 a, but as KRAPP-DOBBIE point out the *h* is by no means certain, and they think it looks more like a *b*. SCHIPPER (Germania XIX, 329) reads *hete to hofe ceose*, but the gap in the MS is not big enough to admit of this conjecture, the meaning of which, by the way, is very obscure. For *weorðan*, earlier edd. read *sprecan* and the facsimile is illegible, but according to KRAPP-DOBBIE, the ultra-violet print "plainly shows *weorðan*". They sum up: "A plausible reconstruction is difficult to find here, and it may be that the text as it stood was corrupt." HOLTHAUSEN, Anglia Beibl. LIV, p. 31, 32 emends to

⟨*ond mynd*⟩ *giað þone þe mon gescop*
þæt he ne ⟨*his cwealm*⟩ *hete *⟨*ge*⟩*ceose* ⟨*wre*⟩*can;*

but this seems too fanciful and uncertain.

Now to begin with ·*ete* I do not think that we should read a *b* here: KRAPP-DOBBIE may have been misled by a slight crease in the parchment. Instead, we seem to be justified in reading *l*, and after *l* an *œ* is not too faintly visible. *Pæt he. ne læte* would then seem to be the reading of 24 a. As for the restoration of *ceose*, we do not get any help from the facsimile. I suggest the reading *to forlore weorðan*. Line 24 ff would then run:

> *pæt he ne læte*   *to forlore weorðan*
> *cearfulra þing* etc.,

'that he may not suffer the crowd of the wretched to come to perdition'. For the phrase cp. Andreas 1423 *ne loc of heafde to forlore wurde*.

59 ff is a praise of Jerusalem, which is blessed and honoured as the city of God. Jesus' stay there is symbolized by God descending from Heaven and taking up His abode in the city:

> *Sioh nu sylfa þe g e o n d*   *þas sidan gesceaft,*
> *swylce rodores hrof*   *rume g e o n d w l i t a n*
> *ymb healfa gehwone,*   *hu þec heofones cyning*
> *siðe geseceð,*   *onð sylf cymeð,*
> *nimeð eard in þe,*   *swa hit ær gefyrn*
> *witgan wisfæste*   *wordum sægdon* etc.

According to GREIN *geond* goes with *þe* (*þe geond* = χατά σε GREIN-KÖHLER p. 257), and all later editors seem to agree with him. But HOLTHAUSEN (Literaturblatt XXI, 371, 72) places the caesura after *þe*, assuming some omission after that line. COOK C says that the only interpretation conforming to the Antiphon (*Leva in circuitu oculos tuos*) is GREIN's, translating *þe geond* 'about thee'. The real difficulty, according to him, is *geondwlitan*, "for which one would like to substitute *geondwlīt*, parallel with *sioh*". *Gesceaft* would then be the object of *sioh* and *hrof* the object of *geondwlīt*. COOK also discusses the possibility of taking *gesceaft* as the object of *geond*, translating *sylfa þe* = 'thyself'. He does not give any acceptable solution of *geondwlitan* but quotes a suggestion by BRIGHT, who "would construe *sioh ... geondwlitan* as formed upon the analogy of expressions like *ga gesittan, cum neosian*, where a verb of *motion* is more specifically defined by a following verb in the inf.". BRIGHT would translate: 'Lift up thine eyes (*sioh*) to look widely (*rume geondwlitan*) over the broad creation'. Cook rightly declines this conjecture as being "too venturesome". Krapp-Dobbie do nothing to explain the crux: according to them *þe geond* belong together, "a thought repeated in l. 61 a", and the "whole passage is consistent and consecutive in meaning"(!)

It cannot be doubted, however, that Holthausen's placing of the caesura is the original one. The Antiphonary passage runs: *O Hierusalem, civitas Dei summi: leva in circuitu oculos tuos ... quia jam veniet solvere te a vinculis.* Jerusalem lifts her eyes towards God approaching from above: *sioh nu sylfa þe | geond þas sidan gesceaft* etc. Only l. 61 a *ymb healfa gehwone*, then, corresponds to *in circuitu*. As Cook alternatively suggested, *þe sylfa* means 'thyself'; cp. Andr. 1348, Gen. 934 etc. As for *geondwlitan*, Cook is certainly right trying to establish a parallelism between this word and *sioh*. Is there no alternative to *geondwlit* which does not land us in metrical difficulties? With a slight alteration I think we can put the text in order, reading

> Sioh nu sylfa þe   geond þas sidan gesceaft
> swylce rodores hrof   rume geondwlite
> ymb healfa gehwone etc.

As regards this combination of imperative and optative in exhortations cp. Chr. 243 b ff *Cum nu, sigores weard ... ond þine miltse her arfœst ywe!*; 251 ff *þa gyldnan geatu ... hat ontynan, ond usic þonne gesece ...*; Gen. 517 b ff *lœste þu georne his ambyhto, nim þe þis ofœt on hand*; Ps. 65, 1 *Ealle eorðbuend ecne drihten wordum wislicum wide herian, and his naman secgeað neode mid sealmum* etc. Ps. 148, 2 *Heriað hine ealle engla ðreatas, lofige hine swylce eall his leodmœgen!* (cp. Behre pp. 16, 28 ff). The copyist's error, to all appearances, was due to a vertical slip from the ending *e* to *an* in *sidan*, which is written immediately above in the MS. The subject must be supplied from the preceding *Hierusalem—þu* ll. 50—58.

152 b ff   *Is seo bot gelong*
> eal œt þe anum, ... ofer þearfum.
> Hœftas hygegeomre   hider ⟨gesec⟩ es;
> ne lœt þe behindan,   þonne þu heonan cyrre,
> mœnigo þus micle etc.

Geseces, Krapp-Dobbie's amendment of Gollancz's conjecture *gesece*, seems certain. The word preceding *oferþearfum* was restored as *for* by Sievers, Btr. X, 453, on the analogy of El. 521 *for ofer-þearfe*, followed by Cosijn, Btr. XXIII, 109; and as *æfter* by Holt-hausen, IF IV, 384, and so Cook C. But, as Krapp-Dobbie remark, the first letter of the missing word seems to have an ascending stroke, so neither of the two suggestions seem appropriate. A close inspection of the facsimile reveals a barely visible *e* in the left part of the gap, so we might read *her for oferþearfum*, which would go well with the following *hider-heonan*.

185 b ff Joseph is upbraiding Maria, thinking she has committed adultery:

> *Is þæt wide cuð*
> *þæt ic of þam torhtan   temple dryhtnes*
> *onfeng freolice   fæmnan clæne,*
> *womma lease,   ond nu gehwyrfed is*
> *þurh nathwylces.   Me nawþer deag,*
> *secge ne swige.*

After *nathwylces* a word must have been left out. Possible restorations are *scyld* (Cosijn, Btr. XXIII, 110) or *nið* (Kock, Anglia XLIV, 104). But *nathwylces mān* would be easier to adopt since *mān* may easily have been dropped by haplography owing to the following *me na-*. *Mān* 'sin', moreover, is better in meaning than *nið* 'wicked-ness' or *scyld* 'guilt'.

206 b ff

> *Nu ic his tempel eam*
> *gefremed butan facne,   in me frofre gæst*
> *geeardode.   Nu þu ealle forlæt*
> *sare sorgceare.*

Punctuation according to editors. But *nu-nu* must be correlative here, the clause introduced by the first *nu* containing the reason for the clause introduced by the second, so we should put a comma instead of full stop after *geeardode*. For the same construction with the same order of clauses cp. Chr. 573 b ff *Nu ge geare cunnon hwæt se hlaford is se þisne here lædeð, nu ge fromlice freondum togeanes gongað glædmode.*

310 b ff Isaiah has been brought to Paradise, where he beholds an enormous door, girt with metal and wondrous fittings:

> Wende swiðe
> þæt ænig elda   æfre meahte
> swa fæstlice   forescyttelsas
> on ecnesse   o inhebban,
> oþþe ðæs ceasterhlides   clustor onlucan,
> ær him godes engel   þurh glædne geþonc
> þa wisan onwrah   ond þæt word acwæð etc.

In the following lines the angel tells him that the Lord will pass through the gate, descending to the earth, and that after His traversing it the door will be for ever shut; only God can open it.

THORPE, GREIN, ASSMANN, COOK C, and KRAPP-DOBBIE read *ne* between *æfre* and *meahte*, only GOLLANCZ keeps the MS reading, translating "he pondered deeply, how any mortal man might ever raise those bolts so firmly fixed etc.". It may seem natural at first to supply a negation but we are, I think, fairly safe in regarding the conservative readings as the lectio difficilior. The poet presents to us the image of the prophet contemplating the wonderful object, meditating on the difficulty for mortal man to open these huge bolts, until the angel informs him that only God can open it. Compared with this the idea 'He did not at all expect any mortal man to be capable of unlocking it till the angel told him that God alone would do so' is logically far less satisfactory. As regards the meaning 'ponder', it can easily be ascribed to a verb so often used in the sense 'think'. A similar significance is to be found in Christ and Satan 89: *Wene(ge) þæt tacen sutol þa ic aseald wes on wærgðu*; I translate "Consider the manifest miracle, when I was given over to condemnation". There does not seem to be any reason, then, to change anything in the MS version.

Christ II

537 b ff

> Ðær wæs wopes hring,
> torne bitolden;   wæs seo treowlufu
> hat æt heortan,   hreðer innan weoll,
> beorn breostsefa.

KRAPP's and DOBBIE's punctuation distorts the context. How can *wopes hring* be *torne bitolden*? With the old editions one must interpret:

> *Ðær wæs wopes hring;*
> *torne bitolden*   *wæs seo treowlufu,*
> *hat æt heortan;*   *hreðer innan weoll ...*

Cynewulf means to say that the apostles' love was mixed with sorrow; as GOLLANCZ translates: "their faithful love was overwhelmed with grief".

554 b ff

> *Gesegon wilcuman*
> *on heahsetle*   *heofones waldend,*
> *folca feorhgiefan,*   *frætwum ealles waldend*
> *middangeardes*   *ond mægenþrymmes.*

The passage has been much criticized. SIEVERS (Btr. X, 515) objects to line 556 b from a metrical point of view, saying that it is "metrisch falsch", and suggests that *waldend* has crept into it as an echo from l. 555. He omits *waldend* and changes to *frætwan ealles*, taking *frætwan* as the acc. of a noun *frætwa*, "Schmücker". Such a noun is however very doubtful. TRAUTMANN (BEV, 89) falls back upon the explanation that a leaf is missing. As *frætwum* is the last word on fol. 15 b, he thinks that the next word on the missing folio 16 a was a hypothetical *blican* and that the text between this word and *ealles waldend* has been lost. HOLTHAUSEN (Anglia Beibl. IX, 355) says that SIEVERS is right, but he himself alters to *fregan ealles*. KRAPP and DOBBIE think that either *waldend* can be omitted or else *frætwum waldend* may be the second part of l. 556 and *ealles* the beginning of line 557. The simplest explanation is that *waldend* was falsely repeated from l. 555b and that it should only be omitted. JOST's theory (English Studies XXVII, p. 175 ff) that ll. 558—85 are a fragment of a lost dialogue, is not convincing.

Christ III

1312 ff

> *Eala, þær we nu magon*   *wraþe firene*
> *geseon on ussum sawlum,*   *synna wunde,*
> *mid lichoman*   *leahtra gehygdu,*
> *eagum unclæne*   *ingeþoncas!*

1316 *Ne þæt ænig mæg oþrum gesecgan*
     mid hu micle elne æghwylc wille
     þurh ealle list lifes tiligan,
     feores forhtlice, forð a ðolian,[3]
1320 *synrust þwean ond hine sylfne þrean,*
     ond þæt wom ærran wunde hælan,
     þone lytlan fyrst þe her lifes sy,
     þæt he mæge fore eagum eorðbuendra
1324 *unscomiende eðles mid monnum*
     brucan bysmerleas, þendan bu somod
     lic ond sawle lifgan mote.

Punctuation according to ASSMANN, and all editors and critics
agree. But who can really believe that an author of such a poem as
Christ III should have been naïve enough to make a statement like
the one beginning on l. 1316 a? There seems, indeed, to be a general
feeling of dissatisfaction with the passage. GREIN changes *wille* to
scyle, followed by COSIJN, Btr. XXIII, 113. COOK C proposes *sceolde*;
HOLTHAUSEN, Literaturblatt XXI, 372, says *wille* may mean 'möchte
wollen', and similarly MOORE, Archiv CXXXI, 312. But none of these
suggestions improves the meaning of the passage in any respect. The
critics take *þær* l. 1312 to mean 'utinam', apart from GOLLANCZ, who
omits it, and combine *mid lichoman* and *eagum* l. 1315: "with our
bodily eyes". This reading is apparently intended to correspond to
ll. 1329 b ff: *We mid þam oðrum ne magun, heafodgimmum* etc. As
COOK interprets: "If we only might (?) see our sins with our bodily
eyes! ... But we cannot see them with our bodily eyes" etc.

Now we may be fairly certain that there is nothing the matter
with the textual tradition. We may further be sure that the poet does
not simply say that everyone zealously wants to pay heed to his
life and free himself from the stain and wound of sin. If we want to
know what the author means, all we have to do is to put a comma
after *ingeþoncas*, taking the clause *þær—ingeþoncas* as subordinate
to *ne þæt ænig mæg* etc., and reading *þær* as 'if'. COSIJN (ibid.)
rejects the possibility of taking *þær* in the conditional sense. But if
þær = gif, *mid lichoman* does not go with *eagum*, for it is expressly
said l. 1328 that we can only penetrate into our souls *heortan eagum*.
Instead *mid lichoman* goes with *leahtra gehygdu*, 'the sinful thoughts

---

[3] The reading of 319 b is KRAPP's and DOBBIE's suggestion and very elegantly
solves the problem of the MS version *forð aðolian*.

of the flesh'; similarly Cott. Ps. 15: *þurh lichaman lene geðohtas*; 41 *ðurh lichaman leðre geðohtas*. *Eagum* goes with *geseon*, a common pleonastic combination; cp. Gen. 106 *eagum wlat*, 820 *minum eagum geseah*, Exod. 278 *eagum ... lociað*, Chr. 536 *eagum segun* etc. So reading, we get at the poet's meaning, namely, that if we can penetrate into our souls and see their sins and unclean thoughts, then the zeal with which everyone will endeavour to wash the stains of sin away and heal the inward wounds will be indescribable — a remark, it will be seen, that testifies to anything but superficial illusions concerning sin and human life.

1559 ff   *Ðonne mansceaða*   *fore meotude forht,*
        deorc on þam dome standeð,   *ond deaðe fah,*
        wommum awyrged,   *bið se wærloga*
        fyres afylled.

Cosijn, Btr. XXIII, 114, reads *fyrena afylled*, and Cook C hesitates between this and the MS version. Krapp-Dobbie and other editors keep *fyres*. But Holthausen, emending to *feres* = *færes* (Literaturblatt XXI, 372) has made an improvement which should certainly be adopted in the text: there can be no question of the sinner being "filled with fire" standing before the Lord, but filled with fear, a parallel to 1559 b. The copyist's mistake is easily explained as an anticipation of *y* in *afylled*.

Guthlac A

22 ff   *Ðider soðfæstra*   *sawla motun*
      cuman æfter cwealme,   *þa þe her Cristes æ*
      lærað ond læstað,   *ond his lof rærað;*
      oferwinnað þa awyrgdan gæstas,   *bigytað him wuldres ræste,*
      hwider sceal þæs monnes   *mod astigan,*
      ær oþþe æfter,   *þonne he his ænne her*
      gæst bigonge,   *þæt se gode mote,*
      womma clæne,   *in geweald cuman.*

This is Krapp-Dobbie's punctuation, with *hwider* as a relative, 'to which'. No doubt this arrangement is preferable to that of the other editors, who regard *hwider* as an interrogative and put a question mark after *cuman*. But we should get closer to the meaning here if we take *Ðider — hwider* to correspond and put a comma after *rœrað*. The idea underlying the lines seems to be: the souls of the just, of those who keep the law of Christ etc., are allowed to arrive, after death, to the place where the spirit of man (*þœs monnes mod*) ascends when on earth here (*her*) he observes spiritual discipline in solitude (*þonne he his œnne . . . gœst bigonge* with hendiadys) so that he may arrive in the Kingdom of Heaven (*þœt se gode mote in geweald cuman*); namely, when in prayer he communicates with God.

181 b ff

> Frome wurdun monge
> godes þrowera;   we þœs Guðlaces
> deorwyrðne dœl   dryhtne cennað.
> He him sige sealde   ond. snyttrucrœft,
> mundbyrd meahta,   þonne mengu cwom
> feonda fœrscytum   fœhðe rœran.

The reading *Guðlaces* is adopted by KRAPP-DOBBIE, following KOCK, JJJ., p. 40, who however proposed *guðlaces*, "of warfare". According to KOCK 181 b—182 a are parenthetic: — "valorous were many among God's sufferers — we of this warfare ascribe a glorious portion to the Lord". The pun *guðlaces*, however, seems anything but to the point and is rightly rejected by KRAPP-DOBBIE. Now, the MS does not read *Guðlaces* but *Guðlace*, and in order to retain the dative COSIJN, Btr. XXIII, 116, adds *eac* before *dryhtne*, translating "Guðlac, nächst Gott" etc., but his suggestion is declined by HOLT-HAUSEN, Anglia Beibl. IX, 356, for metrical reasons. GOLLANCZ reads as in the MS but translates "wherefore we ascribe Guthlac's dear-worth lot unto the Lord".

The textual tradition, I think, is authentic and gives good context. We should retain *Guðlace* and put a comma after *dœl*, taking *Guðlace* and *dryhtne* as dependent on *cennað* constructed ἀπὸ κοινοῦ. In this way we get the connection between *Frome wurdun monge godes þrowera* and the rest: many of God's martyrs became bold, and we ascribe a considerable share in this fact to Guthlac, as a model, and to the Lord, because the latter *him sige sealde ond snyttrucrœft*. A few lines earlier on the saint's importance as a model of holy life has been pointed out:

> *Ðær he mongum wearð*
> *bysen on Brytene,   sippan biorg gestah*
> *eadig oretta,   ondwiges heard.* (174 b ff)

Our passage, then, may be read as follows:

> *Frome wurdun monge*
> *godes prowera: we pæs Guðlace*
> *deorwyrdne dæl,   dryhtne cennað* etc.

269 ff The demons are mocking Guthlac because he thinks he can lead his life in the desert:

> *No we oferhygdu   anes monnes*
> *geond middangeard   maran fundon.*
> *Ðu pæt gehatest   pæt ðu ham on us*
> *gegan wille,   eart ðe godes yrming.*
> *Bi hwon scealt pu lifgan,   peah pu lond age?*
> *Ne pec mon hider   mose fedeð* etc.

The somewhat puzzling *eart ðe* made THORPE emend to *eart ðu.* GOLLANCZ, reading with the MS, translates "thou art God's starveling". KRAPP-DOBBIE admit this as a possibility, but prefer the alteration *ðe eart,* thinking a relative has been misplaced. Alternatively, they suggest the much inferior reading *ðeah* for *ðe,* which hardly gives any sense at all.

The text may be retained as it stands, and *ðe* explained as a reflexive dative, as in the Phoenix 287 b ff *Bið him edniwe pære sunnan pegn* (cp. p. 86).

393 b ff

> *Symle Cristes lof*
> *in Guðlaces   godum mode*
> *weox ond wunade,   ond hine weoruda god*
> *freoðade on foldan,.   swa he feora gehwylc*
> *healdeð in hælo,   pær se hyra gæst*

398

> *pihð in peawum.   He wæs peara sum;*
> *ne won he æfter worulde,   ac he in wuldre ahof*
> *modes wynne.   Hwylc wæs mara ponne se?*
> *An oretta   ussum tidum*
> *cempa gecyðeð   pæt him Crist fore*

403   *woruldlicra m a   wundra gecyðde.*
        He hine scilde   wið sceðþendra
        eglum onfengum   earma gæsta etc.

This arrangement of the text is KRAPP-DOBBIE's, and their version of l. 400 b is decidedly preferable to the odd displacements of earlier critics. Thus ASSMANN, following GREIN, unnecessarily ended l. 400 with a *he* supplied after *þonne*, reading *se an oretta* in l. 401 a. GOLLANCZ read the half-line in the same way but supplied nothing.

As for the rest of the passage, KEMBLE emended *gecyðeð*, 402 a, to *gecyðed*, and was followed by GOLLANCZ and HOLTHAUSEN, Anglia Beibl. IX, 356; the latter also changing *mara* 400 b to *ma*. GOLLANCZ's translation of the emended text containing *se an oretta* and *gecyðed* l. 402 a runs "What man was greater than he, the one hero, the one champion, known in our times, so that, on his behalf, Christ showed forth more wonders in this world?"; but this rendering does not make much sense.

As a matter of fact, the suggestions referred to here do not really suffice to put the text in order, and the critics are silent about the main problem of the passage. Why *woruldlicra m a wundra*? More than what? If *ma* means 'more miracles than those hitherto related', we look in vain for any earlier mention of such miracles: up to line 403 we hear nothing but that Guthlac is steadfast, resists the devils and speaks to them, and that his spirit is strengthened by the Lord. It is not until after these lines that we hear about the real miracle, i. e. that *no god wolde þæt seo sawl þæs sar þrowade in lichoman, lyfde sepeana þæt hy him mid hondum hrinan mosten* (l. 407 b ff) etc.; which results in the wonderful flight through the air ll. 412 ff. If, on the other hand, *ma* means 'more miracles than he showed to anyone else', we are at great pains of supplying a *þonne*-clause, and *ma* is always used in such a way that a *þonne*-clause is either expressed or can easily be supplied from the context. A connection with omitted links like the one between *him Crist ... ma wundra gecyðde* and *Hwylc wæs mara þonne se* (Christ showed more miracles to him (than to anybody else, so) who was greater than he?) is therefore much too far-fetched to be possible in our poem. Nevertheless, although *ma* gives doubtful sense it seems to be authentic, and the fault is apparently to be found in some other word in the passage. *An oretta* appears to be the weak point, and probably these words are the result

of a slight corruption distorting the meaning of the whole sentence.
After the restoration of a lost letter we may read:

Hwylc wæs mara þonne se?

A ne oretta	*ussum tidum*
cempa gecyðeð	*þæt him Crist fore*
woruldlicra ma	*wundra gecyðde.*

Here we can easily supply *þonne (Crist) Guðlace gecyðde*: *oretta*,
then, does not refer to the hero of the poem. The emended sentence
now also agrees in a natural way with the preceding rhetorical
question. The *woruldlicu wundor*, as was pointed out above, are
related at ll. 407 ff.

508 ff are the end of the saint's severe scolding of the demons:

Gefeoð in firenum,	*frofre ne wenað,*
þæt ge wræcsiða	*wyrþe gebiden.*

Oft ge in gestalum stondað; þæs cymeð steor of heofonum.

Me þonne sendeð	*se usic semon mæg,*
se þe lifa gehwæs	*lengu wealdeð.*

So the MS. The reading *semon*, 'reconcile' (HOLTHAUSEN Anglia Beibl.
IX, 356), is the final result of a discussion that need not be summed
up here, and has been accepted by KRAPP-DOBBIE. They also read
me þonne ⟨sige⟩ sendeð etc.; *sige* was originally added by GREIN
(Germania X, 424), but the other earlier editions read with the MS.
The addition obscures the meaning, which depends chiefly on the two
words *gestalum* and *semon*, and which does not seem to have been
made quite clear.

GREIN-KÖHLER, p. 631, and BOSWORTH-TOLLER, p. 444, think that
gestalum is < *gestǎlu*, 'theft', and GOLLANCZ translates "oft are ye
engaged in theft". Quite apart from the oddity of portraying the arch-
enemies of man as thieves, this interpretation of the word does not
agree with *semon*; nor does a reading *gestǎlu* = 'stealth', which
KRAPP and DOBBIE seem to have in mind when they refer to *stal-
gongum* l. 1140. *Semon* makes us expect a word for 'dissension',
'quarrel', so *gestalum* seems to be < *gestāl*, related to *stǣlan*,
'accuse', and *onstāl*, 'accusation'. "You are often occupied with
quarrels", the poet makes Guthlac say to the devils; that is why the
Lord sends a peacemaker like the saint as a *steor of heofonum*. To
make the context clearer, a colon may be put after *heofonum*.

541 ff The holy man is not exempt from the demons' torture, but like Andrew, he has his refuge from pain in God:

> *He þa sar forseah,   a þære sawle wel*

           *   *

            *

> *þæs mundboran*   *þe þæt mod geheold,*
> *þæt him ne getweode*   *treow in breostum,*
> *ne him gnornunga*   *gæste scodun,*
> *ac se hearda hyge*   *halig wunade,*
> *oþþæt he þa bysgu*   *oferbiden hæfde.*

GREIN, GOLLANCZ, ASSMANN, and KRAPP-DOBBIE all assume a gap in the text after l. 541, but the only one to try a restoration was GREIN, who suggested the emendation *on frean fultum forð getreowde*, which seems fairly hazardous.

I do not think there is a gap but rather that the text of the passage is corrupt. The MS reads *mond* for *mod* l. 542, and departing from this copyist's error, the only part of the corruption corrected by the editors, we may restore the passage thus:

> *He þa sar forseah,   a þære sawle h æl*
> *wæs mundbora   þe þæt mod geheold*
> *þæt him ne getweode   treow in breostum* etc.

Þæs may quite easily have been miswritten for *wæs*, which called for the *n*-ending in *mundbora*, and then the *n* also cropped up in *mod*. As for *wel* it is, to all appearances, a repetition by dittography of the last three letters in *sawle*. All the errors are typical slips of negligence. To the phrase *hæl wæs mundbora* (*hæl* = salvation), some Bible passages correspond, i. e. Ex. 15, 2 *Dominus ... factus est mihi in salutem*, repeated also in Ps. 117, 14 and Isaiah 12, 2. *Hæl* is mostly used in the religious sense. In the emended passage *hæl* forms the contrast of *sar*, and l. 541 b ff contain the reason for 541 a, in the same way as for instance Jul. 211 b ff:

> *(ne ondræde ic me) ... þinra wita bealo.*
> *Hæbbe ic me to hyhte   heofonrices weard* etc.

Guthlac B

1278 b ff   *Ða se æpela glæm*
   setlgong sohte,   swearc norðrodor
   won under wolcnum,   woruld miste oferteah,
   þystrum biþeahte,   þrong niht ofer t i h t,
   londes frætwa.

Tiht is taken by GOLLANCZ to mean 'expanse', and KLAEBER (Anglia Beibl. XV, 345) has a similar idea, thinking it means 'tract', developed from the original sense of *tiht*, 'motion'. He compares it to the Latin *'tractus'*, which presents such a semasiological curve. GREIN-KÖHLER quote the passage under the heading 'Zug', 'Bewegung', ASSMANN makes no comment, and KRAPP-DOBBIE say that l. 1281 b may be treated as a parenthesis.

It does not seem necessary to assume a development of meaning in *tiht*: it may meen simply 'motion', and *þrong niht ofer tiht* would signify "night fell over the stir (of the earth)". In that case *londes frætwa* cannot be a variation of *tiht*, as it is in KLAEBER's interpretation, but of *woruld*, and *þrong niht ofer tiht*, as KRAPP-DOBBIE suggest, is a parenthetical half-line.

The Phoenix

13 ff   *Ðæt is wynsum wong,   wealdas grene,*
    rume under roderum.   Ne mæg þær ren ne snaw,
    ne forstes fnæst,   ne fyres blæst,
    ne hægles hryre,   ne hrimes dryre,
    ne sunnan hætu,   ne sincaldu,
    ne wearm weder,   ne winterscur
    w i h t e gewyrdan ...

GOLLANCZ, translating the last half-line "may there work any harm", assumes an intransitive use of *gewyrdan*, and so do KRAPP and DOBBIE, who alternatively suggest the reading *wiht gewyrdan*. SCHLOTTEROSE takes the object of *gewyrdan* to be *wealdas*, the beginning of the sentence in his version, putting a comma after *roderum*. According to BRIGHT, *wihte* is acc. sing. of *wiht*.

It is difficult to see why *gewyrdan* cannot be used in its ordinary transitive sense here, and why *wihte* cannot be its object in acc. plur.

as GREIN-KÖHLER suggest (p. 796): wind and weather cannot harm the creatures. The same thought is repeated at l. 59 (*ne se hearda forst* etc.) *cnyseð œnigne.*

28   *Is þœt torhte lond   twelfum herra ...*

ETTMÜLLER reads *hearre,* SCHLOTTEROSE and COOK EPh. *herre* to agree with *lond,* other editors keep *herra.* Lactantius' *ille locus* l. 8 may account for the form.

60 ff   *Đœr ne hœgl ne hrim   hreosað to foldan,*
          ne windig wolcen,   ne þœr wœter fealleþ,
          lyfte gebysgad,   ac þœr lagustreamas,
          wundrum wrœtlice,   wyllan onspringað
          fœgrum foldwylmum.   Foldan leccaþ
          wœter wynsumu etc.

L. 61 a is translated by GOLLANCZ "... nor windy cloud", and TUPPER defends the MS tradition (PMLA, XXV, 173), reading "... nor cloud driven by the wind". All editors keep *windig* except SCHLOTTEROSE, who emends to *winneþ* declaring "eine windige wolke, die zur erde fällt, kann ich mir nicht vorstellen". I agree with this objection and with SCHLOTTEROSE's reference to the corresponding Lactantius line (23) *nulla super campos tendit sua vellera nubes,* where there is no mention of the wind. But I cannot see the justification of his emendation ("noch wütet eine wolke"), which was originally suggested by TRAUTMANN, nor can I understand his hesitation in proposing no less than three other alternatives: *windeþ* "bewegt sich" (as in Andr. 372), or *wœðeþ* 'jagt dahin' (as in El. 1273), or *ne wind wēdeþ* ("noch wütet der Sturm"), which is also TRAUTMANN's invention. Context and palæography admit of only one of these four proposals: *ne windeþ wolcen. Windan* is exactly the word demanded here, used for 'fly', 'soar'; cp. Exod. 80 *dœgsceades hleo* (the pillar of cloud) *wand ofer wolcnum*; Met. 31, 12 *sume fleogende windað under wolcnum* etc. The ending *-eþ* was, it seems, exchanged for *-ig* on account of a vertical slip: the middle syllable in an *œnigne* just above the word in question distracted the scribe's attention.

The MS *foldwylmum* l. 64 is changed by all editors except SWEET and Gollancz to *flodwylmum.* "The presence of *Foldan* in l. 64 b indicates that the MS is in error here", say Krapp and Dobbie. But repetition is so common a phenomenon in Anglo-Saxon poetical style that it must not disturb this excellent MS reading, 'spring-water', agreeing with *wyllan-wæter wynsumu. Flodwylm* is only used of the raging sea (in Andreas l. 516).

287 b ff the Phoenix, resurrected from the fire, has returned to his native island:

> *Bið him edniwe*
> *þære sunnan þegn,   þonne swegles leoht,*
> *gimma gladost,   ofer garsecg up,*
> *æpeltungla wyn,   eastan lixeð.*

As early as in Thorpe's edition the emendation *segn* for *þegn* was suggested, and subsequently adopted by Ettmüller, Bright, Gollancz, Assmann, and Krapp-Dobbie. Grein retained *þegn* but translated "Leuchtglanz"; only Cook, ibid., and Schlotterose read *þegn* in its usual sense. But Cook does not attempt an interpretation, and Schlotterose's "Es ist sich wieder neu der degen der sonne" does not explain the construction. Emerson, p. 20, thinks the reading *segn* is convincing enough to be taken as a support for his thesis that the Phoenix poet worked fairly independent of his Latin original, which speaks of the Phoenix as an attendant of the sun.

Yet *þegn* is no doubt the lectio difficilior. It is the bird that is renewed, the worshipper and servant of the sun, its *satelles* as Lactantius puts it (l. 33). The construction may seem puzzling, but is not too uncommon; a reflexive dative is used in a similar pleonastic manner with *beon* in the prose Exodus 14, 14 *Beoð eow stille*; Anglo-Saxon Chr. 1009 *þone lencten wæron him on Cent*; in poetry Gen. 367 a *wesan him on wynne*; Met. 20, 45 ff *eart þe selfa þæt hehste good* cp. Voges pp. 331, 332; Gu. 272 b *eart ðe godes yrming.* 'The attendant of the sun' is apparently the authentic reading, so here, at least, the poet followed his original. We need not, like Schlotterose, take any trouble to render the dative at all.

293 ff   *Is him þæt heafod   hindan grene,*
          wrætlice wrixleð,   wurman geblonden.

THORPE changed to *wrixled*, followed by KLIPSTEIN, GOLLANCZ, translating 'variegated', and KRAPP-DOBBIE. But this alteration is needless; the reference is to the gleaming of the feathers on the bird's head and the word is used in the same way as in El. 759 *heardecg ... bleom wrixleð*.

404 b ff Adam and Eve have succumbed to the temptations of the devil and tasted the forbidden fruit:

>   *Ðær him bitter wearð*
> *yrmþu æfter æte   ond hyra eaferum swa,*
> *sarlic symbel   sunum ond dohtrum.*
> *Wurdon teonlice   topas idge*
> *ageald æfter gylte.   Hæfdon godes yrre,*
> *bittre bealosorge.*

The passage, punctuated with KRAPP-DOBBIE, is the most interesting one in the Phoenix from a critical point of view, and conjectures have sprouted in abundance here. Two of the earliest editors, THORPE and ETTMÜLLER, assume a gap in 407 b, reading *to þas ... idge*. SCHLOTTE-ROSE prefers to emend, changing to *torne scyldge*, an alteration made, it seems, at random. COOK, ibid., thinks that 407 b is "hopelessly corrupt". GREIN was the first to read *topas* for the MS *to þas* and to accept the *idge* of the text. GREIN-KÖHLER, p. 385, suggest the sense 'avidus' and compare an *icge* with Swedish *idog*. HART, according to BRIGHT, suggests *idæge*, 'that same day', for *idge* on the analogy of *idæges*, and BRIGHT, though he keeps the MS version in his text, remarks in a note that *idge* may possibly be a remnant of *grædige*. KLAEBER, JEG Ph XII, 258, asks himself whether there may not be a connection between *idge* and *icge, incge-* Beow 1107, 2577; but this does not help us to understanding either. BRETT, MLR XXII, 259, suggests that *idge* is a corrupt or late form of the adj. *ecge, icce* in the Kentish Glosses on Prov.; and interprets "their teeth were grievously set on edge". KRAPP-DOBBIE do not quite believe in the word *idge*, and, while retaining it in their text, seem to prefer BRIGHT's hypothesis about a corrupt *grædige*.

Ageald has also been questioned, and SCHLOTTEROSE emends to *agæled*, "gehemmt", followed by KLAEBER, ibid. BRETT, ibid., proposes taking *ageald* as a noun, and, punctuating *... idge; ageald æfter gylte hæfdon, godes yrre*, translates "they had reward after sin,

God's wrath". Or, with *ageald* as a verb: "he repaid them after their guilt" etc. But "he" as the subject is not easily supplied in this context. GREIN-KÖHLER p. 283 think that *agyldan* means 'punish', and so does GOLLANCZ: "it (?) requited them according to their guilt". KRAPP-DOBBIE combine *wurdon-ageald* (!), translating "their teeth were requited in accordance with their guilt".

The doubts concerning the authenticity of *idge* do not appear very well founded. Whether it is related to *icge* or not is an open question, but *idig* may without greater difficulty be explained as a Zero Grade form derived from a root **ai-dh* 'burn', related to αἶθος, 'fire', and *ād*, 'pyre'; with a development of meaning we get Icel. *ið*, 'activity', *iðinn*, 'zealous' etc., and with this sense 'desirous' would fit in well (cp. WALDE-POKORNY I, 5). So GREIN seems right in glossing *idig* as 'avidus' and GOLLANCZ in translating 'greedy'. *Ageald* and its connection with what precedes is more problematic. The alteration *agæled* is inappropriate; 'checked' or 'restrained' teeth have nothing to do in the context, and *ageald* as a noun must be rejected.

Our starting-point in an attempt to make the context clear ought to be a negative one: in a poem of such smooth and lofty style we may take for granted that *topas* does not occupy a prominent position and that consequently there is no connection, broken or preserved, between *topas* and *ageald*. *Ageald* is rather connected with *symbel*, and, I think, means 'repay', as BRETT would suggest. It is, then, used with the dative here: "a grievous banquet repaid their sons and daughters after their guilt". *Wurdon teonlice topas idge* is a complete sentence and stands back, in the context, as a causal parenthetical clause, asyndetically coordinate. We should then get the version:

> Ðær him bitter wearð
> yrmþu æfter æte   ond hyra eaferum swa:
> sarlic symbel   sunum ond dohtrum
> (wurdon teonlice   topas idge)
> ageald æfter gylte.

567 b ff   (weoruda god ... sawle alyseð) ...   Me þæs wen næfre
> forbirsteð in breostum,   ð e ic in brego engla
> forðweardne gefean   fæste hæbbe.

GRUNDTVIG's alteration to *þæt* is unnecessary, but GOLLANCZ's and KRAPP-DOBBIE's reading *ðe = ðy*, 'because', is inferior to SCHLOTTE-

ROSE's taking it as a relative, with commas after *engla* and *gefean*. *Wen* and *gefea* are so closely linked up psychologically that the latter can be considered a variation of the former here.

646 b ff contain an elaborate exposition of the different ideas united in the Phoenix symbol:

Swa fenix beacnaƌ,
geong in geardum,   godbearnes meaht,
ƿonne he of ascan   eft onwæcneƌ
in lifes lif,   leomum geƿungen.
650   *Swa se hælend us   helpe gefremede*
ƿurh his lices gedal,   lif butan ende,
swa se fugel swetum   his fiƿru tu
ond wynsumum   wyrtum gefylleƌ,
654   *fægrum foldwæstmum,   ƿonne afysed biƌ.*
Ƌæt sindon ƿa word,   swa us gewritu secgaƌ,
hleoƿor haligra,   ƿe him to heofonum biƌ,
to ƿam mildan gode,   mod afysed
in dreama dream,   ƿær hi dryhtne to giefe
659   *worda ond weorca   wynsumne stenc*
in ƿa mæran gesceaft   meotude bringaƌ,
in ƿæt leohte lif.

GREIN, ASSMANN, SCHLOTTEROSE, COOK ibid., and KRAPP-DOBBIE all agree in putting full stop after *geƿungen* l. 649 (SCHLOTTEROSE semi-colon), comma after *ende* l. 651, and full stop after *biƌ* l. 654; besides, GREIN, ASSMANN, SCHLOTTEROSE, and COOK agree in putting quotation-marks after *biƌ*, apparently influenced by the following *Ƌæt sindon ƿa word, swa us gewritu secgaƌ* etc. COOK makes l. 655 ff begin a new section under the headline "Epilogue".

Such an arrangement of the text, however, conceals the symbolism here and perverts the meaning. As for the first section, the opening phrase *swa fenix beacnaƌ ... godbearnes meaht* is explained in the succeeding four lines, where the symbolic connection between the bird's rebirth after the conflagration and the martyr-death of Christ is pointed out:

Swa fenix beacnaƌ   .... godbearnes meaht,
ƿonne he of ascan   eft onwæcneƌ

in lifes lif,   leomum geþungen,
swa se hælend us   helpe gefremede
þurh his lices gedal,   lif butan ende.

After l. 651 a new sentence should begin, and the context in this section has been quite deleted by the editors referred to. It is plain from the context that l. 654 b cannot be the end of a quotation. Again, there can hardly be any doubt that *afysed* l. 654 corresponds to *afysed* l. 657, and that *Ðæt* l. 655 refers to the *swetum wyrtum-fægrum foldwæstmum*: the sweet herbs carried by the wings of the Phoenix, when he is prepared for death in the flames (*þonne afysed bið*), symbolize the words (prayers) of holy people with which their spirits prepare themselves for (going) to Paradise (*þe him to heofonum bið ... mod afysed*). GOLLANCZ alone came pretty close to an acceptable interpretation of the lines in his translation: "And as for the sweet herbs ... wherewith the bird filleth its two wings, and is then impelled away, these are the words and utterances of saints (as Scripture telleth us), whereby their spirits are impelled to heaven etc." But the construction is better taken as an anacoluthon and *swa* as loosely connected with what precedes: 'in like manner' (just as the Phoenix signified God's power, so do the herbs signify ... etc.). *Afysed* cannot mean 'impelled' here, and *gewritu* is not Scripture but obviously some apocryphal writing conveying the fairly esoteric tradition. Anyhow, the text should be thus rearranged, from l. 652:

Swa se fugel swetum   his fiþru tu
ond wynsumum   wyrtum gefylleð,
fægrum foldwæstmum,   þonne afysed bið:
þæt sindon þa word,   swa us gewritu secgað etc.

It is quite probable that the tradition about the connection between the *swete wyrta* and the *word haligra* was somehow linked up with the Physiologus cycle; as COOK ibid. has shown, *hi ... worda ond weorca wynsumne stenc ... meotude bringað* ll. 658 ff has a direct correspondence in the last section of the Greek Physiologus Phoenix chapter (cp. COOK ibid. p. 123): "that we with holy prayers may ... send up spiritual fragrance by means of our good lives" (ἵνα ἡμεῖς δι᾽ εὐχῶν ἁγίων ... ἀναπέμπωμεν εὐωδίαν πνευματικὴν διὰ πολιτειῶν ἀγαθῶν), cp. LAUCHERT p. 238. A fairly close parallel is Christ and Satan 355 ff;

Ðonne beoð þa eadigan   þe of eorðan cumað,
bringað to bearme   blostman stences,

wyrte wynsume   (*þœt synd word godes*),
þonne hie befœðmeð   *fœder mancynnes* ...
... lœdeð to lihte ...

Cp. CLUBB pp. 94, 95; ZIEGLER p. 165. (Quotation according to KRAPP.) In the Old English Phoenix l. 465 b ff, the sweet herbs also represent the good deeds of the righteous, but the double symbolism with the herbs now standing for good deeds, now for prayers, is characteristic of this poem with its complexity of symbols.

667 ff   *Hafað us alyfed*   *lucis auctor*
           þœt we motun her   *m e r u e r i,*
           goddœdum begietan   *gaudia in celo* ...

Different proposals have been made for the improvement of the mysterious *m e r u e r i* in the macaronic epilogue of the poem. ETT-MÜLLER suggested *meruisse*, HOLTHAUSEN (Archiv CXII, 132) *meri* & *ueri*, SCHLOTTEROSE and COOK ibid. *meritare*, and KALUZA (Der alt-englische Vers I, 18) altered *her* to *hic* and placed the caesura after *motun*. Neither of these emendations is convincing, and there is every reason to believe that the poet wrote *mereri*, as ASSMANN reads in his text and as KALUZA suggests. To *mereri* corresponds exactly *goddœdum begietan*, and the *u* was probably a mere repetition from *motun*.

Juliana

149 ff   *Nœfre þu gelœrest*   *þœt ic leasingum,*
           dumbum ond deafum   *deofolgieldum*
           g œ s t e geniðlum   *gaful onhate* ...

The form *gœste* has caused trouble. The alteration *gœsta* is a strong temptation, and all editors fall into it except GOLLANCZ, who retains *gœste* although without explanation. Also CONRADI (p. 26) has *gœsta geniðlum*. The change is of course a safe normalization; cp. *feond moncynnes* Jul. 317; *Fynd syndon eowere* Jud. 195; *Him fynd godes fœcne leogað* Ps. LXXX, 14, etc. But an adnominal dative instanced in the passage here dealt with is fairly common in Latin. It is quite possible, then, that Cynewulf was influenced by some expression like *animo hostibus* in his source. In view of the Latin tendency it is thus perhaps best to retain the *gæste geniðlum* of the MS, "the enemies of the soul", and regard it as a sort of linguistic licence on the part of the poet.

201 b ff Juliana, persisting in her Christian faith, is being threatened by the heathen Heliseus:

> *Gif þu leng ofer þis*
> *þurh þin dolwillen   gedwolan fylgest,*
> *þonne ic nyde sceal   niþa gebæded*
> *on þære grimmestan   godscyld wrecan ...*

Cosijn, Btr. XXIII, 124, thinks *þære grimmestan* refers to Juliana and emends *on þe þa grimmestan*. v. d. Warth, p. 35, has the same idea, but according to him the MS version may be retained if translated: "An der grimmigsten (sc. sünderin) die schuld gegen Gott rächen". But *grim* is not very appropriate if it refers to Juliana, not even when applied to her by her enemies. *Grim* is rather the word for the cruel treatment with which she is being menaced, and probably *on þære grimmestan* is an ellipsis for *on þære grimmestan wisan*; cp. *on wisum* Ps. 140[8]. *On þære grimmestan* is contrasted with the two superlatives ll. 206, 207: *þa selestan, þa mildestan (godu)*.

350 b ff

> *Hyre se feond oncwæð,*
> *wræcca wærleas,   wordum mælde:*
> *"Ic þe, ead mæg,   yfla gehwylces*
> *or gecyðe   oð ende forð ...*

Ettmüller changes to *eaðe mæg*, which he took to go with his second alteration, *gecyðan* l. 353, and so Sievers Btr. X, 517, Cosijn Btr. XXIII, 124. Trautmann BEV, p. 96, prefers *eadge mæg*, Gollancz reads as in the MS, considering *eadmæg* a compound, "blessed maiden", and Grein, Assmann, and Krapp-Dobbie also follow the MS, though reading as above. But *mæg* ought to be more strongly emphasized, and the best thing, I think, would be to read *Ic þe, eade mæg*, as a vocative.

483 b ff

> *Sume ic larum geteah,*
> *to geflite fremede,   þæt hy færinga*
> *ealde æfþoncan   edniwedan ...*

All editors have this punctuation except GOLLANCZ, who has none at all. KOCK (JJJ, 30), however, proposes

> Sume ic larum geteah
> to geflite, fremede,   þæt hy ...

and translates "some I through promptings drew and urged to strife". He compares the constructions Sal. 158 ff *hwilum he gefeteraŏ fæges mannes / handa, gehefegaŏ*, 'at times he fetters and weighs down the hands of fated man'; Sat. 67 ff *Crist heo afirde / dreamum, bedælde*, 'Christ had removed and severed them from joys'; Met. 28, 72 *þæt hit weas come / niwan, gesælde*, 'that it perhaps had come and happened now'(?). I prefer KOCK's punctuation to that of the editors, but I doubt whether he and they rightly interpret the passage in Juliana. *Fremman* means either to "advance", "further", cp. Andr. 933 ff: *ic eaŏe mæg anra gehwylcne fremman ond fyrþran ... on landa gehwylc*, but this sense has not much to do with that of *fremman* in the Juliana passage, as SIMONS (p. 44) and BOSWORTH-TOLLER p. 333 seem to believe. Or it means to "perform" or "effect". Now *fremman* in its former sense involves the assent of the object; cp. also Beowulf 1830 ff "*Ic on Higelace wat ... þæt he mec fremman wile wordum ond weorcum, þæt ic þe wel herige*" etc. As for the meanings of *fremman* in the other Germanic languages FICK-TORP (p. 233) give: befördern, vorwärts bringen, fördern, ausführen, vollführen. FINNUR JÓNSSON (Lex. poet. p. 152) enumerates the following characteristic meanings in ON poetry: 1) stille noget frem, 2) føre en videre ved hædersbevisninger, 3) fremme, ophjælpe, støtte, 4) hædre en ved gaver, 5) udstyre, 6) bringe til udførelse, bedrive. We here see the same main meanings as in Old English. That the word may be a parallel to *geteon*, 'draw', 'constrain', is therefore highly improbable and KOCK's structural comparisons are irrelevant. The most plausible explanation of *fremman* in our passage is that it means 'bring about' and is comparable with *gefremman* in Beowulf 953 ff: '*Ðu þe self hafast dædum gefremed, þæt þin dom lyfaŏ*' etc. Consequently

> Sume ic larum geteah
> to geflite, fremede,   þæt hy færinga
> ealde æfþoncan   edniwedan ...

would mean: 'Some through my doctrines I compelled to strife and brought about that they suddenly renewed old grudges.'

490 b ff The devil is telling Juliana the record of his crimes:

> *Sume, þa ic funde*
> *butan godes tacne,   gymelease,*
> *ungebletsade,   þeah ic bealdlice*
> *þurh mislic cwealm   minum hondum*
> *searoþoncum slog.*

Instead of *þeah, þa* was early suggested (THORPE), and ETTMÜLLER, GREIN, STRUNK, WILLIAMS, and KRAPP-DOBBIE agree. COSIJN (Btr. XXIII, 124) reads *þe*, strongly objecting to the MS version as "unsinn", TRAUTMANN, BEV, p. 97, reads with COSIJN. Only GOLLANCZ, translating "nevertheless", and V. D. WARTH, p. 39, read as in the MS besides GREIN, who alternatively proposed *þeah* as a preterite of *þicgan*, a very unlikely suggestion. However tempting an emendation here may be — both THORPE and COSIJN obviously hold, as it is natural to do, that the devil attached his victims b e c a u s e they were defenceless — it is nevertheless not necessary to emend. For reading with the MS, and taking, with GOLLANCZ, *þeah* to be an adverb, we find the poet expressing his moral indignation by making the devil mean: "they were heedless and unblessed, yet I killed them ... w i t h c u n n i n g". The contrast *gymelease — searoþoncum* is effaced if we sacrifice *þeah*.

556 b ff

> *Wiste he þi gearwor,*
> *manes melda,   magum to secgan,*
> *susles þegnum,   hu him on siðe gelomp.*

*   *

*

> *"georne ær*
> *heredon on heahþu   ond his halig ⟨word⟩,*
> *sægdon soðlice   þæt he sigora gehwæs (ana weolde"* etc.)

Much of the text has been lost here. Judging from the other Juliana legends, the following incidents, perhaps with some omissions, happen in the gap: after the devil has been released Juliana is again dragged before Heliseus who asks by what witchcraft she can endure his torture; then she is tormented by fire and a wheel with swords in it; she is however still unharmed and thanks God. When the heathens see and hear this they convert themselves, except Heliseus and his men, and praise God, but are all beheaded by the heathen emperor, five hundred men and one hundred and thirty women. The quotation marks round the lines 559—563 of the sequel to these events in Cynewulf are KRAPP's and DOBBIE's invention. They think that the lines are part of a prayer to God, said by Juliana after the occurrences described above, which, in the Acta Sanctorum, ends by: *Tu enim es Deus benedictus in secula*, and that the Old English lines are a "very free expansion of the idea underlying the Latin". This piece of criticism is quite impossible since *heredon* and *sægdon* cannot refer to Juliana. The two editors are apparently misled by the fact that immediately after Juliana's prayer the words: *Et dum hæc diceret, ecce subito venit angelus Domini et separavit ignem* etc. follow in the Acta Sanctorum, which correspond to *Ða cwom engel godes ... ond þæt fyr tosceaf* ll. 563 ff in Cynewulf's poem. The passage put between quotation marks by KRAPP and DOBBIE is of course the end of a description of the converted heathens' glorification of God and cannot possibly be a quotation. This is the only and last thing we hear about the converts in the Old English legend, which means that the episode about their execution, as has previously been intimated, was omitted by Cynewulf.

699 b ff

Min sceal of lice

sawul on siðfæt,   nat ic sylfa hwider,

eardes uncyðþu;

This simple melancholy reflection has not been duly appreciated: if critics do not emend, they force the periods into some syntactical strait-jacket. STRUNK reads *eardes uncyðgu* "devoid of a country", applying to *sawul*. HOLTHAUSEN (Literaturblatt XXVIII, 11) believes in *uncyðig*, referring to *ic*. v. D. WARTH (p. 44), following BOSWORTH-TOLLER's translation "in ignorance" p. 1095, takes *uncyðþu* to be an instrumental. TRAUTMANN (BEV, 137) regards *eardes uncyðþu* as a genitive to *hwider*.

All these comments are unnecessary. *Uncyðþu* does not mean 'ignorance' but has the same sense as in Guthlac 852 ff: *Siþþan se eþel uðgenge weard Adame ond Euan ... þa hy on uncyððu ... scofene wurdon* etc., cp. GREIN-KÖHLER, p. 737. 'An unknown country' is the simple notion here, recurrent in elegiac poetry where the incertitude of the life to come is pondered: so in all probability Seaf. 37 ff: "*pæt ic feor heonan | elþeodigra eard gesece*" (cp. ARNGART passim). As for the syntactical context, *eardes uncyðþu* is neither genitive nor instrumental but an answer loosely attached to *hwider*: "I know not myself whither; some unknown country of the earth". This lax construction is an excellent stylistic device rendering the uncertainty and vagueness of the soul's destiny.

IV. Style and Manner

1. Previous discussion

The enormous literature on the various Cynewulf questions is not, to such a degree as one might expect, concerned with the style of the poems connected with Cynewulf or his school. The works that do deal with the style, chiefly discuss the vocabulary and the phraseology of the texts. There are also some brief syntactical monographs of a descriptive character, such as PROLLIUS, "Ueber den syntactischen Gebrauch des Conjunctivs in den Cynewulfschen Dichtungen Elene, Juliana und Crist" (Marburg 1888); CONRADI, "Darstellung der Syntax in Cynewulf's Gedicht Juliana" (Halle 1886); RÖSSGER, "Über den syntaktischen Gebrauch des Genitivs in Cynewulfs Crist, Elene und Juliana" (Halle 1885); REUSSNER, "Untersuchungen über die Syntax in dem angelsächsischen Gedichte vom heiligen Andreas" (Halle 1889, only verbal syntax); ROSE, "Darstellung der Syntax in Cynewulfs Crist" (Halle 1890); SCHÜRMANN, "Darstellung der Syntax in Cynewulf's Elene" (Paderborn 1884); AHRENS, "Darstellung der Syntax im angelsächsischen Gedicht Phönix" (Rostock 1904). Some of these authors have touched upon some point which will be of value in our examination of certain stylistic features.

G. JANSEN's thesis on the Cynewulf poems is a concentrated description of the style of these texts; it deals with the vocabulary and the synonyms, with alliteration, rhyme, and various rhetorical devices such as accumulation, tautology, parallelism, anaphora, antithesis, parenthesis, asyndeton and polysyndeton, various kinds of discourse, personification, litotes, allegory etc. G. JANSEN's work, though valuable, is, however, only a short descriptive catalogue of salient features; there is no systematic comparison and no real analysis.

An interesting study of the structure of the plot in Elene, Juliana, and Christ, as compared with Beowulf and some medieval Latin texts was made by SMITHSON. He analysed the relations between main action, discourse, digressions, episodes, and the greater or lesser degree of coherence between these parts of the plot. SMITHSON, however, is concerned with content, not with style, and we hear nothing about the influence of the former on the latter.

S. K. DAS makes an important, though not exhaustive, investigation of the style in his studies on the Cynewulf canon. After a thorough analysis of the metre, the author demonstrates the predominance of ideas and reflection in Cynewulf's poetry. The abstract side of a thing is generally emphasized, and a fact often represented in its abstract aspects. This characteristic quality of the Cynewulfian poetry may be studied, above all, in the poet's use of appositions (apparently = variations). Cynewulf is also fond of sentence-periods and of the effect produced by summing up and closing such periods. The style in his poem is strongly marked by emotion. Some particular features are noted: relative clauses are sometimes used as resolution or conclusion; the position of adverbial clauses in the middle of sentences is pointed out; longwinded periods are frequent; "ideas or personalities are the only important things which draw to themselves all weight of thought and feeling" (p. 164). Sound-variation is a common feature in Cynewulf's poetry. Nature is only dealt with incidentally; there are no minute descriptions of natural phenomena as in for instance Beowulf and Andreas. A strong spiritual energy, and struggles between good and evil powers are characteristic of the Cynewulf canon.

We shall return to S. K. DAS's work after a survey of what he, and others, have to say about the other poems of the Cynewulf group as compared with the signed poems.

The style of these texts has been analysed chiefly in connexion with a debate on authorship, which deals with all of them, and on unity, which deals with the three Christ poems and the two Guthlac texts. We will, in the following survey, also consider some arguments of a palæographic and literary kind, which are of importance in the discussion.

The Andreas Problem

An animated if somewhat arbitrary controversy on the problem whether Andreas is Cynewulf's work, raged particularly in the eighties and nineties. The problem has generally been linked up with the minor question whether Fata Apostolorum, the short poem ascribed to Cynewulf immediately following Andreas in the manuscript, should be regarded as the end of that epic or as an independent piece.

We are here only concerned with clearly documented opinions. The first to raise relatively substantial objections against the attribution of Andreas to Cynewulf, a position then held by most scholars, was FRITZSCHE in 1879. He compares the treatment of the sources, the subject-matter, the verse, the style and language, the vocabulary, and some parallel passages of the different texts. FRITZSCHE ascribed the Riddles and the whole of Christ to Cynewulf, but this we can disregard in only taking into account what he says about the signed poems. In his time Cynewulf's signature in Fata Apostolorum had not yet been discovered, but the poem was nevertheless generally held to be Cynewulf's work. He thought he found that the author of Andreas follows his source, which FRITZSCHE believed to be Greek, much more closely than Cynewulf his Latin originals. But FRITZSCHE's knowledge of the sources of the texts was far too limited to enable him to see a possible difference clearly. He also points out that the thaumaturgical character of Andreas is not so accentuated in Cynewulf's undobuted works but without giving convincing reasons why this is an objection to Cynewulf's authorship. The verse in Andreas he finds more perfect than in the Cynewulf poems. As for the style FRITZSCHE tells us, without proving it, that the language is "breiter". He says that "repetition" is more common in Andreas than in Cynewulf and mentions some cases of the type *hie-hæleð hellfuse* yet without showing their frequency in the different texts or why they are arguments against attribution. In his chapter on vocabulary he enumerates what words are to be found in Cynewulf and not in Andreas, and vice versa. It is however of little avail for us to know that for example *onsecgan* does not exist in Andreas as Cynewulf uses it only in Juliana, or that *flacor* and *flangeweorc* are met with only in Christ. The important parallels between the texts are only partly quoted and imperfectly commented on; still FRITZSCHE thinks they point to Andreas being an imitation of Cynewulf's work and even more so of Beowulf.

In 1884 HOLTBUER (pp. 39—40) came to the conclusion that the vocabulary of Andreas is similar to that of Cynewulf's works but "nur an sehr wenigen stellen fand sich eine annähernd formelle übereinstimmung der verschiedenen genitivverbindungen" and that many kennings, metaphors, and periphrases in Andreas are rare or nonexistent in Cynewulf's works. As some verbs and adjectives in Andreas are further missing in the other texts HOLTBUER "vom sprachlichen Standpunkte aus" denied the identity of the Andreas author with Cynewulf.

CREMER, after a thorough metrical and superficial linguistic analysis, finds that Andreas from a metrical point of view comes close to Cynewulf's poems but that "sprachliche Abweichungen", i. e. the dative *fœder* in Andreas, *fœdere* in Cynewulf and the consistent shortening of *eo, ea* in the oblique cases of *feorh* and *mearh* in Andreas, point to different authors.

In 1888 NAPIER discovered the end of Fata Apostolorum, which was till then regarded as lost, on page 54[b] of the Vercelli Book. Since on the one hand this fragment contains Cynewulf's acrostic, and since on the other the whole poem Fata Apostolorum follows Andreas in the manuscript, a supposed connection between the two poems became an argument for those who defended the attribution of Andreas to Cynewulf, alleging the existence of a long poem ending with his signature, just as was the case with his other works. This view was contested by WÜLKER, who in his paper "Die Bedeutung einer neuen Entdeckung für die ags. Literaturgeschichte" 1888, drew attention to the fact that Andrew and Matthew are separated in the enumeration of the fates of the apostles, which, he argued, is not to be expected in the epilogue of a legend partly devoted to the two apostles' joint adventures among the heathens. Neither was SIEVERS (Anglia XIII, p. 25) convinced that NAPIER's discovery proved the attribution of Andreas to Cynewulf, and he did not even believe that the acrostic belonged to the Fates. According to SIEVERS there is a double epilogue in the Fates: one part at ll. 88—106, another at ll. 107—122, and the latter of these parts contains a slightly altered repetition of the other (ll. 107—114). SIEVERS thinks that ll. 88—106 belonged to a lost poem written by Cynewulf and crept into the Fata Apostolorum.

MATHER in 1892 thought that the slightly greater frequency of double alliteration in the a-lines and of D- and E-verses in the b-lines in Andreas prevents the attribution of the poem to Cynewulf, without explaining what latent qualities in these metrical details endow them with such a fatal effect.

An interesting investigation refusing to identify the author of Andreas with Cynewulf was made by BUTTENWIESER in 1899. Her booklet, in spite of its obvious methodical looseness and subjective æstheticism, has none the less a certain value and no doubt indicates some of the right lines to be taken up by anyone dealing with Old English problems of authorship. It is possible that her book is only a preliminary sketch as she says she intends to publish a second volume on the same subject, containing her main material, which, however, never appeared. What did actually appear, was, above all, one of the most exhaustive lists of passages and phrases common to Andreas on the one hand and to the rest of Old English poetry on the other, particularly to Cynewulf's works and Beowulf (cp. further p. 235 ff). She emphasizes the necessity of examining whether these parallels point to identity or imitation, but apart from a few cases she does not make this examination in her published work. She further mentions some passages in the first 150 verses of Andreas which according to her show imperfect style compared with Cynewulf's art. But we hardly ever learn whether or not such imperfections occur in Cynewulf's work as well and never in what proportions. What is essential in her book is her opinion of Old English poetical style as subject to individual modifications, which can be discovered in an analysis of the usage and stylistic habits of the poets, and which are not wholly obscured by the uniformity of Old English poetical language.

In BARNOUW's study of 1902, the author concludes, from the great frequency of the weak adjektive + substantive of the type *hadre sœgl, hleoleasan wic* in Andreas, as compared with Cynewulf's poems and from the absence of the Andreas formula *œfter þissum wordum* in Cynewulf's works, that the former epic cannot have been written by the famous poet but is earlier than his works.

KRAPP A (p. XXXIII ff) is convinced that the Fates is not the end of Andreas; as for the question of authorship he declares, after an investigation of certain forms (such as the use of the periphrastic preterite) and of the use of words and particles (*butan* common in Cynewulf, rare in Andreas; *œninga* only found in Andreas; *ða gen* rare in Andreas, frequent in Cynewulf, etc.) that it seems "impossible to assign *Andreas* to Cynewulf" (p. LI).

S. K. DAS shows that, unlike Cynewulf, the Andreas author is not occupied with ideas or abstractions; his style gives no sublime effects, we do not find the syntactical features characteristic of the Cynewulfian poetry in Andreas; there are no studied periods. There is no assonance or sound-variations to make the verse mellifluous; there are marked metrical differences. S. K. DAS further points out that the poet is not preoccupied with wisdom and learning, as Cynewulf is, and he makes the important observation that the author of Andreas and Cynewulf do not present to us the same God: Cynewulf's God is the Christian Deity, the Andreas poet's God "is no more than a haughty king who does his best to make his cause successful" (p. 229). In this poem God is rather like a Saxon chieftain.

On the strength of the various divergencies of style and manner, S. K. DAS concludes that Andreas cannot be the work of Cynewulf.

Many scholars hold that Cynewulf is the author of Andreas, still, following the same principles for a survey here as in the former section, we shall have to disregard a good many sweeping assertions. In 1885 RAMHORST maintained that Cynewulf was the author of Andreas, pointing out some similarities of vocabulary and some parallel passages. In order to show correspondences of vocabulary RAMHORST quotes the words existing in Beowulf, Andreas, and Cynewulf exclusively and then those confined to Andreas and Cynewulf only, as well as words that are rare outside Andreas and Cynewulf. In order to show that too much importance must not be given, on the part of those who refuse to ascribe Andreas to Cynewulf, to the non-existence in Andreas of words found in Cynewulf and vice versa, he enumerates words met with in Elene only and not in Christ and Juliana, in Christ but not in Juliana and Elene, and so on. In so doing he is the first to take into account what is different in Cynewulf's genuine works, which is highly important for a treatment of the problem. He further collects a series of parallel phrases which he, unlike Fritzsche, considers to indicate one and the same author for Andreas and Cynewulf's works. A more extensive collection of parallels was made by SARRAZIN (Anglia IX, 515 ff, BS) who, in his attempts to prove that Cynewulf was both the author of Andreas and the last redactor of Beowulf, quoted many passages which some of the texts have in common, as *glædmod, geong*, Beow. 1784, *gangað glædmode* Chr. 576, *sweg up astag*, Beow. 782, Jul. 62 *reord up astag*, Beow. 38 *ne hyrde ic cymlicor ceol gegyrwan*, Andr. 360 *æfre ic ne hyrde þon cymlicor ceol gehladenne heahgestreon* etc. Such combinations torn out of their context, however, cannot be considered a decisive argument (cp. further p. 235 ff).

WACK, somewhat rashly, thought that as *se, þeo, þæt* are "syntaktisch vollkommen gleich verwandt" in Andreas and Elene as well as the pronouns *þes, þeos, þis*, the two poems are by the same author. TRAUTMANN (Anglia Beibl. VI, 17 ff) like SARRAZIN, takes up parallels between the texts trying to prove that Fata Apostolorum is the end of Andreas, and compares formulas occurring in the short poem and Cynewulf. We can proceed to Simons, who declares that the words common to Andreas and Cynewulf are sufficiently numerous to prove that the author was the same man. A more important contribution to the defence of Cynewulf as the author of Andreas was made by Bourauel. This scholar thinks that the author of Fata Apostolorum drew from several sources (cp. p. 34), and points out the similarity between the Andreas poet's free manner of treating his sources and Cynewulf's gleaning from several texts in composing Fata Apostolorum. He also thinks that *pisne sang* in line 1 of F. A. points to the preceding poem and that F. A. is a harmonious epilogue of A. His analysis suffers from containing more objections to earlier research than convincing positive argumentation. In 1901 Skeat takes up Sievers' idea of the double epilogue in the Fates, though, unlike Sievers, he holds that Andreas is Cynewulf's work. He suggests the following solution of the problem about the end of the poem: the author first intended to write an epilogue without runes, i. e. ll. 107—122. But when this epilogue was written he composed another, this time with a runic acrostic. Now a scribe is introduced who adds the two epilogues to the finished poem — in the wrong order.

In the second class of commentators on the Andreas problem there remains perhaps to mention Colton, whose results in an "unpublished investigation" are given by Cook in the shape of some figures in his edition of Christ. Colton is said to have found some correspondences in vocabulary between Andreas and Cynewulf's poems by "dividing the total number of correspondences by the number of lines in the poem" (p. LXI), but this method of his seems to me to have a great deal more to do with arithmetic than with philology.

I shall, here, only make one comment: it seems to me to be obvious that the arguments in favour of the Fates as the close of Andreas cannot be upheld. Palæographic facts give us nothing to go on. Stylistic arguments are not conclusive, and as for further evidence I fully agree with Krapp, who regards Andreas and the Fates as two poems on the following grounds (p. XXXVII): "Andreas has a single source, ... and there is no evidence that the author of Andreas endeavored to manipulate or to enlarge the structure of the narrative as his source gave it. The Fates of the Apostles has a different but quite as definite a source, although the exact text which the Anglo-Saxon poet used has not been discovered." This is the only important fact to reckon with, and its weight in favour of different authorship seems conclusive.

The problem of the Christ trilogy

We must here distinguish between two questions: are the texts nowadays known as Christ I (the Nativity), Christ II (the Ascension), and Christ III (the Judgment) three sections of the same poem or different poems; and are all of these texts Cynewulf's work or only one or some of them?

The first to make a detailed study of the Christ trilogy was DIETRICH, as early as 1853. According to him, there is a unity of composition and of subject-matter that indicates that the three parts (I = v. 1—439, II = v. 440—778, III = v. 779—1664 in his division) are links in a single whole (the Christ), and that this whole was composed by Cynewulf. DIETRICH chiefly devoted himself to an investigation of the content and the composition of the poems, but also made a few remarks on the style, noting a number of words that only are to be found in Christ and in poems signed by Cynewulf. DIETRICH's views were accepted by several scholars; however, no more detailed study of the poems was made until SIEVERS pointed out (Btr. XII, p. 454 ff) that the metrical difference between the three parts is too considerable to admit of the assumption that the Christ is a single unit. Thus the first two parts have only one hypermetrical line (621), whereas the third is very rich in this device. Further, Cynewulf's acrostic is only to be found in the second part. The conclusion is that, if Cynewulf is the author, the three parts are different poems. CREMER's metrical study gives the result that the Christ is made up of two parts (1—778, 779—1693), these parts are the works of different poets, and the second part is probably composed by Cynewulf. MATHER's metrical analysis, however, tends to show that the three parts distinguished by DIETRICH are really Cynewulf's work.

In a note to his essay on Old Germanic verse (Anglia Beibl. V, p. 93) TRAUTMANN declared that the three parts of the Christ, for metrical reasons, cannot be composed by Cynewulf. Only the second part shows his technique, the first and the third must have been written by another poet. A few years later TRAUTMANN (Anglia XVIII, p. 382 ff) suggested another division of Christ than DIETRICH's.

According to TRAUTMANN, Christ I comprises ll. 1—439, Christ II 440—867, Christ III 868—1693. These parts are different poems, and TRAUTMANN repeats his opinion that only part II can be Cynewulf's work: the vocabulary of the other parts differs too much from Cynewulf's usage; the source of part II is known, not so the sources of the other parts; the general style and the metre are different. The division between part I and part II and between part II and part III has found favour with most scholars; thus COOK and KRAPP-DOBBIE adopt it in their editions, and, in fact, it is the most natural of the divisions that have been suggested. But the actual end of Christ III is a more difficult problem; we shall deal with it after we have completed our survey of the discussion on the other questions connected with "Christ".

BLACKBURN (Anglia XIX, 89 ff) was of opinion that Christ is made up of three different parts. Part I ends with l. 438, part II with l. 865, part III with l. 1663. This is apparent from the division of the MS; further the subject-matter of the parts is different: part I is almost purely lyric, part II a poetical homily, part III is descriptive. All three parts are in themselves complete poems. BLACKBURN also pointed out some differences of style: Christ III, for example, has a simple word for "God" such as god, crist, frea, drihten, in about 65 % of all cases, part I has such words in 21 % and part II in 32 %. Part I has 68 kennings, II has 80, and III 60, which makes a considerable difference between I and II on one hand, and III on the other, in view of the respective length of the texts. BLACKBURN concluded that there are only slight differences between I and II, but III differs from the other parts in such a way that difference of authorship must be assumed.

COOK C, however, (p. XXI ff) defends the unity of Christ. He remarks that the distinct plan and style of each part is not conclusive against the unity. Further, too much weight must not be attached to the evidence of the MS division; the sources of all three parts are of a similar nature; some points of language and style are found uniformly in all three parts (rhyme in II and III, to + abstract nouns in I, II, and III, pleonasms in I and II; verbal resemblances between all the parts). There are also no marked dialectal differences between the sections. From these and similar arguments COOK inferred that all three divisions have an organic relation to one another and that all of them are Cynewulf's work. COOK's view was supported by GEROULD (Engl. Stud. XLI, p. 13 ff). In a criticism that is very much to the point and of great methodical interest, he questioned the value of TRAUTMANN's argument against single authorship of Christ, notably difference of vocabulary which was the main reason for TRAUTMANN's objections. "The vocabulary of an author", says GEROULD, "may vary somewhat from work to work, words may be used in one that do not occur in another, an idea may be couched now in this form and now in that ... Differences in vocabulary are, then, to be somewhat discounted as proof of lack of unity or diversity of authorship" (p. 15). GEROULD proceeds to show how Cynewulf, in the 427 lines in Christ II, employs 128 words that are not elsewhere to be found; such a fact, naturally, tends to invalidate TRAUTMANN's arguments which were founded on the absence, in Cynewulf's works, of certain words that are used in part I and III of Christ. There are no serious objections, according to GEROULD, to the assumption that Cynewulf wrote all three parts of Christ.

On the basis of a thorough metrical analysis, SCHWARZ concluded that Christ is made up of three parts (I: 1—439, II: 440—866, III: 867—1664), that owing to differences of for instance alliteration, types of verse, rhyme, and hypermetrical lines, all three are written by different authors and part II by Cynewulf. MOORE (JEGPh XIV, p. 550 ff) answers the question: "The Old English Christ: Is It a Unit?" by yes, after having quoted passages from Augustine, St. Leo, St. Maximus, and Bede, which tend to prove that there was an "intimate correlation of the three great mysteries of the In-carnation, Ascension, and Last Judgment" (p. 563). On the whole, "little or no evidence can be brought forward in favor of the independence of the three parts" (p. 567). BROTHER AUGUSTINE PHILIP on palæographic grounds, however, rejects the idea about the unity of the Christ poems. A study of the divisions made by the Exeter scribe, notably the use of spacing, capitalization, and endmarking, leads him to the conclusion that the scribe regarded the first three pieces as independent poems. DUBOIS (p. 30) holds that Christ is a single poem, and that Cynewulf is the author. MILDENBERGER, in an interesting though somewhat brief article, introduces quite a new element into the discussion on the unity of Christ. He points out that while a unit between the motifs of the different parts of Christ, the Nativity, the Ascension, and the Judgment, is difficult to find in literary docu-ments, such a unit actually exists in iconographic tradition. "The iconography which combines these three motifs found its way to Northumbria ... by the end of the seventh century." MILDENBERGER sums up: "Both the poetic material and the icon seem to indicate the working of some unifying idea nowhere explicit but inherent in the recurrent combination of the motifs, a unifying idea undoubtedly apparent to contemporary Christians. Such an explanation of unity may ... (by analogy) be reasonably ascribed to the three-part Christ poetry" (p. 432). MILDENBERGER has nothing to say about authorship.

S. K. DAS had earlier found considerable differences between Christ II, on the one hand, and Christ I and III on the other. Apart from differences of metre, there are important divergencies of style. Thus, unlike the poems signed by Cynewulf, "no particular abstract attribute is brought into special prominence" (p. 182) in the appositions of Christ I; no prepositional appositions give suggestions of abstract meaning, and there are no verbal appositions as in Cynewulf's poems. The same is true of Christ III; and neither of the two parts show the same concentration on ideas as the Cynewulfian poetry. Neither of them have the same artistic qualities as Cynewulf's poems, consequently, neither is the work of that author.

As for the end of Christ III, TRAUTMANN, as was pointed out above, held that the last line of the poem was l. 1693, in other words, that Guthlac A begins with the line *Monge sindon geond middangeard*. This is the opinion of many scholars and causes a great deal of confusion in references to lines in the Guthlac text. The disputed 29 lines between *Se bið gefeana fægrast* and *monge sindon geond middangeard* are general reflections on Paradise and the destiny of the souls of the holy, and are therefore, it might seem, equally suitable as the introduction to a poem on a saint and as the close of a poem on the Day of Judgment. COSIJN (Btr. XXIII, p. 114) thinks that they form "ein selbständiges Stück über das Schicksal der frommen Seele", and KRAPP-DOBBIE admit that this is a possibility, though, on the evidence of the MS, they take *Se bið gefeana fægrast* to be the first line of Guthlac A: "there can be little doubt that he (the compiler of the Exeter Book) intended this passage, Guthlac 1—29, to be part of the major division of the manuscript which begins at this point and continues with the life of Guthlac" (p. XXX). A similar opinion had earlier been put forward by GOLLANCZ C, p. 191: the lines in question are, "if the original scribe may be credited, the opening lines of the *Legend of St. Guthlac*; there is absolutely no break in the MS between these lines and the passage usually printed as the first section of the latter poem".

It seems to me that there may be some further reasons for assigning the 29 lines on Paradise to the Guthlac A poet. For *seo eadga sawl* that is the centre of these pious reflections, goes much better with the legend that follows than with Christ III: in the latter poem it is mostly the sinners that are referred to as individuals, not the righteous, which are depicted as a group. But if we assume that Guthlac A begins with *Se bið gefeana* etc., the poet, when speaking about *seo eadge sawl*, is obviously thinking of the model of holy life that he is about to describe. There is, therefore, also some internal evidence that the Paradise passage really forms the opening section of Guthlac A and that GOLLANCZ and KRAPP-DOBBIE have the correct division between Christ III and this poem. When, in the chapters that follow, I quote other scholars' references to lines in Guthlac, I shall, as far as possible, quote according to KRAPP-DOBBIE's division.

The Guthlac problem

Guthlac is nowadays generally considered to consist of two parts. This view was first taken by RIEGER in 1869, (p. 325 ff), who held that the second part begins with l. 791 (= 819, if we take Christ III to end on l. 1664). RIEGER was also convinced that both parts were composed by Cynewulf, on account of certain similarities between Guthlac, Wanderer (which RIEGER regarded as Cynewulf's work), and other poems written by Cynewulf. TEN BRINK (p. 73) had a similar opinion, but according to him Guthlac B is a later addition made by Cynewulf, an addition which "überragt den ersten Theil durch dichterischen Gehalt". An important contribution to the discussion on the Guthlac poem was made in 1879 by CHARITIUS. Whereas earlier scholars contented themselves with rather sweeping and not very well supported statements, CHARITIUS subjected the texts to a more thorough examination of metre, syntax, and style. He found that Guthlac B, from a metrical point of view, is stricter than the A poem and that it is close to the Cynewulf canon in this respect. He also pointed out that certain metrical formulas, common in Guthlac B and in Cynewulf's poetry, are not at all to be found in Guthlac A. CHARITIUS further made an examination of the frequency of substantival compounds: Cynewulf's poems and Guthlac B present strong similarities in the use of such compounds, but in Guthlac A they are much rarer than in the other texts. Further differences, according to CHARITIUS, can be noted in the phraseology of the poems. Combinations such as *on þas lænan tid, on þas seocnan tid, in þa æðelan tid; leof mon leofum, yfel yfele, god of gode; londes frætwe; fira cyn,* are found in Cynewulf and Guthlac B, not in Guthlac A; superlative with the genitive (type *hyhta hyhst*) is very rare in Guthlac A, very common in Guthlac B and the Cynewulfian poetry. There are also frequent parallels between Guthlac B and Cynewulf. Differences of this kind lead CHARITIUS to the conclusion that Guthlac B, but not Guthlac A, is Cynewulf's work. When the poet composed the B poem, he was, however, acquainted with the A poem, which appears from certain parallels; finally, the latter poem is earlier than the former since the poet of Guthlac A refers to the oral tradition about the saint, the author of Guthlac B only to the literary tradition.

Another detailed investigation of the style of Guthlac was carried out by LEFÈVRE, who divides the poem into three sections: G I = v. 1—500 (1—529), G II v. 501—790 (530—818), v. 791—the end (818—1379). LEFÈVRE concentrates on the metre of the text, the vocabulary and phraseology, the characteristic passages, and the composition and relation to the source. He remarks that in a metrical analysis of the poem the question of rhyme is of chief importance, and the use and frequency of rhyme does not raise any doubts as to Cynewulf's authorship. LEFÈVRE makes a more detailed examination of the vocabulary than CHARITIUS and employs a better method: he takes the conceptions, not the words, as starting-points. He is, then, not liable to the common error of concluding different authorship from the fact that a certain word that is to be found in one text, happens to be missing in another. Only if the conception expressed by this word occurs in both texts are we in a position to draw conclusions, otherwise the difference is of no value as a criterion. But LEFÈVRE also makes a comparison of the more ordinary type, quoting words and combinations of words that are used in Guthlac but not in the poetry ascribed to Cynewulf. Both investigations tend to show that the differences of vocabulary between the Cynewulf canon and Guthlac are very slight but that the similarity is striking. Again, there are several parallels between Guthlac and the Cynewulf poems, especially Christ. LEFÈVRE, finally, finds that there is a certain difference between the composition and the relation to the source in Guthlac I and II, on the one hand, and Guthlac III on the other. This, however, is chiefly due to the difference of subject-matter. LEFÈVRE'S opinion on the question of the source has been referred to on p. 39. His analysis leads up to the conclusion that Guthlac I, II, and III are all composed by one author, and that this author must have been Cynewulf. On the other hand, Guthlac III presents formal qualities which surpass those of the other two texts; however, this does not justify the conclusion that this part was not Cynewulf's work but only that it was written later than the two other sections.

CHARITIUS and LEFÈVRE, then, have different views of the problem connected with the Guthlac text. However detailed their studies on style and composition may be, and however interesting some of the points they have demonstrated, they are, on the whole, fairly un-satisfactory as arguments in a discussion of authorship and neither of the theories put forth by the two scholars is very plausible.

The next thorough examination of the text was CREMER'S, who, after his metrical analysis, concluded that Guthlac A and B were written by different authors but that the latter poem, since there is nothing in the language and the metre inconsistent with the usage in Elene and Juliana, must no doubt be regarded as Cynewulf's work. MATHER also made a metrical investigation of the texts; he agreed with CREMER that Guthlac A and B have different authors, but as to the authorship of the latter poem he took a more prudent view: "there is not sufficient ground for excluding Guthlac B from the Cynewulfian poems. On the other hand, there is nothing that amounts to con-vincing proof of its Cynewulfian authorship. ... In view of the ab-scence of evidence against it, I am inclined to attribute the poem provisionally, and with little certainty to Cynewulf" (p. 103).

TRAUTMANN, K, called attention to the use of certain phrases and words in Guthlac B, such as *folcum gefræge, frymða god, ælda cynnes, cyning ælmihtig, ælda tudres* etc; and declared that the poem, in respect of phraseology, had many points in common with the Cyne-wulfian poetry. Also the metrical similarity, according to TRAUTMANN, is striking, and the result of his examination was that Guthlac B, in all probability, must be considered a Cynewulf poem.

S. K. DAS's metrical analysis gives the result that neither Guthlac A nor Guthlac B can be Cynewulf's work. As for the style of the poems, both are different from the Cynewulf canon. Unlike these poems, the Guthlac texts do not contain abstractions and preponderance of ideas: Guthlac B, it is true, like Cynewulf's poems, is fairly rich in vari-ations, but "no particular aspect of an idea is brought into special prominence" (p. 184), and nowhere do we perceive a deeper meaning or an emotional tension suggested by abstractions. The feeling for nature in Guthlac B is hardly in keeping with the atmosphere in

Cynewulf's poetry. Guthlac A, unlike the poems signed by Cynewulf, has few variations, and there are no abstractions in the language. The sentences are simpler than in the Cynewulf poetry; of complication in structure we see nothing at all. Neither Guthlac A nor B have periods leading up to a climax. The B poem does not reveal any artistic skill like the signed poems, and the subject-matter of Guthlac A is different from the themes used by Cynewulf. S. K. DAS concludes that neither Guthlac A nor B can have been composed by Cynewulf.

We may, in fact, still agree with KÖRTING, who, in 1887, passed the following verdict on the attempts to solve the problem of authorship (p. 50): "Die Verfasser der beiden Guðlac-Dichtungen sind völlig unbekannt; dafür, dass beide oder doch die zweite von Cynewulf geschrieben sei, sind ausreichende Beweise bis jetzt nicht erbracht worden."

The Phoenix

A minute examination of the style of this text was made by GAEBLER as early as 1880. In this investigation he found nothing in the poet's way of utilizing his source that is inconsistent with the theory that Cynewulf is the author of the Phoenix. Again, there are some words in the Phoenix that are not used by Cynewulf, such as *œsce, abywan, œlmesse, basu, brœd, brid, cleowen, domlic, edwenden* etc., but still more words that are to be found in that poem and the Cynewulf canon exclusively, such as *œppled, bedeglian, bibyrgan, bisorgian, dwœscan, fnœst*; or words that are rare outside this group, such as *afœran, afysan, amerian, anhaga* etc. There are further certain phrases that are common in the Phoenix and the Cynewulf canon (*on þa halgan tid, on þa snudan tid, blissum hremig, geong in geardum, forht on ferhðe* etc.), and parallels between Cynewulf and the Phoenix are common. These parallels, in GAEBLER's opinion, cannot be regarded as simple borrowings. GAEBLER finally stresses the fact that the Judgment plays an important part in the Phoenix as well as in Cynewulf's poems, especially Christ, which proves the close relations between his poetry and the legend about the holy bird. The Phoenix, according to GAEBLER, is probably to be assigned to Cynewulf.

HOLTBUER's examination, however, led to the result that the Phoenix cannot be Cynewulf's work. This is also the opinion of CREMER and

MATHER, whose metrical investigations established obvious differences between Cynewulf's poems and the Phoenix. Also FULTON is convinced that the poem was composed by some other author. After a minute criticism of GAEBLER's arguments, especially the conclusions drawn from similarity of vocabulary and parallel passages, FULTON remarks that the atmosphere of Cynewulf's poetry and the Phoenix is different: Cynewulf is disposed to be "somewhat gloomy and reflective", the Phoenix poet is of "a sunnier disposition" (p. 81). FULTON further found metrical differences between the Phoenix and the other poems, and divergencies of language: the Phoenix has *fœder* as the dat. sing. but Cynewulf *fœdere*, the Phoenix *fotas*, Cynewulf *fet*, the Phoenix *glæd* (92, 289, 303, 593), Cynewulf *glåd* (Chr. 1286). There is, in FULTON's opinion, "absolutely no strong evidence which makes for a Cynewulfian authorship" (p. 85).

BARNOUW's examination of the use of article, weak adjective, and noun in the Phoenix tends to show that this poem, if Cynewulf wrote it, must be his last work. AHRENS's detailed study of the syntax of the Phoenix (parts of speech, parts of sentence, sentence-structure) led the author to the conclusion that, if syntactical characteristics are of any value as criteria, the Phoenix poet must have been strongly influenced by Cynewulf even if he was not identical with that author. AHRENS, however, is on the whole sceptical of the possibility to solve an attribution problem solely on syntactical grounds.

According to SCHWARZ, the metre of the Phoenix shows that it cannot be a work of Cynewulf's but must be later than his poetry.

S. K. DAS finds that the period in the Phoenix "falls short of the effectiveness of a Cynewulfian period", and, unlike the Cynewulf poetry, no particular idea is brought into prominence (p. 179). The poem, further, contains no appositions such as we are used to in the signed poems, and there is a general lack of abstractions. The attention of the poet is not concentrated to ideas but to actions (p. 184). Again, the Phoenix poet does not, like Cynewulf, construct periods working up to a climax but prefers, like the Andreas poet, series of paragraphs. S. K. DAS also stresses differences of a more literary nature: the Phoenix, unlike Cynewulf's poems, is an allegory; there is no hint of struggle between the good and the evil powers, and there is no fighting against the devil as in Cynewulf's poetry. There is reason to believe, consequently, according to the author. that the Phoenix is not Cynewulf's work.

The Dream of the Rood

Among the studies on this poem that pay some attention to style, we first notice an article by TEN BRINK (Anz. f. d. A., V, p. 61 ff). Apart from the similarity of tenor and thought in the Dream and in the final section of Elene, TEN BRINK pointed out some phraseological details common to the Dream and the Cynewulf canon, such as *menn ofer moldan* and *leohte bewunden*; further the common use of certain words, such as *hilderinc* and *reordberend*. Some passages are also strongly suggestive of one another; on, for instance, El. 1252 and the Dream 126 ff. TEN BRINK remarks that "... hier wie dort eine auch für die altenglische zeit keineswegs gewöhnliche, sondern sehr besonders geartete, bedeutende individualität redet" (p. 61). TEN BRINK, accordingly, thinks there are reasons to believe that the Dream of the Rood is Cynewulf's work. EBERT also studied the relations of the poem to Cynewulf's poetry. His essay, which deals only little with vocabulary and phraseology, gives the following results and observations: *hwæðre* occurs 9 times in the Dream and twice the phrase *mæte weorode* = alone (p. 91). The main part of EBERT's investigation, however, is devoted to a somewhat superficial literary analysis. On these and on similar grounds EBERT refused to assign the poem to Cynewulf. HOLTBUER found that the Dream of the Rood contains adjectives, adverbs, and verbs with the genitive that do not occur in Cynewulf's signed poems; accordingly, Cynewulf cannot have been the author of that poem.

A more detailed investigation of the style and manner of the Dream of the Rood is S. K. DAS's analysis. This scholar remarks that there are no abstract appositions in the poem and no periods leading up to a climax. As for the theme of the poem he remarks that unlike the case in Cynewulf's poems, the Crucifixion does not take place on the instigation of the devil and that the poet does not mention that Christ, before the Ascension, vanquished the devil. The style and manner of the Dream of the Rood being different from the Cynewulf canon, S. K. DAS concludes that it is not the work of that author.

What is striking in most of the works surveyed above is the almost impressive optimism on the part of the scholars as to the possibility of solving a problem of attribution by drawing extensive conclusions from a few isolated details chosen at random and without regard to critical principles. Few of the scholars have asked themselves the necessary question: What features of an author's style and manner are so personal to him that similar features in a certain text indicate it as being his work, or that the absence of these features in another text prevents it from being attributed to him? This, however, is no objection to the fact that some of the critics have really found differences which are of value in an attempt to solve the question of authorship. Metrical differences, for instance, must be considered important: metre is so delicate and supple a thing that it is well protected from imitation; it does not strike the eye, unlike certain features of vocabulary or phraseology. Homogeneity of metre, therefore, strongly points to identical authorship, different metre to different authors. Now as for style, BUTTENWIESER and S. K. DAS are the only scholars who call attention to divergencies of a psychological kind: the former when pointing out passages in Andreas that testify to a taste different from Cynewulf's, the latter when stressing the important fact that Cynewulf's signed poetry, unlike the disputed texts, reveal a certain preoccupation with abstract conceptions — the most important observation, it seems to me, that has been made in the discussion of Cynewulf's style and manner. (Before S. K. DAS it was made, though quite incidentally, by BRANDL (p. 1042).

The stylistic part of S. K. DAS's work, however, suffers from two serious defects: a subjectivity that is much too pronounced (frequent remarks about the musical and emotional qualities of the style) and a lack of thoroughness (no methodical comparisons; the author too often contents himself with hints and intimations). Nevertheless, and owing chiefly to the result of S. K. DAS's metrical analysis, it is now more than only probable that the number of poems written by Cynewulf must be limited to four: the texts signed by the author.

But it is time to pass on from this survey to a few more positive methodical speculations.

2. Method and definitions

The objective of our stylistic study, as was pointed out in the first chapter, p. 9, is to find and analyse 1) features of the style in our texts which we may suppose to be stamped by the poets' individualities to a greater extent than other features; 2) features which we may suppose to be due to traditional influence. These two aspects of style can in some cases be fused into one since, of course, we may learn a great deal about the poetic personalities of our authors from their attitude to stylistic tradition.

When we try to evolve a method for dealing with a problem of this kind we must begin by making some general observations.

In an analysis of an author's style — whether he is deeply indebted to a literary convention or not — we find that we may distinguish between such features as may be looked upon as reflecting his manner of combining and developing conceptions and ideas, and such as seem to represent stylistic likes and dislikes which have nothing to do with logical qualities. These points of view, then, will determine our choice of stylistic criteria, but we will not classify these according to the two groups referred to, since some features of style may be regarded from both points of view.

When dealing with the features belonging to the first group, we shall first concentrate on those elements in a poet's style that are indicative of his capacity for distinguishing between vital and subordinate epic matter in a given context, namely, between the incidents, on the one hand, and their motives, their background, their consequences, and explanations of their nature, on the other. We can decide to what extent such distinctions are made when we analyse the use of what we shall call compound and complex clause-series (p. 118 ff).

On a minor scale the ability to distinguish between essential and subordinate matter is apparent from an author's way of expressing causal relations: he may subordinate cause to effect or he may put both on the same level. The capacity referred to may also be judged from the extent to which an author expresses incidents vital to the plot in subordinate clauses. These two points will be treated in the chapter on causal parataxis and essential hypotaxis (p. 153 ff).

The extent of a similar faculty can be defined by a study of adversative asyndeton and syndesis: here we see how often, if at all, the difference between opposite statements is expressed by the poet (p. 172 ff).

We also see a more or a less highly developed discriminative talent in the extent to which an author stresses unimportant elements of a sentence by means of variation. An examination of this point is given in ch. 6, p. 194 ff.

Again, a poet's power of analysing and understanding a given context is apparent from the use he makes of borrowings from other poems (ch. 7).

In our chapter on narrative looseness we shall examine the more or less developed sense of narrative coherence as reflected in the different poems (p. 318 ff).

Different ways of associating and developing conceptions and ideas will be examined in our analysis of the choice between close and loose variation (ch. 6).

The elements of a poet's style and manner belonging to our second group are of great importance when it comes to examining his poetical technique and personal taste and schooling. In the first place we propose to study such elements made up of variations in so far as the use of this stylistic device points to a greater or a lesser poetical variety and precision. This analysis will be made in the sections dealing with variational accumulation and variational chiasmus (ch. 6). The quality of a poetical technique may also be evaluated by the use made of borrowings, just as the ability to understand a certain context, as was just pointed out, appears from such a use.

Further, the vocabulary is of interest in this connexion inasmuch as any choice of words must reflect the poet's general taste and his predilection for certain ideas.

Our study of the influence of poetical tradition will chiefly be restricted to the vernacular tradition. We shall, in examining the different characteristics of style just referred to, also see in how far they are representative of the poet's attitude to this tradition.

So much for the general method. We have still a word to say about the application of this method. First, a thing which ought to go without saying but which nevertheless, as we have seen, has far from always been observed by earlier critics dealing with similar problems: our starting-point must always be a complete comparison. It is of no use whatever to point out, for example, this deficiency or that clumsiness in the style of Andreas or Guthlac A, if one does not at the same time ascertain whether a similar deficiency does or does not, in fact, occur in the other poems. For instance, the fact that a certain word occurs in Cynewulf's poetry but not in Andreas is no reason for drawing conclusions concerning differences of style unless there is a genuine place in the context in Andreas for the conception expressed by the word.

A few words on the proportion of our material: the respective

ngth of our poems varies considerably. In order to realize fully
e significance of the different points of our analysis, one should
eep in mind that Andreas comprises 1722 lines, Elene 1321, Juliana
31, Christ II 427, The Fata Apostolorum 122, The Dream of the
ood 156, Christ I 439, Christ III 798, Guthlac A 818, Guthlac B
61, and the Phoenix 677 lines.

We have, further, to consider some questions of chronology, which
ill be of importance to our conclusions in chapters 3 and 7.
ow the chronology of the Anglo-Saxon poems is notorious for being
ne of the most difficult fields in English philology, and, at best, we
nay only arrive at approximate and relative datings. After con-
idering, however, the arguments put forth by GROTH, BARNOUW,
SARRAZIN (Engl. Stud. XXXVIII, 170 ff), RICHTER, BLACKBURN ED
. XXIII, THOMAS, KLAEBER (MLN XXXIII, 218 ff and Anglia L, 202),
SCHÜCKING (St. E. Ph. Kl., 213 ff), and RICCI (RES, V, 257 ff) — though
the latter does not attempt a classification — I think we may
assume, with some degree of certainty, that Genesis A, Exodus, and
Daniel, are earlier than Beowulf, and that Beowulf is earlier than
the Cynewulf group.

The texts of KRAPP and KRAPP-DOBBIE will be used for the
examination of the Cynewulf and the Cædmon groups, and Beowulf
will be quoted from KLAEBER's third edition. When necessary, the
punctuation of these editors will be altered.

It need hardly be said, finally, that when I speak of inconsistencies
and deficiencies in the following analysis, it is from the point of
view of comparison between the different poems, not out of modern
standards for literary judgment.

Before we pass on to the treatment of the problem itself, we must
pause for a moment to consider a matter of no small importance.
Since certain linguistic and stylistic terms are used in different ways
by different scholars, since further I intend to use some in may own
way, and since I shall have to invent others, we must dwell for a
moment on the definition of certain terms.

In the chapter on the use of compound and complex series we
shall take the clause as a basis. The centre or the whole of a clause
I take to be any finite verbal expression of an idea, whether its
subject is stated or only implied. Thus in Elene 1246 b ff *gife unscynde mægencyning amæt ond on gemynd begeat, torht ontynde,*

tidum gerymde, bancofan onband, breostlocan onwand etc., the verbs
ontynde, gerymde, onband, onwand are each the centres of a clause.
The reason why I regard a construction like the above as a series of
clauses, and not as a sequence of predicates with a single subject,
is that the omission of a subject is extremely common in Old English
(cp. POGATSCHER). In a great many constructions the subject is either
implied in the verb or must be supplied from an earlier noun or
pronoun, and it seems that in all such cases the presence of the
subject is very strongly felt. It seems natural, therefore, to interpret
finite forms like those referred to, as real clauses.

A clause is called secondary when its volume is less than that of
two or more clauses of the opposite kind in one and the same series.
If in a series composed chiefly of main clauses, there is one secondary
sub-clause, then the main clauses, amounting as they do to a greater
volume than the secondary clause, are called predominant; and on
the other hand, if we have a series with many sub-clauses and only
one main clause, this latter is secondary and the sub-clauses are
predominant. The terms compound and complex series will be
explained in detail in ch. 3.

The term parallel is used to designate a certain, sometimes
extensive, combination of words occurring in more than one poem.
The combinations need not be exactly identical but their similarity
must be so marked that we have to do with an actual borrowing or
a reminiscence.

The terms "essential" and "unessential" are often used. "Unessential" applies to clauses and variations which are of second-rate
importance in the course of the narrative. "Essential" applies to
clauses and variations which are of first rate importance.

Other terms are used in conformity with the general usage or are
explained in the places where they occur.

3. The use of compound and complex series

A study of types of clause-series in the Cynewulf group establishes
certain differences of style which testify, in some of the poems, to a
deliberate poetical technique, in others, to a somewhat random method
of composition.

Anglo-Saxon poets frequently work with two types of clause-series.
The one — here called the compound series — consists of short main

clauses, syndetically or asyndetically coordinate. It is sometimes intermixed with a secondary sub-clause so that the units which make up the series consist of either main clause or main clause + sub-clause The sub-clauses are secondary not in relation to the main clause with which they are connected but in relation to the whole series. The other type of clause-series — here called the complex series — is made up of one or a few secondary main clauses and a more or less elaborate system of predominant sub-clauses. We have then, here, two extremes of clause-series, two radically different structures. So much for the division between these types of series. Now as for the difference between compound and complex series, on the one hand, and such parts of a text, on the other, as are neither compound nor complex but make up a zone between these two extremes, it is quite obvious that we cannot make absolute distinctions, separating, sharply, "short" units from "not short", "complex" from "not complex". The extension of series and units must be relative: in the following examination the compound series is a series that stands out in the context, making up a whole, as a specially prominent sequence of short, chiefly main clauses; the complex unit as one that differs from the context in respect of elaborateness of subordination. Departing from this main difference, we find that the compound series, generally, can be said to consist of units of up to 6, occasionally 7 half-lines. The extension of the complex series varies greatly, but it seldom comprises less than 10 half-lines. Units with more than 6 and less than 10 half-lines constitute, roughly, the great mass of sentence-types enlarged by complements, adverbials, and variations, and made up of even proportions of main- and sub-clauses. These sentences will be called "full', and the units· in a compound series that are more extensive than the rest of the units in the series, "fuller" than these other units.

If, in a complex series, there are two or, very seldom, three main clauses, the second and the third are either parenthetically inserted, or correspond to the first, or are syndetically coordinate with it, or variations.

Finally, before we leave the definitions of the terms used in this connexion, a vital point must be cleared up. How do we know the difference between coordination and subordination? In most cases the context, easily enough, answers this question, but sometimes it is hard to say whether a certain word introduces a main clause or a sub-clause. This is especially true of *þær*. In this chapter we shall try to overcome this difficulty by regarding a *þær*-clause as part of a complex series when it is to be found in a system of sub-clauses. Such a *þær*-clause may naturally be considered a relative sub-clause.

The two types of series here indicated have casually been referred to, in other terms, by scholars such as FRITZSCHE, who speaks of "ein kahler aneinanderreihen von Hauptsätzen" in Andreas (p. 35), having in mind, apparently, what we call compound series; or S. K. DAS, who draws our attention to "longer periods" in Cynewulf, "having their roots in feelings and emotions rather than in reason" (p. 159), which seems to refer, in some cases, to our complex series.

We are not, in the following investigation, primarily concerned with the mere occurrence of these types of clause-series, but with the way in which they are used, i. e. what kind of matter they express.

Compound series, standing out in the context, occur first in Elene ll. 18 b—30 a: the heathens are preparing an attack on the realm of the Christian emperor Constantine. Their martial doings are described in short, vivid strokes: the dazzle of weapons, the movements of armies, accompanied by the ravenous wolf and eagle. To this section corresponds a sequence ll. 50—56 a, setting forth the measures of defence on the part of the Romans: the stir and bustle, the clang of shield and spear, the shouts of heralds. The raven, eager for prey, is here the counterpart of the wolf and the eagle. Ll. 75 b—98: the emperor starts up out of his sleep; a celestial messenger speaks to him: "have no fear of the advancing enemy but look to Heaven for help". So doing, he sees a cross adorned with gems and bearing an inscription which promises him victory. 109 b—113 details of the battle: the trumpets sound; raven, eagle, and wolf now appear together as grim symbols of savagery; the horror of battle prevails. After two fuller units dwelling on the fall of men, the close combat, and the showers of darts and arrows, we get another series ll. 121— 143. The fight is still raging until the fullest unit of the series (6 half-lines ll. 127 b—130 a), which describes the climax of the battle, when the Roman king orders his people to rear the Cross among them. The rest of the series tells us of the disordered flight and complete overthrow of the panic-stricken enemies. 189—202 a: Constantine has been told of the Christian truth; he is baptized, rejoices, and devotes himself to the service of God. Some of the compound series here mentioned seem to have been composed on the model of similar sections in the Cædmon poems; cp. p. 251 ff. 225—240 a the voyage to the land of the Jews: the men prepared for the expedition, the ships ready to sail, the loading of weapons, men, and corslets, the ships running through the onset of the waves; everything described, as BROOKE remarks (I, 234), "as if it were a Viking expedition", and probably inspired by a similar passage in Beowulf (cp. p. 240 ff). 332—349 the prophecies of Moses and David concerning the birth of Christ are quoted by the queen. 481 b—494 a Simon's story about what happened after the Crucifixion: the Lord is taken down from the Cross, rests for three nights in the grave, rises from the dead and appears before His followers; Judas's brother is baptized, Stephen is stoned to death. 547—558 a the confusion after Judas's revelation that he knows the secret about the Cross, told in a series beginning with short, restless units in one and two half-lines: the Jews are discussing and trying to find an expedient; heralds summon them to the queen, they feel anxious and go to the court. 632—641 Judas refuses stubbornly to betray the hiding-place of the Cross: "I remember nothing about it; it happened too long ago." This section corresponds to ll. 699—705 a: Judas, overcome by torture, offers to tell the secret. The passages are linked up with split anaphoras: *Is-ic-is-ic-ic* : *ic-ic-is-ic*. The dramatic significance of the correspondence is striking. A series found at 652 b—666 contains the dispute between Judas and Elene, connecting statements to the opposite effect, and is therefore a case analogous to the one at ll. 632—641 and 699—705 a. 750—762 a a praise of God and a description of Seraphim, the armed guard of Heaven. 802—809 a the events after Judas's prayer: smoke rises on the spot where the Cross is hidden, Judas rejoices and thanks God. 842 b—851 the Cross is taken out of the earth and brought to the queen; she rejoices and asks for the Cross of Christ. 867—893 the people exult over the three crosses, a dead boy is carried to them; two of the crosses are lifted up over him; there is no change until the third is erected; then he is recalled to life; the people praise the Lord. Here we find the two climaxes of this incident, the two tests with the crosses, set forth in fuller units with 6 half-lines (878 b—881 a and 884 b—887 a), a device similar to the one at 127 b—130 a. 898 b—929 the devil speaks: earlier on he was powerful, now his strength has been broken by Judas's conversion, he has again been defeated in his fight against Christ, but he threatens his adversary with future destruction. 1026 b—1042 the Cross becomes a remedy for sufferings; Judas is baptized; he preferred good to evil. 1186 b—1200 the nails from Jesus' Cross will give victory in fight; this was declared by prophets; Elene sends the nails, fastened to bridles, to Constantine.

Complex series occur ll. 157—165: Constantine asks if anyone knows the God who sent the propitious cross. 172—188 the wise men tell the emperor about the Cross and about the Passion, the Harrowing of Hell, and the Resurrection. 202 b—210 a Constantine finds information in the Scriptures about the place where Christ was crucified, an event caused by the devil's deceits. 419 b—425 Judas explains the reason for the Roman expedition; the sub-clauses here enlarge on Christ's sufferings. 426 b—432 a Judas warns his people that the secret about the Cross must not be revealed. 432 b—439 Judas: "the power of the Jews will be broken if the mystery of the Cross is revealed". 441—447 form a contrast to this section in the form of a quotation: Judas is told by his father to disclose the mystery before he dies. 456—461 Judas: how could the Jews harm Christ, knowing that He was God's son? 511—516 Judas: the Lord is gracious, though we have sinned, if we repent. 558 b—564 the queen enquires for the place where Christ died. 574—581 the queen threatens the Jews with death unless they make known their secret. 611—618 how is it possible that a man in the desert should choose stones instead of bread if both are given him? 673 b—682 a Judas must divulge the hiding-place of the Cross in order that the divine wish may be fulfilled. 772—783: a prayer that the Cross shall be discovered, the mazy intricacy of which, balanced by the extensive chiasmus, is an outstanding example of the elaborateness of Cynewulf's art:

Gif þin willa sie,   wealdend engla,
þæt ricsie   se ðe on rode wæs,
ond þurh Marian   in middangeard
acenned wearð   in cildes had,
þeoden engla,   (gif he þin nære
sunu synna leas,   næfre he soðra swa feala
in woruldrice   wundra gefremede
dogorgerimum;   no ðu of deaðe hine
swa þrymlice,   þeoda wealdend,
aweahte for weorodum,   gif he in wuldre þin
þurh ða beorhtan   bearn ne wære),
gedo nu, fæder engla,   forð beacen þin.

784—792 a just as God heard Moses, so He is now asked to reveal the treasure. 813—818 a Judas asks forgiveness for his sins. 859—866 Judas does not know which is the right Cross before he places them all in the city, waiting for miracles. 967—975 the news about the finding of the Cross is spread everywhere. 981 b—988 a the messengers are charged to bring the news about the finding of the Cross so long hidden in the earth, to the emperor Constantine. 1006— 1014 a corresponds to this section; Constantine gives orders that a church shall be built, for the glory of Christ, on the spot where the Cross was found. 1049 b—1060 a it is made known that Judas is ordained bishop under the name of Cyriacus. 1175 b—1181 a the nails of the Cross will be famous, giving victory in battle. 1204 b—1211 a Elene exhorts the people to obey the laws of God and the Church. 1217 b—1226 a Elene, about to depart, bestows precious gifts on the people and appoints the day of the finding of the Cross as a memorial day.

In Juliana the first compound series occurs at ll. 8 b—35 a, setting forth a series of incidents and facts forming the beginning of the story to come: the heathens persecute the Christians; Heliseus' idolatry and power are mentioned; his desire for the Christian Juliana; her faithfulness to Christ; her compulsory betrothal and resistance. 58—71 a Heliseus sends for Juliana's father and complains to him about the refusal. 158—168 Juliana is handed over to Heliseus, who greets her with exclamations on her beauty. 225—246 Juliana is hanged by the hair and lashed; she is sent to prison, remains steadfast; the false angel appears. 464 b—486 a an account of the devil's crimes: acts of deceit and violence. 581 b—606 Juliana is plunged into boiling lead; the lead does not harm her but flows out over the surrounding crowd, killing seventy-five heathens. The saint stands unharmed and thanks God; Heliseus, in fury, curses his impotent gods and orders Juliana's execution.

Complex series are to be found ll. 71 b—77: the reason for Heliseus' wrath: Juliana tells him to desert his old gods and adopt the Christian faith. Further 80—86: the oath of Juliana's father to give her over to destruction. 108—113 a Juliana refuses Heliseus unless he confesses Christ, the Creator of the universe. 119—127 a Juliana's father threatens her with a martyr's death unless she abandons her heresy and adopts the heathen faith. 169—174 Heliseus: if Juliana foregoes her religion she will escape the punishment in store for her. 176—183 Juliana: no punishment will make her accept Heliseus unless he turns to the Christian Lord. 201 b—208 Heliseus: Juliana will be chastised if she persists in her refusal to acknowledge his gods. 272—277, 278—282 a Juliana prays God not to desert her and to tell her who the mysterious messenger really is. 352—356 the devil assures the saint that his account of the crimes is true; 357—362 a he intended to entice her from God into a life of evil. The next case, 382—397 a, contains a series with asyndetically coordinate conditional sub-clauses alternating with syndetic ones (the devil explains in what manner he can be defeated):

> Gif ic ænigne   ellenrofne
> gemete modigne   metodes cempan
> wið flanþræce,   nele feor þonan
> bugan from beaduwe,   ac he bord ongean
> hefeð hygesnottor,   haligne scyld,
> gæstlic guðreaf,   nele gode swican,
> ac he beald in gebede   bidsteal gifeð
> fæste on feðan,   ic sceal feor þonan
> heanmod hweorfan,   hroþra bidæled,
> in gleda gripe,   gehðu mænan
> þæt ic ne meahte   mægnes cræfte
> guðe wiðgongan,   ac ic geomor sceal
> secan oþerne   ellenleasran,
> under cumbolhagan,   cempan sænran,
> þe ic onbryrdan mæge   beorman mine,
> agælan æt guþe.

In these seemingly uncouth periods we have, it will be observed, a fairly skilful pattern of correspondences: the two nele-clauses are complementary, as are the two first ac-clauses. The second main clause ac ic geomor sceal secan (oþerne ellenleasran) etc. corresponds with ic sceal feor þonan heanmod hweorfan. Without this network of correlations the artistic value of the periods would of course be inferior, an accumulation of similar clauses being the only effect. 446—453 the devil begs Juliana, by the Grace of the Lord, to have mercy on him in spite of his deceits. 494 b—505 a: time would not suffice for the demon to tell all the crimes he committed ever since the beginning of the world. 518 b—525 a: a continuation of the devil's speech: never did any human being break his power as Juliana has done. 539—545 a a repetition of the demon's prayer for mercy. 718 b—729 a the poet asks the reader of his legend to pray for the salvation of his soul on Judgment Day.

The use of the two types in Christ II is to some extent influenced by the style of Gregory in the 29th homily. The compound series occurs ll. 470 b—494 a: the apostles praise the Lord; He orders them under His protection to preach the Gospel among the heathens and persecute idolatry. The angels appear. The narrative broadens, describing the Ascension and the sadness of the apostles, and narrows again, ll. 502 b—513 a, in a more detailed account of the different events during the Ascension. 527—532 Christ ascends to Heaven; there is joy at His arrival; He sits down on His Father's right hand. 633—650 Job compared Christ to a bird; the heathens did not know its flight; sometimes it rose to Heaven, sometimes it descended to the earth. 664—685 the Lord has endowed humanity with many qualities. The enumeration that follows is an extensive *sum*-series:

> Sumum wordlaþe wise sendeð
> on his modes gemynd þurh his muþes gæst,
> æðele ondgiet. Se mæg eal fela
> singan ond secgan þam bið snyttru cræft
> bifolen on ferðe. Sum mæg fingrum wel
> hlude fore hæleþum hearpan stirgan,
> gleobeam gretan. Sum mæg godcunde
> reccan ryhte æ. Sum mæg ryne tungla
> secgan, side gesceaft. Sum mæg searolice
> wordcwide writan. Sumum wiges sped
> giefeð æt guþe, þonne gargetrum
> ofer scildhreadan sceotend sendað,
> flacor flangeweorc. Sum mæg fromlice
> ofer sealtne sæ sundwudu drifan,
> hreran holmþræce. Sum mæg heanne beam
> stælgne gestigan. Sum mæg styled sweord,
> wæpen gewyrcan ...

This is inspired by Gregory, (MIGNE, P. L. 76, 1218), who, in his turn, is influenced by a passage in 1 Cor. 12, 8—11. Thus the Latin here supports a tendency in Anglo-Saxon poetical language (cp. p. 33). The series at 736b—746a is an echo of ll. 495—511 and 527—532: the Ascension motif reappears with the Lord ascending to Heaven and the joy at His arrival. 804 b—810 a the transitoriness of life and joy; the Doom. 833 b—840 a the terror at Judgment Day.

Complex series are no less common in Christ II. The opening section 440—449 a belongs to this type: the poet wants the unknown *mon se mæra* to know what truly happened on the birth of Christ when no angels appeared. 460 b—467 the apostles are together at Bethania, where the Lord blesses them before He ascends to Heaven.

564—570 a part of the hymn on the power of Christ: the power of the devils is broken after the Harrowing of Hell. 586—598 a the result of the mission of the Lord: He delivered the human race so that, henceforth, man has the freedom to choose between good and evil. One of the sub-clauses is expanded into a sequence of *swa*-coordinations, worked out as a series of contrasts linked up at the end by rhymes:

> ..... *þæt nu monna gehwylc*
> *cwic þendan her wunað,   geceosan mot*
> *swa helle hienþu   swa heofones mærþu,*
> *swa þæt leohte leoht   swa ða laþan niht,*
> *swa þrymmes þræce   swa þystra wræce,*
> *swa mid dryhten dream   swa mid deoflum hream,*
> *swa wite mid wraþum   swa wuldor mid arum,*
> *swa lif swa dead* ... (589 b—596 a).

611 b—618 a: we ought to thank the Lord because He gave us salvation and averted misery. 759 b—765 the angels protect mankind from the arrows of the devils. 815—820 a an admonition to man about spiritual discipline. 840 b—847 a security on the Day of Judgment will be more precious to everyone than life. 858 b—863 man is supported by God in the perilous voyage of life.

The Fates of the Apostles opens with a compound series, ll. 1—17, describing the heroism of the apostles; their decision to go out and preach the Gospel; the destinies of Peter, Paul, and Andrew. 63—79 a Matthew, Irtacus, James, Simon, and Thaddeus fall as warriors. 98 b—106: a concentrated vision of the Doom in the form of Cynewulf's acrostic. The poem contains nothing like a complex series apart from the prayer ll. 115—120 a: let us pray that we may enjoy the bliss of Paradise.

The material here considered is comprehensive and homogeneous enough to enable us to draw certain conclusions as to the main tendencies in the use of compound and complex series in Cynewulf. Compound series are reserved for descriptions of incidents and actions important to the plot and implying a change in the situation; as for example in Elene the battle-scenes, Constantine's vision, his baptism, the voyage to the land of the Jews, the finding of the Cross, the incident of the dead boy, the Cross as a remedy for disease, the baptism of Judas, the sending of the wondrous nails to Constantine.

In Juliana we see this use in the persecutions of the Christians, Heliseus' desire for Juliana, different stages of the martyrdom: Heliseus' complaints, the arrest, the torture, the imprisonment; the false angel; the miraculous escape from the second torture. Christ: the apostles are ordered to preach the Gospel; the Ascension; the flight of Christ. The use in the Fates of the Apostles reminds us of the opening parts of Elene: the battles of the apostles against evil and paganism.

We further observe that the compound series is employed for matter which is dramatic in a different way: incidents to come or such as do not form part of the main plot; drastic speech, dialogue, vivid description. Instances are, in Elene, the prophecies about the birth of Christ, Simon's story about the events after the Crucifixion, the anxiety of the Jews after Judas's tale, Judas's speech before and after the torture, his dispute with the queen, the devil's complaints and threats. In Juliana we note the vivid account of the devil's crimes, in Christ, the scenes from the Day of Judgment. We must, however, take care not to force our interpretation: the description of Seraphim has nothing particularly dramatic about it, and the section about the propitious nails is repeated in a complex series. Neither does the description of Heliseus' power fit in with the use hinted at above. As for the sum-series, Chr. 664—685, it is a special case, being a formula section, supported by the Latin original.

In the study of the use of the complex series we can notice, first, that it is especially common in speeches. As such it gives the background or reason for some part of the plot to follow or expounds a preceding section. The former is for instance the case with Judas's warnings and Juliana's and Heliseus' dialogue, the second with the conclusion of the devil's description of his sins in Juliana 494 b— 505 a. Constantine's investigations into the secret of the Cross, it will be observed, form the conclusion of the preceding battle-scene as well as the background of the story to come. Prayers are common in the complex type, and in speeches, it is used to convey questions and explanations of various kinds of minor importance to the plot. When not used in speeches, the type has a similar explanatory function, which is, of course, especially perceptible in Christ II. The series of this type is also used to check the flow of action, waiting, as it were, for some imminent event; this is seen in El. 859—866: Judas waiting for a sign from God. The complex type also gives the result or consequence of what precedes; for example the spreading of the news El. 967—975; man's freedom, a result of Christ's mission Chr. 586—598 a. In one case the complex series clearly does not fit into the use here outlined: the section dealing with Judas's appointment as bishop El. 1049 b—1060 a.

As we have seen, similar series may correspond so that similar matter is set off against the background (El. 18 b—30 a—50—56 a; 632—641—699—705 a).

When we turn to Andreas it is to a poem in which the use of the structural types here considered differs considerably from the Cynewulf canon. The compound series occurs ll. 45—53, the Mermedonians attack Matthew and blind him; he is given a poisonous drink but praises God. 88—112 after Matthew's prayer a light is seen in the prison and the voice of God is heard, promising the rescue of Matthew and his fellow-prisoners through Andrew. 118—128 the Lord disappears after having delivered the message, Matthew rejoices, dawn appears; the Mermedonians gather. 275 b—285 the helmsman tells Andrew about the danger of the island of Mermedonia. 329 b—342 (Andrew is telling the Lord about his master): Christ ordered His apostles to go out preaching His religion, forbidding them to bring any possessions with them. God will always be in their presence. 369 b—381 a storm arises, Andrew's disciples are frightened. After an interval of four lines to the effect that Andrew thanked the Lord, his speech follows ll. 386—395. Andrew wishes God to reward the helmsman; his disciples are sick, the sea is raging. 433 b—454 a Andrew: God protects the voyagers, the sea will calm itself; when the apostles were terrified during a stormy voyage Christ appeased the winds and waves. 461—470 Andrew preaches and comforts his disciples until they fall asleep; the sea calms down, Andrew rejoices and begins to speak. 505 b—520 a (the end of Andrew's admiring speech to the helmsman): the wisdom of so young a man is praised; the Lord answers that He and His men were often in danger on the sea but always fared well; no one is harmed against the will of God; His power is described. 537—544 a Andrew praises God. 577—594 Andrew enumerates the best known miracles of Christ. 609 b—617 the Lord speaks: the Jews were sinful and obeyed the devil; they will suffer punishment. 669 b—698 Andrew: the high priest insults the disciples because of their belief in Christ; His origin was not divine; the priest names His relatives. Thus spoke the priests, but the Lord goes into the desert with His disciples. 716 b—728 Andrew: Christ shows the two images, representing Cherubim and Seraphim, to His disciples, and describes their praising God in Heaven. 735—746 a the image comes to life and begins to reprove the priests. After four and a half lines, setting forth the creation of the universe, the short clauses continue 751—762, dealing with the relations between God and the patriarchs; after the words of the image everyone is silent. 847—891 Andrew, on the shore of Mermedonia, sees his disciples asleep at his side, he awakens them and tells them that Christ was in the boat; they describe their dream: eagles carried them to Heaven, where they saw splendour and heard divine music; the angels, the patriarchs, the martyrs, king David, and the apostles praising God. Blessed are those who enjoy Paradise, the others sink into perdition. 902—919 Andrew, in a prayer, repents of not having recognized the Lord; praises Christ as a helper; the latter appears and promises to protect the apostle. 950—959 a Christ tells Andrew the torments he must endure among the cannibals and warns him not to desert God. In a fuller unit Christ asks the apostle to remember the torments of the Lord; in 963 b—972 these are described. 981—1003 Andrew goes into the city, invisible, arrives at the prison, sees the guards, who fall dead to the ground; he praises God. The door opens. 1007 b—1023 a Andrew and Matthew meet in the prison, embrace and kiss, thank God, Andrew speaks. A gap in the text follows. 1041 b—1053 a Matthew's fellow-prisoners rejoice and hurry out of the prison; Matthew leads them out of town, hidden by a cloud. The apostles talk together before parting, comforting one another. 1093—1118 (the Mermedonians have discovered the dead guards) the citizens are summoned and draw lots to decide which of them is to be killed. An old man is selected but offers his son instead. The people, overcome with hunger, are eager to kill the boy. In 1125 b—1134 (.. astah. Đa ..) the boy begs for his life, but the man-eaters are inexorable. Their swords will take his life. 1155—1172 (The miracle about the sword has happened). There is great commotion among the Mermedonians; they take counsel together. A good piece of advice is needed. The devil appears and begins to speak. 1179—1214 (continuation of the devil's speech) Andrew has done a lot of harm to the people; they are told to kill him. Andrew answers: "the devil, a prisoner in hell, urged the people to battle. Christ defeated him and bound him." The devil points out that Andrew is speaking. The cannibals rush to battle; the Lord speaks to Andrew, telling him to stand firm: his torments will soon begin. A fuller unit concludes the speech of Christ: the man-eaters will not be able to kill the apostle.

1236 b—1265 a (the men drag Andrew on the ground) the city is in an uproar; the apostle's blood is flowing; he is nevertheless steadfast; evening comes and he is locked up in the dungeon; his belief is unshaken; he is valiant; snow and ice cover the land; the prisoner remains staunch. A fuller unit (1265 b—1269 a) interrupts the series: Andrew praises God till morning. 1269 b—1283 the compound series continues: the cannibals enter the prison, the torture of Andrew begins anew and is described; he complains of his sufferings: God must know them. Ll. 1284—1290 a complex interruption; he invokes God for help. The short clauses continue 1291—1310: God is asked to protect the apostle. The devil appears and encourages the people; the torture recommences, night draws on, Andrew is imprisoned. 1324—1336 the devil with six attendants visits Andrew in prison and scorns him. Herod crucified Christ; the devil's servants will now kill his apostle. They are told to attack him and do so, but God protects their victim. 1341—1368 a (after a fuller unit describing how the devil's servants flee from Andrew when they see the Cross on his forehead): The devil urges them on; they tell their master to attack the apostle himself if he can, they are content to scoff at him. The devil blames Andrew for his power; now, however, he will suffer punishment. An interruption (the devils are ready to kill him); 1372—1406 a (end of the devil's speech): who is mighty enough to deliver Andrew?; the latter replies that he is preserved by God, who fettered the devil. To the demon there will be nothing but misery. The devils run away; the Mermedonians appear and resume the torture. Andrew is badly hurt and in a prayer to God laments his pain. 1425—1435 a Andrew complains that his body is destroyed; the Lord comforts him. 1441—1450 God tells Andrew to look at the ground where he was tortured; he sees flowering trees. 1455—1470 (After Andrew has thanked God) he continues his praise till night falls; then is imprisoned; God appears in the prison and foretells the end of his sufferings; Andrew thanks Him. 1520—1557 Water rushes forth from the mouth of the image, drowning the Mermedonians; a grim mead-banquet ensues; the water floods the whole city; the inhabitants try to escape but a girdle of fire surrounds the town. There is a general wailing; a poor man begins to speak. 1569—1590 the people are punished; the flood increases; Andrew stills the waves; the water flows back into a crevice; the land is dry. 1620—1632 a the apostle calls to life those who were drowned by the waves. They are baptized. 1669—1681 a the Lord orders Andrew to return to

Mermedonia; this he does for the benefit of the Christians; he preaches to the people. 1695—1722 the day for Andrew's parting is at hand; he makes ready for the voyage; the devil flees in sorrow to hell. The converted people accompany Andrew to the shore and see him leave. Their hymn on the glory of God concludes the poem.

Complex series occur in Andreas at ll. 33—39: the Mermedonians generally give their prisoners a poisonous drink that makes them lose their wits. 70—75 (part of Matthew's prayer): the apostle is willing to suffer anything that God imposes upon him. 147—154 a (the Mermedonians visit Matthew in the prison): three days remain till the cannibals carry out their sinister intentions. 161—167 a God remembers how Matthew, who has served Him among many tribes, is in distress. 205—210 the power of God is great enough to move whole cities. 344—348 (the helmsman): if you are God's servants then I will take you where you like. 408—414 (Andrew's disciples refuse to leave their master in the lurch):- if they did, they would be loathsome to everyone who is eager for the reputation of having served his lord well. 483 b—488 (Andrew is speaking to the helmsman): he asks him to reveal his art in navigating the vessel. 526—531 a (the Lord is speaking): it is obvious that Andrew is God's servant since the sea obeys him. 603—609 a Christ asks Andrew whether his master worked any miracles before the high priests and the scribes (cp. p. 55). 786—791 the stone image goes to Mambre, as the Lord ordered him, where the patriarchs are buried. 897—901 (the beginning of Andrew's prayer): he realizes that God was in the boat though he did not recognize Him. 926—932 a (the Lord's reply to Andrew's apology): the latter's demeanour in the boat is a peccadillo as compared with his hesitation to carry out the order about the expedition to Mermedonia. 1265 b—1269 a Andrew does not cease to praise God until dawn. 1284—1290 the apostle trusts that God will never desert him; (this series is probably taken over from Guthlac, cp. p. 292). 1418—1424 (part of a prayer) God had promised the apostles that not a hair on their heads would be touched if they kept His law. 1435 b—1440 truly the universe shall perish rather than God's word be made to fail. 1483 b—1487 a (the poet speaks): a wiser man than he shall tell all the apostle's adventures.

It is not difficult to see the essential difference between the use of the two kinds of series in Cynewulf's poems and in Andreas, a difference that is especially interesting in poems with such resemblance of subject-matter. The compound series, in Andreas, is

used almost indiscriminately. Even if it may be used, as in Cynewulf, in dramatic sections and parts essential to the plot (45—53,
369 b—381, 433 b—454 a, 461—470, 735—746 a, 981—1003, 1041 b—
1053 a, 1093—1118, 1269 b—1283, 1455—1470, 1520—1557, 1569—
1590, 1620—1632 a, 1695—1722) it has, besides, the most various
functions. Thus it happens that a series, containing a dramatic
element, is also used to describe some incidental circumstance connected with it. In ll. 88—112, for instance, except for the future
rescue of Matthew, the text also, and chiefly, deals with God's
promise that Paradise will be Matthew's reward and that he must
not lose his courage. The fact that God's voice was suddenly heard
is not treated as a single link in a chain of events but lengthily
repeated throughout nine lines. One should compare the concentrated
description of Constantine's dream in Elene 69—71, which is logically developed. Similarly, at ll. 1007 b—1023 a the important fact
that Andrew catches sight of Matthew in prison is set forth in the
same language as the account of their joy and hope. Ll. 1041 b—
1053 a treat of the conversation between the two apostles as if it
were as important as the flight of Matthew and the other prisoners.
1236 b—1265 a Andrew's moods and belief in Christ, and the change
in the weather, are told in the same manner as the torture of the first
day. 1291—1310 Andrew's prayer and the devil's encouragement are
taken together with the events of the second day. The same strange
blending of different matter in the same series is met with in 1372—
1406 a, where the torture of the third day is broadly limited by the
apostle's speeches.

Nothing like this is to be found in Cynewulf. Exceptions like Jul.
18—26 and 238—241, which are incidental passages that have made
their way into a larger whole, do not fall into the same category as
the lines in Andreas here referred to. In Andreas they fill a considerable space, are often much more extensive than the essential section
they are linked up with in the series, and the inevitable impression
is that the poet does not care to make any difference between fundamental and unessential points.

This impression is intensified if we take a look at the cases where
the compound series is used without any dramatic motivation whatever. Ll. 118—128, for example, are only a sort of interlude between
the disappearance of God and the entrance of the man-eaters, but the
passage is written as if this link between two episodes were the main
point. 386—395 Andrew's hope is couched in a slightly fuller

language than the following statement about the weather and the
condition of the disciples, but not full enough to distinguish the
obviously different parts from one another. BUTTENWIESER (p. 85) has
called attention to ll. 391—395, which she cites as an instance of
"der eintönige Bau aufeinander folgender Sätze"; this may be true,
but for this kind of clauses Cynewulf can equally well be blamed.
What is essential here is the fact that the poet is repeating and
trying to quicken, in a manner unknown to Cynewulf, his earlier
dramatic description of the raising of the storm. (Cynewulf, on the
contrary, prefers to take up a previous short statement in a fuller
language; cp. El. 56b—57a and 61b—65a; Jul. 26b—28a as
compared with 38—41.) Further the reflections ll. 505b—520a are
expressed in the same way as are the descriptions of the cruelty of
the Mermedonians. So is also the high priest's information ll. 669b—
691, although the beginning of his speech is more dramatic. Other
instances are ll. 751—762; here, to all appearance, Cynewulf would
have used a fuller language (cp. El. 784ff, 500—510). 847—891,
with the description that follows after the short incident, can be
compared with a similar description El. 731—742. 902—919 can
also be mentioned, and between the prophecy and warning 950—
959a no difference is made. 1125b—1134 there is another curious
case like the one at 118—128: the lines should slowly have lead up
to the climax 1135—1154, but the latter lines, linguistically, must
play the subordinate part. As for Cynewulf's way of handling
analogous situations, cp. El. 859ff, Jul. 573ff. In the same way
1179—1214 are only a prelude to the following episode; nevertheless
the style makes them more important than what succeeds. 1324—
1335a: the one line and a half about the attack of the devils cannot
detach itself from the preceding speech.

Ll. 1341—1368a are likewise a mixture of dialogue (reflections,
threatenings, digressions) forming the background of the plot, but
the real culmination of the section, the unsuccessful attack of the
devils, falls outside the series (ll. 1335b—1340) — a technique
highly different from Cynewulf's. Ll. 577—594, 963b—972 relate
episodes from the life of Christ. But there is a considerable difference
between these passages and the Genezareth episode ll. 433b ff as
well as El. 481b ff, 898b ff; Jul. 464b ff, which sections also contain
biblical and religious matter. The two former passages in Andreas
have rather frail connections with the plot — the enumeration of the
miracles is loosely attached to the narrative, the Passion of Christ is

an association caused by the imminent sufferings of His apostle. Contrary to this, the Genezareth episode has direct relations to the calming of the sea by Andrew's presence; the Passion of Christ in Elene to the finding of His Cross and the resistance of the Jews; the fight between Christ and the devil in the same poem to the waverings and the final conversion of Judas; the fight between the devil and mankind in Juliana to the whole plot of that poem; and similarly the instances of compound series in Christ — these are made up of biblical material just as is the whole poem.

One can mention, further, as an instance of the difference between the ways of handling the same material in Cynewulf and in Andreas, ll. 329 b ff in the latter poem compared to Chr. 481 ff: here a vivid and vigorous admonition, there a faint and imperfectly concentrated speech, ruined by an irrelevant borrowed passage (cf. pp. 273, 278). The rarity of complex series in Andreas is in accordance with the extensive use of the compound type — one cannot expect much interest in the function of the complex series in an author with so pronounced a sympathy for expressing vital as well as subordinate matter in compound series. The proportion of compound series in A. is 43 per cent.; in El. 22, Jul. 16, Chr. 24, and Fata 34 per cent. Complex series: in A. 6 per cent; El. has 14, Jul. 17, Chr. 15, and Fata 4 per cent. As for skill in constructing the fullest series of the complex type, the short complex series in Andreas have little in common with the ingenious interlacements in El. 772—783, Jul. 382—397, Chr. 586—598.

Even from the rare occurrence of complex series in Andreas it appears that its functions must be limited compared to the functions in Cynewulf. The case where the type gives the reason or background of a following section is the most evident. Thus in ll. 33—39: a preparation for the cruel treatment of Matthew, 147—154 a and 161—167 a the background of Andrew's expedition. 786—791 an event. Otherwise the complex series conveys questions, assertions, prayer. One notices, finally, that the subordinate system of the complex type in Cynewulf is more elaborate than in Andreas.

The significance of the difference here demonstrated is plain enough. In Cynewulf the epic matter is allowed to come apart into its constituents; the form, as it were, classifies the matter. Monotony is avoided; the style is subtle enough to mark the change from action to reflection, from cause to effect. In Andreas, on the contrary, we do not see anything of the kind: the different components of this epic are fused together almost indiscriminately into a single mass; and this mass, owing to the deterioration of the studied complex type series, makes an impression of crudity. One should beware of modern standards when it comes to the criticism of poetry bordering on antiquity, but one thing it is nevertheless possible to assert: it is easier to write Old English poetry in compound than in complex series. A set of current phrases, some poetic words, an episode to stick to — and even a mediocre poet can satisfactorily describe a battle or a voyage in a series of short and abrupt clauses. But for the complicated interlacement of ideas, the expression of the various feelings in a prayer or an elegiac reflection, cast in a system of subordinate periods, the poet needs a great deal more than this simple linguistic equipment. There is not only less art in the structure of Andreas; the frequent use of the compound type points to a temperament for which incidents and drama are essential. This goes well with the choice of subject-matter. It must be borne in mind, however, that the subject does not oblige a poet to use a style like the Andreas poet's — there is frequently enough reason for the fuller style, as has been shown above.

In the Dream of the Rood we meet with a use of the structural sequences which is more similar to that of the Cynewulf canon than to Andreas. The Dream of the Rood consists for the most part of compound sequences, the first of which runs from the first line as far as l. 94 before we get a fuller unit. The brief staccato units of this series often comprise no more than one or two half-lines, the conciseness of which, however, is balanced by the hypermetrical structure of many lines. The author begins his poem by saying that he wants to tell a dream, and continues with a description of it. He saw a Cross, adorned with gems; all creation, angels and men, beheld Christ on it; it was radiant with splendour but bore traces of ancient evil; now it sweated blood, now it was decked with treasures. The dreamer felt sad and frightened when gazing at the Cross, and suddenly he heard it speak; it tells its mournful story: how it was hewn down in the forest, made into a cross for the execution of criminals and carried to a hilltop. There it saw the Lord coming to ascend on it; it trembled with terror but dared not move or fall. It had to hold the Lord and was pierced by nails; blood flowed over it; then darkness fell over the earth and all creation wept and lamented the death of the Lord. Strangers came, took the body of the Lord and buried it, lamenting the lifeless body. The Cross was taken down and hidden in the earth, later on it was found and adorned with gold and silver. The Cross continues: it has seen sad and terrible things, but was honoured by the Lord just as He honoured His mother Mary. Then follow two complex series 95—100 and 103 b—109: the poet is asked to make known his dream about the Cross; and a short description of the Day of Judgment. Ll. 110—135 a we get the compound series again, setting forth the Doom in more detail (110—121): the terror of the unjust, the calm of the righteous. In the rest of the section the poet tells us that he prayed to the Cross, that he will henceforth live for it. He has no longer any friends, they live with the Lord in Heaven. In a complex section the poet turns to his own hopes for a life in eternal bliss (135 b—144 a). A final sequence of this type (150—156) contains a reflection on the glory of Christ when he came to Paradise with saints and angels. (Compound series 76 %, complex 18 %.)

It has often been maintained in the literature on the Dream of the Rood that the poem is lyrical in character. Thus Bütow remarks (pp. 91, 92): "Vor allem aber scheint sich uns ein hoher literarischer Wert darin erkennen zu lassen, dass des Dichters Kreuzverehrung nirgends in christlicher Konvention stecken bleibt, sondern als Ausdruck einer persönlichen Erschütterung wirkt." Recently Kennedy has spoken of "this lovely lyric of the Cross" and remarked that "a stark vigor of imagination fuses with lyric emotion to make the description notable" (pp. 262, 263). S. K. Das has even the impression that "concise expression breathes forth suppressed feeling" (p. 186). Now there is no accounting for tastes, and the search for feeling in a poem like this is to a great extent a matter of taste, but it is certain that if there is any meaning in the word "lyric", then we cannot look upon the Dream of the Rood as a thoroughly lyrical poem. The emotional element is restrained to a few points: the dreamer's fear and sorrow, the feelings of the Cross at the execution, the poet's hopes connected with the Cross and his expectations of Paradise. Otherwise the subjective ingredient, the experience of the Cross, is a mere setting for the description of the Crucifixion and the Passion, which are the main themes of the poem. The use of the two sentence-types are also indicative of this; the compound series is employed, chiefly, to tell us what happened. We are reminded of the occurrence of this type in the description of Constantine's dream in Elene. The sections in the two poems differ in that the Cynewulf passage is more concentrated and only deals with the emotions of the dreamer in a short concluding unit; the Dream passage is very extensive and contains more descriptions of feelings. The second compound series in the Dream, ll. 110—135 is equally divided, it may be said, between the feelings of others on the Day of Judgment, and the feelings of the poet worshipping the Cross. This section consequently differs from what we are used to in Cynewulf, being rather suggestive of the application of the type in Andreas. The complex series are employed in the manner we expect: the command of the Cross to the poet; the poet's longing for eternal bliss; Christ, His angels, and the saints in Paradise. The portion about the arrival of Christ on Judgment Day ll. 103 b—109 dwells on the intentions of the Lord.

In Christ I the first compound series runs from l. 9 to 17: in an indirect speech the Lord is asked to restore the ruinous house, to deliver wretched mankind from fear and enemies. 85 b—94 a Man will reap as he has sown; the Virgin Mary asks: why are the son and the daughter of Salem surprised and mournful, asking how I, a mother, could preserve my maidenhood? 146 b—159 a corresponds to the first compound series: the Lord is besought to come and save mankind, the prisoners; to give them life and have mercy upon them. This portion is made up of shorter, more restless units than the first; it is a more impassioned invocation, in a direct speech, from creatures in spiritual distress. Ll. 173 b—185 a a part of Mary's and Joseph's dialogue: J: only God can help me; M: why do you complain? You are faultless, yet you speak like a sinner; J: I find no defence against calumny. In a shorter compound series ll. 189 b—196, the conclusion of Joseph's speech, alternatives are contrasted: what happens if he reveals the supposed adultery, what happens if he keeps it secret? 233—261 a a speech addressed to Christ: a light shone to mankind; the Son existed before anything was created; He is the wisdom that wrought creation; no one can tell His origin; He is asked to deliver mankind and open the golden gates; the devil has scattered His flock and subdued what he bought with His blood. 326—336 a speech to the Virgin Mary: She is the door through which the Saviour passed, Christ found Her pure; the Lord closed Her, unsullied, with a key; She must show us the Grace that Gabriel brought to Her. 363—373 a a third version of the prayer to Christ for help: come and deliver us, comfort us though we have sinned. 403—415 a praise addressed to the Lord: He is holy, His glory eternal, He is the God of hosts, the Lord of Creation; blessed be He and praised eternally.

The first complex series occurs ll. 22—32: a prayer that the Lord shall not desert the human race confined in a prison, waiting for the sun, for the Lord to bring the light and make them worthy of glory when they must wander to this gloomy land. Ll. 43—49 Many things were made manifest by the Lord of life which were earlier on hidden in darkness, prophecies (came true) when He appeared who enriches the power of speech of those who praise Him. 71—77 the Virgin Mary, the noblest Maiden that ever the human race heard of, is asked to reveal the secret how She could be pregnant and yet spotless. 109—117 a the Lord, who was for ever without beginning, is asked to send us light and to come Himself that light may appear to those who live in darkness. 140 b—146 a He brought the law to those who hoped for His arrival since they had been promised that He would purify the world. 261 b—274 another, more extensive prayer: the Lord is implored to bring help to the sinners so that the devil may perish and the human race ascend to the realm of glory, from where it was enticed by the evil spirit to live in misery. 282—290 a a praise of the Holy Virgin: the angels proclaim her the Lady of the races in Heaven, on earth, and in hell, because She was willing to give Her virginity to the Saviour, cp. p. 164. 294 b—300 God sent Her word that She should bear His son and yet remain unblemished. 310 b— 316 Isaiah was wondering how anybody could open the large door until the angel addressed him, cp. p. 75; 317—325 the angel's speech: God alone will pass through it and visit the earth and then it will be for ever locked so that only He can open it. 378—384 a hymn to Trinity, holy and blessed, whom men must extol now that God revealed Himself to us so that we may know Him. 421 b—425 it was an even greater accomplishment than anyone knows how He could bring help for the human race through His mother's womb. (Compound series 25 %, complex 21 %.)

In this poem we notice that the difference in the use of the two types of series is less clear than in the Cynewulf canon and the Dream. We can perceive some instances which remind us of Cynewulf: the part of Joseph's and Mary's dialogue, which is given a certain vividness by the compound form (173 b—185 a) and is similar to Constantine's and Elene's dispute; the speech to the Virgin in which She is compared to a door and which sets forth, symbolically, the birth of Christ as a chain of events (326—336). This portion corresponds to compound series in Cynewulf and Andreas in which various doings of the Lord are described, but there is this difference that we more easily recognize the passages in the latter poems as accounts of real events than in the Christ I section, in which one single fact is symbolized as a series of occurrences. Otherwise the Christ I poet employs the compound type for matter which would have given Cynewulf reason for digressions and associations in complex series. This is the case with the prayers and invocations in compound series — in the one at ll. 146b—159a there is no time, so to speak, for anything but short exclamations.

This is also the case with the reflections on the destiny of man, placed between good and evil. The complex series are used in a more natural way: in prayers to Christ and the Virgin, in hymn and praise, which give the poet occasion for reflections and deviations of different kinds. Apart from these instances we find this type in explanations of the relation between God and man and of the birth of Christ. The subject-matter of the poem makes the use of complex and fuller series seem most natural, exegetical and lyrical as it is, and perhaps the compound portions were used chiefly for the sake of variety.

In Christ III, on the contrary, we find a manner of handling the structural sequences which is far more in the Cynewulf tradition. Since the poem deals with the Day of Judgment, we know what to expect from the compound series. Ll. 881 b—892 a: the earth quakes; angels blow their trumpets from the four quarters of the world; they blow towards the stars, from south and north, from east and west; they rouse the dead from their sleep; then we may hear the laments of a sad and frightened multitude. 930—940: all the world resounds; a conflagration spreads over the earth; the flame roars, the sky bursts, the stars fall, the sun darkens, even the moon goes down and the stars sink from Heaven. 941—955 the Lord will come; His host accompanies Him; holy souls go with Him; the celestial trumpet resounds; the winds roar from seven quarters; they devastate the earth; they frighten the world; there is a terrible thunder. 981 b—1014 the fire consumes all living creatures; it rages throughout the earth; the fishes swim in a fire-bath instead of rivers; the water burns; the storm and wind overthrow the world; the men moan; the flame destroys the sinners; there is general wailing; no escape is possible; the fire consumes everything on earth, searching within and without; the King of Heaven comes; He shines in glory; the angels gleam around Him; they tremble with fear of the Lord. The series is interrupted by a complex series 1015—1021 a containing a reflection on man's fear, so natural when even the angels are frightened. 1021 b—1048 the Day will be terrible when the Lord oppresses the races, bids them rise from the graves and come to the Doom; their rest is over; everyone shall rise and take flesh and be renewed; he shall have with him all evil and good that he has done; his soul and body; all shall be revealed before God; mankind is renewed; it rises to the Doom; the air is on fire; the stars fall; the souls go to the eternal home; the deeds of man are manifest; they cannot be concealed. 1069—1082 the multitude appears before the Lord, everyone brings the treasures of his bosom; the Lord will see the good souls; those are bold who bring Him a fair countenance; they shall be happy. 1137—1152 a (the events on the Crucifixion): the veil of the temple was rent in twain; walls fell down; the earth trembled, the sea overflowed its banks; the stars fell from the sky; Heaven realized who it was who adorned it with stars; therefore it sent heralds when He was born. 1225—1231 (after a fuller unit on the destiny of the good on Judgment Day): the sinners shall be gathered on the left hand of the Lord; they shall moan and tremble; they expect no grace. 1259—1267 (the lot of the good): Hell is shut to them, Heaven is open: this is granted to the righteous; the others will see their sins; suffering shall adhere to them from three quarters (a description of these in fuller units follows). 1336—1343 the Lord speaks to the happy and promises them peace; He comforts them and bids them to go blessed to the joy of angels and enjoy it blissfully. 1358 b—1369 (the conclusion of the speech to the righteous): "you did all this for me when you comforted them (the destitute), therefore you will enjoy reward"; otherwise He speaks to the sinners; they cannot expect Grace; their reward will come according to their deeds; they shall suffer a terrible doom. 1376 b—1385 a the Lord begins to speak to the sinful: "I wrought you with my hands; I gave you limbs and spirit; I honoured you more than anyone; I gave you a shape like mine own; I gave you wealth and richness; you knew nothing of woe; you were not grateful for all this." 1418 b—1425 a: "I descended as a son to his mother; I was born alone; they wrapt me and laid me in the dark; I suffered this for the world; I lay on stone." 1433—1445 "I suffered blows, I was spat on, they gave me a bitter drink; I received their wrath; they pursued me; they struck me; I endured this torment for thy sake; they pressed a thorny crown upon my head." Ll. 1460—1464, from 1469—1479, from 1495—1498 we get a series of short units built as antitheses: the sufferings of the Lord are contrasted with the happiness they were intended to

bring to mankind, or with the crimes by which they have been re-
warded; of the type:

> Ic onfeng þin sar   þæt þu moste gesælig
> mines eþelrices   eadig neotan (1460—1461)

and

> Wurde þu þæs gewitleas   þæt þu waldende
> þinre alysnesse   þonc ne wisses? (1472—1473).

1510—1518 "You did not seek the sad; you did not comfort them;
this you did in contempt of me; therefore you shall suffer punishment." The Lord shall pronounce a terrible doom. 1524—1529: they
may not scoff at His decree; they shall fall into the abyss; the Lord is
terrible; no foe will be left on earth. 1536b—1548 they will not
thenceforth escape sin, they are fettered by fire, the vengeance is
manifest; the sin will never be consumed by fire; eternally they will
remain in the abyss, gnawed by torments and serpents. 1591—1598 a
a summing up of the events of the Doom: Heaven and Hell shall be
full of souls; the pit shall swallow the unjust; the flame shall torment
the sinners.

Complex series: 867—874 Judgment Day falls terribly upon the
world as a thief in the dead of night. 921—929 A warning for punishment to him who does not feel afraid before God. 960—968 a indeed,
at the Doom, Adam's kin does not wail for nothing when the fire consumes earth, sea, and heaven. 1015—1021 a (cp. p. 139). 1056 b—1060
he must think in time of the spirit who wants to be pure when the fire
tries the souls. 1090—1099 a (the sight of the Cross) shall be the ruin
of those who felt no gratitude when the Saviour was hanged on the
Cross where He, being free from sin, bought us life and freedom. 1167 b
—1173 the water dared not touch His feet, even the trees announced
who it was who created them when the Lord descended on one of
them to suffer for mankind. 1199—1203 What can he expect who
neglects the sufferings of the Lord who would give us eternal life?
1207 b—1212 a they see, in sorrow, how the King delivered them
from evil that they might live in Paradise. 1284—1290 (after a
description of two kinds of torture for the damned): a third sorrow
is that they will see the rigtheous enjoy the good deeds which they
themselves used to despise. 1312—1326 (cp. p. 77): if we can see
the sins of our souls no one can tell the ardour with which everybody
will give heed to his life and purify his soul that he may live sinless
in the world. 1329 b—1335 we cannot penetrate, with our ordinary

eyes, into the mind and see whether evil or good dwells there that it may please the Lord when He shines in glory on Judgment Day. 1370—1376 a the Almighty will have no compassion on the Day when, in wrath, He will accuse the sinners and ask for their life's account. 1386—1393 Christ: "When I had created you and given you wealth and the fair earth to enjoy, then you disobeyed my law." 1399—1404 "When I had given you happiness and it seemed too little to you unless you became God's equals, then you were severed from eternal joys." 1489—1494 "The cross of your sins is worse than that other Cross which I ascended when your misery grieved me and I delivered you from hell, where you would keep it yourself." 1549—1554 we may say that the soul's guardian, who does not care whether his soul be miserable or happy, has lost the wisdom of life. 1580 b—1590 (what is proper for him who wants eternal life): let him take care of the beauty of his soul and of his words and actions as long as he lives, that he may not lose the joy of life and the reward of glory which the Lord gives to the righteous. 1615 b—1622 wretched shall he be who is such a sinner that he shall be severed from the Lord and thrown into the fire of hell, where limbs are scourged and consumed by flames.

In this poem, then, the two types have fairly specialized functions. The compound sequence deals almost exclusively with the outward incidents on and after Judgment Day: the ravagings of fire, wind, and water; the appearance of the Lord; the raising of the dead; the innumerable host gathers in fear; what happened on the Crucifixion; what will happen to the sinners and to the just. In Christ's speeches their deeds are related and the stories of His birth and of the Passion are told. True, the compound type also mentions the fear of those to be condemned, but it dwells on the outward tokens of their terror, the moaning and the trembling. The complex series, on the other hand, delves, as it were, underneath this dramatic surface: it tells us either about the feelings of mankind and of the Lord (921—929, 960—968 a, 1015—1021 a, 1207 b—1212 a, 1284—1290, 1312—1326, 1370—1376 a); or of the condition of the wretched, the blessed, and the Lord (867—874, 1056 b—1060, 1090—1099 a, 1199—1203, 1329 b—1335, 1489—1494, 1549—1554, 1580 b—1590, 1615 b—1622). In these two cases we find that the subordinate parts of the series develop or give the reason for the feeling and the state of God and man. The cases at 1167 b—1173, 1386—1393, and 1399—1404 are exceptional, being descriptions of events, but we have seen matter of this kind regularly moulded in the compound type. Compound series 30 %, complex 17 %.

We pass on to Guthlac A. Compound series ll. 1—21: the fairest joy shall be the meeting between the angel and the happy soul when it has left the pleasures of this world; the angel speaks: "you shall go to the place you longed for; I shall lead you; the road will be agreeable, a light shall appear; you are going to Paradise"; there is never sorrow, but bliss and rest; the holy will be happy with the Lord; He gives them eternal reward; what is built there lasts for ever; there is eternal life and eternal youth. 30—38 a there are many ranks of holy people; if we keep the commandments we may belong to one of them; a wise man may be happy in the world and yet be careful for the soul; the world is agitated, the love of Christ cools down. 53 b—64 the world is divided; the Lord knows where the just live; He sees his commandments disobeyed; He shall find many, few shall be chosen; some want the reputation of their Order only by words, not by deeds; wealth is more to them than eternal life. 73 b—92 they are oppressed by the highest majesty; they enjoy this life by order; they wish for a better one; they buy glory, give alms, comfort the poor, are liberal with their belongings, give to the needy, serve God; He sees their action. Some live in the desert; they wait for Paradise; the devil vexes them; sometimes he brings them terror, sometimes glory; angels stand before them, they guard them; these are the really holy. 114—123 a (the struggle for Guthlac's soul): the time had come; two guardians fought for him; their teaching was not alike; one taught him the transitoriness of this life and praised Heaven where the souls of the holy enjoy the bliss of the Lord. 133—153 a God destined the end of their fight; the devil fled; the angel remained and taught Guthlac to love his life on the hill; the devils often came there with horror; earlier on they had lived there; now they were cut off from glory; that land was unknown to man; then the builder came there and took his abode; not because he cared for wealth, but he kept that land for his God. 170—191 a Guthlac was good; he cherished a heavenly hope; he aimed at salvation; the angel was near him; he was a model for many a man in Britain; he prepared himself in spirit; he raised the Cross of Christ; many martyrs grew bold; we ascribe a share in this to Guthlac and to the Lord; He gave him victory when foes attacked him; their hatred did not cease, they tempted him; an angel was his support. 215—232 the Lord had that place in mind; it awaited a better dweller; the foes were envious; they must not have a home anywhere; they long for a dwelling; they wish God to put an end to their sufferings by death; they cannot harm Guthlac but are mournful, being vanquished; they must leave that place. 242—279 (Guthlac speaks to the devils): "There is one Almighty God; He protects me; I can keep this dwelling; I am not destitute but powerful; I build myself a house here; an angel supports me; go away from this spot; I want peace with God; my spirit shall not suffer from you; God protects me; my dwelling shall be here." There is a general noise and cry; the devils shout; "we have known many a man; no one was prouder than you; you say you will live here; you will have nothing to eat; hunger and thirst will assault you. Abandon this spot!" 284b—338 "we can trample down your dwelling; furious crowds will destroy you; we shall attack you; go away!"; Guthlac is supported by God, he does not flinch: "the desert is wide; it is inhabited by evil spirits; with all your efforts you will not be victorious; I will not take up arms against you but sacrifice to Christ; you have threatened me[1]; I am not afraid; you cannot harm me; I am God's servant; I do not yearn or mourn; I trust to God; He comforts me." So spoke the saint; the devils fled; Guthlac was brave, he did not care for transient joys; he was merciful to men; his spirit was incited from above; he often thought of renouncing the world. 390—411 the hate of the foes is violent, there is another cry; Guthlac praises God and is preserved as are all righteous souls; Guthlac is the greatest; he defended himself against the demons; they were eager to attack him; they must not harm his soul but were allowed to touch him. 460—497a (the demons speak about monastic corruption): "many seem to live in righteousness but they do not live for God, but for the body in foolish pleasures; all this shall come to light; we have made you see it yourself; you have gained suffering"; God wanted to thank him for his pain; He gave him wisdom; he was steadfast among his enemies, he said that they must leave the spot. "You are guilty; you get no Grace from the Lord; though you were allowed to have me in your power you could not accept it patiently; you brought me through the air; the light of Heaven was revealed to me; you blamed me for tolerating bad morals; you intended to defame the saints; I will tell you the truth: youth in its prime is not mature." A fuller unit on the years of

---

[1] Cosijn's emendation *ermða* for *earda* l. 308a seems conclusive.

discretion; 502 b—517 a "wisdom comes when youth passes; you only care for guilt and sin; you are engaged in quarrels; I am sent as a peacemaker"; so spoke the saint, free from sin. 547—556 (Guthlac is oppressed by the devils): the torture was severe, the demons cruel; they could not kill him; the soul waited for a better time; they understood that God protected him as He can protect all the blessed ones. 691 b—702 (the devils have been ordered to bring the saint back from the door of hell): the demons were frightened; the angel spoke; he protected Guthlac; he commanded the fiends: "you shall do him no harm; you shall bring him back; he shall sway over that plain." A fuller unit: God had ordered him to interfere; 707—714 "I will not conceal who I am; I am God's servant, one of the twelve; He has sent me seeing your actions; this is my brother; his distress grieves me." A fuller unit: "you shall often see me with him, my friend." 719—748 a "now I will visit him; I shall make his words and deeds known to the Lord; He knows him;" Guthlac rejoiced; the slaves were ready; they brought him back; their way was easy; the builder came to his abode; birds greeted him; he had often given them to eat; Guthlac renounced the world; served God; rejoiced at the wild beasts; the plain was beautiful; the saint might enjoy it; God preserved it. 773—789 Guthlac fought against sin; he prayed to God; he thanked God for his martyrdom; his spirit was brought to Heaven; he got his reward there; the Lord is his protector. 796 b—810 these (the righteous) are the communicants, warriors dear to Christ; they have shining belief, pure heart; they worship the Lord; have wise thought; take care of their souls; fight fiends and sins; love their brethren; humiliate themselves; meditate; observe God's commandments; love fasting; avoid hatred; seek prayer; resist sin; keep truth.

Complex series: 22—29 the souls of the righteous will come, after death, to the place where the spirit of man ascends in prayer. 46 b— 53 a we may not hope for a change in the world, that it shall bring us more joys than griefs, before the end of all that God created. 98 b—105 a the hope of Guthlac was turned to Heaven ever since God gave him Grace so that he sought solitude and gave his prime, formerly spent in pleasures, to God. 127—132 (the doctrine of the evil spirit) he urged him that he should join malefactors and live by crime just as those who do not care about man's life if they only gain by it. 153 b—159 a he was tempted, as those remember who revere him for his wonders and his fame which he gained, boldly.

alone in the desert. 160 b—167 a he often brought God's word to those who loved martyrs' lives when the Lord gave him Grace so that he despised worldly pleasures. 192—199 (the devils threaten him): they said that he should burn on the hill and flames consume his body, that his misery should be extended to his race if he did not return to the world and abandon the struggle. 206—214 they said that of all men Guthlac had caused them most trouble since he came to that desert where they, earlier on, had enjoyed their rest after miseries. 233—238 they said that he would suffer death, when they came with a greater host, if he awaited another, more sinister, meeting. 412—420 the demons fly with Guthlac through the air so that he can see the life of men in monasteries, of those who indulge in pleasures before old age has come. 440—445 it seemed to Guthlac that that man was happy who was careful about his life so that the enemy might not harm him when the Lord had decided his departure. 452—459 the devils: "we should not have tormented you if you had listened to friends when you came here and said that the Holy Ghost would preserve you on account of your tonsure." 497 b—502 a Guthlac: "young people enjoy the world until, in old age, the spirit gets higher ideals". 637—644 "I believe in the Father, that He will never desert me because of the deeds with which I have long served Him." 645—651 a "I trust Trinity, who holds Heaven and earth, that you may not harm me. 651 b—662 I am filled with faith and love of God and longing for Paradise where the glorious Home is, and where hope of life will never be granted you for your pride. 673—679 a you must not expect that you may bring me to hell where your home is; where, mourning, you suffer torments." 763—768 the Lord wants us to accept wisdom so that His truth is known to us, which He gave us for our glory. 811—818 it shall not grieve them (the righteous) when they go to the Holy City where they see God's face brilliantly abiding. (Compound series 47 %, complex 17 %.)

Before we analyse the use of the series in this poem we shall examine the cases in Guthlac B. Compound series 907—915 the devils howled; now they changed to human beings, now to serpents spitting venom; Guthlac was steadfast. 953 b—966 a hope and bliss were renewed; disease inflamed his body; his limbs were heavy; God visited him; he was unshaken by the illness; he was not afraid of death but praised and loved the Lord. 976—985 a he was physically weak but spiritually strong; the illness was severe; the drink was prepared that Eve brewed for Adam; the devil gave it to Eve; she gave it to Adam. 1007 b—1034 a (the servant of the saint pays a visit to his sick master): he found him ill; sadness seized him: "why are you so distressed; never did I see you thus afflicted; can you speak; methinks illness has overcome you; this is the greatest sorrow to me; do you know how this will end?" Guthlac could not draw his breath; illness oppressed him; finally he spoke: "disease attacked me this night; my limbs are heavy; the body shall be in the grave; death approaches." 1044 b—1072 a (the end of Guthlac's speech): "the soul is ready to depart; now you know my end"; the youth lamented and was sad; his mind was heavy; he shed tears; God[2] might not retain man's life longer than was destined. The saint noticed his sorrow; he began to cheer him: "do not be sad; it is not hard for me to obey God's will; I do not mourn for death; I do not fear the ministers of hell; the devil cannot accuse me of sins. 1086 b—1098 a "I know that the reward is free from defect; my heart and soul is longing for the eternal joy; this world is no pain for me; I know there is eternal reward." He ceased to speak; he had to rest; night drew near. 1137 b—1158 a (the saint is still on his sick-bed): he did not mourn; death approached; the seventh day after his falling ill came; the servant came to visit him; he found him dying in God's temple; it was the sixth hour; death was near; he could hardly draw his breath or speak. 1262 b—1273 a (Guthlac is holding his last long speech): "I will always keep friendship with you; my soul is longing for the true bliss; it is late; my body is weak; the soul yearns for the eternal home; I am weary." He sank to the wall, still brave; he drew his breath; a sweet odour came from his mouth. A fuller unit follows, dwelling on the sweetness of the odour. 1278 b—1289 a sunset came; night closed in; a light began to shine; the dying man awaited his end; the light shone during the night; the shadows vanished. A fuller unit about the light follows. 1293 b—1309 a the holy man arose and spoke to his servant: "perform your commission; the soul is ready to depart." He received the Eucharist; he looked towards Heaven and expired, his soul was brought to Heaven; a light shone there. 1325 b—1335 a the island quaked; the servant was frightened; he went to his boat and put out to sea; the sun shone; the boat hurried over the sea to the harbour.

---

[2] TIMMER rightly assumes this meaning of *wyrd* l. 1057 (p. 226).

Complex series: 865 b—870 a no man was ever so just that he could escape the drink that Eve gave to Adam. 881 b—888 a Guthlac's miracles, his healing of sick people, became famous in Britain. 925 b —932 a the holy man healed both body and soul of those who visited him as long as he lived. 970 b—975 the time was near that his work should come to an end through death, just as our parents suffered it long ago. 985 b—991 a the children had to pay for the deed so that thenceforth no one could escape the deadly drink. 1098 b—1104 the day came when the Almighty rose from the dead, when He ascended to Heaven from Hell. 1114—1123 a Guthlac preached the Gospel to his servant in such a way that he had never heard any one preach before. 1158 b—1162 the servant asked Guthlac, if he could speak, to tell him what he thought of his condition. 1178 b— 1189 a (Guthlac to his servant): "Go and tell my sister when I am dead and say to her that I avoided her in this life because I wanted us to meet in Heaven." 1227—1234 a (Guthlac is revealing the secret about the angel's visit): "you ask me about a thing which I never told anyone, except you, lest people should have wondered and spread it abroad." 1238—1254 since I took my dwelling here the Lord sent me an angel, every evening and morning, who healed my sorrows and gave more wisdom to me than to any other man, so that I know men's thoughts, a thing that I must not reveal to anybody. (Compound series 30 %, complex 15 %.)

The style of Guthlac A, as far as the use of the compound series is concerned, is markedly different from that of the other poems hirtherto examined. We find a diction of great abruptness, a mosaic of style put together by small units often consisting of only one or two half-lines. It is difficult to see how S. K. DAS can call this a "flowing style of narrative" (p. 180), if by "flowing" we mean that the parts of the style are connected so as to avoid jerky transitions. The compound parts remind us of Andreas. If these series, in the latter poem, are used almost indiscriminately, the same is even more true of Guthlac A, in which poem they have many various functions. True, events are told of in ll. 114—123 a (the struggle for Guthlac's soul); 691 b—702 (the devils are frightened by the angel's intervention); the part of ll. 719—748 a that deals with Guthlac's return; 773—789 (Guthlac dies and his soul is brought to Heaven). Sometimes also a small fragment of a series deals with some event; for instance the first lines of 133—153 a (God ordains the end of the struggle between the angel and the devil, and the devil flees) and the end of this section (Guthlac came to the desert). Further, Guthlac's preparation and raising of the Cross in 170—191 a, the flight of the devils in 284 b—338 and their fury in 390—411, the account of their deeds in 488—497. But apart from these cases, and from those which express commands and threats as parts of the sections ll. 242—279, 284 b—338, 691 b—702, the rest of the compound series expresses something static; circumstances and situations. In the compound form we get descriptions of Guthlac's condition as a dweller in the desert, a faithful and steadfast Christian, a patient martyr, a hopeful seeker for the bliss of Heaven. We also get reflections on the life of the holy men or sinners in general, on the wretchedness of the demons, on the eternal joys of Paradise. Such matter is also found in complex parts, e. g. 22—29, 46 b—53 a, 98 b—105 a, 127—132, 153 b—159 a, 160 b—167 a, 206—214, 440—445, 452—459, 637—644, 645—651 a, 651 b—662, 673—679 a, 763—768, 811—818. But in the complex form we also have threats (192—199, 233—238) and events (412—420). Explanatory speeches are quite as common in the compound as in the complex type. There is no great difference, then, in the use of the types in Guthlac A.

The usage in Guthlac B is not very different from that of the A poem. Thus in the story of Guthlac's illness, the compound type may be employed to describe his condition (ll. 953 b—966 a, 976—980 a, 1150 b—1155 a, 1269 b—1273 a). However, the use of the series in descriptions of events occurs ll. 907—915 (the doings of the devils); 982 b—985 a (Adam and Eve accept the drink of sin), 1007 b—1010 (the servant finds his master ill), 1139 b—1150 a (the end approaches), 1278 b—1289 a (night falls, a light begins to shine), 1300—1309 a (Guthlac dies), 1325 b—1335 a (the island trembles, the servant flees). But we also find compound series in speeches: ll. 1027—1034 a, 1064—1072 a, 1086—1093, 1262 b—1269 a, 1295 b—1299 contain the brief and jerky utterances of the saint, ll. 1011—1022 those of the servant. The complex cases in the poem are heterogeneous: circumstances (ll. 865 b—870 a, 970 b—975, 985 b—991 a), events (881 b—888 a, 925 b—932 a, 1098 b—1104, 1238—1254), exhortations (1158 b—1162, 1178 b—1189 a), explanations (1227—1234 a).

In the Phoenix, finally, the compound series occur ll. 1—14 a: far away there is a fair country; no man lives there; it is beautiful and blessed; noble its maker; there the door of Heaven is often open; a delightful plain and green woods are there. 20 b—27 it is full of flowers; there are no hills or mountains or anything ragged, and the fair plain flourishes there. 60—73 there is no hail, frost, or rain, only clear brooks; they irrigate the ground, flow through the forests; the Lord ordained that the streams should run through the land twelve times; the woods are hung with everlasting fruit. 153—164 a (the Phoenix has grown old): he becomes sad; he leaves the flowering place and seeks a district where no men live; there he rules the birds and lives with them; then they fly westwards; the birds surround their lord. 199 b—208 a (the Phoenix gathers herbs and leaves in the tree where he has taken his abode): he carries them to the tree; he builds a nest and lives there; he surrounds himself with fragrance and flowers. 213—222 a the herbs catch fire; bird and nest are burned; the flames consume the Phoenix; his life vanishes. 265—274 a the bird grows up from the ashes; his life is renewed; then he collects his body; he brings together ashes and bones and covers them with herbs. Some fuller units follow: the bird returns to his island, he becomes young again. 291—301 a he is fair; his head, tail, wings, and neck are beautifully coloured. A fuller unit: the beauty of his eyes. 305—325 his neck and belly, the shield over his back, his legs and feet are bright and variegated; he is beautiful and like the peacock. He is not slow but swift; his maker is eternal; then he departs for his own land; he appears to men; they gather from all quarters. 331—341 a they admire its beauty; they write the occurrence on marble; birds gather, praise the Phoenix, surround him. 350—357 a he visits his old country; the birds return to the earth; the noble bird is in his home; only God knows its sex. 539—551 holy spirits praise God; the souls of men will be purified by fire; the poet: do not think that I am lying; listen to Job; thus he speaks. 614 b—626 a (the souls in Paradise) the Lord gives them every good; they praise Him; they sing hymns around His throne; "peace be with thee, and wisdom, and thanks for thy gifts; thy strength is great".

Complex series occur ll. 28—32: according to what wise men say, the noble land is higher by twelve fathoms than any hill on this earth. 240 b—247 a the flesh of the Phoenix is renewed just as the harvest is stored before the coming of winter lest rain destroy it. 341 b—349 the people marvel at the birds' adoration of the Phoenix, how they praise him as their king and lead him to his nest until they cannot follow him any more when he seeks his abode. 368—374 a the Phoenix does not fear death since he knows that new life is in store for him when he rises from the ashes. 393—400 a we know that God created man and woman and placed them in Paradise, where they were happy as long as they kept His word. 411 b—417 a therefore they had to abandon joy when the serpent deceived them so that they went into the vale of death. 482—490 a blissful man earns joy in Heaven until his days' end when death comes and sends the lifeless bodies into the earth, where they remain for a long time. 552—561 a "I do not regret that I must die, and then, like the Phoenix, have new life". 655—661 a (the herbs) are the words by which the holy prepare themselves for Heaven, where they bring the odour of words and deeds. 667—677 the Maker of life has permitted us to earn delights in Heaven where we may live in bliss and see the Lord. Compound series 22 %, complex 11 %.

The compound series describes events at ll. 153—164 a (the Phoenix grows old and visits the land of birds); 199 b—208 a (he builds his nest); 213—222 a (he is burnt in his nest). 265—274 a (he becomes young again); 320—325 (he departs from his land, the people gather); 331—341 a (the people's admiration, the attention of the birds); 350—354 a (his visit to his country; the return of the birds). But it is also used, in a striking manner, in descriptions: 1—14 a, 20 b—27, 60—73 (the wonderful island); 291—301 a, 305—325 except for the last few lines (the beauty of the Phoenix). Conditions and states are depicted ll. 354 b—357 a (the Phoenix in its home), 539—551, 614 b—626 a (the souls in Paradise).

The complex series set forth circumstances and sometimes the reasons for these. But ll. 341 b—349 (the Phoenix and the birds) give events reflected in the minds of the people; 393—400 a, 411 b—417 a likewise events: the story of Adam and Eve; and also 485 b—490: the coming of death.

If we look back at the use of the structural types in the poems discussed, they may be said to fall into three groups. The first group includes the Cynewulf canon, the Dream of the Rood, and Christ III. In all these poems — though least in the Dream of the Rood — we meet with a highly developed feeling for the form, which is adapted, in a subtle manner, so as to suit the subject-matter, being different for different sorts of themes. This group forms the contrast to the second, which comprises Andreas and Guthlac A: in these poems the compound type is used for the expression of all kind of matter, encroaching, as it were, on the field of complex series. In Guthlac A, however, the complex series is more frequent (17 %) than in Andreas (6 %). In the third group, finally, (Christ I, Guthlac B, The Phoenix), we notice the same use of the compound series, without regard to the subject-matter, as in the second, but with this difference that the compound type is less frequent (Chr. I 25 %, Gu. B 30 %, Ph. 22 %; but Andr. 43 %; Gu. A 47 %). The complex series are used more indiscriminately in Guthlac B and the Phoenix than in Christ I.

We have here referred to the use of the series that is found in the Cynewulf canon, the Dream of the Rood, and Christ III, as a more natural use than the treatment of the series in the other poems. We have a further reason for this judgment than the mere fact that in the former poems the subject-matter is classified, by the form, according to its character. This reason is apparent from an examination of the use of the series in the earliest poetry.

We may notice that the compound series in descriptions of events are extremely common especially in Beowulf and Exodus. In the former poem they occur ll. 1—19, 32—42, 47—63, 74—85, 90 b—110, 115—149 a, 154 b—174, 178 b—193, 198 b—216, 244—272 a, 312—343, 364 b—376, 381 b—390, 395—410, 456—472, 510 b—519, 530—564, 569 b—583 a, 607—619, 651 b—676, 702 b—730, 734 b—749, 753 b—775 a, 814 b—828 a, 884 b—906, 913 b—931, 946 b—979, 1008 b—1029, 1035—1045, 1113 b—1132 a, 1157 b—1180 a, 1207 b—1220, 1224 b—1243 a, 1263 b—1282 a, 1288—1306 a, 1376 b—1407, 1455—1464, 1516 b—1549, 1563—1575 a, 1615 b—1637 a, 1652—1686, 1703 b—1739 a, 1745—1762 a, 1782—1793, 1799—1821, 1863 b—1899, 1957 b—1966 a, 2009 b—2019, 2076—2100, 2105—2171, 2177—2196 a, 2247—2270 a, 2283 b—2315, 2327 b—2341 a, 2426—2434, 2455—2471, 2482 b—2493 a, 2503—2512 a, 2546 b—2575 a, 2580 b—2610, 2618 b—2632, 2672 b—2682 a, 2702 b—2719, 2732 b—2743 a, 2762 b—2793, 2809—2820, 2850—2863, 2873—2886 a, 2897 b—2910, 2928—2941 a, 2946—2960, 2967 b—2976, 2980 b—2998, 3028—3046, 3120—3136, 3156—3172 (46 %). Complex series are not so frequent; instances are ll. 67 b—73, 217—223 a, 277 b—285, 293—300, 426 b—432, 874 b—882, 907—913 a, 1085 b—1094, 1096 b—1103, 1448—1454, 1550—1556, 1576 b—1584 a, 1845 b—1853 a, 1855—1861, 1946—1951 a, 2200—2206, 2348—2354 a, 2638 b—2646 a, 2802—2808, 2836—2842 a, 2864—2872, 2999—3007 a, 3021 b—3027 (5 %). Nearly all the compound series in Beowulf describe events and actions except 244—272 a and 381 b—390 (dialogue), 1169—1180 a (Wealhþeo's thanks), 1376 b—1396 (dialogue), 1455—1464 (description), 1703 b—1739 a, 1745—1762 a (reflections), 2247—2270 a, 2455—2471 (elegies). The complex series have various functions. In Exodus we find compound series at ll. 33—48, 68—80 a, 98—115, 129 b—140 a, 162—182, 187—202, 220 b—233 a, 247—261 a, 299—314 a, 331—355, 374 b—388, 447—469 a, 482—502 a, 530 b—542 a, 565—590 (43 %); all these cases describe events. Complex series occur 22 b—29, 80 b—87 a, 420 b—425, 432—442, 506 b—512, 519 b—525, 558—564 (8 %); these contain explanations, comments and speeches.

The use of the compound type for the description of events and of the complex type for subordinate matter seems, then, to have a traditional background. This background is clearly discernible in the Cynewulf canon, the Dream, and Christ III; the other poets, making indiscriminate use of the series, are less aware of the tradition, and their style is less adapted to the content.

4. Causal parataxis and essential hypotaxis

Connected with the different development, in our texts, of compound clause systems, is the difference consisting of the frequent use, in some poems, of parataxis as compared with the more restricted use in other texts. We shall also note the difference between the use of parataxis, in some poems, in cases when other poems prefer conjunctional adverbs and hypotactical combinations. Naturally, the more developed the syntax of a text, the less common is the encroachment of parataxis on the province of hypotaxis. KELLNER may be right in pointing out that what is formally paratactical juxtaposition is "hypotaxis of subordination" from a logical point of view (p. 53); what is of interest for us here is the extent to which the logical relations between sentences get their formal expression, and we must not underestimate the difference between a style in which this extent is great and a style in which it is inconsiderable.

SCHÜRMANN quotes instances of what he regards as parataxis for relative and temporal hypotaxis in Elene (p. 383); however, such cases I prefer to leave out since they seem fairly obscure. Instead we shall concentrate on cases with causal parataxis, which are more conspicuous and only incidentally referred to by SCHÜRMANN (l. 836, hardly possible; ibid.).

KOPAS, p. 83, gives isolated instances of causal parataxis (Andr. 215, 1121, 1134, 1547; Chr. II 827; El. 547 b, 703; Chr III 1541, 941; Ph. 492; Gu. A 302, 692, 746, Gu. B 1033). These cases are very doubtful except for El. 703, Gu. 746, and Ph. 492. AHRENS (p. 79) quotes Ph. 9—10, 163—64, 188—89, 317 ff, 404 ff, 432 ff, 460 ff, 491 ff, 667 ff as cases of causal parataxis; only 163—64, 188—89, 432 ff, 491 ff are possible instances.

In an examination of hypotaxis we shall concentrate on what is here called essential hypotaxis, i. e. the introduction of an episode, vital to the plot, in a subordinate clause. Such cases will be found almost exclusively in Andreas.

There are, in Elene, the following cases of causal parataxis:

35 b ff
                                              Feðan trymedon
    eoredcestum,   *þæt on ælfylce*
    deareðlacende   *on Danubie*
    stærcedfyrhðe,   *stæðe wicedon*
    ymb þæs wæteres wylm.   *W e r o d e s   b r e a h t m e*
    w o l d o n   R o m w a r a   *r i c e   g e þ r i n g a n ...*

61 b ff
                                              Modsorge wæg
    Romwara cyning,   *rices ne wende*
    for werodleste,   *hæfde wigena to lyt,*
    e a x l g e s t e a l n a   *w i ð   o f e r m æ g e n e,*
    h r o r a   t o   h i l d e.

It should be observed, however, that this sentence contains the repetition of an earlier idea, introduced l. 48 b by means of hypotaxis: (*Wæron Romware ... sona gegearwod ...*) *þeah hie werod læsse hæfdon to hilde þonne Huna cining.*) The use of parataxis l. 63, therefore, may be a deliberate arrangement for the sake of variation. Ll. 148 f, the causal clause is parenthetic:

    Gewat þa heriga helm   *ham eft þanon,*
    huðe hremig,   (*hild w æ s g e s c e a d e n*) ...

The causal element is here mixed with a temporal ingredient. Ll. 588 b ff.

                        He þe mæg soð gecyðan,
    onwreon wyrda geryno,   *swa ðu hine wordum frignest,*
    æriht from orde   *oð ende forð.*
    He is for eorðan   *æðeles cynnes,*
    wordcræftes wis   *ond witgan sunu,*
    bald on meðle.

In 591—593 a we have, it will be noticed, two sets of reasons why the queen can get the information asked for from Judas: first because his ancestors, as his speech has led the Jews to believe, knew all about the passion of Christ, secondly because of his own wisdom, manifest in his advice to his fellow-tribesmen.

635 ff   *Ic ne mæg areccan,   nu ic þæt rim ne can.*
           Is nu feala siðþan   forðgewitenra
           frodra ond godra   þe us fore wæron,
           gleawra gumena.

Part of the reason set forth in ll. 636 ff is inherent in the causal relative clause l. 632 b: (*Hu mæg ic þæt findan*) *þæt swa fyrn gewearð wintra gangum?*

701 b ff   *Ic þæt halige treo*
      lustum cyðe,   nu ic hit leng ne mæg
      helan for hungre.   Is þes hæft to ðan strang,
      þreanyd þæs þearl   ond þes þroht to ðæs heard...

769 b ff   *Ðær he þin ne mæg*
      word aweorpan,   is in witum fæst,
      ealre synne fruma,   susle gebunden.

867 ff   *Gesæton sigerofe,   sang ahofon,*
           rædþeahtende,   ymb þa roda þreo
           oð þa nigoðan tid,   hæfdon neowne gefean
           mærðum gemeted.

ll. 869 b—70 a contain the reason for *sigerofe* and *sang ahofon.*

939 ff   *Ne þearft ðu swa swiðe,   synna gemyndig,*
           sar niwigan   ond sæce ræran,
           morðres manfrea,   þec se mihtiga cyning
           in neolnesse   nyðer bescufeð ...

For this instance compare p. 68.

1077 b ff   *Mec þæra nægla gen*
      on fyrhðsefan   fyrwet myngaþ.
      Wolde ic þæt ðu funde   þa ðe in foldan gen
      deope bedolfen   dierne sindon .....

In another form the same ideas are hypotactically repeated in ll. 1081 b ff: *A min hige sorgað ... ærþan me gefylle fæder ælmihtig ... willan minne ... þurh þara nægla cyme.*

There are 11 cases of causal hypotaxis (ll. 534, 635, 702, 811, 814, 822, 956, 962, 1139, 1170, 1317), and 7 instances of conjunctional adverbs (210, 309, 517, 522, 767, 1250, 1319). Ll. 811, 962, 1139 *þæs* and *þæs þe* are originally genitives governed by *þanc(ian)* but practically equivalent to conjunctions, coinciding with *þæs* (*þe*) = because.

There is one certain instance of essential hypotaxis in Elene, ll. 1049 b ff:

> Ðæt gecyðed wearð,
> siððan Elene heht   Eusebium
> on rædgeþeaht,   Rome bisceop,
> gefetian on fultum,   forðsnoterne,
> hæleða geræðum   to þære halgan byrig,
> þæt he gesette   on sacerdhad
> in Ierusalem   Iudas þam folce
> to bisceope   burgum on innan ...

Causal parataxis occurs in Jul.:

105 ff
> Him þa seo eadge   ageaf ondsware,
> Iuliana   (hio to gode hæfde
> freondrædenne   fæste gestaþelad):
> "Næfre ic þæs þeodnes   þafian wille
> mægrædenne,   nemne he mægna god
> geornor bigonge" ... etc.

A similar case is met with l. 210 ff:

> Ne ondræde ic me   domas þine,
> awyrged womsceaða,   ne þinra wita bealo.
> Hæbbe ic me to hyhte   heofonrices weard,
> mildne mundboran,   mægna waldend,
> se mec gescyldeð   wið þinum scinlace ...

420 b ff
>   Ðu wið Criste geo
> wærleas wunne   ond gewin tuge,
> hogdes wiþ halgum.   Ðe wearð helle seað
> niþer gedolfen ...

Jul. has 3 instances of causal hypotaxis ll. 427, 599, 660. *Forþon* in the latter case is regarded by KRAPP and DOBBIE as an adverb, but there can be no doubt that it is a conjunction. There are 3 cases of conjunctional adverbs (103, 446, 647). Instances of parataxis in Christ are:

738 b ff

                Đa wæs engla þreat
on þa halgan tid   *hleahtre bliþe*
wynnum geworden.   *Gesawan wuldres þrym,*
æþelinga ord,   *eðles neosan* ...

756 ff

Forþon we a sculon   *idle lustas,*
synwunde forseon,   *ond þæs sellran gefeon.*
Habbað we us to frofre   *fæder on roderum*
ælmeahtigne.

Forþon in 756 a connects the sentence with the preceding *þæt þæt hælobearn heonan up stige*, but the causal relation of 758 to 756—757 is still stronger.

797 f   *Đonne ħ cwacað,*   *gehyreð cyning mæðlan,*
           rodera ryhtend,   *sprecan reþe word* ...

Chr. has 4 instances of causal hypotaxis (501, 573, 792, 828), and six of conjunctional adverbs (598, 611, 756, 766, 815, 829).

The Fata Apostolorum has one case of parataxis:

107 ff

Sie þæs gemyndig,   *mann se ðe lufige*
þisses galdres begang,   *þæt he geoce me*
ond frofre fricle.   *Ic sceall feor heonan,*
an elles forð,   *eardes neosan* ...

Causal hypotaxis is found l. 47; essential hypotaxis l. 18 ff:

Ne þreodode he fore þrymme   *ðeodcyninges,*
æniges on eorðan,   *ac him ece geceas*
langsumre lif,   *leoht unhwilen,*
syþþan hildeheard,   *heriges byrhtme,*
æfter guðplegan   *gealgan þehte.*

Among the cases of causal parataxis in Cynewulf we notice a special group with inversion in the clause containing the reason. This is to be found in Elene ll. 636, 703, 770; Jul. 212; Chr. 758. Inversion in this position is common in both Old English verse and prose and gives a certain emphasis to the causal clause.

In Andreas causal parataxis is frequent. There are the following cases:

107 b ff

                               Nis seo þrah micel
þæt þe wærlogan   witebendum,
synnige ðurh searocræft,   swencan motan.
Ic þe Andreas   ædre onsende
to hleo ond to hroðre   in þas hæðenan burg.

125 b ff

                             Duguð samnade,
hæðne hildfrecan,   heapum þrungon …
Woldon cunnian   hwæðer cwice lifdon
þa þe on carcerne   clommum fæste
hleoleasan wic   hwile wunedon …

194 ff

Ðæt mæg engel þin   eað geferan,
halig of heofenum   con him holma begang,
sealte sæstreamas   ond swanrade …

337 ff

Ne ðurfan ge on þa fore   frætwe lædan,
gold ne seolfor.   Ic eow goda gehwæs
on eowerne agenne dom   est ahwette. Cp. p. 52.

391 ff

Nu synt geþreade   þegnas mine,
geonge guðrincas.   Garsecg hlymmeð,
geofon geotende.

401 ff

Edre him þa eorlas   agefan ondsware,
þegnas þrohthearde,   þafigan ne woldon
ðæt hie forleton   æt lides stefnan
leofne lareow   ond him land curon:
("Hwider hweorfað we …. gif we swicað þe"?)

420 b ff

                             Lang is þes siðfæt
ofer fealuwne flod;   frefra þine
mæcgas on mode.

516 b ff

                             Flodwylm ne mæg
manna ænigne   ofer meotudes est
lungre gelettan;   ah him lifes geweald
se ðe brimu bindeð etc.

613 b ff

                         Hie seo wyrd beswac,
forleolc ond forlærde.   Nu hie lungre sceolon,
werige mid werigum,   wræce þrowigan …

672 b ff

               He on gewitte oncneow
þæt we soðfæstes   swaðe folgodon,
læston larcwide.   He lungre ahof
woðe wiðerhydig   wean onblonden ...

Ll. 672 b—674 a contain the reason also for 669—672 a (*Huscworde
ongan* ... *ealdorsacerd herme hyspan*), which idea is repeated ll.
674 b—75.

676 ff

Hwæt, ge syndon earme   ofer ealle menn!
Wadað widlastas,   weorn geferað
earfoðsiða,   ellþeodiges nu
butan leodrihte   larum hyrað etc.

692 ff

Swa hleoðrodon   hæleða ræswan,
dugoð domgeorne,   dyrnan þohton
meotudes mihte.

763 ff

... ða ða yldestan   eft ongunnon
secgan synfulle,   (soð ne oncneowan),
þæt hit drycræftum   gedon wære ...

802 b ff

             Forlætan moldern wunigean
open eorðscræfu,   woldon hie ædre gecyðan
frumweorca fæder.

969 b ff

             Ic adreah feala
yrmþa ofer eorðan.   Wolde ic eow on ðon
þurh bliðne hige   bysne onstellan ...

985 ff

... stop on stræte,   (stig wisode),
swa him nænig gumena   ongitan ne mihte,
synfulra geseon.   Hæfde sigora weard
on þam wangstede   wære betolden
leofne leodfruman   mid lofe sinum.

1068 b ff

           To þam fæstenne
wærleasra werod   wæpnum comon.
hæðne hildfrecan,   to þæs þa hæftas ær
under hlinscuwan   hearm þrowedon.
Wendan ond woldon   wiðerhycgende
þæt hie on elþeodigum   æt geworhton ...

1139 b ff   *Ðrymman sceocan,*

modige maguþegnas,   *morðres on luste,*
woldon æninga,   *ellenrofe,*
on þam hysebeorðre   *heafolan gescenan,*
garum agetan.

We have here a parataxis of motive, of the same kind as in ll. 802, 969 and 1068 ff.

1158 b ff   *Hornsalu wunedon,*

weste winræced,   *welan ne benohton*
beornas to brucanne   *on þa bitran tid ...*

The fact that the mead-halls were empty was due to the lack of riches: there were no gifts or treasures for the chieftain to bestow on his men. This seems to be the idea underlying the parataxis here.

ll. 1215   *Ne magon hie ond ne moton*   *ofer mine est*
          þinne lichoman,   *lehtrum scyldige,*
          deaðe gedælan,   *ðeah ðu drype þolige,*
          mirce manslaga.   *Ic þe mid wunige.*

1291 ff   *Ðu eart gescyldend*   *wið sceaðan wæpnum,*
          ece eadfruma,   *eallum þinum;*
          ne læt nu bysmrian   *banan manncynnes ...*

1364 b ff   *Nu leng ne miht*

gewealdan þy weorce.   *Ðe synd witu þæs grim*
weotud be gewyrhtum.

1390 b ff   *Heton lædan ut*

þrohtheardne þegn   *þriddan siðe,*
woldon aninga   *ellenrofes*
mod gemyltan.

Another parataxis of motive.

1431 ff   *Ne wep þone wræcsið,*   *wine leofesta,*
          nis þe to frecne.   *Ic þe friðe healde*
          minre mundbyrde,   *mægene besette.*

1458 ff   *Ða þa folctogan*   *feorðan siðe,*
          egle ondsacan,   *æðeling læddon*
          to þam carcerne,   *woldon cræfta gehygd,*
          magoræddendes   *mod oncyrran ...*

Cp. 802, 969, 1068, 1139, 1390 ff.

1537 b ff

                          Wæs him ut myne
fleon fealone stream,   woldon feore beorgan,
to dunscræfum   drohtað secan ...

Cp. the similar cases above and p. 171.

1558 ff   *(Nu ge magon sylfe   soð gecnawan,)*
               þæt we mid unrihte   ellþeodigne
               on carcerne   clommum belegdon,
               witebendum.   Us seo wyrd scyðeð,
               heard ond hetegrim,   þæt is her swa cuð!

1581 ff   *Smeolt wæs se sigewang,   symble wæs dryge*
               folde fram flode,   swa his fot gestop.
               Wurdon burgware   bliðe on mode ...

1595 b ff   *Ða wearð acolmod,*
               forhtferð manig   folces on laste.
               Wendan hie wifa   ond wera cwealmes,
               þearlra geþinga   ðrage hnagran ...

Parataxis of motive; as in the last instance in Andreas:

1698 ff   *Ongan hine þa fysan   ond to flote gyrwan,*
               blissum hremig,   wolde on brimþisan
               Achaie   oðre siðe
               sylfa gesecan ...

Along with these 30 instances of parataxis, Andreas has only 9 cases of causal hypotaxis. Three occur after *þanc* and forms of *þancian* 1012, 1151, 1453; one l. 529 *(forþan)*; *nu* ll. 317, 485, 644, 1504; *þæt* l. 276. Conjunctional causal adverbs are used ll. 458 and 526. Inversion in the causal clause is used 11 times: 420, 518, 803, 970, 987, 1072, 1141, 1159, 1365, 1581, 1597.

If, finally, we look at essential hypotaxis, clauses combined in this way are more frequent and more awkward than in Cynewulf, where the only instances seem to be El. 1049 ff and Fata 19 ff, which are both fairly innocuous. The cases in Andreas are:

ll. 48 ff   *Hie þam halgan þær   handa gebundon*
               ond fæstnodon   feondes cræfte,
               hæleð hellfuse,   ond his heafdes segl
               abreoton mid billes ecge.   Hwæðre he in breostum þa git
               herede in heortan   heofonrices weard,
               þeah ðe he atres drync   atulne onfenge.

If, for instance, the last line had run: *þeah ðe him dægcandel dyrned wære*, it would have been more comprehensible. As it now stands it introduces, as if it were an incidental circumstance, an important detail which has not been mentioned before. It is true that a few lies above we are informed that the Mermedonians used to give their prisoners a poisonous drink, but not that such a drink was given to the apostle. Anyhow the drink is more important than the blinding: of the latter particular there is no more mention, but the dangerous drink proves God's Grace, the apostle's wits being unharmed even after he has accepted it.

239 b ff
> *Se beorn wæs on hyhte,*
> *syðþan he on waruðe   widfæðme scip*
> *modig gemette.*

Andreas catches sight of the boat with the Lord and his angels, which will bring him to the hostile country, but this essential fact is less important to the poet than the apostle's feelings on the occasion. True, the event is repeated, a few lines further down, in a main clause, but one expects the repetition to tbe couched in a fuller style, so the thing is said in a manner, compared to Cynewulf's, as unhappy as it is undramatic. The poet's way of describing this episode is decidedly different from Cynewulf's technique.

1074 b ff
> *Him seo wen gelah,*
> *syððan mid corðre   carcernes duru*
> *eorre æscberend   opene fundon,*
> *onhliden hamera geweorc,   hyrdas deade.*

The common short asyndetic sentences otherwise so favoured by the Andreas poet would have come in well here. The dramatic and vital significance of the episode is not reflected in the language; even less are the ensuing doings of the panic-stricken guards, which are described in a complex series. Especially the last two words, the appalling discovery relegated to the very end of the period, ll. 1077 b, inevitably reveal an inferior poet as compared with Cynewulf.

1219 ff
> *Æfter þam wordum com   werod unmæte,*
> *lyswe larsmeoðas,   mid lindgecrode,*
> *bolgenmode;   bæron ut hræðe*
> *ond þam halgan þær   handa gebundon,*

sippan geypped wæs   æðelinga wynn,
ond hie andweardne   eagum meahton
gesion sigerofne ...

Even if the passage is not so defective language as some critics will have it (cp. p. 58), it can hardly claim much admiration since the fact that Andrew became visible, the indispensable connecting link between the speech of the Lord and the attack of the heathens, is all but spoilt. But a construction such as the above is not likely to surprise a reader of Andreas, who has to put up with enough instances of it. It must be admitted, however, that for awkwardness this case probably stands first.

Causal parataxis is to be found in the Dream of the Rood:

ll. 55 b f   *Weop eal gesceaft,*
        cwiðdon cyninges fyll.   Crist wæs on rode.

ll. 147 ff *He us onlysde   ond us lif forgeaf,*
        heofonlicne ham.   Hiht wæs geniwad
        mid bledum ond mid blisse   þam þe þær bryne þolodan.

We have one instance of conjunctional causal adverb l. 84; none of essential hypotaxis.

Christ I contains the following instances of causal parataxis:

68 ff   *... bringeð blisse þe,   benda onlyseð*
        niþum genedde.   Nearoþearfe conn,
        hu se earma sceal   are gebidan.

Christ's knowledge of man's sufferings is the motive for his mission in the world.

189 b ff   *Me nawþer deag,*
        secge ne swige.   Gif ic soð sprece,
        þonne sceal Dauides   dohtor sweltan ...

The omission of the causal conjunction is quite in conformity with the style of Joseph's reproach; the strong emotional tension of the passage would not bear too elaborate a system of subordinations.

255 b ff   *Us is þinra arna þearf!*
        Hafað se awyrgda   wulf tostenced,
        deor dædscua,   dryhten, þin eowde ...

Parataxis here makes an exclamation of the passage. If hypotaxis had been used, the style would have been calmer and we should have had argument rather than emotion. Of this more tranquil diction we have an instance in the complex prayer following at l. 261 b ff (*Forþon we, nergend, þe biddað* ...), a less emotional, more reflective section. Inversion occurs in one case (l. 256).

There are 10 cases of causal hypotaxis (*þæs þe* l. 129, *forþon* l. 169, 287, 408; *nu* 83, 206, 247, 341, 383; *þæt* 210. In KRAPP-DOBBIE's and COOK's editions *forþon* l. 287 is taken as a conjunctional adverb, but clearly the Virgin's intention to bear the Lord is the reason for the angel's praise, so we must put a comma after l. 285:

```
283 ff      ... Cristes þegnas      cweþað ond singað
            þæt þu sie hlæfdige      halgum meahtum
            wuldorweorudes,      ond worldcundra
            hada under heofonum,      ond helwara,
            forþon þu þæt ana      ealra monna
            geþohtest þrymlice,      þristhycgende,
            þæt þu þinne mægðhad      meotude brohtes ...
```

As an adverb *forþon* occurs 8 times (ll. 33, 94, 148, 241, 261, 294, 385, 429).

There is no instance of essential hypotaxis.

Causal parataxis in Christ III:

```
968 b ff                      Teonleg somod
            þryþum bærneð      þreo eal on an
            grimme togædre.      Grornað gesargad
            eal middangeard      on þa mæran tid.
```

The fire of the *þreo*, earth, sea, heaven, cause the mourning of the earth.

```
991 b ff                      Beornas gretað,
            wepað wanende      wergum stefnum,
            heane, hygegeomre,      hreowum gedreahte.
            Seoþeð swearta leg      synne on fordonum ...
```

These instances fit in well with the compound style of the description of the Judgment Day horrors; the poet is only concerned with the events, the connexion between them is of less interest to him.

1045 b ff
                          Opene weorþað

    ofer middangeard   monna dæde.

    Ne magun hord weras   heortan geþohtas,

    fore waldende   wihte bemiþan.

The negative sentence is the equivalent of *sceolon nyde geþohtas onwreon* or the like, thus containing the cogent reason for the disclosure of the thoughts.

1280 ff *magun þurh þa lichoman,   leahtra firene,*

        geseon on þam sawlum.   Beoð þa syngan flæsc

        scandum þurhwaden   swa þæt scire glæs ...

1424 f *Lytel þuhte ic leoda bearnum,   læg ic on heardum stane,*

      cildgeong on crybbe.

Lytel, here, must not be taken too literally but is rather the equivalent of *hean* or *feasceaft*; the whole passage deals with the contrast between man's disregard for Christ and Christ's great mission.

1527 ff *Bið þonne rices weard   reþe ond meahtig,*

      yrre ond egesful.   Ondweard ne mæg

      on þissum foldwege   feond gebidan.

We have 8 cases of hypotaxis (1093, 1202, 1235, 1257, 1294, 1427, 1476, 1637); and 9 instances of conjunctional adverb (1015, 1099, 1151, 1165, 1214, 1360, 1513, 1578, 1630). Inversion occurs ll. 994, 1047, 1281, 1424, 1527. Essential hypotaxis is not used in the poem.

In Guthlac A causal parataxis occurs:

86 f   *eaweð him egsan,   hwilum idel wuldor,*

        brægdwis bona   hafað bega cræft ...

181 b ff   *Frome wurdun monge*

      godes þrowera; we þæs Guðlace

      deorwyrðne dæl,   dryhtne cennað,

      He him sige sealde   ond snyttrucræft ...

                                    (cp. p. 79).

218 ff   *To þon ealdfeondas   ondan noman,*

      swa hi singales   sorge dreogað.

      Ne motun hi on eorþan   eardes brucan ...

244 b ff

                  Mæg ic þis setl on eow
butan earfeðum   ana geðringan.
Ne eam ic swa fealog,   swa ic eow fore
                             stonde ...

274 ff   *Ne þec mon hider   mose fedeð;*
beoð þe hungor ond þurst   hearde gewinnan,
gif þu gewitest   swa wilde deor
ana from eþele.

292 f   *Gearo wæs Guðlac,   hine god fremede*
on ondsware   ond on elne strong.

312 b ff

                    Nis me wiht æt eow
leofes gelong,   ne ge me laþes wiht
gedon motun.   Ic eom dryhtnes þeow,
he mec þurh engel   oft afrefreð.

There is a clear causal relation between the two last sentences and what precedes; there is also such a relation between 314 b—315 and the following lines, but there the connexion is indicated by the conjunctional adverb: *Forðon mec longeþas lyt gegretað* etc.

349 b ff

                    ... *þonne flygereowe*
þurh nihta genipu   neosan cwoman
þa þe onhæle   eardas weredon,
hwæþre him þæs wonges   wyn sweðrade;
woldun þæt him to mode   fore monlufan
sorg gesohte ...

The reason for their question is the hope that the saint might get a liking for a life of worldly pleasures.

467 f   *We þec in lyft gelæddun,   oftugon þe londes wynna,*
woldun þu þe sylfa gesawe   þæt we þec
                          soð onstældun.

470 ff   *Ða wæs agongen   þæt him god wolde*
æfter þrowinga   þonc gegyldan
þæt he martyrhad   mode gelufade,
sealde him snyttru   on sefan gehygdum ...

478 ff   *Ge sind forscadene,   on eow scyld siteð!*
Ne cunnon ge dryhten   duguþe biddan,
ne mid eaðmedum   are secan ...

488 ff   *Setton me in edwit   þæt ic eaðe forbær*
           rume regulas   ond reþe mod
           geongra monna   in godes templum;
           woldan þy gehyrwan   haligra lof ...

541 f   *He þa sar forseah,   a þære sawle hæl*
           wæs mundbora   þe þæt mod geheold ...

                                            (cp. p. 83).

569 ff   *Ongunnon gromheorte   godes orettan*
           in sefan swencan,   swiþe geheton
           þæt he in þone grimman gryre   gongan sceolde,
           hweorfan gehyned   to helwarum,
           ond þær in bendum   bryne þrowian.
           Woldun hy geteon   mid torncwidum
           earme aglæcan   in orwennysse ...
           meotudes cempan.

579 ff   *Ne eart ðu gedefe,   ne dryhtnes þeow*
           clæne gecostad,   ne cempa god,
           wordum ond weorcum   wel gecyþed,
           halig in heortan.   Nu þu in helle scealt
           deope gedufan ...

Nu l. 582 is, of course, an adverb: hell, according to the devils, justly awaits the prisoner because he is not a worthy servant of God.

We should have expected *Forþon þu* etc. *Forþon* l. 585 b is subordinate to the clause 582 b—585 a (cp. p. 221).

629 ff   *Ge þa fægran gesceaft   in fyrndagum,*
           gæstlicne goddream,   gearo forsegon,
           þa ge wiðhogdun   halgum dryhtne.
           Ne mostun ge a wunian   in wyndagum ...

711 ff   *He mec of heofonum   hider onsende,*
           geseah þæt ge on eorðan   fore æfstum
           on his wergengan   wite legdon.

714   *Is þæt min broþor,   mec his bysgu gehreaw.*

719 ff   *Nu ic his geneahhe   neosan wille;*
           sceal ic his word ond his weorc   in gewitnesse
           dryhtne lædon.

744 b ff
$\qquad$ *Guþlac moste*
eadig ond onmod   eardes brucan.
Stod se grena wong   in godes wære;
hæfde se heorde,   se þe of heofonum cwom,
feondas afyrde.

There are 20 instances of causal parataxis, 6 of hypotaxis (150, 317, 469, 472, 585, 778), 7 of conjunctional adverbs (ll. 46, 65, 316, 378, 526, 645, 754). Inversion is used ll. 220, 246, 470, 574, 579, 714, 720, 746. There does not seem to be any instance of essential hypotaxis

Guthlac B has the following instances of parataxis:

944 b ff
$\qquad$ *Wæs se bliþa gæst*
fus on forðweg.   Nolde fæder engla
in þisse wonsælgan   worulde life
leahtra leasne   longfyrst ofer þæt
wunian leton ...

1005 f   *ond þa in eode   eadgum to spræce,*
wolde hyrcnigan   halges lara ...

1023 ff   *Him þa sið oncwæð,   sona ne meahte*
oroð up geteon;   wæs him in bogen
bittor bancoþa.

1091 b ff
$\qquad$ *Nis þes eþel me*
ne sar ne sorg.   Ic me sylfum wat
æfter lices hryre   lean unhwilen.

1094 ff   *Ða se wuldormaga   worda gestilde,*
rof runwita;   wæs him ræste neod,
reonigmodum.

1203 ff   *Ic þec halsige,   hæleþa leofost*
gumena cynnes,   þurh gæsta weard,
þæt þu hygesorge   heortan minre
geeþe, eorla wyn.   Nis þe ende feor ...

1295 b ff
$\qquad$ *Tid is þæt þu fere,*
ond þa ærendu   eal biþence,
ofestum læde,   swa ic þe ær bibead,
lac to leofre.   Nu of lice is,
goddreama georn,   gæst swiðe fus.

There is a remote possibility that *nu* means 'now that', but I feel almost certain that it is an adverb. It corresponds to *tid*: "it is time that you go, for now I am prepared to die". *Nu* as a conjunction would be much too unstressed in this context.

There is, along with 7 instances of parataxis, only two of hypotaxis (1053, 1185), and one with conjunctional adverb (985). In the use of parataxis for the expression of causal relations, the poem is then more radical than Guthlac A. There is no instance of essential hypotaxis. Inversion occurs ll. 945, 1024, 1095, 1206, 1298.

Parataxis is used in the Phoenix:

163 b ff
          Fuglas þringað
  utan ymbe æþelne; *æghwylc wille*
  wesan þegn ond þeow *þeodne mærum . . .*

188 ff
  . . . ðonne on þam telgum *timbran onginneð,*
  nest gearwian. *Bið him neod micel*
  þæt he þa yldu *ofestum mote*
  þurh gewittes wylm *wendan to life . . .*

The causal connexion here is obvious: the nest is the means by which the Phoenix brings about his rebirth, so the clause beginning by *bið him* introduces the motive for his building this nest.

406 ff
  Sarlic symbel *sunum ond dohtrum*
  (wurdon teonlice *to þas idge)*
  ageald æfter gylte.   (Cp. p. 88.)

430 ff
  . . . in þam (holtes hleo) he getimbreð *tanum ond wyrtum*
  þam æþelestum *eardwic niwe,*
  nest on bearwe. *Bið him neod micel*
  þæt he feorhgeong eft *onfon mote*
  þurh liges blæst *lif æfter deaþe . . .*

This case corresponds to l. 189 b ff.

491 ff
  Ðonne monge beoð *on gemot læded*
  fyra cynnes; *wile fæder engla,*
  sigora soðcyning, *seonoþ gehegan . . .*

611 ff
  Ne bið him on þam wicum *wiht to sorge,*
  wroht ne weþel *ne gewindagas,*
  hungor se hata *ne se hearda þurst,*
  yrmþu ne yldo. *Him se æþela cyning*
  forgifeð goda gehwylc.

This case is analogous to Andreas ll. 337 ff. Inversion is used ll. 189, 407, 432, 492. Conjunctional adverbs occur at ll. 368, 409, 411, 472; hypotaxis at ll. 410, 476. It may be observed that most cases of causal connexions, whether paratactical, hypotactical, or indicated by adverbs, fall in that section of the poem in which the symbolism of the Phoenix is explained. There we hear about the cause and effect of man's sin, of God's grace, and about the hope for a life to come. In the earlier part of the poem, on the contrary, we get a description sticking to the main events of the Phoenix's life and death; there is little room for reflection on reasons and motives. Only in two cases, in this earlier section, do such reflections occur, and we get the instances of parataxis. Otherwise the poet is more interested in the temporal succession of his narrative; we notice the frequent *þonne*-clauses in the story about the Phoenix ll. 125—365.

The proportion of causal parataxis, as we have seen, is 10 in Elene, 3 in Juliana, 3 in Christ II, 1 in Fata; hypotaxis (including conjunctional adverb): Elene 18, Juliana 6, Christ II 10, Fata 1. Essential hypotaxis: Elene 1, Fata 1. Andreas: parataxis 30, hypotaxis 11, essential hypotaxis 4. The Dream of the Rood: parataxis 2, hypotaxis 1; Christ I: parataxis 3, hypotaxis 18; Christ III: parataxis 6, hypotaxis 17; Guthlac A: parataxis 20, hypotaxis 13; Guthlac B: parataxis 7, hypotaxis 3; the Phoenix: parataxis 6, hypotaxis 6. What strikes us first, here, is the extensive use of causal parataxis in Andreas and Guthlac A, which two poems stand out as a separate group in this respect, just as they did in the use of clause-series. Guthlac A has a few more cases than Andreas, being not quite half so long. The use of causal hypotaxis, however, is more developed in the shorter poem. This use is more restricted in Guthlac B. Essential hypotaxis is a feature characteristic of Andreas. Cynewulf's poetry is homogeneous in its preference for hypotaxis; a preference most manifest in Elene. Most similar to these texts is Christ III. Christ I, of all the poems, has the most developed causal hypotaxis. The Phoenix has equal proportions. The Dream of the Rood and Fata are similar.

The connection between the difference as to causal parataxis and hypotaxis in our poems, and the difference in these same poems as to the use of clause-series, has already been hinted at. In both cases we see in some of the texts the same tendency to describe, on the same level, matter of varying value and importance, and to reduce fundamental things to inferior rank. Such texts are, above all, Andreas and Guthlac A.

Of particular interest in this connexion is the parataxis of motive with *wolde*-clauses. Guthlac B has one instance. Cynewulf, apart from El. 40, avoids this stereotyped construction, and his ways of expressing motive are various. He can work it into the narrative in a *þonne*-clause as El. 473 or in the whole of a full sentence such as Jul. 409 or in a sub-clause of a complex series such as El. 420 ff. On the whole, however, Cynewulf takes a very faint interest in continually informing the reader of the reason for this action and that speech. He employs instead the more developed, and, we may say, the more artistic method of letting the motives appear, without giving special prominence to them, in the very course of the narrative. But one is not for that reason entitled to look upon a frequent use of paratactical causal *wolde*-clauses as an earlier and more primitive stage of development: Genesis, although its syntax is not very advanced, contains 6 instances of them but makes more use of *forðon*. Exodus, as far as I can see, has 4 cases, Daniel has 2.[1] But in Beowulf the situation is different: there the extensive use of *wolde*-clauses is striking. As instances one can mention ll. 154, 664, 755, 796, 1010, 1292, 1339, 1494, 1546, 1791, 1805, 2294, 2315, 2858, 3171. It is obvious that even if causal parataxis as a rule must be considered one of the features of style which are fairly well protected from imitation, its simplicity escaping attention, the same can hardly be said about the *wolde*-clauses, the formulary character of which strikes the eye. It is highly probable, therefore, that the frequent occurrence of *wolde*-clauses in Andreas, 10 cases, is an imitation of Beowulf. In itself, the correspondence need not point to such a conclusion, but taken along with the other numerous instances of imitation of Beowulf in Andreas (cp. pp. 275—287) it supports this inference. In one case not only the construction but the whole passage seems to be imitated:

B. 755 ff   *Hyge wæs him hinfus,*   *wolde on heolster fleon,*
            secan deofla gedræg;   *ne wæs him drohtoð þær ...*

A. 1537 ff   *Wæs him ut myne*
            fleon fealone stream,   *woldon feore beorgan,*
            to dunscræfum   *drohtað secan ...*

---

[1] Gen. ll. 855, 1732, 1975, 2047, 2684, 2906; Ex. 150, 256, 400, 505; Dan. 83, 246.

Now we also notice that Guthlac A, containing 4 cases, has, comparatively, as many instances as Andreas. We have then, here, another feature linking these two poems up, besides the extensive use of compound series and of causal parataxis in general. But it is not probable that the author of Guthlac A, like the Andreas poet, imitated the *wolde*-constructions from Beowulf since he is otherwise not directly influenced by it.

Parataxis is generally regarded as an earlier stage of development than hypotaxis. The question is therefore whether Guthlac A and Andreas, which are especially rich in parataxis, are earlier than the other texts. Now a study of parallels tends to show that the Andreas poet borrowed from Cynewulf's poetry and from Guthlac A (pp. 261 ff, 291 ff). The fact that it cannot therefore be earlier than these poems is not contradicted by the poet's extensive use of weak adjective + noun, which BARNOUW (p. 135 ff) takes to indicate an earlier date, for this use may have been a deliberate archaism, just as the frequent parataxis may have been. Guthlac A, on the other hand, does not contain borrowings which, clearly, show dependence on other poems. Its author, like the Andreas poet, makes frequent use of weak adjective and noun. We cannot, however, exclude the possibility that the use of parataxis and weak adjective and noun, which in Andreas seems to be an archaic feature, indicates, in Guthlac A, a comparatively early date since there is nothing else in the poem incompatible with such an assumption. RICHTER concludes, in fact, from a study of linguistic and metrical details of the poems, that Guthlac A is earlier than Cynewulf's poetry and Andreas (pp. 18, 88).

However, these chronological hypotheses are uncertain, and we had better content ourselves with the psychological aspects of the use of parataxis hinted at above.

5. Adversative asyndeton

The use and treatment of opposite statements in the Cynewulf group has been largely neglected in earlier examinations of the style. Attention has in a few cases been paid to antithesis; thus HUCHON mentions some "antithèses isolées" in Cynewulf (I, 314), and G. JANSEN refers to a few instances of this stylistic device in Elene (917, 306) and Christ III (908, 1496, 1576 p. 99). SCHÜRMANN quotes instances of adversative asyndeton in Elene (p. 381 ll. 491, 917, 388, 477, 565).

Mätzner also briefly refers to "asyndetische Anreihungen" in Anglo-Saxon poetry (III, 407, 413; Gu. 59). Ahrens (p. 78) thinks that ll. 518—520 in the Phoenix are an instance of adversative asyndeton, but he has no doubt misunderstood the context.

In the following chapter we shall deal with the juxtaposition of sentences contrasted with one another without any combining links such as *ac* (nearly always used after a negative sentence), *hwæðre*, *þeah*, or the like. We shall also compare these instances with cases when such links occur. *Ac*, it may be pointed out, is not always adversative in our texts; in Guthlac A 259, 310, it is = *forðon*, in the Phoenix 5 and 26 it is = copulative *ond*.

In Elene there are the following cases:

14 b ff

Hine god trymede

> *mærðum ond mihtum,   þæt he manegum wearð*
> *geond middangeard   mannum to hroðer,*
> *werþeodum to wræce ...*

The attempts to emend *wræce* to *wræþe* or *wraþe* (Ekwall Anglia Beibl. XXXIII, 65; Kock Anglia XLVII, 264; Holthausen Anglia Beibl. XXXV, 276) are unnecessary and would spoil the contrast here, which is borne out by the subsequent events in the legend. Antitheses of this kind are rare but they exist: cp. Andr. 116, Chr. III 907—08.

366 b ff

Moyse sægde

> *hu ge heofoncyninge   hyran sceoldon,*
> *lare læstan.   Eow þæs lungre aþreat,*
> *ond ge þam ryhte   wiðroten hæfdon ...*

386 ff
> *Oft ge dyslice   dæd gefremedon,*
> *werge wræcmæcggas,   ond gewritu herwdon,*
> *fædera lare,   næfre furður þonne nu ...*

474 ff
> *... on sefan sohton   hu hie sunu meotudes*
> *ahengon, helm wera,   hlaford eallra*
> *engla ond elda,   æðelust bearna.*
> *Ne meahton hie swa disige   deað oðfæstan,*
> *weras wonsælige,   swa hie wendon ær ...*

491 b ff

Ða for lufan dryhtnes

> *Stephanus wæs   stanum worpod;*
> *ne geald he yfel yfele ...*

916 b ff

                                Is his rice brad
ofer middangeard.   *Min is geswiðrod*
ræd under roderum.

924 b ff

                                Gen ic findan ne can
þurh wrohtstafas   *wiðercyr siððan*
of ðam wearhtreafum;   *ic awecce wið ðe*
oðerne cyning ...
(cp. p. 67).

1265 b ff

                              ⋂ *wæs geara*
geogoðhades glæm.   *Nu synt geardagas*
æfter fyrstmearce   *forð gewitene ...*

Adversative *ac* in the poem is used ll. 222, 355, 450, 469, 493, 569, 1304), *hwæðre* l. 719, adversative *ond* ll. 357, 361, 664, 922, *þeah* l. 500. The instances in Juliana are:

26 b ff

                              Đa his mod ongon
fæmnan lufian   (*hine fyrwet bræc*)
Iulianan.   *Hio in gæste bær*
halge treowe,   *hogde ...* (*þæt hire mægðhad ...*
                                          clæne geheolde).

38 ff

Đa wæs se weliga   *þæra wifgifta,*
goldspedig guma,   *georn on mode,*
þæt him mon fromlicast   *fæmnan gegyrede,*
bryd to bolde.   *Heo þæs beornes lufan*
fæste wiðhogde ...

587 b ff

                              Đær on rime forborn
þurh þæs fires fnæst   *fif ond hundseofontig*
hæðnes herges.   *Đa gen sio halge stod*
ungewemde wlite.

590 b ff

                              Næs hyre wloh ne hrægl,
ne feax ne fel   *fyre gemæled,*
ne lic ne leoþu.   *Heo in lige stod*
æghwæs onsund ...

This latter case of contrast is a special one, different from the rest in that the whole of the two clauses are not contrasted but only part of them — they really mean the same thing —; *wloh-hrægl-feax-fel-fyre gemæled* is opposed to *æghwæs onsund.* Such contrasts

are generally linked up with *ac*, as for instance the description of
the island in the Phoenix (ll. 14 b—20 a, 60—64 a, 74—76 etc.); we
shall return, in the chapter on variation, to this common and interesting construction (p. 232 f). Adversative *ac* occurs ll. 85, 153, 385,
388, 393; *hwœðre* is to be found l. 517, *þeah* l. 492.

Christ II only contains one instance:

681 b ff   *Swa se waldend us,*
          godbearn on grundum,   his giefe bryttað.
          Nyle he œngum anum   ealle gesyllan
          gœstes snyttru ...

Here the second clause is a restriction of the first, a modification
which might have been introduced by *hwœðre.*

Ac occurs twice in Christ, ll. 477, 707, *hwœðre* likewise twice, ll.
453, 709, *þeah* l. 523.

The Fata Apostolorum has one case:

98 b ff   Ϝ *þœr on ende standeþ,*
          eorlas þœs on eorðan brucaþ.   Ne moton hie awa œtsomne,
          woruldwunigende.

Ac is used ll. 19, 34, and 115.

Looking at these cases of adversative asyndeton in Cynewulf, we
see that most of them — seven cases in Elene, and two in Juliana —
are passages of marked vividness and emotion. In Elene they are all,
with the exception of 14 b ff, to be found in speeches full of emotional
tension: Elene's reproach of the treacherous Jews, Judas's description
of the fates of Christ and Stephen, the vanquished devil's laments,
melancholy due to the transitoriness of youth. In Juliana the two
cases occur in the dramatic description of the saint's miraculous
rescue from torture (587 b ff, 590 b ff).

In Andreas asyndeton is found:

64 b ff   *A ic symles wœs*
          on wega gehwam   willan þines
          georn on mode;   nu ðurh geohða sceal
          dœde fremman   swa þa dumban neat.

113 ff   *Is to þœre tide   tœlmet hwile,*
          emne mid soðe   seofon ond twentig
          nihtgerimes,   þœt ðu of nede most,

    sorgum geswenced, sigore gewyrðod,
    hweorfest of henðum in gehyld godes,
    Antithesis l. 116.

194 ff Ðæt mæg engel þin eað geferan,
    halig of heofenum con him holma begang,
    sealte sæstreamas ond swanrade,
    waroðfaruða gewinn ond wæterbrogan,
    wegas ofer widland. Ne synt me winas cuðe,
    eorlas elþeodige, ne þær æniges wat
    hæleða gehygdo, ne me herestræta
    ofer cald wæter cuðe sindon.

424 b ff   Sund is geblonden,
    grund wið greote. God eaðe mæg
    headoliðendum helpe gefremman.

The dangers of the sea are contrasted with the help from above.

505 b ff   Ðu eart seolfa geong,
    wigendra hleo, nalas wintrum frod,
    hafast þe on fyrhðe, faroðlacende,
    eorles ondsware.

681 ff Secgað soðlice þæt mid suna meotudes
    drohtigen dæghwæmlice. Ðæt is duguðum cuð
    hwanon þam ordfruman æðelu onwocon.
    (He wæs afeded on þysse folcsceare ...)

800 ff Ne dorston þa gelettan leng owihte
    wuldorcyninges word. Geweotan ða ða witigan þry
    modige mearcland tredan.

This instance is analogous to Jul. 590 b ff; the contrast lies here between *dorston gelettan word* = *sæne wurdon*, and *geweotan*.

887 ff Ðær wæs wuldres wynn, wigendra þrym,
    æðelic onginn, næs þær ænigum gewinn.
    Ðam bið wræcsið witod, wite geopenad,
    þe þara gefeana sceal fremde weorðan ...

903 b ff   Ic on brimstreame
    spræc worda worn, wat æfter nu
    hwa me wyrðmyndum on wudubate
    ferede ofer flodas.

The apostle means to say: *spræc worda worn swa þæt ne wiste þætte meotod on scipe wære*; thus 903 b—904 a are contrasted with the following sentence.

951 b f

                 Is þe guð weotod,
heardum heoruswengum   scel þin hra dæled
wundum weorðan,   wættre geliccost
faran flode blod.   Hie þin feorh ne magon
deaðe gedælan,   þeh ðu drype ðolie ...

1072 ff   *Wendan ond woldon   wiðerhycgende*
þæt hie on elþeodigum   æt geworhton,
weotude wiste.   Him seo wen gelah
syððan mid corðre   carcernes duru
eorre æscberend   opene fundon ...

1112 b ff

               Ðeod wæs oflysted,
metes modgeomre,   næs him to maðme wynn,
hyht to hordgestreonum.

1126 ff   *Ða se geonga ongann   geomran stefne,*
gehæfted for herige,   hearmleoð galan,
freonda feasceaft,   friðes wilnian.
Ne mihte earmsceapen   are findan ...

1159 b ff

               welan ne benohton
beornas to brucanne   on þa bitran tid,
gesæton searuþancle   sundor to rune ...

The case is similar to 800 ff; *to rune* is contrasted with *welan* 1159 b, and we should have expected *ac gesæton* etc.

1334 f   *Hie wæron reowe,   ræsdon on sona*
gifrum grapum.   Hine god forstod ...

1363 b ff   *Hwæt, ðu leoda feala*
forleolce ond forlærdest!   Nu leng ne miht
gewealdan þy weorce.

1392 f   *woldon aninga   ellenrofes*
mod gemyltan.   Hit ne mihte swa!

1418 ff   *Ðu ðæt gehete   þurh þin halig word,*
þa ðu us twelfe   trymman ongunne,
þæt us heterofra   hild ne gesceode,

> *ne lices dæl*   *lungre oððeoded,*
> *ne synu ne ban*   *on swaðe lagon ....*
> *... Nu sint sionwe toslopen,*   *is min swat adropen,*
> *licgað æfter lande*   *loccas todrifene ...*

1538 b ff
> *woldon feore beorgan,*
> *to dunscræfum*   *drohtað secan,*
> *eorðan ondwist.*   *Him þæt engel forstod ...*

1609 ff
> *Ne beoð ge to forhte,*   *þeh þe fell curen*
> *synnigra cynn.*   *Swylt þrowode,*
> *witu be gewyrhtum.*   *Eow is wuldres leoht*
> *torht ontyned,*   *gif ge teala hycgað.*

1701 b ff
> *Ðær he sawulgedal,*
> *beaducwealm gebad.*   *Ðæt þam banan ne wearð*
> *hleahtre beworfen,*   *ah in helle ceafl*
> *sið asette ...*

Along with these cases of asyndeton, we find instances of *ac* at
ll. 23, 38, 232, 281, 634, 637, 736, 1083, 1209, 1476, 1592, 1670, 1703.
Of *hwæðre* there are three instances ll. 51, 504, 1487, and two of the
adverb *þeah* (ll. 813, 1250). Adversative *ond* occurs l. 1414. Both adversative syndesis and asyndeton, consequently, are more frequent
in Andreas than in Cynewulf's poems; the Andreas author likes con-
trasting parts of the narrative with each other. But asyndeton is
used more indiscriminately than it is by Cynewulf, who prefers to
intensify only certain situations in his stories by this device.

The poet of the Dream of the Rood is almost indifferent to the
effect produced by adversative asyndeton. There seems to be only
one case of this device:

46 ff   *Ðurhdrifan hi me mid deorcan næglum.*   *On me syndon þa*
> *dolg gesiene,*
> *opene inwidhlemmas.*   *Ne dorste ic hira nænigum sceððan.*

Ac is used ll. 11, 43, 115, 119, 132, *hwæðre* ll. 18, 24, 38, 42, 57, 59,
70, 75, 101, thus very frequently for a 156 line poem; *ond* l. 13.

In Christ I, the adversative asyndeton is likewise very rare. Instances are:

18 ff   *Eala þu reccend*   *ond þu riht cyning,*
> *se þe locan healdeð,*   *lif ontyneð,*
> *eadgan upwegas,*   *oþrum forwyrneð*
> *wlitigan wilsiþes,*   *gif his weorc ne deag.*

172 b ff

Ic tearas sceal

geotan geomormod.   God eape mæg

gehælan hygesorge   heortan minre ...

Ac occurs ll. 56, 95, 156, 200, 345, 421, adversative *ond* ll. 76, 84, 93, 179, 188, 299; *sepeah* 211. Instances in Christ III:

905 ff   Cymeð wundorlic   Cristes onsyn,
            æpelcyninges wlite,   eastan fram roderum,
            on sefan swete   sinum folce,
            biter bealofullum ...

910 ff   He bið þam godum   glædmod on gesihþe,
            wlitig, wynsumlic,   weorude þam halgan ...
            ... He bið þam yflum   egeslic ond grimlic ... (918)

1183 b ff

Ðeah hi ferðgewit

of hyra æþelum   ænig ne cuþen,

wendon swa þeah wundrum,   þa hyra waldend for

of lichoman.   Leode ne cuþon,

modblinde men   meotud oncnawan ...

The attitudes of the soulless creatures of the universe and of man towards the passion of Christ are here contrasted.

1260 ff   Swa sceal gewrixled   þam þe ær wel heoldon
            þurh modlufan   meotudes willan.
            Ðonne bið þam oþrum   ungelice
            willa geworden.

The sentence 1260—1261 gets its full significance from the description of the joys of Paradise contained in the preceding section.

1383 b ff

Geaf ic þe eac meahta sped,

welan ofer widlonda gehwylc,   nysses þu wean
                                ænigne dæl,

ðystra þæt þu þolian sceolde.   Ðu þæs þonc ne wisses.

1420 b ff

Wearð ic ana geboren

folcum to frofre.   Mec mon folmum biwond,

biþeahte mid þearfan wædum,   ond mec þa on þeostre
                                    alegde ...

The poet's intention must be to contrast the greatness of Christ's mission with the poor and trivial circumstances of his Nativity. We may compare ll. 1424 ff, p. 165.

1499 ff   *Bibead ic eow*   *þæt ge broþor mine*
               in woruldrice   *wel aretten*
               of þam æhtum   *þe ic eow on eorðan geaf,*
               earmra hulpen.   *Earge ge þæt læstun* ...

In these 7 cases it is either the attitude of Christ towards the good and the bad or God's grace and man's evil that are contrasted. More often the poet uses *ac*-constructions: ll. 963, 1002, 1049, 1054, 1293, 1366, 1393, 1428, 1476, 1544, 1567, 1576, 1597, 1640, 1662. *Ðeah*, as an adverb, occurs ll. 1090, 1185, 1308, 1419; *hwæðre* l. 1377.

Guthlac A:

59   *He fela findeð,*   *fea beoð gecorene.*

84 b ff   *Oft him brogan to*
               laðne gelæded   *se þe him lifes ofonn,*
               eaweð him egsan ...   *Fore him englas stondað,*
               gearwe mid gæsta wæpnum ...

200 ff   *Swa him yrsade*   *se for ealle spræc*
               feonda mengu.   *No þy forhtra wæs*
               Guðlaces gæst,   *ac him god sealde*
               ellen wiþ þam egsan ...

260 b f   *Her sceal min wesan*
               eorðlic eþel,   *nales eower leng.*

301 ff   *... ge her ateoð*   *in þa tornwræce*
               sigeleasne sið.   *No ic eow sweord ongean*
               mid gebolgne hond   *oðberan þence* ... *(ac ic minum*
                                       Criste cweman þence ...)*

325 b ff   *Gewat eal þonan*
               feonda mengu.   *Ne wæs se fyrst micel*
               þe hi Guðlace   *forgiefan þohtan.*

330 ff   *Forlet longeþas*   *lænra dreama.*
               No he hine wið monna   *miltse gedælde,*
               ac gesynta bæd   *sawla gehwylcre* ...

The poet means that Guthlac absented himself from the joys of the world, but he did not abandon the world altogether: he still prayed for the welfare of souls.

353 ff
woldun þæt him to mode   fore monlufan
sorg gesohte,   þæt he siþ tuge
eft to eþle.   Ne wæs þæt ongin swylc ...
        ... (ac he on þæs lareowes
wære gewunade) 359 b—60 a.

406 ff
Wæron hy reowe   to ræsanne
gifrum grapum.   No god wolde
þæt seo sawl þæs   sar prowade
in lichoman,   lyfde seþeana
þæt hy him mid hondum   hrinan mosten ...

465 f
Fela ge fore monnum miþað   þæs þe ge in mode
             gehycgað;
ne beoð eowre dæda dyrne,   þeah þe ge hy in dygle
             gefremme.

502 b ff
          Ðeodum ywaþ
wisdom weras,   wlencu forleosað,
siððan geoguðe geað   gæst aflihð.
Ðæt ge ne scirað,   ac ge scyldigra
synne secgað ...

514 ff
Wæs se martyre   from moncynnes
synnum asundrad.   Sceolde he særes þa gen
dæl adreogan,   ðeah þe dryhten his
witum weolde.

547 ff
Ðrea wæron þearle,   þegnas grimme,
ealle hy þam feore   fyl gehehton.
No hy hine to deaðe   deman moston,
synna hyrdas,   ac seo sawul bad
in lichoman   leofran tide.

574 ff
Woldun hy geteon   mid torncwidum
earme aglæcan   in orwennysse,
meotudes cempan.   Hit ne meahte swa!

608 ff
... ond ic bletsige   bliðe mode
lifes leohtfruman,   ond him lof singe ...
... Ðæt eow æfre ne bið   ufan alyfed
leohtes lissum,   þæt ge lof moten
dryhtne secgan,   ac ge deaðe sceolon
weallendne wean   wope besingan ...

663 ff
> *Wendun ge ond woldun,   wiþerhycgende,*
> *þæt ge scyppende   sceoldan gelice*
> *wesan in wuldre.   Eow þær wyrs gelomp ...*

With these instances of adversative asyndeton Guthlac A, with its 818 lines, is richer in this device than any of the poems examined. It is employed in various connexions, chiefly in contrasts between Guthlac's bliss and the wretchedness of the devils, and between the demons' evil designs and their frustration. But the most interesting thing about the cases here listed is the frequent combination of asyndeton on the one hand and syndetic constructions with *ac* or *seþeana*, or hypotactic ones with *þeah*, on the other. This stylistic feature is characteristic of Guthlac A; we find *ac* in 7 cases, *seþeana* in one, and hypotaxis in two cases. We notice that whereas the asyndetic contrast is the most important, advancing the narrative a step further, the syndetic contrast, introduced by *ac*, is chiefly formal, being a positive statement completing a preceding negative one. Adversative *ac*-constructions are, on the whole, much favoured by the poet; apart from the cases in combination with asyndeton here referred to, there are the following instances: (11, 20, 151, 188, 222, 228, 247, 294, 321, 372, 378, 399, 422, 462, 484, 497, 545, 633, 701, 756). Adversative *ond* is used ll. 36, 61, 520, 637, 680, *hwæðre* ll. 233, 352, 446, 557, *þeana* l. 110 and *þeah* 493.

Things are different in Guthlac B. Adversative asyndeton occurs:

842 ff
> *... gif hy halges word   healdan woldun*
> *beorht in breostum,   ond his bebodu læstan,*
> *æfnan on eðle.   Hy to ær aþreat*
> *þæt hy waldendes   willan læsten,*
> *ac his wif genom   wyrmes larum*
> *blede forbodene ...*

899 ff
> *... on þam westenne   woðe hofun*
> *hludne herecirm,   hiwes binotene,*
> *dreamum bidrorene.   Dryhtnes cempa,*
> *from folctoga,   feonda þreatum*
> *wiðstod stronglice.*

976 ff
> *Ða wæs Guðlace   on þa geocran tid*
> *mægen gemeðgad,   mod swiþe heard,*
> *elnes anhydig.*

1024 b ff

Wæs him in bogen
bittor bancopa.   Beald reordade,
eadig on elne ...

Ac-constructions occur, apart from l. 846, at ll. 831, 836, 925, 963, 991, 995, 1055, 1072; adversative *ond* l. 1210; *peah* 940, *sepeah* 961. Adversative constructions are thus restricted to the beginning of the poem and to contrasts between worldly and heavenly life, the saint and the devils, the illness and Guthlac's boldness. Only the second of these themes is abandoned by the poet towards the end of the narrative, and about the other two he gets tired, it seems, of speaking in terms of opposition. We may notice that adversative constructions fit in well with a predominantly compound style, such as that of Guthlac A, and is less likely to be favoured by a poet with a more subtle style such as the author of the B poem.

The Phoenix poet hardly makes any use at all of the adversative asyndeton. There is only one clear case:

355 b ff

God ana wat,
cyning ælmihtig,   hu his gecynde bið,
wifhades þe weres;   þæt ne wat ænig
monna cynnes ...

Adversative *ac*-constructions appear ll. 19, 35, 62, 75, 180, 317, 596, 609); *hwæðre* is used ll. 222, 366, 443, and 640; *peah* 565.

In Cynewulf's poetry Elene has asyndeton 8 times, *ac* 7, *hwæðre* 1, *ond* 4, *peah* 1. Juliana: asyndeton 4, *ac* 5, *hwæðre* 1, *peah* 1. Christ II: asyndeton 1, *ac* 2, *hwæðre* 2, *peah* 1. Fata: asyndeton 1, *ac* 3. Andreas: asyndeton 21, *ac* 13, *hwæðre* 3, *ond* 1, *peah* 2. The Dream of the Rood: asyndeton 1, *ac* 5, *hwæðre* 9, *ond* 1. Christ I: asyndeton 2, *ac* 6, *ond* 6, *sepeah* 1. Christ III: asyndeton 7, *ac* 15, *peah* 4, *hwæðre* 1. Guthlac A: asyndeton 16, *ac* 27, *hwæðre* 4, *ond* 5, *peana* 1, *peah* 1. Guthlac B: asyndeton 4, *ac* 9, *ond* 1, *peah* 1, *sepeah* 1. The Phoenix: asyndeton 1, *ac* 8, *hwæðre* 4, *peah* 1.

Let us look at the psychological significance of the facts dealt with in this chapter. A poet making frequent use of combinations of opposite statements without any transitional link, seems more interested in these statements as such, as links in a narrative chain, than in the relation between them. His language does not convey to us the connection between the isolated epic details. It is, consequently, deprived of characterization, and this produces a certain stiffness.

Especially Andreas and Guthlac A, with their abundance of asyndeton, give us this impression, the same as they gave us in the examination of compound and complex series and of parataxis and hypotaxis. The latter poem, however, with its 16 cases, is richer in adversative asyndeton than Andreas with 21, in view of the respective length of these texts.

As for the other texts, the Cynewulf poetry is fairly restricted in the use of adversative asyndeton and syndesis and has, on the whole, equal proportions of both. The Dream of the Rood, Christ I, and the Phoenix have a marked tendency towards syndetic combinations. In Christ III and Guthlac B this tendency is also clear, though somewhat less pronounced.

What has been said about the chronological aspect of the use of parataxis is also true of the same aspects of asyndeton. This type of combination was, without a doubt, an earlier stage of development than syndesis, but any conclusions drawn from this fact as to the age of Andreas and Guthlac A, both poems rich in asyndeton, are uncertain and had better be avoided.

We have, in the last two chapters, been dealing with the expression of combinations of different ideas; we shall now, in a study of variations, proceed to examine the development of the same conception or idea.

6. The Use of Variation

Ever since HEINZEL's study on the style of Old Germanic poetry, the device known as "variation" has rightly been considered one of the salient features of this style. Definitions of the conception of "variation" are various, i. e. in the cases when scholars have at all taken the trouble to define this term so abundantly used by them. A tolerable definition is the one given by PAETZEL (p. 3): "Ein für das Verständnis genügend gekennzeichneter Begriff wird, entgegen dem Gebrauch der Prosa, noch einmal und zwar oft mit Unterbrechung des syntaktischen Zusammenhanges dem Hörer oder Leser vor die Seele gerückt". But this definition does not sufficiently stress the fact that the conception is repeated by means of another word or other words than that or those used for the original expression of the conception. This follows from the very term "variation" and is emphasized by HEUSLER (ZfdA LVII, 32): "noch eh der dichter eine ruhepunct erreicht

hat, wiederholt er das gesagte, aber mit einem neuen, 'variieren-
den' ausdruck" etc. Further, the variation very often occurs more
than "einmal". PAETZEL also divides the variations into different
groups: variation of words and variation of clauses. These two groups
are further devided into classes: the word-group into variations of
substantives, adjectives, and verbs, and their respective position in
the sentence; the clause-group into different kinds of clauses and
complements. However detailed it may be, this purely formal classification does not tell us all that we should like to know about the
poet's way of dealing with variation and we may, I think, attempt
another classification which pays attention, not only to form, but
also to the effect of certain formal patterns on the style.

We shall divide the variations into two main groups. The first
group is called close variation and is, in the main, identical with
the variation defined by PAETZEL and HEUSLER. It comprises variations which correspond in a direct way to their correlatives, as we
shall call the expression for the original conception which is not in
itself a variation. This direct correlation means that conception
corresponds to conception; substantive to substantive, adjective to
adjective, verb to verb and so on; clauses to similar clauses. Constructions, likewise, correspond to one another although a direct
object may correlate with an indirect one. It may be noted that a
variation is often preceded by ond. We must be careful in ascertaining
from the context when we have to do with a real variation and not
with an expression of a new conception.

In the second group of variations the correspondence between
correlative and variation is looser. This group we shall call loose variation. Here not only conceptions, but whole ideas correlate. The same
idea is repeated by means of variation in such a way that the variation
is either a negative version of the correlative, or the correlative of
the variation; or the variation states the significance, which we know
already, of the correlative, or the reverse; or the variation enumerates
the constituents of the correlative, or it is a summing up of several
correlative elements. From the formal point of view it deviates in
different respects from the correlative. PAETZEL mentions a few instances of this kind of variation as "Grenzfälle" (p. 33). G. JANSEN
speaks, p. 90, of "Parallelismus", which means that "der gleiche
Gedanke in verschiedener Art der Auffassung und des Ausdrucks
doppelt gesetzt wird" (Tautologie der Gedanken). The few instances
of "Parallelismus" referred to by JANSEN, however, afford no clear

illustrations of his definition (only Christ III 1366 ff, 587 ff, Jul. 468 ff, are possible instances). ZIEGLER (p. 64) refers to "Begriffs-parallele Wendungen in ungleicher Form"; his seven quotations from Genesis, however, are not well chosen. BARTLETT does not distinguish between what we are here calling close and loose variation; in her chapter about "Repetition Parallels" (p. 33), however, she touches upon our loose variation when referring to Ph. 355 ff.

In dealing with the loose variation, which will be found to form an extensive and interesting group, one must be careful not to mix it up with such epexegetic clauses as introduce an explanation of the cor-relative, thus adding an element which cannot simply be deduced from this correlative. The loose variation repeats something that we know already, for instance

Juliana:

134 ff   *Næfre ic me ondræde*   *domas þine,*
            ne me weorce sind   *witebrogan,*
            hildewoman.

But in Elene:

673 b ff   *Ðu scealt geagninga*
            wisdom onwreon,   *swa gewritu secgaþ,*
            æfter stedewange   *hwær seo stow sie,*

l. 675 b explains to us the meaning of *wisdom*, it does not repeat, by variation, something we have already heard.

I do not, in the first place, intend to give a full list of all the close variations in our texts though the proportions of them in the different poems, according to PAETZEL, will be given at the end of the chapter. What is aimed at here, is a study of the poets' manner of using these variations. Variation is a kind of repetition, and this repetition, some-times, becomes excessive through the poet's accumulating variations of the same parts of speech. Such monotony is frequent in some of our poems, rare in others, and this will be demonstrated in an examination of instances with three or more successive variations, here called variational accumulation (cases with a smaller number of variations, such as those mentioned by BUTTENWIESER (pp. 82 ff) are common in all poems and have little interest). On the other hand, the monotony impending in texts where variation is common, may be counter-balanced by an arrangement of the variations in an order opposite to the order of the correlatives. BUTTENWIESER, pp. 68, 69, quotes Jul. 1 ff, El. 243 ff, Chr. 502 ff as instances of this; PAETZEL's material contains isolated cases. The difference between our poems in the use of this device will be shown in a study of variational chiasmus. Finally, more or less important elements in a sentence may be stressed by variations; this point will be considered in more detail on p. 193 f. When less important elements are stressed in this way, we speak of unessential variation. It is from these three points of view, then, that we will regard the close variation. Another way of examining the use of variation is to see what sort of notions are varied and how often; this has been done by PAETZEL and we shall return to his results later on.

Variational accumulation occurs in Cynewulf:

Elene:

459 b ff

        ... gif hie wiston ær
 þæt he Crist wære, cyning on roderum,
 soð sunu meotudes, sawla nergend?

474 ff

 ... on sefan sohton hu hie sunu meotudes
 ahengon, helm wera, hlaford eallra
 engla ond elda, æðelust bearna.

Juliana:

140 f

 Ða wæs ellenwod, yrre ond reþe,
 frecne ond ferðgrim, fæder wið dehter.

641 f

 Gemunað wigena wyn ond wuldres þrym,
 haligra hyht, heofonengla god.

It may be observed that accumulation in Cynewulf occurs in only a few cases and that mostly words for God and Christ are stressed in this way. This is in confirmity with the general usage in religious poetry; as MARQUARDT points out: "Mehr als zweigliedrige Variationen werden in erster Linie ... in der geistlichen Dichtung für Gott gebraucht" (p. 313).

As a parallel to the scarcity of variational accumulation in Cynewulf one can notice a greater frequency in his poems of diversity in the arrangement of groups of variations, consisting in a chiastic organization of corresponding parts. Instances of variational chiasmus in Cynewulf are:

Elene:

79 f
  Constantinus, heht þe cyning engla,
  wyrda wealdend ...

92 b ff
         Mid þys beacne ðu
  on þam frecnan fære feond oferswiðesð,
  geletest lað werod.

107 b ff
       ... ond þæt halige treo
  him beforan ferian on feonda gemang,
  beran beacen godes.

126 b f
       Hæðene grungon,
  feollon friðelease.

166 ff a chiastic variation of clauses:
  Hio him ondsware ænige ne meahton
  agifan togenes, ne ful geare cuðon
  sweotole gesecggan be þam sigebeacne.

173 b f
      him wæs leoht sefa,
  ferhð gefeonde ...

186 b f
      ... beorna wuldor
  of deaðe aras, dryhten ealra
  hæleða cynnes.

245 b f
  (Ðær meahte gesion) ... sæmearh plegean,
  wadan wægflotan.

273 ff
  (Swa hit siððan gelamp ... þæt) ...
  guðrofe hæleþ to Hierusalem
  cwomon in þa ceastre corðra mæste,
  eorlas æscrofe ...

290 b ff
      ... þæt ge geardagum
  wyrðe wæron wuldorcyninge,
  dryhtne dyre ...

337 b f
      Be þam Moyses sang,
  ond þæt word gecwæð weard Israhela ...

342 f   *Be ðam Dauid cyning   dryhtleoð agol ...*
            ond þæt word gecwæþ   wigona baldor ...

369 ff   *ond ge þam ryhte.   wiðroten hæfdon,*
           onscunedon þone sciran   scippend eallra,
           dryhtna dryhten ...

380 b ff   *... þa ðe leornungcræft*
           þurh modgemynd   mæste hæfdon,
           on sefan snyttro.

404 b ff   *... ond for eorlum spræc,*
           undearninga   ides reordode
           hlude for herigum ...

454 f   *Ða ic fromlice   fæder minum,*
           ealdum æwitan,   ageaf ondsware ...

460 f   *(þæt he Crist wære ...)*
           soð sunu meotudes,   sawla nergend.

486 ff   *ealles leohtes leoht   lifgende aras,*
           ðeoden engla,   ond his þegnum hine,
           soð sigora frea,   seolfne geywde ...

529 b f   *(Ðus mec fæder min) ...   wordum lærde,*
           septe soðcwidum ...

558 b ff   *Ða sio cwen ongan*
        weras Ebresce   wordum negan,
        fricggan fyrhðwerige   ymb fyrngewritu ...

583 b f   *... ne magon ge þa wyrd bemiðan,*
        bedyrnan þa deopan mihte.

The chiasmus is here placed at the end of the queen's speech and
the rhetorical artifice, along with the expanded half-lines, give an
emphatic close to the queen's menaces.

588 b f   *He þe mæg soð gecyðan,*
        onwreon wyrda geryno ...

615 b f   *(þæt he þone stan nime) ...   hlafes ne gime,*
           gewende to wædle,   ond þa wiste wiðsæce ...

679 b f   *þæt me halig god*
        gefylle, frea mihtig ...

In 726 ff we have a studied triple nominal chiasmus, marking the solemn opening of Judas's great invocation to God:

> *... ond þu geworhtest   þurh þines wuldres miht*
> *heofon ond eorðan   ond holmþræce,*
> *sæs sidne fæðm,   samod ealle gesceaft,*
> *ond þu amæte   mundum þinum*
> *ealne ymbhwyrft   ond uprador ...*

The group 728 b, close to the centre of the figure, serves as a summing up of all the rest.

757 b f

> *Heardecg cwacaþ,*
> *beofaþ brogdenmæl ...*

813 f

> *Nu ic þe, bearn godes,   biddan wille,*
> *weoroda willgifa ...*

840 f

> *... hige onhyrded,   þurh þæt halige treo,*
> *inbryrded breostsefa ...*

934 f

> *Him ða gleawhydig   Iudas oncwæð,*
> *hæleð hildedeor ...*

954 ff

> *(hu se feond ond se freond   geflitu rærdon),*
> *tireadig ond trag,   on twa halfa,*
> *synnig ond gesælig.*

967 f

> *Ða wæs gefrege   in þære folcsceare,*
> *geond þa werþeode   wide læded ...*

1022 b ff

> *Heo þa rode heht*
> *golde beweorcean   ond gimcynnum,*
> *mid þam æðelestum   eorcnanstanum*
> *besettan searocræftum ...*

1047 ff

> *... þæt he swa geleafful   ond swa leof gode*
> *in worldrice   weorðan sceolde,*
> *Criste gecweme.*

1076 b f

> *godes agen bearn,*
> *nerigend fira.*

1120 f

> *Nu we seolfe geseoð   sigores tacen,*
> *soðwundor godes ...*

1181 b ff

He ah æt wigge sped,

sigor æt sæcce,   ond sybbe gehwær,

æt gefeohte frið ...

1229 ff

(Sie þara manna gehwam) ...

behliden helle duru,   heofones ontyned,

ece geopenad   engla rice ...

The variational chiasmus forms a pattern with 1230 a.

Juliana:

1 f
We ðæt hyrdon   hæleð eahtian,

deman dædhwate ...

14 b ff

Feondscype rærdon,

hofon hæþengield,   halge cwelmdon,

breotun boccræftge ...

48 b f
(Gif þu soðne god lufast ond gelyfest)   ond his lof

rærest,

ongietest gæsta hleo ...

51 b ff

... gif þu to sæmran gode

þurh deofolgield   dæde biþencest,

hætsð hæþenweoh ...

109 b ff

... nemne he mægna god

geornor bigonge   þonne he gen dyde,

lufige mid lacum   þone þe leoht gescop ...

170 f
ond þe to swa mildum   mundbyrd secest,

hyldo to halgum ...

172 f
wraþe geworhtra   wita unrim,

grimra gyrna,   þe þe gegearwad sind ...

181 b f

gæsta scyppend,

meotud moncynnes ...

233 b ff

Hyre wæs Cristes lof

in ferðlocan   fæste biwunden,

milde modsefan,   mægen unbrice.

249 b ff

Ðe þes dema hafað

þa wyrrestan   witu gegearwad,

sar endeleas ...

298 b ff

                     ... *þæt he sacan ongon*
wiþ þa gecorenan   Cristes þegnas,
ond þa halgan weras   hospe gerahte
þurh deopne gedwolan ...

361 b f

(þæt þu heofoncyninge wiðsoce) ...   ond to sæmran
                                             gebuge
onsægde synna fruman.

400 f

... *hu gefæstnad sy   ferð innanweard,*
wiðsteall geworht.

420 b ff

                       Ðu wið Criste geo
wærleas wunne   ond gewin tuge,
hogdes wiþ halgum.

579 f

... *ond þa onbærnan het   bælfira mæst,*
ad onælan ...

667 f

... *meotud moncynnes   milde geweorþe,*
sigora sellend.

Christ II:

471 f

lufedon leofwendum   lifes agend,
fæder frumsceafta.

499 b f

                     Him wæs geomor sefa
hat æt heortan,   hyge murnende ...

503 b f

                     æþeling heredun,
lofedun liffruman

508 b ff

                     Cleopedun of heahþu
wordum wrætlicum   ofer wera mengu
beorhtan reorde ...

539 b f

                       hreðer innan weoll,
beorn breostsefa.

609 b f

(deaw ond ren) ...   *duguðe weccaþ* ...
... *iecað eorðwelan.*

621 b ff

(Ic þec ofer eorðan geworhte),   on þære þu scealt
                                         yrmþum lifgan,
wunian in gewinne   (ond to þære ilcan scealt eft
                                         geweorþan

We here see the same arrangement with long half-lines and chiasmus as in El. 726 ff; the passage in Christ has a similar solemn significance, rendering Gregory's *Terra es, et in terra ibis*, which is inspired by Gen. III, 19: *In sudore vultus tui vesceris pane, donec reuertaris in terram de qua sumptus es.*

634 (Iob)   *herede helm wera,   hælend lofede.*

640 b f   *þam þe deorc gewit*
       hæfdon on hreþre,   heortan stænne.

649 b f   *... grundsceat sohte,*
       wende to worulde.

716 ff   *meotud meahtum swið   munt gestylleð,*
       gehleapeð hea dune,   hyllas ond cnollas
       bewrið mid his wuldre ...

773 f   *utan us to fæder   freoþa wilnian,*
       biddan bearn godes ...

Fata Apostolorum:

19 b f   *... ac him ece geceas*
       langsumre lif,   leoht unhwilen ...

28 f   *engla ordfruma   eorðan sohte*
       þurh fæmnan hrif,   fæder manncynnes.

91 b ff   *Hu, ic freondu beþearf*
       liðra on lade,   þonne ic sceal langne ham,
       eardwic uncuð,   ana gesecan ...

115 f   *Ah utu we þe geornor   to gode cleopigan,*
       sendan usse bene   on þa beorhtan gesceaft ...

As is apparent, this fairly simple stylistic device plays an important part in Cynewulf and is often used to give a touch of the serious or the sublime; in such cases it is sometimes coupled with other stylistic contrivances. It is occasionally so simple that it extends over two parallel half-lines, but more frequently it runs from a b-line to the following a-line, thus forming a sort of enjambement. Very often it is intermingled with non-variational parts of the period. Not seldom it has the form ab-ba-ab or abc-cba.

We turn to unessential variation. BUTTENWIESER points out (p. 67) that "die Variation wird sinngemäss angewandt; darum ist es der wichtigste Begriff oder Gedanke, der nochmals in anderen Worten wiederholt oder durch Appositionen erweitert wird, welche im Satze eine Stellung erhalten, die sie beim Vortragen am wirksamsten erscheinen lässt". Even if this is an exaggeration — it is not always easy to say which is "der wichtigste Begriff' in an Old English poetical sentence — the remark can be said to hold good inasmuch as clearly unessential elements, in the best Anglo-Saxon poetry, are seldom emphasized by variation. In the following survey of Cynewulf's poems cases are given where an unimportant element has variation but not an important one. Poetical formulas are not taken into account.

Elene has unessential variation l. 67: (*Here wicode*) ... *egstreame neah, on neaweste* ...

223 b f
                       swa hire weoruda helm,
    byrnwiggendra,   *beboden hæfde.*

240 b ff
                       Ne hyrde ic sið ne ær
    on egstreame   *idese lædan,*
    on merestræte,   *mægen fægerre.*

589   (*He þe mæg soð gecyðan*),   *onwreon wyrda geryno;*

here the verbal variation is chosen to make up the hypermetrical half-line.

1147 ff   *Ongan þa geornlice*   *gastgerynum*
            on sefan secean   *soðfæstnesse*
            weg to wuldre.

Juliana:

1 f   *We ðæt hyrdon*   *hæleð eahtian*
      deman dædhwate   *þætte* ...

675   (*Heliseus*   *ehstream sohte*)
     leolc ofer laguflod   *longe hwile*
     on swonrade.

Both instances in Juliana, however, are fairly innocuous: after l. 2 there follows a clause containing a variation for Maximianus, and the unsuccessful suitor is elaborately called *se synscaþa* — *sceohmod* — *Heliseus* (ll. 671 ff).

Christ II:

520 ff   *ealra sigebearna   þæt seleste*
          ond æþeleste,   þe ge her on stariað
          ond in frofre geseoð   frætwum blican.

662 f   *ond eac monigfealde   modes snyttru*
       seow ond sette   geond sefan monna.

The few cases in Cynewulf can be considered not very happy attempts to fill in the half-lines; sometimes it is not difficult to replace the variations by more suitable words.

Loose variation:

Elene:

134 ff   ... *flugon on fæsten   ond feore burgon*
        æfter stanclifum,   stede weardedon
        ymb Danubie.

150 b ff   *Com þa wigena hleo*
        þegna þreate   þryðbord stenan,
        beadurof cyning   burga neosan

194 ff   *Ða wæs on sælum   sinces brytta,*
       niðheard cyning.   Wæs him niwe gefea
       befolen in fyrhðe ...

219 b ff   *Elene ne wolde*
        þæs siðfates   sæne weorðan ...
               ... ac wæs sona gearu ...

252 ff   ... *ald yðliodu,*[1]   *oncrum fæste,*
       on brime bidan   beorna geþinges,
       hwonne heo sio guðcwen   gumena þreate
       ofer eastwegas   eft gesohte.

366 b ff   *Moyse sægde*
        hu ge heofoncyninge   hyran sceoldon,
        lare læstan.

368 a is a variation of *hyran*.

---

[1] ARNGART's conjecture (English Studies XXVII, p. 19), seems conclusive.

370 ff   *... onscunedon þone sciran   scippend eallra,*
dryhtna dryhten,   ond gedwolan fylgdon
ofer riht godes.

Chiastic arrangement.

493 ff   *ne geald he yfel yfele,   ac his ealdfeondum*
þingode þrohtherd,   bæd þrymcyning
þæt he him þa weadæd   to wræce ne sette ...

663 f   *Wiðsæcest ðu to swiðe   soðe ond rihte ...*
                  ... ond nu on lige cyrrest.

Chiastic arrangement.

887 b ff   *He sona aras*
gaste gegearwod,   geador bu samod
lic ond sawl.

902 ff   *Hwæt is þis, la, manna,   þe minne eft*
þurh fyrngeflit   folgaþ wyrdeð,
iceð ealdne nið,   æhta strudeð?

Chiastic arrangement.

928 f   *ond he forlæteð   lare þine*
ond manþeawum   minum folgaþ ...

Chiastic arrangement.

1038 b f   *He þæt betere geceas,*
wuldres wynne,   ond þam wyrsan wiðsoc ...

1117 b ff   *... þeah hie ær wæron*
þurh deofles spild   in gedwolan lange,
acyrred fram Criste.

1228 b f   *Sie þara manna gehwam*
behliden helle duru,   heofones ontyned ...

Chiastic arrangement.

Juliana:

3 b ff   *... se geond middangeard,*
arleas cyning,   eahtnysse ahof,
cwealde cristne men,   circan fylde,

> *geat on græswong   godhergendra,*
> *hæþen hildfruma,   haligra blod ...*

Ll. 5, 6, and 7 explain in detail *eahtnysse ahof.* Chiastic arrangement in 4 b—5 a—5 b—6.

85 ff   *þæt ic hy ne sparige,   ac on spild gieſe ...*

120 ff   *gif þu unrædes   ær ne geswicest,*
            ond þu fremdu godu   forð bigongest
            ond þa forlætest   þe us leofran sind ...

134 ff   *Næfre ic me ondræde   domas þine,*
            ne me weorce sind   witebrogan,
            hildewoman ...

360 b ff   *... þæt þu heofoncyninge*
            wiðsoce, sigora frean,   ond to sæmran gebuge,
            onsægde synna fruman.

Chiastic arrangement.

373 ff   *... þæt he byrnende   from gebede swiceð,*
            steped stronglice,   staþolfæst ne mæg
            fore leahtra lufan   lenge gewunian
            in gebedstowe.

410 f   *... þæt he monþeawum   minum lifge,*
            acyrred cuðlice   from Cristes æ ...

Chiastic arrangement.

468 b ff   *Oft ic syne ofteah,*
            ablende bealoþoncum   beorna unrim
            monna cynnes,   misthelme forbrægd
            þurh attres ord   eagna leoman ...

L. 469 forms a chiasmus with 468 b.

564 b f   *(engel godes)   ... þæt fyr tosceaf,*
             gefreode ond gefreoðade   facnes clæne ...

Chiastic arrangement.

590 b ff   *Næs hyre wloh ne hrægl,*
            ne feax ne fel   fyre gemæled,

ne lic ne leoþu.   Heo in lige stod
æghwæs onsund.

610 b ff   *... þæt hyre endestæf*
of gewindagum   weorþan sceolde,
lif alysed.

Christ II:

458 b ff   *Hy þæs lareowes*
on þam wildæge   word ne gehyrwdon,
hyra sincgiefan.   Sona wæron gearwe,
hæleð mid hlaford,   to þære halgan byrg ...

They did not despise his command, in other words, they were ready
to go.

476 b f   *Næfre ic from hweorfe,*
ac ic lufan symle   læste wið eowic ...

486 b f   *feondscype dwæscað,*
sibbe sawað   on sefan manna ...

586 b ff   *... hu þæt hælubearn*
þurh his hydercyme   hals eft forgeaf,
gefreode ond gefreoþade   folc under
wolcnum ...

Cp. Juliana 565. Chiastic arrangement.

639 ff   *Wæs þæs fugles flyht   feondum on eorþan*
dyrne ond degol,   þam þe deorc gewit
hæfdon on hreþre,   heortan stænne.

Ll. 640 b—650 = *feondum.*

676 b ff   *Sum mæg fromlice*
ofer sealtne sæ   sundwudu drifan,
hreran holmþræce.

To stir the sea is to drive the ship. Chiastic arrangement.

776 b f   *... se us lif forgeaf,*
leomu, lic ond gæst.

818 f   *... þæt he her in worulde   wunian mote,*
somed siþian   sawel in lice.

The Fata Apostolorum:

65 b ff

Dæges or onwoc,
leohtes geleafan, land wæs gefælsod
þurh Matheus mære lare.

The loose variations with their correlatives, it will be seen, do not form very large patterns but are nearly always concentrated to less than seven half-lines. Juliana 3 b ff, 468 b ff, and Christ II 458 b ff, have patterns in seven half-lines. We notice the frequent chiastic devices, which, as it were, make up for the formal looseness that is characteristic of this type of variation.

In Andreas there are the following cases of accumulation, chiefly limited to the first half of the poem:

A 102 b ff

Ðe is neorxnawang,
blæda beorhtost, boldwela fægrost,
hama hyhtlicost, halegum mihtum
torht ontyned.

194 ff

Ðæt mæg engel þin eað geferan,
halig of heofenum con him holma begang,
sealte sæstreamas ond swanrade,
waroðfaruða gewinn ond wæterbrogan ...

232 ff

ah he wæs anræd ellenweorces,
heard ond higerof, nalas hildlata,
gearo, guðe fram, to godes campe.

324 b ff

He is cyning on riht,
wealdend ond wyrhta wuldorþrymmes,
an ece god eallra gesceafta ...

526 f

Forþan is gesyne, soð orgete,
cuð, oncnawen ...

Ll. 700 ff there is an exact repetition of the accumulation at ll. 324 ff:

cræfta gecyðde þæt he wæs cyning on riht
ofer middangeard, mægene geswiðed,
waldend ond wyrhta wuldorþrymmes,
an ece god eallra gesceafta.

1514 ff

... swa hit soðfæste syðþan heoldon
modige magoþegnas, magas sine,
godfyrhte guman, Iosua ond Tobias.

It may be observed that accumulation in Cynewulf occurs in a few cases when God and Christ are stressed by variations; in Andreas, on the contrary, apart from two similar cases, one of which is an identical repetition of the other, variations of diverse kinds of words are accumulated. An accumulation like the one at ll. 526 ff is apparently caused only by a desire to create a mass of syllables big enough to fill up some half-lines.

When we compare Cynewulf's instances of chiasmus with those in Andreas, we find that the latter differ not a little both in respect of quantity and quality:

20 b f   *folcstede gumena,*
         hæleða eðel.

92 ff   *ða wearð gehyred   heofoncyninges stefn*
         wrætlic under wolcnum,   wordhleoðres sweg
         mæres þeodnes.

118 b f   *helm ælwihta,*
         engla scyppend.

171 b f   *cininga wuldor,*
         meotud mancynnes …

279 f   *Ne magon þær gewunian   widferende,*
         ne þær elþeodige   eardes brucað …

290 b f   *engla þeoden,*
         neregend fira …

434 b f   *scyppend engla,*
         weoruda dryhten.

453 f   *sæ sessade,   smylte wurdon*
         merestreama gemeotu.

902 f   *Weorð me nu milde,   meotud ælmihtig,*
         bliðe, beorht cyning.

1006 f   *(Geseh he Matheus) secgan dryhtne lof,   dom-*
                               weorðinga engla ðeodne.

1075 b ff   *carcernes duru*
         eorre æscberend   opene fundon,
         onhliden hamera geweorc.

1113 b f   *næs him to maðme wynn,*
hyht to hordgestreonum.

1213   *herd hige þinne,*   *heortan staðola …*

1554 f   *Ðær wæs wop wera*   *wide gehyred,*
earmlic ylda gedræg.

1572 b f   *Wæter fæðmedon,*
fleow firgendstream,   *flod wæs on luste …*

·The fact that the figure is relatively rare in Andreas — Juliana, which is shorter by less than a half, has one more instance — shows that the poem, in respect of the use of variations, has the same lack of variety that characterizes nearly all the details of its style. Variation in Andreas being as extensive as it is Cynewulf's poems, a section like ll. 455—902 is crude and uninteresting. It should also be noted that the Andreas poet employs chiefly the simple forms of the figure, and of Cynewulf's interlacements we see hardly anything at all. Only ll. 1572 b ff form a comparatively elaborate pattern, ab—ba—ab.

In Andreas, the instances of unessential variation are not, as in Cynewulf's poetry, occasional slips. Instances are:

11 a   (*þonne rond ond hand*)
on herefelda   *helm ealgodon*
on meotudwange.

Helm is the most important element in the sentence.
35—36 a   (*Syððan him geblendan … dryas …*)   *drync unheorne,*
se onwende gewit,   *wera ingeþanc,*
heortan on hreðre …

This instance is also quoted by BUTTENWIESER (p. 75). The reader's attention is distracted from the essential *drync*.

49   *Hie þam halgan þær*   *handa gebundon*
ond fæstnodon   *feondes cræfte …*

We should have expected a variation of *þam halgan*.

52   *Hwæðre he in breostum þa git*
herede in heortan   *heofonrices weard …*

No variation of 53 b.

64 b   *A ic symles wæs*
              on wega gehwam   *willan þines*
              georn on mode ...

72 a   *(Gif þin willa sie,*   *wuldres aldor),*
              þæt me wærlogan   *wæpna ecgum,*
              sweordum, aswebban ...

Wærlogan is the important notion.

124 a   *(Nihthelm toglad,)*   *lungre leorde.*
       Cp. the continuation: *Leoht æfter com, dægredwoma.*

134 b   *Hæfdon hie on rune*   *ond on rimcræfte*
              awriten, wælgrædige ...

187 a   *(Nu bið fore þreo niht*   *þæt he on þære þeode sceal)*
              fore hæðenra   *handgewinne*
              þurh gares gripe   *gast onsendan* ...

L. 187 a is not essential in the context.

233—34 a   *(ne wæs him bleað hyge)*
              ah he wæs anræd   *ellenweorces,*
              heard ond higerof,   *nalas hildlata*
              gearo, guðe fram,   *to godes campe.*

Apart from being an accumulation, this is a repetition of an
element completely irrelevant to the context and makes the passage
even more inferior than it would be without such a repetition
(cp. p. 320).

383 a   *(Him þa se halga)*   *on holmwege*
              ofer argeblond,   *Andreas* ...

526—27   *Forþan is gesyne,*   *soð orgete,*
              cuð, oncnawen,   *þæt* ...

693 a   *(Swa hleoðrodon*   *hæleða ræswan),*
              dugoð domgeorne,   *dyrnan þohton*
              meotudes mihte.

Dugoð domgeorne is not only a conventional expression which
ruins consistency here (the evil *ræswan* are speaking), but also takes
the stress instead of *meotudes mihte.*

759 a   *(Is seo wyrd mid eow)*   *open, orgete* ...

This case comes close to the one at 526—27; the main point here is *wyrd*.

825 b   *(Đa gelœdan het   lifes brytta*
         ofer yđa geþrœc ...   fœđmum ferigean) ...
         leofne mid lissum   ofer lagufœsten ...

1077 a   *... syđđan mid corđre   carcernes duru*
         eorre œscberend   opene fundon,
         onhliden hamera geweorc,   hyrdas deade.

The sentence does not gain from the fact that the least striking part of the alarming discovery is heavily stressed. Cp. p. 268.

1114 a   *(Đeod wœs oflysted,*
         metes modgeomre),   nœs him to mađme wynn,
         hyht to hordgestreonum.

The simple fact that the people were frantic with hunger is obscured by the unnecessary cumbersome addition.

1140 a   *Đrymman sceocan,*
         modige maguþegnas,   morđres on luste ...

This is an eccentricity of the same kind as the one at l. 693; contrary to the demands of the context a conventional heroic variation is used.

1235—36 a *(Drogon deormodne   œfter dunscrœfum)*
         ... efne swa wide swa   wegas to lagon,
         enta œrgeweorc,   innan burgum,
         strœte stanfage.

The attention is diverted from the act of torture to the streets. This is a typical instance of the poet's inability to distinguish between principal and accessory, of his tendency to be enticed from a vital point to an unimportant detail, which in itself may possess some poetical quality. The *strœte stanfage* are probably due to influence from Beowulf, cp. p. 282.

1571 a   *... þœr wœs modigra   mœgen forbeged,*
         wigendra þrym.

The punishment is not emphasized.

1656—57 a (*Sægde his fusne hige*),
　　　þæt he þa goldburg　　ofgifan wolde,
　　　secga seledream　　ond sincgestreon,
　　　beorht beagselu.

This is a case similar to the one at ll. 1235—36 a.

In Andreas, then, variation is used indiscriminately, as a general way of making the lines ponderous, quite irrespective of whether narrative coherence and the harmony of the sentence is retained or not. The author of the poem comes close to losing sight of the original function of variation.

In Andreas loose variation is much more common than in the Cynewulf canon.

45 f　　　*Eodon him þa togenes,　　garum gehyrsted,*
　　　　　lungre under linde,　　(nalas late wæron) ...

123 b ff　　　　　　　　　　*Nihthelm toglad,*
　　　　　lungre leorde.　　Leoht æfter com,
　　　　　dægredwoma.

139 b ff　　　　　　　　　　*Rihtes ne gimdon,*
　　　　　meotudes mildse.　　Oft hira mod onwod
　　　　　under dimscuan　　deofles larum ...

150 f　　　*... þæt hie banhringas　　abrecan þohton,*
　　　　　lungre tolysan　　lic ond sawle ...

Chiastic arrangement.

231 b f　　　　　　　　　*... ne wæs him bleað hyge,*
　　　　　ah he wæs anræd　　ellenweorces ...

256 ff　　*Hwanon comon ge　　ceolum liðan,*
　　　　macræftige menn,　　on merepissan,
　　　　ane ægflotan?　　Hwanon eagorstream
　　　　ofer yða gewealc　　eowic brohte?

308 ff　　*... ðæt ðu sæbeorgas　　secan woldes,*
　　　　merestreama gemet,　　maðmum bedæled,
　　　　ofer cald cleofu　　ceoles neosan?

366 b f　　*(heht his engel gan) ...　　ond mete syllan,*
　　　　frefran feasceafte　　ofer flodes wylm ...

Chiastic arrangement.

422 b ff
                            Mycel is nu gena
     lad ofer lagustream,   *land swiðe feorr*
     to gesecanne.

Chiastic arrangement.

431 f   *ond for dryhtnes lufan*   *deað þrowodon,*
         ... sawle gesealdon;

To 'suffer death' and 'give up the ghost' are common combinations; logically the latter is a loose variation of the former.

471 f   *Næfre is sælidan*   *selran mette,*
         ... rowend rofran,   *rædsnotterran,*

523 b ff
                        Wuldras fylde
     beorhtne boldwelan,   *swa gebledsod wearð*
     engla eðel   *þurh his anes miht.*

578 ff   *healtum ond hreofum*   *hyge blissode,*
         ða þe limseoce   *lange wæron,*
         werige, wanhale,   *witum gebundene ...*

587 f   *(He gehalgode)*
         ... win of wætere   *ond wendan het,*
         beornum to blisse,   *on þa beteran gecynd ...*

609 b ff
                     Me þæt þinceð,
     ðæt hie for æfstum   *inwit syredon*
     þurh deopne gedwolan.   *Deofles larum*
     hæleð hynfuse   *hyrdon to georne,*
     wraðum wærlogan.

645 ff   *(Nu ic on þe sylfum*   *soð oncnawe)*
         wisdomes gewit ...   *snyttrum bloweð,*
         beorhtre blisse,   *breost innanweard.*

669 b ff
                    Huscworde ongan
     þurh inwitðanc   *ealdorsacerd*
     herme hyspan,   *hordlocan onspeon,*
     wroht webbade.

679 f   *butan leodrihte*   *larum hyrað,*
      eadiges orhlytte   *æðeling cyðað ...*

735 f   *Ne dorste þa forhylman   hœlendes bebod*
         wundor fore weorodum,   ac of wealle ahleop ...

It obeyed the Lord, which means that it lept from the wall.

800 ff   *Ne dorston þa gelettan   leng owihte*
          wuldorcyninges word.   Geweotan ða ða witigan þry
          modige mearcland tredan.

They obeyed his words, which means that they went through the
country.

851 ff   *Ic eow secgan mœg   soð orgete,*
          þœt us gystrandœge   on geofones stream
          ofer arwelan   œðeling ferede.
          In þam ceole wœs   cyninga wuldor ...

887 f   *Ðœr wœs wuldres wynn,   wigendra þrym,*
          œðelic onginn,   nœs þœr œnigum gewinn.

890 f   *þe þara gefeana sceal   fremde weorðan,*
          hean hwearfian ...

938 ff   *(swa þe beorht fœder)*
          geweorðað wuldorgifum   to widan aldre,
          crœfte ond mihte.

951 b ff   *Is þe guð weotod,*
          heardum heoruswengum   scel þin hra dœled
          wundum weorðan ...

1042   *lungre leordan,   nalas leng bidon* ...

1051 ff   *Ægðer þara eorla   oðrum trymede*
          heofonrices hyht,   helle witu
          wordum werede.

Chiastic arrangement.

1099 ff   *Leton him þa betweonum   taan wisian* ...
          ... hluton hellcrœftum,   hœðengildum
          teledon betwinum.

1239 b f *(Wœs þœs halgan lic)   ... swate bestemed,*
          banhus abrocen;   blod yðum weoll ...

1258 ff   *(hrim ond forst)* ...   *hæleða eðel*
           lucon, leoda gesetu.   L a n d   w æ r o n   f r e o r i g
           c e a l d u m   c y l e g i c e l u m,   c l a n g   w æ t e r e s   þ r y m;
           o f e r   e a s t r e a m a s   i s   b r y c g a d e
           b l æ c e   b r i m r a d e.

Chiastic pattern ll. 1259 b—62 a: ab—ba—ab.

1324 ff   *Ðone Herodes   ealdre besnyðede* ...
                      ... o n d   h i n e   r o d e   b e f e a l g,
           þæt he on gealgan   h i s   g a s t   o n s e n d e.

1365 b ff   *Ðe synd witu þæs grim*
           weotud be gewyrhtum.   Ð u   s c e a l t   w e r i g m o d,
           h e a n,   h r o ð r a   l e a s,   h e a r m   þ r o w i g a n ...

1383 b ff   *Ðu scealt widan feorh*
           ecan þine yrmðu.   Ðe   b i ð   a   s y m b l e
           o f   d æ g e   o n   d æ g   d r o h t a þ   s t r e n g r a.

1405 f   *... banhus blodfag,   b e n n e   w e a l l a ð,*
           s e o n o d o l g   s w a t i g e.

This clumsy sort of variation is quite without parallel in Cynewulf.

1465 ff   *ond frofre gecwæð   fæder manncynnes,*
                      ... h e h t   h i s   l i c h o m a n
           h a l e s   b r u c a n.

Chiastic arrangement.

1471 ff   *Næs him gewemmed wlite,   ne wloh of hrægle*
           lungre alysed,   ne loc of heafde,
           ne ban gebrocen,   ne blodig wund
           lice gelenge,   ne laðes dæl,
           þurh dolgslege   dreore bestemed,
           ac wæs eft swa ær   þurh þa æðelan miht
           lof lædende,   o n d   o n   h i s   l i c e   t r u m.

1530 b f   *Fæge swulton,*
           geonge on geofene   guðræs fornam ...

1538 b f   *woldon feore beorgan,*
           to dunscræfum   drohtað secan ...

1609 b f   *... þeh þe fell curen*
           synnigra cynn.   S w y l t   þ r o w o d e ...

1625 ff   *Ða þær ofostlice   upp astodon*
           manige on meðle,   mine gefrege,
           eaforan unweaxne,   ða wæs eall eador
           leoðolic ond gastlic ...

1654 b f   *Sægde his fusne hige,*
           þæt he þa goldburg   ofgifan wolde ...

Variation in Andreas, as compared with Cynewulf's poetry, is then characterized by monotony and excess, and the greater frequency of loose variation introduces a certain amount of vagueness, less perceptible in Cynewulf, into the style of this epic. Chiastic arrangements are less frequent than in Cynewulf, and the pattern formed by the loose variation and its correlative is sometimes more extensive than in the Cynewulf canon: 256 ff, 1258 ff 8 half-lines, 1471 ff 14 half-lines. 7 half-lines are found ll. 609 b ff, 1625 ff.

The Dream of the Rood.

Chiasmus:

23 b f   *hwilum hit wæs mid wætan*
                                        bestemed,
           beswyled mid swates gange ...

52 b ff   *Ðystro hæfdon*
           bewrigen mid wolcnum   wealdendes hræw,
           scirne sciman   sceadu forðeode ...

96 f   *... þæt ðu þas gesyhðe   secge mannum,*
       onwreoh wordum   þæt hit is wuldres beam ...

104 ff   *... on þysne middangeard   mancynn secan*
       on domdæge   dryhten sylfa,
       ælmihtig god ...

142 b ff   *... þær ic syþþan mot*
       wunian on wuldre,   well mid þam halgum
       dreames brucan.

Loose variation:

133 b f   *... sohton him wuldres cyning,*
       lifiaþ nu on heofenum   mid heahfædere ...

147 f   *He us onlysde   ond us lif forgeaf,*
            heofonlicne ham.

There are no instances of accumulation or unessential variation.

Christ I.

Accumulation occurs:

50 ff   *Eala sibbe gesihð,   sancta Hierusalem,*
        cynestola cyst,   Cristes burglond,
        engla epelstol . . .

204 b ff   *sceolde ic lifes þrym*
        geberan, beorhtne sunu,   bearn eacen godes,
        torhtes tirfruman.

The effect of accumulation is here counter-balanced by the chiasmus of the last variation.

Chiasmus:

5 f   *. . . ond gesomnige   side weallas*
       fæste gefoge,   flint unbræcne . . .

166 f   *. . . nu þu freode scealt   fæste gedælan,*
        alætan lufan mine.

243 b f   *Cum, nu, sigores weard,*
        meotod moncynnes . . .

308 b ff   *Eal wæs gebunden*
        deoran since   duru ormæte,
        wundurclommum   bewripen.

408 ff   *. . . forþon þu gefyldest   foldan ond rodoras,*
        wigendra hleo,   wuldres þines,
        helm alwihta.

426 ff   *Ond swa forðgongende   folca nergend*
        his forgifnesse   gumum to helpe
        dæleð dogra gehwam,   dryhten weoroda.

Unessential variation:

221 ff   *. . . þe þæt asecgan mæge   sundbuendum,*
        areccan mid ryhte,   hu þe rodera weard
        æt frymðe genom   him to freobearne.

The essential point, Christ as the son of God, gets less attention from the poet than the unimportant *areccan*.

282 ff
> *Swylce þa hyhstan   on heofonum eac,*
> *Cristes þegnas,   cwepað ond singað*
> *þæt þu sie hlæfdige   halgum meahtum*
> *wuldorweorudes,   ond worldcundra*
> *hada under heofonum,   ond helwara …*

The central *hlæfdige* is without stress of variation unlike the less weighty verb in the preceding half-line.

289 f
> *þæt þu þinne mægðhad   meotude brohtes,*
> *sealdes butan synnum.*

Another instance of the same kind.
Loose variation:

27 ff
> *… hwonne us liffrea   leoht ontyne,*
> *weorðe ussum mode   to mundboran,*
> *ond þæt tydre gewitt   tire bewinde …*

56 f
> *ac þe firina gehwylc   feor abugeð,*
> *wærgðo ond gewinnes.*

67 ff
> *awæcned to wyrþe   weorcum Ebrea,*
> *bringeð blisse þe,   benda onlyseð*
> *niþum genedde.*

Gollancz and Kennedy have misunderstood the meaning of l. 67; Gollancz translates: '(Now the Child is come), awakened to destroy the Hebrews' works', and Kennedy (p. 239): '(Now is the Child come), born to demolish the works of the Hebrews.' But the line must mean: 'born to make an end of the Hebrews' sufferings', and ll. 68 b—69 a then enter in more detail on the result of His mission. Bosworth-Toller (p. 1238), and Jost (Review of Kennedy, English Studies XXVIII, p. 117), give the correct interpretation. *Niþum genedde* (for MS *geneðde*) probably means, as Klaeber suggests (JEGPh IV, 108), 'forced by hostility'.

124 b ff
> God wæs mid us
> *gesewen butan synnum;   somod eardedon*
> *mihtig meotudes bearn   ond se monnes sunu*
> *geþwære on þeode.*

Chiastic arrangement.

173 b ff
> God eaþe mæg
> gehælan hygesorge   heortan minre,
> afrefran feasceaftne.

203 ff
> Sægde soðlice   þæt me swegles gæst
> leoman onlyhte,   sceolde ic lifes þrym
> geberan, beorhtne sunu ...

206 b ff
> Nu ic his tempel eam
> gefremed butan facne,   in me frofre gæst
> geeardode ...

343 ff
> ... þæt he us ne læte   leng owihte
> in þisse deaðdene   gedwolan hyran,
> ac þæt he usic geferge   in fæder rice ...

373 b ff
> Us is lissa þearf,
> þæt þu us ahredde   ond us hælogiefe
> soðfæst sylle ...

419 ff
> ond sio weres friga   wiht ne cuþe,
> ne þurh sæd ne cwom   sigores agend
> monnes ofer moldan.

The author of this poems shows, then, a certain inclination for the loose variation; he takes little interest in the effect produced by accumulation but more in chiasmus. The poet, consequently, aims at avoiding monotony in his variations. The pattern of the loose variation does not extend 6 half-lines.

Christ III.

Accumulation:

910 ff
> He bið þam godum   glædmod on gesihþe,
> wlitig, wynsumlic,   weorude þam halgan,
> on gefean fæger,   freond ond leoftæl,
> lufsum ond liþe   leofum monnum ...

953 ff
> Ðonne heard gebrec,   hlud, unmæte,
> swar ond swiðlic,   swegdynna mæst,
> ældum egeslic,   eawed weorþeð.

997 ff
> Ðær bið cirm ond cearu,   ond cwicra gewin,
> gehreow ond hlud wop   bi heofonwoman,
> earmlic ælda gedreag.

1531 ff   *... þæt on þæt deope dæl   deofol gefeallað*
               in sweartne leg,   synfulra here
               under foldan sceat,   fæge gæstas
               on wraþra wic,   womfulra scolu
               werge to forwyrde   on witehus,
               deaðsele deofles.

The deliberate arrangement of the variations in this passage, with the expressions for hell in the first, for the damned in the second half-line, is in a manner that reminds us of Cynewulf's inclination for stylistic patterns.

1617 ff   *... from his scyppende   ascyred weorðan*
               æt domdæge   to deaðe niþer,
               under helle cinn   in þæt hate fyr,
               under liges locan ...

The variational accumulations, then, are frequent. They mostly serve to emphasize the horrors of hell and damnation.
Chiasmus:

873 f   *semninga forfehð   slæpe gebundne,*
              eorlas ungearwe   yfles genægeð.

910 f   *He bið þam godum   glædmod on gesihþe,*
              wlitig, wynsumlic   weorude þam halgan.

928 f   *... ymbutan farað   ælbeorhtra scolu,*
              hergas haligra ...

1011 f   *... ond hine ymbutan   æþelguð betast,*
              halge herefeðan,   hlutre blicað.

1085 ff   *beacna beorhtast,   blode bistemed*
             heofoncyninges   hlutran dreore,
             biseon mid swate ...

1172 f   *... geþolade fore þearfe   þeodbuendra,*
              laðlicne deað   leodum to helpe.

1237 ff   *An is ærest   orgeate þær*
             þæt hy fore leodum   leohte blicaþ,
             blæde ond byrhte   ofer burga gesetu.

1380 b f   *... ond þe ondgiet sealde.*
       Of lame ic þe leoþo gesette,   geaf ic ðe lifgendne
                                 gæst.

1446 f   *Ða ic wæs ahongen   on heanne beam,*
          rode gefæstnad ...

1513 b f   *Ðæs ge sceolon hearde adreogan*
          wite to widan ealdre,   wræc mid deoflum gepolian.

Unessential variation is rare:

1515 ff   *Ðonne þær ofer ealle   egeslicne cwide*
          sylf sigora weard,   sares fulne,
          ofer þæt fæge folc   forð forlæteð ...

A momentary lack of inspiration seems to be the reason for the padding at l. 1517 a, where we should have expected a variation for the *egeslicne cwide.*

1549 ff   *Ðæt we magon eahtan   ond on an cweþan,*
          soðe secgan,   þæt se sawle weard
          lifes wisdom   forloren hæbbe,
          se þe nu ne giemeð ...

An isolated instance of unessential verbal variation.
Loose variation is a feature characteristic of Christ III:

907 ff   *on sefan swete   sinum folce,*
          biter bealofullum,   gebleod wundrum,
          eadgum ond earmum   ungelice.

908 a and 910 form a chiastic pattern.

910 ff   *He bið þam godum   glædmod on gesihþe,*
          wlitig, wynsumlic,   weorude þam halgan,
          on gefean fæger,   freond ond leoftæl,
          lufsum ond liþe   leofum monnum
          to sceawianne   þone scynan wlite,
          weðne mid willum,   waldendes cyme,
          mægencyninges,   þam þe him on mode ær
          wordum ond weorcum   wel gecwemdun.

Ll. 916 b—917 repeat, in another form, *þam godum, weorude þam halgan,* and *leofum monnum.*

918 ff   *He bið þam yflum   egeslic ond grimlic*
          to geseonne,   synnegum monnum,
          þam þær mid firenum cumað,   forð forworhte.

A variation similar to the case ll. 916 b—917.

956 ff   *Ðær mægen werge   monna cynnes*
          wornum hweorfað   on widne leg,
          þa þær cwice meteð   cwelmende fyr.

972 ff   *Swa se gifra gæst   grundas geondseceð;*
          hipende leg   heahgetimbro
          fylleð on foldwong   fyres egsan,
          widmære blæst   woruld mid ealle ...

985 b ff   *þonne on fyrbaðe*
          swelað sæfiscas;   sundes getwæfde
          wægdeora gehwylc   werig swelteð ...

Chiastic arrangement.

999 b ff   *Ðonan ænig ne mæg,*
          firendædum fah,   frið gewinnan,
          legbryne losian   londes ower,
          ac þæt fyr nimeð   þurh foldan gehwæt,
          græfeð grimlice,   georne aseceð
          innan ond utan   eorðan sceatas ...

1018 b ff   *heagengla mægen*
          for ðære onsyne beoð   egsan afyrhte,
          bidað beofiende   beorhte gesceafte
          dryhtnes domes.

1027 ff   *Ðonne eall hraðe   Adames cynn*
          onfehð flæsce,   weorþeð foldræste
          eardes æt ende.   Sceal þonne anra gehwylc
          fore Cristes cyme   cwic arisan,
          leoðum onfon   ond lichoman,
          edgeong wesan.

Between the two loose variations we have here a line (1031) corresponding more closely to l. 1028 a.

1049 ff   *Ne sindon him dæda dyrne,   ac þær bið dryhtne cuð*
          on þam miclan dæge,   hu monna gehwylc
          ær earnode   eces lifes ...

1053 b ff   *Ne bið þær wiht forholen*
          monna gehygda,   ac se mæra dæg
          hreþerlocena hord,   heortan geþohtas,
          ealle ætyweð.

1066 ff   *folcdryht wera*   *biforan bonnað,*
        sawla gehwylce   *þara þe sið oþþe ær*
        on lichoman   *leoþum onfengen.*

1127 b f   *Gesegun þa dumban gesceaft,*
        eorðan ealgrene   *ond uprodor* ...

1155 ff   ... *þætte eorðe ageaf*   *þa hyre on lægun.*
        Eft lifgende   *up astodan*
        þa þe heo ær fæste   *bifen hæfde,*
        deade bibyrgde ...

1162 b f   *Hyge wearð mongum blissad,*
        sawlum sorge toglidene.

1170 a   *monge, nales fea* ...

1174 ff   *Ða wearð beam monig*   *blodigum tearum*
        birunnen under rindum,   *ræde ond þicce;*
        sæp wearð to swate.

1225 ff   ... *ond þær womsceapan*   *on þone wyrsan dæl*
        fore scyppende   *scyrede weorþað,*
        hateð him gewitan   *on þa winstran hond* ...

Chiastic arrangement.

1242 ff   *Oþer is to eacan*   *ondgete swa some,*
        þæt hy him in wuldre witon   *waldendes giefe,*
        ond on seoð,   *eagum to wynne,*
        þæt hi on heofonrice   *hlutre dreamas*
        eadge mid englum   *agan motun.*

1255 ff   *Ðonne hi þy geornor*   *gode þonciað*
        blædes ond blissa   *þe hy þu geseoð,*
        þæt he hy generede   *from niðcwale*
        ond eac forgeaf   *ece dreamas.*

1259   *bið him hel bilocen,*   *heofonrice agiefen.*

1344 ff   *Onfoð nu mid freondum*   *mines fæder rice*
        þæt eow wæs ær woruldum   *wynlice gearo,*
        blæd mid blissum,   *beorht eðles wlite* ...

1365 ff   *Ne þurfon hi þonne to meotude*   *miltse gewenan,*
        lifes ne lissa,   *ac þær lean cumað*

> *werum bi gewyrhtum   worda ond dæda,*
> *reordberendum;   sceolon þone ryhtan dom*
> *anne geæfnan,   egsan fulne.*

We have here two consecutive loose variations; first the positive equivalent (l. 1366 b—68 a) of the negative statement l. 1365—66 a, then the real significance (1368 b—69) of this positive equivalent.

1392 ff   *... ða þu lifes word   læstan noldes,*
ac min bibod bræce   be þines bonan worde.
Fæcnum feonde   furþor hyrdes ...

Again two variations of the same kind as l. 1365 ff: first a restatement in a positive form, then its significance.

1403 ff   *... ða þu of þan gefean   fremde wurde,*
feondum to willan   feor aworpen.
Neorxnawonges wlite   nyde sceoldes
agiefan geomormod ...

1407 f   *... earg ond unrot,   eallum bidæled*
dugeþum ond dreamum ...

1409 b ff   *... þær þu þolades siþþan*
mægenearfeþu   micle stunde,
sar ond swar gewin   ond sweartne deað ...

1439 ff   *Ðonne ic fore folce onfeng   feonda geniðlan,*
fylgdon me mid firenum,   fæhþe ne rohtun,
ond mid sweopum slogun.

1443 b ff   *Ða hi hwæsne beag*
ymb min heafod   heardne gebygdon,
þream biþrycton,   se wæs of þornum geworht.

1476 ff   *... ac forgield me þin lif,   þæs þe ic iu þe min*
þurh woruldwite   weorð gesælde;
ðæs lifes ic manige ...

The pattern is chiastic.

1480 ff   *For hwan þu þæt selegescot   þæt ic me swæs on þe*
gehalgode,   hus to wynne,
þurh firenlustas,   fule synne,
unsyfre bismite   sylfes willum?

Ge þu þone lichoman   þe ic alysde me
feondum of fæðme,   ond þa him firene forbead,
scyldwyrcende   scondum gewemdest.

þone lichoman þe ic alysde me feondum of fæðme and *þa him firene forbead* are both summed up in *þæt selegescot þæt ic me swæs on þe gehalgode.*

1487 ff   *For hwon ahenge þu mec hefgor   on þinra honda rode*
þonne iu hongade?   Hwæt, me þeos heardra þynceð!
Nu is swærra mid mec   þinra synna rod
þe ic unwillum   on beom gefæstnad,
þonne seo oþer wæs   þe ic ær gestag ...

Ll. 1489 and 1491 repeat, in another form, the idea of l. 1487—88 a.

1519 ff   *Farað nu, awyrgde,   willum biscyrede*
engla dreames,   on ece fir ...
... On þæt ge hreosan sceolan!
(1523 b)

The same curse in two different forms. Chiastic pattern.

1540 b ff   *... þæt is ece cwealm.*
Ne mæg þæt hate dæl   of heoloðcynne
in sinnehte   synne forbærnan
to widan feore,   wom of þære sawle,
ac þær se deopa seað   dreorge fedeð,
grundleas giemeð   gæsta on þeostre ...

Ll. 1541—43 dwell on the ghastly meaning of *ece cwealm*, and ll. 1544—45 repeat, in a positive form, the negative statement of 1541—43 a.

1559 ff   *Ðonne mansceaða   fore meotude forht,*
deorc on þam dome standeð ...
... won ond wliteleas   hafað werges bleo,
facentacen feores (1564—65 a).

The meaning of *deorc* is stressed.

1575 ff   *Ne bið þær ængum godum   gnorn ætywed,*
ne nængum yflum wel,   ac þær æghwæþer
anfealde gewyrht   ondweard wigeð.

1580 b ff
                            He his sawle wlite
    georne bigonge   on godes willan,
    ond wær weorðe   worda ond dæda,
    þeawa ond geþonca ...

1594 ff
    lacende leg   laðwende men,
    þreað þeodsceaþan,   ond no þonan læteð
    on gefean faran   to feorhnere,
    ac se bryne bindeð   bidfæstne here ...

1612 b ff
                         Ðonne hel nimeð
    wærleasra weorud,   ond hi waldend giefeð
    feondum in forwyrd;   þa þrowiað
    ealdorbealu egeslic.

1641 ff
    (synna lease) dream weardiað,   dryhten lofiað,
    leofne lifes weard,   leohte biwundne,
    sibbum bisweðede,   sorgum biwerede,
    dreamum gedyrde,   dryhtne gelyfde.

1652 ff
    Ðær is leofra lufu,   lif butan endedeaðe,
    glæd gumena weorud,   gioguð butan ylde,
    heofonduguða þrym,   hælu butan sare,
    ryhtfremmendum   ræst butan gewinne,
    domeadigra   dæg butan þeostrum,
    beorht blædes full,   blis butan sorgum ...

We find that the loose variations in this poem are often extensive and intricate; in these cases two variations follow the correlative, positive and negative versions alternately. The most expanded patterns are: 12 half-lines: 1652 ff; 11 half-lines: 999 b ff, 1027 ff, 1540 b ff; 10 half-lines: 1365 ff, 1242 ff; 8 half-lines: 972 ff, 1594 ff; 7 half-lines: 1487 ff, 1480 ff, 1403 ff, 1155 ff. Chiastic arrangement is comparatively rare.

Guthlac A.

Accumulation:

11 b f
                         ac þær biþ engla dream,
    sib ond gesælignes,   ond sawla ræst ...

787 b ff
                      Is him bearn godes
    milde mundbora,   meahtig dryhten,
    halig hyrde,   heofonrices weard.

Chiasmus:

84 b ff
                     Oft him brogan to
laðne gelædeð,   se þe him lifes ofonn,
eaweð him egsan ...

571 f   *... þæt he in þone grimman gryre   gongan*
                                        sceolde,
hweorfan gehyned   to helwarum ...

599 f   *Eom ic eaðmod his   ombiehthera,*
þeow geþyldig.

729 f   *Hy hine bæron   ond him bryce heoldon,*
hofon hine hondum ...

775 b ff
                     oft his word gode
þurh eaðmedu   up onsende,
let his ben cuman   in þa beorhtan gesceaft ...

Unessential variation:

159 b f
                     Ðær he dryhtnes lof
reahte ond rærde ...

766 ff   *(gife) ... ða he us to are   ond to ondgiete*
syleð ond sendeð,   sawlum rymeð
liþe lifwegas   leohte geræhte.

Loose variation:

10 b ff
                     Ðær næfre hreow cymeð,
edergong fore yrmþum,   ac þær biþ engla dream,
sib ond gesælignes,   ond sawla ræst ...

Sawla ræst is the contrast to *edergong*, and *hreow* to *sib ond gesælignes*. Ll. 11 b—12 form a positive version of l. 10 b.

22 ff   *Ðider soðfæstra   sawla motun*
cuman æfter cwealme,   þa þe her Cristes æ
læraðð ond læstað,   ond his lof rærað,
oferwinnað þa awyrgdan gæstas,   bigytað him
                                        wuldres ræste ...

24 b—25 a form a chiastic pattern.

43 f   *Ealdað eorþan blæd   æþela gehwylcre*
          ond of wlite wendað   wæstma gecyndu.

66 ff   *... ða þe him to heofonum   hyge staþeliað,*
          witon þæt se eðel   ece bideð
          ealra þære mengu   þe geond middangeard
          dryhtne þeowiað ...

77 ff   *sellað ælmessan,   earme frefrað,*
          beoð rummode   ryhtra gestreona,
          lufiað mid lacum   þa þe læs agun ...

95 ff   *... hu Guðlac his   in godes willan*
          mod gerehte,   man eall forseah,
          eorðlic æþelu,   upp gemunde
          ham in heofonum.   Him wæs hyht to þam ...

Two variations: 96 b—97 a varies 95—96 a; 98 b varies 97 b—98 a.

163 b ff   *þæt he his lichoman*
          wynna forwyrnde   ond woruldblissa,
          seftra setla   ond symbeldaga,
          swylce eac idelra   eagena wynna ...

189 b f   *Him wæs fultum neah,*
          engel hine elne trymede ...

192 f   *cwædon þæt he on þam beorge   byrnan sceolde*
          ond his lichoman   lig forswelgan ...

220 ff   *Ne motun hi on eorþan   eardes brucan,*
          ne hy lyft swefeð   in leoma ræstum,
          ac hy hleolease   hama þoliað

223 b ff   *cwealmes wiscað,*
          willen þæt him dryhten   þurh deaðes cwealm
          to hyra earfeða   ende geryme.

262 ff   *Ða wearð breahtm hæfen ...*
                                  ... Woð up astag,
          cearfulra cirm.   Cleopedon monige ...

   Chiastic arrangement.

364 ff   *... þæt he þæs latteowes   larum hyre,*
          ne lete him ealdfeond   eft oncyrran
          mod from his meotude.

371 f   *Ne mæg min lichoma*   *wið þas lænan gesceaft*
             deað gedælan,   *ac he gedreosan sceal* ...

399 f   *ne won he æfter worulde,*   *ac he in wuldre ahof*
             modes wynne.

400 b ff   *Hwylc wæs mara þonne se?*
        A ne oretta   *ussum tidum*
        cempa gecyðeð   *þæt him Crist fore*
        woruldlicra ma   *wundra gecyðde.*

Cp. p. 81. The rhetorical question 1. 400 b = *nænig wæs mara þonne se,* and this idea is worked out in greater detail ll. 401—03.

421 f   *No þær þa feondas*   *gefeon þorfton,*
             ac þæs blædes hraðe   *gebrocen hæfdon* ...

434 b f   *Guðlac sette*
         hyht in heofonas,   *hælu getreowde* ...

Chiastic pattern.

543 ff   ... *þæt him ne getweode*   *treow in breostum,*
        ne him gnornunga   *gæste scodun,*
        ac se hearda hyge   *halig wunade* ...

579 ff   *Ne eart ðu gedefe,*   *ne dryhtnes þeow*
        clæne gecostad,   *ne cempa god,*
        wordum ond weorcum   *wel gecyþed,*
        halig in heortan.   *Nu þu in helle scealt*
        deope gedufan,   *nales dryhtnes leoht*
        habban in heofonum,   *heahgetimbru,*
        seld on swegle,   *forþon þu synna to fela,*
        facna gefremedes   *in flæschoman.*

Ll. 585 b—86 are the positive equivalent of 579—82 a: *Ne eart ðu gedefe ... ne clæne gecostad, ne ... wordum ond weorcum wel gecyþed, halig in heortan = þu synna to fela, facna gefremedes in flæschoman.*

582 b ff   *Nu þu in helle scealt*
         deope gedufan,   *nales dryhtnes leoht*
         habban in heofonum ...

599 ff   *Eom ic eaðmod his*   *ombiehthera,*
        þeow geþyldig.   *Ic geþafian sceal*
        æghwær ealles   *his anne dom* ...

612 ff
 Ðæt eow æfre ne bið ufan alyfed
 leohtes lissum, þæt ge lof moten
 dryhtne secgan, ac ge deaðe sceolon
 weallendne wean wope besingan,
 heaf in helle, nales herenisse
 halge habban heofoncyninges.

"You shall not praise God in Heaven; that means that you shall
bemoan misery in hell; that means you shall not sing God's praise."

623 ff
 Sindon ge wærlogan, swa ge in wræcsiðe
 longe lifdon, lege bisencte,
 swearte beswicene, swegle benumene,
 dreame bidrorene, deaðe bifolene,
 firenum bifongne, feores orwenan.

A set of negative equivalents for positive terms.

632 ff
 Ne mostun ge a wunian in wyndagum,
 ac mid scome, scyldum, scofene wurdon
 fore oferhygdum in ece fyr ...

752 ff
 Hwæt, we þissa wundra gewitan sindon!
 Eall þas geeodon in ussera
 tida timan.

781 ff
 Swa wæs Guðlaces gæst gelæded
 engla fæðmum in uprodor,
 fore onsyne eces deman
 læddon leoflice.

Formal looseness; chiastic pattern.

792 b ff
    ... þa þe ræfnað her
 wordum ond weorcum wuldorcyninges
 lare longsume, on hyra lifes tid
 earniað on eorðan ecan lifes ...

802 ff
 gearwaþ gæstes hus, ond mid gleawnesse
 feond oferfeohtað ond firenlustas
 forberað in breostum, broþorsibbe
 georne bigongað, in godes willan
 swencað hi sylfe ...

The meaning, set forth in detail, of *gearwian gæstes hus.*
802 a and 803 a are a chiastic arrangement.

810   *swincað wið synnum,   healdað soð ond ryht.*

The loose variations in the beginning of the poem are less extensive
than those of the second half, which remind us of the instances in
Christ III. Ll. 612 ff comprise 12 half-lines, 579 ff: 10, 802 ff: 9,
95 ff: 8, 66 ff, 400 b ff, 781 ff, 792 b ff: 7 half-lines.

Guthlac B.

Accumulation:

1259 b ff   *nelle ic lætan þe*
     æfre unrotne   æfter ealdorlege
     meðne, modseocne   minre geweorðan,
     soden sorgwælmum.

1322 b ff   *... hu se stenc ond se sweg,*
     heofonlic hleoþor   ond se halga song
     gehyred wæs,   heahþrym godes,
     breahtem æfter breahtme.

1357 b ff   *Is hlaford min,*
     beorna bealdor,   ond broþor þin,
     se selesta   bi sæm tweonum
     þara þe we on Engle   æfre gefrunen
     acennedne   þurh cildes had
     gumena cynnes,   to godes dome,
     werigra wraþu,   worulddreamum of,
     winemæga wyn,   in wuldres þrym,
     gewiten, winiga hleo,   wica neosan
     eardes on upweg.

This passage, with its studied interlacement of accumulated variations and attributes stands out, in the otherwise fairly smooth style
of the poem, as a highly emphasized paragraph — there is no mis-
taking the strong emotion the poet tries to convey to the servant's
words about his departed master.

Chiasmus:

819 f   *Ðæt is wide cuð   wera cneorissum,*
     folcum gefræge ...

869 f   ... þone Eue fyrn   Adame geaf,
    byrelade bryd geong.

979 b f   Hreþer innan weol.
    born banloca.

996 b ff   Swa wæs Guðlace
    enge anhoga   ætryhte þa
    æfter nihtscuan   neah geþyded,
    wiga wælgifre.

1055 b ff   ac he hate let
    torn þoliende   tearas geotan,
    weallan wægdropan.

1132 b f   ... þe him meotud engla,
    gæsta geocend   forgiefen hæfde.

1160 b f   ... þæt him on spellum gecyðde,
    onwrige worda gongum ...

1208 f   Oft mec geomor sefa   gehþa gemanode,
    hat æt heortan,   hyge gnornende ...

1212 f   Symle ic gehyrde,   þonne heofones gim,
    wyncondel wera,   west onhylde ...

1216 b ff   Ic þæs þeodnes word,
    ares uncuþes   oft neosendes,
    dægwoman bitweon   ond þære deorcan niht,
    meþelcwide mæcges,   ond on morgne swa,
    ongeat geomormod,   gæstes spræce ...

1325 b f   Beofode þæt ealond,
    foldwong onþrong.

1333 b ff   ... þæt se hærnflota
    æfter sundplegan   sondlond gespearn,
    grond wið greote.

1335 b ff   Gnornsorge wæg,
    hate æt heortan,   hyge geomurne,
    meðne modsefan ...

1371 ff   ... þæt git a mosten   in þam ecan gefean
    mid þa sibgedryht   somudeard niman,
    weorca wuldorlean,   willum neotan
    blædes ond blissa.

In Guthlac B we find more instances of close variations, arranged in a chiastic pattern, than in any of the non-Cynewulfian poems. But the device is handled with less skill; of Cynewulf's intricacies in working the variations into the periods we see nothing, and a more studied instance such as ll. 1216 b ff is exceptional. There are no clear cases of unessential variation.

Loose variation:

827 b ff
               ... *þær him nænges wæs*
willan onsyn,   ne welan brosnung,
ne lifes lyre   ne lices hryre,
ne dreames dryre   ne deaðes cyme,
ac he on þam lande   lifgan moste
ealra leahtra leas,   longe neotan
niwra gefeana.   Ðær he no þorfte
lifes ne lissa   in þam leohtan ham
þurh ælda tid   ende gebidan ...

Three variations: 831—32 a is a summing up of the preceding negative details, 832b—33 a a positive repetition of the summing up, l. 833b—835 a negative restatement of this summing up, corresponding back to the first set of negations ll. 827b—830.

839 ff   ... *ond þær siþþan a   in sindreamum*
to widan feore   wunian mostun
dryhtne on gesihðe,   butan deaðe forð ...

1047 b ff
               Ða wæs wop ond heaf,
geongum geocor sefa,   geomrende hyge,
siþþan he gehyrde   þæt se halga wæs
forðsiþes fus.   He þæs færspelles
fore his mondryhtne   modsorge wæg,
hefige æt heortan.

1074 b ff   (*sceolon wræcsið wepan*),   *wilna biscirede*
in þam deaðsele   duguða gehwylcre,
lufena ond lissa.

1077 b ff
               Ic eom siþes fus
upeard niman,   edleana georn
in þam ecan gefean,   ærgewyrhtum
geseon sigora frean ...

1078b—79a are a variation of 1077b—78a; 1079b—80a are a definition of *edleana. Georn* l. 1078b holds together this loose variation, corresponding closely to *fus*.

1142 b ff
                                  ... þæs þe him in gesonc,
        hat, heortan neah,   hildescurum
        flacor flanþracu,   feorhhord onleac ...

1279 b ff
                            swearc norðrodor
        won under wolcnum,   woruld miste oferteah,
        þystrum biþeahte,   þrong niht ofer tiht ...

1305 ff
        Ða wæs Guðlaces   gæst gelæded
        eadig on upweg.   Englas feredun
        to þam longan gefean ...

1314 b ff
                          Engla þreatas
        sigeleoð sungon,   sweg wæs on lyfte
        gehyred under heofonum,   haligra dream.

1345 b f
                        He þa wyrd ne mað,
        fæges forðsið.   Fusleoð agol ...

The difference from Guthlac A in the use of variation is striking in this poem, not least as regards comparative scantiness of loose variation. This latter kind of variation is sometimes handled with great skill, as for instance the extensive variation of the Paradise theme ll. 827 b ff, a subject which the poet seems to abandon only reluctantly. The pattern here comprises 17 half-lines; 1047 b ff form a 10 half-line pattern. There are no chiastic instances.

The Phoenix.

Accumulation:

307 f
        Wrætlic is seo womb neoþan,   wundrum fæger,
        scir ond scyne.

420 b ff
                          ... oþþæt wuldorcyning
        þurh his hidercyme   halgum togeanes,
        moncynnes gefea,   meþra frefrend,
        ond se anga hyht,   eft ontynde.

Chiasmus:

95 f
        fæder fyrngeweorc   frætwum blican
        torht tacen godes.

131 b ff   *Biþ þæs hleoðres sweg*
eallum songcræftum   swetra ond wlitigra
ond wynsumra   wrenca gehwylcum.

154 b f   *grene eorðan*
aflyhð, fugla wyn,   foldan geblowene

268 ff   *... lic leoþucræftig,   þæt ær lig fornom,*
somnað, swoles lafe,   searwum gegædrað
ban gebrosnad ...

361 ff   *Ðær se eadga mot   eardes neotan,*
wyllestreama   wuduholtum in,
wunian in wonge ...

444 f   *(meotude) gehyrdun under heofonum   halgum*
                                                 ðeawum,
dædum domlicum ...

492 b f   *wile fæder engla,*
sigora soðcyning,   seonoþ gehegan ...

497 f   *... beodeð, brego engla,   byman stefne*
ofer sidne grund,   sawla nergend.

539 f   *Ðonne hleoþriað   halge gæstas,*
sawla soðfæste ...

547 f   *... þæt ic lygewordum   leoð somnige,*
write woðcræfte.

616 b f   *... ond heofoncyninges*
meahte mærsiað,   singað metude lof.

The cases of chiasmus are all very simple; the only extensive instance being ll. 131 b ff.

Unessential variation:

276 ff   *Ðonne fotum ymbfehð   fyres lafe,*
        clam biclyppeð,   ond his cyþþu eft,
        sunbeorht gesetu,   seceð on wynnum.

One would have expected a variation for *fyres lafe* to correspond with the *feorh ond feþerhoma* l. 280 a; *ymbfehð* is not essential in this connexion.

Loose variation:

34 b ff

                              Wæstmas ne dreosað,
beorhte blede,   ac þa beamas a
grene stondað,   swa him god bibead.
Wintres ond sumeres   wudu bið gelice
bledum gehongen;   næfre brosniað
leaf under lyfte,   ne him lig sceþeð
æfre to ealdre ...

The loose variations and their correlative are here arranged in
a chiastic pattern; a negative statement is varied by a positive one;
then follows another positive variation followed by a negative one.

62 b ff

                           ... *ac þær lagustreamas,*
wundrum wrætlice,   wyllan onspringað
fægrum foldwylmum.   Foldan leccaþ
wæter wynsumu   of þæs wuda midle.

74 ff

Ne feallað þær on foldan   fealwe blostman,
wudubeama wlite,   ac þær wrætlice
on þam treowum symle   telgan gehladene,
ofett edniwe ...   ... *grene stondaþ* ...

Chiastic pattern.

96 b ff

                        Tungol beoþ ahyded,
gewiten under waþeman   westdælas on,
bideglad on dægred,   ond seo deorce niht
won gewiteð.

121 b ff

                   ... *swa se haswa fugel*
beorht of þæs bearwes   beame gewiteð,
fareð feþrum snell   flyhte on lyfte ...

Chiastic arrangement.

130 f

wuldres wyrhta   woruld staþelode,
heofon ond eorþan.

179 b ff

                   Ne mæg him bitres wiht
scyldum sceððan,   ac gescylded a
wunað ungewyrded ...

182 ff

Ðonne wind ligeð,   weder bið fæger,
hluttor heofones gim   halig scineð,

beoð wolcen towegen, wætra þryþe
stille stondað, biþ storma gehwylc
aswefed under swegle, suþan bliceð
wedercondel wearm ...

190 ff   *... þæt he þa yldu ofestum mote*
þurh gewittes wylm wendan to life,
feorg geong onfon.

216 b ff   *Ðonne brond þeceð*
heorodreorges hus, hreoh onetteð,
fealo lig feormað ond fenix byrneð ...

314 ff   *Nis he hinderweard, ne hygegælsa,*
swar ne swongor, swa sume fuglas,
þa þe late þurh lyft lacað fiþrum,
ac he is snel ond swift ond swiþe leoht ...

339 f   *ond swa þone halgan hringe beteldað*
flyhte on lyfte; fenix biþ on middum ...

355 b ff   *God ana wat,*
cyning ælmihtig, hu his gecynde bið,
wifhades þe weres; þæt ne wat ænig
monna cynnes, butan meotod ana,
hu þa wisan sind wundorlice,
fæger fyrngesceap, ymb þæs fugles gebyrd.

371 b ff   *... þonne fromlice*
þurh briddes had gebreadad weorðeð
eft of ascan, edgeong weseð
under swegles hleo.

383 b ff   *... þæt he dryhtnes mot*
æfter geardagum geofona neotan
on sindreamum, ond siþþan a
wunian in wuldre weorca to leane.

416 ff   *... in þas deaðdene drohtað sohton,*
sorgfulran gesetu. Him wearð selle lif
heolstre bihyded ...

456 ff   *lænan lifes leahtras dwæsceþ,*
mirce mandæde, healdeð meotudes æ

beald in breostum,   ond gebedu seceð
clænum gehygdum,   ond his cneo bigeð
æpele to eorþan,   flyhð yfla gehwylc ...

L. 457 b—458 a repeat, in a positive form, l. 456, and so, in a less positive form, does 460 b; we notice the chiastic pattern *leahtras dwæsceþ—healdeð æ*. Ll. 459 b—460 a, finally, repeat 458 b—459 a.

470 ff   *Swa nu in þam wicum   willan fremmað*
             mode ond mægne   meotudes cempan,
             mærða tilgað.

476 ff   *... þæs þe hi geheoldan   halge lare*
             hate æt heortan,   hige weallende
             dæges ond nihtes   dryhten lufiað,
             leohte geleafan   leofne ceosað
             ofer woruldwelan ...

476—478 b: chiastic arrangement.

554 b ff   *... gewite hean þonan*
             on longne sið,   lame bitolden,
             geomor gudæda.   in greotes fæðm ...

561 b ff   *Ic þæs lifes ne mæg*
             æfre to ealdre   ende gebidan,
             leohtes ond lissa.

575 b f   *Bana lafe,*
             ascan ond yslan,   ealle gesomnað ...

607 b ff   *þær se longa gefea,*
             ece ond edgiong,   æfre ne sweþrað,
             ac hy in wlite wuniað,   wuldre bitolden
             fægrum frætwum,   mid fæder engla.

Ll. 34 b ff (12 half-lines), 355 b ff (11 half-lines) are especially remarkable achievements among these cases; we may also notice 182 ff (11), 456 ff (10), 476 ff (9); 74 ff and 314 ff have 8 half-lines each; 62 b ff, 383 b ff, 607 b ff: 7 half-lines. Chiastic patterns are rare.

We have found the following proportions of variations examined from our special points of view:

	Accumulation	chiasmus	unessential v.	loose v.	loose v. with *ac*
Elene	2	37	5	15	1
Juliana	2	16	2	11	1
Christ II	—	12	2	8	1
Fata	—	4	—	1	—
Andreas	7	15	21	41	3
Dream	—	5	—	2	—
Christ I	2	6	3	10	1
Christ III	5	10	2	41	8
Guthlac A	2	5	2	30	8
Guthlac B	3	14	—	10	1
The Phoenix	2	11	1	23	5

Extensive patterns of loose variation
(more than 6 half-lines).

	half-lines	instances		half-lines	instances
Juliana	7	2	Gu A	12	1
				10	1
Christ II	7	1		9	1
				8	1
				7	4
Andreas	14	1			
	8	2	Gu B	17	1
	7	2		10	1
			Ph.	12	1
Christ III	12	1		11	2
	11	3		10	1
	10	2		9	1
	8	2		8	2
	7	4		7	3

Chiastic loose variation.

Elene	Juliana	Christ II	Andreas	Christ I	Christ III	Gu A	Ph.
5	5	2	6	1	5	5	5

PAETZEL gives the following proportions of variation in our texts: 18.3 % in Elene, 12.9 % in Juliana, 19.9 % in Christ II; Andreas has 19.0 %, The Dream 14.1 %, Christ I 13.7 %, Christ III 15.6 %,

Guthlac A 6.9 %, Guthlac B 23.3 %, and The Phoenix 16.1 % (p. 160). The only remarkable thing about this survey is the scantiness of variations in Guthlac A (a feature that has also been pointed out by S. K. Das, p. 185) and the great difference, in this respect, from Guthlac B. This difference, then, supports the difference we have found in the examination above. Paetzel also observes, p. 200 ff, that variations of Christian conceptions are common in Cynewulf's poetry and Guthlac A. Guthlac B contains variations chiefly for natural objects and phenomena, and so do Christ III and the Phoenix. Andreas has fewer variations for Christian words and more for words denoting natural phenomena than Cynewulf.

We find, in our analyses in this chapter, that there is a clear division between the use of variation in the Cynewulf canon, Guthlac B, and the Dream of the Rood, on the one hand, and the rest of the texts, on the other. In Cynewulf's signed poems, the Guthlac B, and the Dream there is a majority of close chiastic variations, in the other texts a majority of loose ones. In the latter group Christ III is richest in this device. Christ I forms an intermediate link between the two groups. Accumulation is especially common in Andreas and Christ III, unessential variation is characteristic of Andreas.

A small sub-groups of loose variations is formed by the *ac*-constructions, which are especially frequent in those poems that have the greatest number of loose variations. Such *ac*-constructions, and their relation to a preceding sentence, do not seem to have received due attention. Kopas speaks about "adversatives, aufhebendes, kausales *ac*" (p. 55); Schücking, Satzverknüpfung, deals chiefly with the causal *ac* (p. 91 ff), Glogauer adds, to the senses referred to by Kopas, "eine vierte, die die Erzählung fortführende, bisweilen einen gewissen Abschluss verleihende" (p. 22). Neither of the senses assumed here explains the special function of the *ac*-construction of the loose variation. If we take an instance such as the Phoenix 179 b ff

> *Ne mæg him bitres wiht*
> *scyldum sceððan,   ac gescylded a*
> *wunað ungewyrded,*

we have in the *ac*-clause, it is true, a kind of annulment of what precedes, but, as was pointed out in the analysis of Juliana 590 b ff on p. 174, this annulment is only partial, it does not affect the whole of the preceding clause. *Gescylded*, in other words, is contrasted only with *sceððan*. Between the clauses there is no contrast; they both tell us that nothing can harm the Phoenix. We may say, therefore, that *ac* in some cases, which we here call loose variations, introduces a clause which is a restatement, in a positive form, of a preceding negative statement.

The different use, in our poems, of close and loose variation is of fairly great importance to the quality of the style. We may say that a restricted use of loose variation in favour of chiastic close variation gives more precision and coherence to the ideas and to the poetical style, and a precision not marred by monotony. A frequent use of loose variation, on the contrary, tends to stress certain motifs and ideas at the expense of precision, although this sort of variation may be handled with a great deal of skill. Apart from the different frequency of close and loose variation, there is also a clear difference, in respect of extension of loose variation, between the Cynewulf canon, the Dream of the Rood, and Christ I, on the one hand, and the other poems on the other. In the former group the loose variation is fairly concentrated: the pattern does not extend seven half-lines and is easy to survey. In the latter group the loose variational pattern tends to grow into longwinded periods, which, although they are not devoid of design and arrangement, do not form a coordinate and structural unity in the same way as the loose periods of the former group. Now it seems as if the greater frequency, in some of our texts, of extensive loose variation, is due to special influence. Whereas the close variation presents the main characteristics of the traditional Germanic variation, as it is described by PAETZEL, HEUSLER, and others, the loose variation seems to have its roots, partly at least, in non-Germanic tradition. The loose variation, in fact, is a rhetorical device common in the homilies and sermons of the Fathers, and since the Anglo-Saxon poets were no doubt well read in this kind of literature, it seems reasonable to assume that especially the extensive forms of the loose pattern were imitated from Latin rhetoric. As an illustration of the Latin device I shall choose some homiletic passages in an author who has been of great importance to religious Anglo-Saxon poetry (Gregory, in Ezech. Lib. I, Hom. II, MIGNE, P. L. 76, 800):

Ignis quippe in terram mittitur cum per ardorem sancti Spiritus afflata terrena mens a carnalibus suis desideriis concrematur. De malo autem igne dicitur: "Et nunc ignis adversarios consumet" (Hebr. X, 27), *quia cor pessimum ex sua malitia tabescit.*

Sicut autem ignis amoris mentem erigit, ita ignis malitiæ involvit ...

801:

Dum enim persecutio in Judæa agitur, sancta apostolorum prædicatio in universo mundo dispersa est, sicut ipsi dicunt ...
Iste itaque ignis malitiæ qui a Judæorum cordibus arsit in persecutione, priusquam sanctos apostolos sæviendo affligeret ...

In Prim. Reg. Expos. Lib. III, MIGNE, P. L., 79, 197:
Viri autem Bethsamitæ obtulerunt holocausta, et immolaverunt victimas in die illa Domino.
In qua die, nisi in illa in qua holocaustum Domino vaccas super plaustri ligna posuere? Quæ est igitur dies illa, nisi illuminatio divinæ prædicationis? Ea namque die Bethsamitæ holocausta Domino offerunt, ea die victimas immolant qua ligna concidunt, qua super ea holocaustum Domino vaccas imponunt ... Quia vero non solum holocausta obtulisse, sed immolasse victimas viri Bethsamitæ relati sunt ... Nam holocausta offerunt ...

In Prim. Reg. Expos. Lib. IV, MIGNE, P. L. 79, 240:

Nam si carnis delectationes iniquæ possessionis agri non essent, Apostolus nequaquam diceret: "Qui seminat in carne, de carne metet corruptionem" (Gal. VI, 8). *In carne quippe seminare, est propositum mentis obruere in delectationes corporis. Qui profecto corruptionem de carne metunt: quia in electorum ressurrectione renovationem æternæ incorruptionis nequaquam recipiunt,* etc.

We here see "the Fourth Doctor of the Latin Church" turn and twist ideas to demonstrate their significance thoroughly, in the same manner as the Anglo-Saxon poets. However, we must content ourselves with the general pattern; exact parallels to the Old English passages seem difficult to find.

7. The testimony of the parallels

One of the most striking characteristics of Old English poetry is the phenomenon known to German scholars as "die Parallelstellen" — combinations of two or more words which are used either as common property in different contexts throughout Anglo-Saxon poetical literature, or are to be found only in a few texts. This unique parallelism was early observed; even CHARITIUS in his "Die ags. Gedichte vom heil. Guðlac" in 1879 discussed parallel passages in different poems, but it was not until SARRAZIN's paper appeared in 1886 (Anglia IX) that wider attention was drawn to the parallels. After him several scholars took an interest in this feature, basing their very positive assertions of attribution of certain texts to Cynewulf or to the redactor of Beowulf on similarities of phrases and formulas. Even if one is grateful for the achievements of KAIL, SARRAZIN, and BUTTENWIESER, it must be borne in mind, first, that only some of the passages they have collected can be looked upon as real parallels (they are often phrases torn out of their context), secondly that theirs is a work of survey and compilation, not one of analysis; and that a collection of material does not solve stylistic problems. In SARRAZIN's opinion, the frequent parallels between Beowulf, on the one hand, and the Cynewulf group, on the other, tend to prove identity of authorship. Highly characteristic of this scholar's view of parallels as criteria is his remark (Anglia XIV, p. 192): "Die natürlichste Deutung grosser stilistischer übereinstimmung ist daher die annahme eines verfassers". KAIL, on the other hand, held that the Anglo-Saxon poetical parallels are rather parts of a large stock of formulas, from which the poets may have drawn independently. BUTTENWIESER distinguished between original passages and borrowings. Of these three, and of others who have discussed parallels, BUTTENWIESER, it is true, has done most to construct a basis for the utilization of parallels for stylistic research, in so far as she has formulated a theory for such a utilization, which, in the main, is quite acceptable: "der einzige Anhaltspunkt bei einer Verfasserschaftsfrage (kann) nur der sein, dass der eine Dichter diese Gedanken (i. e. those expressed in the parallel passages) logischer und passender einführt als der andere, dass er beim Auswählen aus dem Ausdrucksvorrat, bei der Anordnung der Formeln mehr Geist und Geschmack zeigt und im Bau seiner Verse grössere Glätte und Vollendung ... zustande bringt" (p. 62). But as has already been pointed out BUTTENWIESER, apart from one or two cases, does not herself make any reasonable use of her theory, and the chief importance of her work, like KAIL's and SARRAZIN's, is to be found in her collection of parallel passages, though it should be readily admitted that her refusal to conclude single authorship from parallels without further ado is a very great improvement on the mechanical attitude of some earlier scholars.

In attempting to make deductions from parallelism in Old English poetry we must carefully differentiate two types of word-combinations. We must distinguish between, first, formulary, often alliterative combinations of a few words such as *heard ond higerof, ofer deop gelad, under wolcnum, halig of hehþo*, which are sometimes almost meaningless and only used in order to delay the march of the narrative and endow it with an archaic and solemn character, and secondly combinations which form part of a greater whole and carry a distinct meaning. To this latter category belong phrases like *onfon æfter fyrste fulwihtes bæð* (El. 490), which is to be found in a very similar form in Andreas, or a clause like *swylce hi me geblendan bitre tosomne unswetne drync* (Chr. 1438) which is also met with, slightly altered, in Andreas. To the latter group also belong extensive passages, the general outline and structure and certain details of which are met with in more than one poem.

It is obvious that whereas the former group must have been part of an easily remembered stock of phrases and of an oral tradition, the latter is a body of real borrowings, bodily taken over by one poet from another, to a certain extent by the same poet from his own work. In this second category, I believe, we have now to do with a literary rather than with an oral tradition. It should be remembered that manuscripts containing tales and legends on Christian subject-matter were collected and accessible in the monasteries, so it cannot have been difficult for the poets to pick out, from the work of their predecessors, passages which might be useful in their own work of composition; such passages, however, may of course also recur in the form of loose reminiscences. I think it is not unimportant to distinguish, as far as possible, between oral and literary tradition as reflected in these different kinds of parallels: the oral tradition, apparently, is mainly the heathen tradition, and it is only natural that with Christian learning and the extensive Christian monastic apparatus the oral tradition should become less important and give way, to a great extent, to the literary one. Another reason for this was, perhaps, that Christian themes were more unfamiliar to the poets, who probably became more dependent on one another's actual writings.

It is not likely that very much difference was made, in the monastic world, between semi-heathen and Christian poetry — one ideology could be interpreted in terms of the other. Thus Beowulf was studied as much as the Cædmon poems, and its influence on Anglo-Saxon poetry became stronger than that of any other poem — not least because the poem contained enough of the original pre-Christian world and ideas to make Anglo-Saxon poets feel at home with it in a way that was perhaps not possible with works of literature wholly grown out of the Christian sphere. What we have said about the importance of Beowulf is in no way inconsistent with KLAEBER's reasonable remark (p. CXIII) that "we should hesitate to attribute to Beowulf a commanding, central position in the development of Anglo-Saxon poetry". It is a matter of great importance to our examination to see how far the different poems are influenced by Beowulf, and in what way — one might say with how much success — the borrowings are adapted to the poet's own style.

It is obvious that in studying parallels in the Cynewulf group we have much less to do with the first group than with the second. The alliterative formulas, since they are not so much borrowings by one poet from another as a general medium, known to all and used by all, tell us hardly anything about the interdependence of the poems and the effect of this interdependence on the style. Whole borrowed phrases, on the contrary, even if they are met with in more than two poems, have a history which can be followed, possess qualities which are altered with the change from originality to imitation. We will, then, in this chapter, devote our attention chiefly to borrowings. But it is of vital importance to consider the parallels in their context, as organic entities, and not, as earlier critics so often did, tear them out of their setting. Now it need hardly be said that at no stage in the investigation of a problem of stylistic quality or priority do we tread on such dangerous, but at the same time, perhaps, such fertile, ground as when we come to consider the significance of parallels. BUTTENWIESER goes so far as to say: "man wird leicht sagen, es liege Gefahr vor, subjektiv zu verfahren, da es schwer ist, für eine tote Sprache das Gefühl wie für seine eigene zu haben und für die Poesie dieser Sprache das Gefühl und das Ohr zu gewinnen, das man seiner eigenen entgegenbringt —-

doch ... einen andern sicheren Anthaltspunkt haben wir nicht"
(p. 63). This, however, is not altogether true; and we may add a
few reflections to modify the pessimism of this declaration which,
although it contains a core of critical soundness, nevertheless makes
priority research appear a good deal more of a *læne gesceaft* than
it actually is — or should be.

First, in a case where it has proved possible to establish with
tolerable certainty that a certain recurring passage is used with less
aptness of context or less stylistic subtlety in one poem than in
another, it seems highly probable that the less logical and consistent
use of this passage is also the later use. For if the contrary is
maintained, one implies the very odd assumption that the imitator,
from among the poetic material at his disposal, picks out incoherent
matter which he then succeeds in moulding into perfect harmony and
accordance with his own work. It must be remembered that we are
here concerned with consciously artistic literature and that, consequently, what was likely to be admired in it was some occasional
superior passage or phrase, which, in the imitator's judgment, stood
out by virtue of the higher stylistic achievement or answered his
own purpose. Such a passage would be in the fullest sense justified
by its context, and it cannot be assumed that an imitator should feel
himself attracted by a passage violating context or syntax. Imitators
were, apparently, poets of less genius and less talent, but even good
poets were borrowers; in this case it is, of course, more difficult to
distinguish original from imitation unless we are enabled to lay down
with certainty, by means of other tests, which poem is the earlier
and which the later. In these cases one can observe the natural fact
that the borrowings of the "good" poets are more easily and more
skilfully fused into their new context.

Secondly, with regard to our possibility of proving what poetic
passages are handled with less consistency and less stylistic subtlety
than others, we are sometimes, with our knowledge of the poet's
manner derived from our previous examination, enabled to say
whether the passage in question is in harmony with this manner or
not. Further, in cases where we cannot take this examination of
style as a basis, we have to do our best to let an objective and logical
analysis take the place of subjective and æsthetic judgment.

There are some cases when we are concerned with passages which
are so similar to one another that it must be assumed that one of the
passages is a borrowing, but when it is impossible to say which

passage is the original and which the imitation. Some instances of this will be quoted.

With these reflections we have chiefly been referring to such cases when the priority of either of two texts examined is not known in advance. This kind of problem will be treated in the studies of the relations between Andreas, on the one hand, and the Cynewulf canon and Guthlac on the other. In these studies, then, we will try to answer two questions: 1) which poem is the earlier, 2) what use does the later poet make of his borrowing; in other words, what is the effect of the borrowing on his style? BUTTENWIESER has not clearly demonstrated the relations between Andreas, on the one hand, and the Cynewulf canon and Guthlac on the other. But we will also, in this chapter, examine the indebtedness of the poets of the Cynewulf group to those Anglo-Saxon poems which, a priori, may be looked upon as belonging to an earlier period. In the first place we shall then, as was mentioned above, study their relations to Beowulf, and, secondly, their relations to the poems known as the Cædmon group (Genesis A, Exodus, and Daniel). These four epics, as we shall find, have been of widely different importance to the composition and the style of the poems in the Cynewulf group.

Many of the parallel passages examined in the following paragraphs have been known for quite a long time, as was just remarked, and the ones I have discovered myself are not very numerous. If the material, mainly, is not new, I hope nevertheless that the analysis of it and the conclusions drawn from it may prove of some interest.

Considering the influence of Beowulf on our poems — of the priority here there can hardly be any doubt — we will begin by seeing how far and in what way Cynewulf is indebted to this epic.

The following passages in Elene seem to be derived from Beowulf (cp. SARRAZIN BS p. 110, Anglia IX, p. 515 ff):

El. 67
    (Here wicode ... egstreame neah)
    on neaweste   nihtlangne fyrst.

Beow. 527 b f
    ... gif þu Grendles dearst
    nihtlongne fyrst   nean bidan.

(SARRAZIN, Anglia IX, p. 546.) The two half-lines of Elene 67 are no natural or formulary combination, so it seems probable that we have an influence from Beowulf there. This would explain the unessential variation *on neaweste* (cp. p. 194).

El. 142 b f

 Lythwon becwom
Huna herges *ham eft þanon.*

Beow. 2365 b f

     lyt eft becwom
fram þam hildfrecan hames niosan!

(SARRAZIN, Anglia IX, p. 516, BS p. 111.) Both passages form part of a compound section; the conclusive statement of the result of Hygelac's war in Friesland is equally applicable to the disastrous effect of the heathens' attack on Rome.

El. 148 ff

Gewat þa heriga helm ham eft þanon,
huðe hremig, (hild wæs gesceaden),
wigge geweorðod ... Com ... burga neosan ...

Beow. 123 b ff

      þanon eft gewat
huðe hremig to ham faran,
mid þære wælfylle wica neosan.

(SARRAZIN, Anglia IX, p. 515.) First, we notice the correspondence in respect of the clause-types; in both poems the passages form part of a compound section, and quite logically: in Beowulf the passage is the centre, in Elene the end of a dramatic episode. It may be noticed that Cynewulf is dependent on the alliterative w-series in Beow. 125, but out of it he makes the appropriate: *wigge geweorðod. Com þa wigena hleo ...*

El. 194 f

Ða wæs on sælum sinces brytta,
niðheard cyning.

Beow. 607 f

Ða wæs on salum sinces brytta,
gamolfeax ond guðrof.

(SARRAZIN, Anglia IX, p. 515, BS p. 110.) The expression of Hroð-gar's elementary joy, if one may say so, when Beowulf proclaims his intention to kill Grendel, is used with more refinement in Elene, where the *sinces brytta* is *on salum* because of the spiritual truth and hope that have just been revealed to him.

El. 226 b ff

     Fearoðhengestas
ymb geofenes stæð gearwe stodon,
sælde sæmearas, sunde getenge.
Ða wæs orcnæwe idese siðfæt,
siððan wæges helm werode gesohte.

El. 231

> Ðær wlanc manig   æt Wendelsæ
> on stæde stodon.   Stundum wræcon
> ofer mearcpaðu,   mægen æfter oðrum,
> ond þa gehlodon   hildesercum,
> bordum ond ordum,   byrnwigendum,

" 236

> werum ond wifum,   wæghengestas.
> Leton þa ofer fifelwæg   famige scriðan
> bronte brimþisan.   Bord oft onfeng
> ofer earhgeblond   yða swengas;
> sæ swinsade.   Ne hyrde ic sið ne ær

" 241

> on egstreame   idese lædan
> on merestræte,   mægen fægerre.

" 247 b

>   Cwen siðes gefeah,
> syþþan to hyðe   hringedstefnan
> ofer lagofæsten   geliden hæfdon
> on Creca land.   Ceolas leton
> æt sæfearoðe,   sunde bewrecene,

" 252

> ald yðliodu,   oncrum fæste
> on brime bidan   beorna geþinges,
> hwonne heo sio guðcwen   gumena þreate
> ofer eastwegas   eft gesohte.

Beow. 207 b ff

>   fiftyna sum
> sundwudu sohte;   secg wisade,
> lagucræftig mon   landgemyrcu.
> Fyrst forð gewat;   flota wæs on yðum,
> bat under beorge.   Beornas gearwe

" 212

> on stefn stigon;   streamas wundon,
> sund wið sande;   secgas bæron
> on bearm nacan   beorhte frætwe,
> guðsearo geatolic;   guman ut scufon,
> weras on wilsið   wudu bundenne.

" 217

> Gewat þa ofer wægholm   winde gefysed
> flota famiheals   fugle gelicost ...

" 293 ff

> ... swylce ic maguþegnas   mine hate
> wið feonda gehwone   flotan eowerne,
> niwtyrwydne   naçan on sande,

arum healdan, oþ ðæt eft byreð
ofer lagustreamas leofne mannan
wudu wundenhals to Wedermearce etc.

Beow. 32 ff   Ðær æt hyðe stod   hringedstefna
isig ond utfus, æþelinges fær;
aledon þa   leofne þeoden,
beaga bryttan   on bearm scipes,
mærne be mæste.   Ðær wæs madma fela

"   37   of feorwegum   frætwa gelæded;
ne hyrde ic cymlicor   ceol gegyrwan
hildewæpnum   ond heaðowædum,
billum ond byrnum;   him on bearme læg
madma mænigo.

Andr. 360 b ff   Æfre ic ne hyrde
þon cymlicor   ceol gehladenne
heahgestreonum.

"   495 ff   ... steoran ofer stæfnan.   Streamwelm hwileð,
beateþ brimstæðo.   Is þes bat ful scrid,
færeð famigheals,   fugole gelicost
glideð on geofone.   Ic georne wat
þæt ic æfre ne geseah   ofer yðlade
on sæleodan   syllicran cræft.

(Beow. 38 — Andr. 360, Beow. 218 — Andr. 479: SARRAZIN, Anglia
IX, p. 519.) The passages in Elene and in Andreas seem both dependent
on Beowulf. It is interesting to notice the difference between the two
former poems as to the treatment of the poetic material. In Elene it
is the general structure of the first Beowulf episode that is reproduced,
and there are allusions to the other two passages. We get the sea-
farers prepared for sailing: El. siððan wæges helm werode gesohte —
wlanc manig ... on stæðe stodon; Beow. fiftyna sum sundwudu
sohte — Beornas gearwe on stefn stigon. The ships ready to sail:
El. Fearoðhengestas ... gearwe stodon ... sunde getenge; Beow.
flota wæs on yðum, bat under beorge, more similarly 32 ff Ðær æt
hyðe stod hringedstefna, which reappears in more detail in the description of the arrival in the Creca land in Elene: syþþan to hyðe
hringedstefnan ... geliden hæfdon. Further the loading of the ships:
El. þa gehlodon hildesercum, bordum ond ordum, byrnwigendum,

werum ond wifum, wæghengestas; Beow. *secgas bæron on bearm nacan beorhte frætwe, guðsearo geatolic.* The sailing: El. *Leton þa ofer fifelwæg famige scriðan bronte brimþisan*; Beow. *Gewat þa ofer wægholm ... flota famiheals fugle gelicost.* The *hyrde*-formula recurs in Elene l. 240 b ff. In Elene, then, we find reminiscences from different episodes in Beowulf concentrated to one episode, handled with great freedom and worked into an extensive and coherent whole. In Andreas, on the contrary, there is more meagreness about the context. We get no full and rich description of the voyage, and the centre of it is the line *færeð famigheals, fugole gelicost glideð on geofone,* which is almost bodily taken over from Beow. 217 ff *Gewat þa ofer wægholm ... flota famiheals fugle gelicost.* As for line 360 b ff *ic ne hyrde* etc. in Andreas, which is obviously taken over from Beow. 38 ff, I must agree with BRANDL (p. 1010) that the *ceol gehladenne heahgestreonum* is a rather inferior imitation of Beowulf. Why should the ship of the Lord, ready to take the apostles on board for their mission to the foreign country, be loaded with treasures? But in Beowulf the phrase is quite appropriate in the account of the chieftain's vessel, containing weapons and ornaments in accordance with his rank.

The end of the description of the voyage in Elene seems also to have a specific source:

El. 250 b ff

<pre>
                                Ceolas leton
            æt sæfearoðe,   sunde bewrecene,
            ald yðliodu,   oncrum fæste
            on brime bidan   beorna geþinges.
</pre>

Beow. 397 f   *lætað hildebord   her onbidan,*
                  wudu wælsceaftas   worda geþinges.

(SARRAZIN, Anglia IX, p. 515, BS p. 110.) Cynewulf is here fairly independent of the earlier poem. The compound series in Beowulf he changes to the full type, in conformity with his usage: in Beowulf the passage is an order, part of the important episode describing Beowulf's arrival in Hroðgar's court; in Elene the voyage is at an end and the full passage is there as a kind of conclusion.

El. 256 ff   *Ðær wæs on eorle   eðgesyne*
                  brogden byrne   ond bill gecost,
                  geatolic guðscrud,   grimhelm manig,
                  ænlic eoforcumbul.

Beow. 1243 b ff

> þær on bence wæs
> ofer æþelinge   yþgesene
> heaposteapa helm,   hringed byrne,
> þrecwudu þrymlic.

(SARRAZIN, Anglia IX, p. 516, BS p. 110.) Here, also, the correspondence is not too striking; Cynewulf employs the passage with a certain freedom. Both sentences are full, as fitting in a description; and Cynewulf uses the depiction of the retainers in the meadhall for an appropriate end: a rapid look at the warriors in the military expedition to the land of the Jews.

El. 332   *Elene maþelode   ond for eorlum spræc*

Beow. 1215   *Wealhðeo maþelode,   heo fore þæm werede spræc.*

(SARRAZIN, Anglia IX, p. 516.) Each half-line may have been a formula, but the combination of both was probably the act of a single poet. Cynewulf's dependence on the Beowulf passage seems fairly certain.

El. 776 b ff

> gif he þin nære
> sunu synna leas,   næfre he soðra swa feala
> in woruldrice   wundra gefremede
> dogorgerimum ...

Beow. 590 ff

> Secge ic þe to soðe,   sunu Ecglafes,
> þæt næfre Grendel swa fela   gryra gefremede,
> atol æglæca   ealdre þinum,
> hynðo on Heorote,   gif þin hige wære ...
>
> (searogrim)

(Beow. 591 — El. 778: SARRAZIN, BS p. 123.) It is tempting to assume an influence from Beowulf here: the structure of the two passages is identical, and verbal correspondences such as *gif he þin nære — gif þin hige wære; næfre he soðra swa feala ... gefremede — ... to soðe ... næfre ... swa fela ... gefremede* are hardly accidental. The interesting point here, if the Elene passage really is a borrowing, is the different context and the different structure to which the borrowing has been adapted. The Beowulf lines are part of the hero's mordant reply to Unferð in the dispute about the swimming-match with Breca, and in the sub-clauses of the complex section the poet accumulates sarcastic sallies; in Elene, on the contrary, the lines are part of an extensive and very intricate series, a prayer telling us, in elaborate yet balanced periods, of God's power and Christ's mission. Thus we see the later poet, as on many other occasions, bending the borrowed poetic material to his own personal basic design.

El. 961 b ff

> *Gode þancode,*
> *wuldorcyninge,   þæs hire se willa gelamp*
> *þurh bearn godes   bega gehwœðres,*
> *ge æt þære gesyhðe   þœs sigebeames,*
> *ge ðœs geleafan ...*

Beow. 625 b ff

> *Gode þancode*
> *wisfæst wordum   þœs ðe hire se willa gelamp,*
> *þæt heo on œnigne   eorl gelyfde*
> *fyrena frofre.*

(SARRAZIN, Anglia IX, p. 516, BS p. 110.) In both passages a woman is the subject; Cynewulf in this borrowing seems considerate of the context in Beowulf. In both passages the sentences are full, but Cynewulf has made his borrowing the object of further elaboration with two members, constructed in different ways, added epexegetically to *bega gehwœðres*. The *æt*-construction interrupts the genitival series, thereby creating a certain variety.

El. 1271 b ff

> *... winde geliccost,*
> *þonne he for hœleðum   hlud astigeð,*
> *wœðeð be wolcnum,   wedende fœreð*
> *ond eft semninga   swige gewyrðeð,*
> *in nedcleofan   nearwe geheaðrod,*
> *þream forþrycced.*

COOK's reference, EPh, to the account of Aeolus and his winds in the Æneid I, 50—63, is interesting and the correspondence especially striking between l. 1275—76 b and the Æneid 54:

> *imperio premit ac vinclis et carcere frenat.*

But the first lines of the passage in Elene seem to correspond more closely to Beow. 1373 ff

> *þonon yðgeblond   up astigeð*
> *won to wolcnum,   þonne wind styreþ*
> *lað gewidru etc.*

(SARRAZIN BS, p. 123.) The metaphor in Elene (*landes frætwe gewitaþ under wolcnum winde geliccost*) is one of the boldest in the poem and hardly equalled in any of the other Cynewulfian texts (apart from the acrostic in the Fates, cp. p. 259). It seems as if the poet was tempted by his erudition to this all but immoderate display of rhetoric, which is rather in the manner of the Andreas author.

Beowulf and Juliana, as may be expected, contain few parallel passages. Apart from some formulas like *gimfæste gife* and *þreaned þolian* one can speak of real parallelism only in the following cases:

Jul. 55 f   *Næfre þu þæs swiðlic   sar gegearwast*
                 þurh hæstne nið   heardra wita

Beow. 1333 b ff   *Heo þa fæhðe wræc,*
       þe þu gystran niht   Grendel cwealdest
       þurh hæstne had   heardum clammum.

(SARRAZIN, Anglia IX, p. 517, BS p. 112.) There is not much to say about this parallel, except that the Juliana passage seems only to be a reminiscence of the phrase in Beowulf.

Jul. 64 b f   *Hæðne wæron begen,*
           synnum seoce,   sweor ond aþum ...

Beow. 769 b f   *Yrre wæron begen,*
      reþe renweardas.

(SARRAZIN, Anglia IX, p. 545.) This parallel is of the same type as Jul. 55 ff.

The author of Christ, certainly, had not much of Beowulf in his mind. (The numerous "parallels" quoted by SARRAZIN BS, pp. 112 ff, 124 ff, seem nearly all to be formularly phrases.) The correspondences here are of the same slight nature as in Juliana and need hardly any comment.

Chr. 520 f   *ealra sigebearna   þæt seleste*
                ond æþeleste,   þe ge her on stariað

Beow. 2794 ff   *Ic ðara frætwa   Frean ealles ðanc,*
                Wuldurcyninge   wordum secge,
                ecum Dryhtne,   þe ic her on starie ...

(SARRAZIN, BS, p. 113.) It is remarkable that the phrase in Beowulf occurs in a context with a Christian note and so fits well into Cynewulf's poem.

Chr. 616 f
ond geþingade   þeodbuendum
wið fæder swæsne   fæhþa mæste ...

Beow. 459   Gesloh þin fæder   fæhðe mæste.

(SARRAZIN, Anglia IX, p. 545; BS p. 124.) Here the heathen idea is reshaped to fit into quite an opposite Christian context.

SARRAZIN, Anglia XIV, p. 409 ff, has called attention to some interesting passages in Christ II and Beowulf. In Chr. 681 b ff Cynewulf speaks about the gifts from God:

Swa se waldend us,
godbearn on grundum,   his giefe bryttað.
Nyle he ængum anum   ealle gesyllan
gæstes snyttru,   þy læs him gielp sceþþe ...

Beow. 1724 b ff   Wundor is to secganne,
hu mihtig God   manna cynne
þurh sidne sefan   snyttru bryttað ...

Here, as also SARRAZIN admits, it is chiefly the ideas of the passages that are similar. However, a few lines further down Cynewulf continues: (759 b ff):

He his aras þonan,
halig of heahðu,   hider onsendeð,
þa us gescildaþ   wið sceþþendra
eglum earhfarum,   þi læs unholdan
wunde gewyrcen,   þonne wrohtbora
in folc godes   forð onsendeð
of his brægdbogan   biterne stræl.

And similarly Beowulf, 1743 b ff:

bona swiðe neah,
se þe of flanbogan   fyrenum sceoteð.
Ðonne bið on hreþre   under helm drepen
biteran stræle   — him bebeorgan ne con —,
wom wundorbebodum   wergan gastes.

A third parallel follows (pointed out by KLAEBER, p. CXII); Chr. 811 b f

Beow. 1755 b ff

Brond biƍ on tyhte,
æleƍ ealdgestreon *unmurnlice ...*

fehƍ oƥer to,
se ƥe unmurnlice *madmas dæleƥ,*
eorles ærgestreon ...

SARRAZIN makes the following comment on the parallels mentioned by him: "Wer nun noch berücksichtigt, dass drei gedanken, welche im Cri. bald aufeinander folgen: 1) die mahnung daran, dass die geistesgaben ein geschenk gottes sind (Cri 681), 2) die warnung vor übermut (Cri 684), 3) die anspielung auf die pfeile des teuflischen feindes (Cri 762 ff) auch im Beow. eng verkettet sind, und zwar in derselben reihenfolge (B. 1725—1740—1744), wird zugeben müssen, dass diese combination von übereinstimmungen nicht zufällig sein kann, dass vielmehr die eine dichtung notwendig durch die andere beeinflusst sein muss" (p. 410). KLAEBER speaks of the same order of the parallels and repeats SARRAZIN's final argument: "the natural supposition had been that the author of a strictly religious poem (Christ) was more likely to have offered the results of a first-hand theological study than the author of our heroic epic, scholar though he was". Though KLAEBER rejects SARRAZIN's theory that Cynewulf was the redactor of Beowulf, he discusses the possibility "that the homiletic part of Hroƍgar's address might have been interpolated by Cynewulf or, in fact, by somebody familiar with Cynewulf's poetry" (p. CXIII). However, KLAEBER seems more inclined to accept COOK's opinion (Trans. Con. Ac. XXVII, p. 385 ff) that the Beowulf redactor, in the passages about the distribution of gifts and the danger of pride, drew directly from passages in Gregory.

Now, SARRAZIN and KLAEBER have overlooked an important fact: the ideas about God's gifts and the danger of pride are also met with in the Gifts of Men, and in the same order as in Beowulf and Christ II (l. 3 b ff:)

... swa her weoruda god,
meotud meahtum swiƍ, *monnum dæleƍ,*
syleƍ sundorgiefe, *sendeƍ wide*
agne spede, *ƥara æghwylc mot*
dryhtwuniendra *dæl onfon.*

(18 ff) ... *Nænig eft ƥæs swiƥe* *ƥurh snyttrucræft*
in ƥeode ƥrym *ƥisses lifes*

forð gestigeð,   þæt him folca weard
þurh his halige giefe   hider onsende
wise geþohtas   ond woruldcræftas,
under anes meaht   ealle forlæte,
þy læs he for wlence   wuldorgeofona ful,
mon mode swið   of gemete hweorfe
ond þonne forhycge   heanspedigran.

It will be seen that the similarity between this passage and Christ II is much closer than the similarity between Christ II and Beowulf: whereas it is expressly said, in the Gifts of Men and in Christ II, that God does not bestow too many gifts on man lest he be arrogant and presumptuous, the Beowulf passage ll. 1728 ff, on the contrary, lets us know that sometimes God distributes wealth and happiness so lavishly that the receiver becomes the victim of pride and haughtiness:

Hwilum he on lufan   læteð hworfan
monnes modgeþonc   mæran cynnes,
seleð him on eþle   eorþan wynne
to healdanne   hleoburh wera,
gedeð him swa gewealdene   worolde dælas,
side rice,   þæt he his selfa ne mæg
his unsnyttrum   ende geþencean.
Wunað he on wiste;   no hine wiht dweleð
adl ne yldo,   ne him inwitsorh
on sefan sweorceð,   ne gesacu ohwær
ecghete eoweð,   ac him eal worold
wendeð on willan;   he þæt wyrse ne con —,
oð þæt him on innan   oferhygda dæl
weaxeð ond wridað etc.

Then the moment for the devil's attack has come. We can, consequently, hardly speak of real correspondences between the passages in Christ II and Beowulf. The ideas referred to may have been a favourite topic in contemporary poetry.

As for the other two passages, there is nothing to prevent us from the natural conclusion that Cynewulf was inspired by Beowulf — I should not say that he b o r r o w e d the passage about the devil's shafts, for there are no verbal correspondences. But finding the passage in Beowulf, it is only natural that he should use the same idea, which, by the way, recurs in Juliana 382 ff, 402 ff, 651 f. It may have been derived from Jerome, cp. p. 30 f. KLAEBER's remark that the priority is more likely to be Cynewulf's is a piece of somewhat theoretical reasoning: if the author of Christ II was inspired by anything in Beowulf, it is natural that he should select passages of a pious nature rather than others, as, in fact, we have often seen him do.

Ll. 811 b f in Christ II seem to be a real borrowing from Beowulf 1755 b ff.

Cynewulf's dependence on Beowulf can be said, on the whole, to be considerable; in the cases where he borrows from the earlier epic, however, the reminiscences are often slight, the borrowed piece of language is sometimes further elaborated, the heathen matter used for Christian ends or fitted into a corresponding warlike context; the adopted matter blends well with Cynewulf's own style.

The Fates of the Apostles suggests a general dependence on the old heroic poetry in its warlike representation of the apostles fighting paganism and idolatry. We chiefly find parallels between this poem and Beowulf, such as

Fates 1 ff
Hwæt! Ic þysne sang   siðgeomor fand
on seocum sefan,   samnode wide
hu þa æðelingas   ellen cyðdon,
torhte ond tireadige.

Beow. 1 ff
Hwæt, we Gar-Dena   in geardagum
þeodcyninga   þrym gefrunon,
hu ða æþelingas   ellen fremedon.

Fates 59 b f
Sweordræs fornam
þurh hæðene hand,   þær se halga gecrang ...

Beow. 557 b f
heaþoræs fornam
mihtig meredeor   þurh mine hand.

Fates 82 b f
... þa gedæled wearð
lif wið lice ...

Beow. 731 f
mynte þæt he gedælde ...   anra gehwylces
lif wið lice ...

(SIEVERS, Btr. IX, 135, KRAPP A p. 160 ff, BRANDL p. 1009.) There may also be some influence from Daniel in ll. 47 f:

forþan he ða hæðengild   hyran ne wolde,
wig weorðian ...

Dan. 207   *þa þis hegan ne willað,   ne þysne wig wurðigean.*

(KRAPP A p. 162.) But isolated phrases that are also to be found in
other poems, such as *dryhtne gecorene* (5 b, Dan. 150), *Lof wide
sprang* (6 b, *blæd wide sprang* Beow. 18), *frame, fyrdhwate* (12 a,
Beow. 1641) etc. may equally well have been common poetical
property.

There are the following parallels between the Cædmon group and
the Cynewulf canon:

El. 69 ff   *Ða wearð on slæpe   sylfum ætywed*
þam casere,   þær he on corðre swæf,
sigerofum gesegen   swefnes woma.
Ðuhte him wlitescyne   on weres hade
hwit ond hiwbeorht   hæleða nathwylc
geywed ...   ... He of slæpe onbrægd,
eofurcumble beþeaht.
                ... Ðu to heofenum beseoh
on wuldres weard;   þær ðu wraðe findest,
sigores tacen.   ... Cyning wæs þy bliðra ...
... Heht þa onlice   æðelinga hleo,
beorna beaggifa ...   ... tacen gewyrcan.
Heht þa on uhtan   mid ærdæge
wigend wreccan ...

Dan. 495 ff   *Ða him wearð on slæpe   swefen ætywed,*
Nabochodonossor;   him þæt neh gewearð.
Ðuhte him þæt on foldan   fægre stode
wudubeam wlitig ...   ... Ðær he to geseah,
þuhte him þæt se wudubeam   wilddeor scylde ...
Ðuhte him þæt engel   ufan of roderum
stigan cwome   and stefne abead,
torhtan reorde.   Het þæt treow ceorfan ...
... Het þonne besnædan   seolfes blædum,
twigum and telgum,   and þeh tacen wesan ...
... Ða of slæpe onwoc,   (swefn wæs æt ende),
eorðlic æðeling,   him þæs egesa stod ...

Dan. 108 ff

Ða þam folctogan   on frumslæpe,
siððan to reste gehwearf   rice þeoden,
com on sefan hwurfan   swefnes woma ...
... Weard him on slæpe   soð gecyðed
þætte rices gehwæs   reðe sceolde gelimpan,
eorðan dreamas,   ende wurðan.
Ða onwoc wulfheort,   se ær wingal swæf.
Babilone weard.   Næs him bliðe hige ...

El. 326 ff

Hio þa on þreate   M manna
fundon ferhðgleawra,   þa þe fyrngemynd
mid Iudeum   gearwast cuðon.
Ðrungon þa on þreate   þær on þrymme bad
in cynestole   caseres mæg,
geatolic guðcwen   golde gehyrsted.

Dan. 88 ff

Ða hie þær fundon   þry freagleawe
æðele cnihtas   and æfæste,
ginge and gode   in godsæde; ...
... Ða þry comon   to þeodne foran,
hearde and higeþancle,   þær se hæðena sæt,
cyning corðres georn,   in Caldea byrig.

It seems difficult to deny that there is a fairly obvious connection between the passages in Elene and those of the earlier epic. Not only do we find that the general structure but also that the details in Daniel recur in Cynewulf's poem. To begin with the first section, the dream; the Elene passage corresponds to two paragraphs in the Cædmon poem, Nebuchadnezzar's two dreams. The Daniel poet, to a great extent, repeats himself, and his two versions are very much alike, but Elene bears closer resemblance to the second version, in general and in detail. El.: *Ða weard on slæpe sylfum ætywed þam casere* — Dan. *Ða him weard on slæpe swefen ætywed, Nabochodonossor*; El. *Ðuhte him wlitescyne on weres hade ... hæleða nathwylc geywed* — Dan. *Ðuhte him þæt on foldan fægre stode wudubeam wlitig*; *Ðuhte him þæt engel ... stigan cwome*; El. *Ðu to heofenum beseoh* — Dan. *Ðær he to geseah*; El. *He of slæpe onbrægd, eofurcumble beþeaht* — Dan. *Ða of slæpe onwoc, eorðlic æðeling*; El. *Heht þa onlice æðelinga hleo ... tacen gewyrcan* — Dan. *Het þæt treow ceorfan ... Het þonne besnædan ... and þeh tacen wesan.* A detail linking the Elene passage up with the first section in

Daniel, is El. *Cyning wæs þy bliðra* — Dan. *Næs him bliðe hige.*
It is interesting to note that this detail gives a different meaning in
Elene. Whereas in Daniel details of the description are repeated:
*Ðuhte him . . . wudubeam — þuhte him þæt se wudubeam . . ., Het . . .
ceorfan — Het . . . besnædan*, the episode is told straightforwardly
and without delay in Elene, from the appearance of the vision to
the command about the Cross. We also notice how the poetic material,
in Cynewulf's hands, is made to yield a significance that it does not
possess in the original: the ominous message in Daniel turns to the
emperor's joy in Elene.

The second section offers striking similarities in details: El. *fundon
ferhðgleawra* — Dan. *fundon . . . freagleawe*; El. *Ðrungon . . . þær on
þrymme bad . . . caseres mæg* — Dan. *comon . . . þær se hæðena sæt,
cyning corðres georn.*

It is quite natural that Cynewulf should have availed himself of
Daniel when composing these episodes. In the Cædmon poem the
context is almost identical and the phrasing suitable for Cynewulf's
purposes. If there really is a borrowing here — and this can hardly
be doubted — we have an instance of how borrowing may improve
poetic matter; how, out of repetitions and barren lines, coherent and
rich poetry may be created.

El. 18 b ff
*Him wæs hild boden,
wiges woma.   Werod samnodan
Huna leode   ond Hreðgotan,
foron fyrdhwate   Francan ond Hugas.*

Gen. 1960 ff
*Ða ic aldor gefrægn   Elamitarna
fromne folctogan,   fyrd gebeodan
Orlahomar;   him Ambrafel
of Sennar   side worulde
for on fultum.*

Dan. 4 ff
*. . . siððan þurh metodes mægen   on Moyses hand
wearð wig gifen,   wigena mænieo,
and hie of Egyptum   ut aforon,
mægene micle.*

The pattern in the description of the beginning of the war in Elene
may be traced to the Cædmon poems. The first unit in the series sets
forth the "declaration of war" in general terms: Elene *wæs hild
boden*. Genesis 1961 *fromne folctogan fyrd gebeodan*, Dan. 5 *wearð*

wig gifen. Then follows a second unit describing the immediate consequence of the state of war, in all three cases containing a form of *faran.* The passage in Elene is most similar to the one in Daniel, but unlike this paragraph, it is part of a compound series.

El. 22 ff
Wæron hwate weras,
gearwe to guðe.   Garas lixtan,
wriðene wælhlencan.   Wordum ond bordum
hofon herecombol . . .
For folca gedryht.   Fyrdleoð agol
wulf on wealde,   wælrune ne mað.
Urigfeðera   earn sang ahof,
laðum on laste . . .

" 109 b ff
　　　　　　　　　Byman sungon
hlude for hergum.   Hrefn weorces gefeah,
urigfeðra,   earn sið beheold,
wælhreowra wig.   Wulf sang ahof,
holtes gehleða.

Ex. 156 ff
(hie gesawon) fyrd Faraonis   forð ongangan,
oferholt wegan,   eored lixan,
(garas trymedon,   guð hwearfode,
blicon bordhreoðan,   byman sungon) . . .
. . . Hreopon herefugolas,   hilde grædige,
deawigfeðere   ofer drihtneum,
wonn wælceasega.   Wulfas sungon
atol æfenleoð   ætes on wenan etc.

" 174 ff
Guðweard gumena   grimhelm gespeon,
cyning cinberge,   (cumbol lixton),
wiges on wenum,   wælhlencan sceoc etc.

Gen. 1982 ff
Foron þa tosomne   (francan wæron hlude)
wraðe wælherigas.   Sang se wanna fugel
under deoreðsceaftum,   deawigfeðera,
hræs on wenan.

Apart from the resemblance in pattern — short compound units — we notice the same order of the descriptions in the Cædmon poems and Elene, and the same details; first the warriors prepared for fight: El. *wæron hwate weras, gearwe to guðe*; Gen. *Foron þa tosomne (francan wæron hlude)*, Ex. *. . . fyrd Faraonis forð ongangan*; then the weapons; El. *garas lixtan, wridene wælhlencan. Wordum ond bordum hofon herecombol*, which seems to be a reminiscence of two Exodus passages: *eored lixan, (garas trymedon)*, and 175 b ff (*cumbol lixton), wiges on wenum, wælhlencan sceoc*. Then follows, in all three poems, the more conventional setting with the beasts of prey following the tracks of the armies. Whereas the Cædmon poems speak more in general of *herefugolas* (Ex.) and *se wanna fugel* (Gen.), Cynewulf goes into detail with *hrefn* and *earn*. The wolf is common with Exodus and Elene, in both cases singing its sinister dirge. In both Elene and the Cædmon poems the scene is very vivid, conveying to us the impression of brisk movement, the bustle and the hurried preparations for fight.

Jul. 563 b ff

                             Đa cwom engel godes
frætwum blican   ond þæt fyr tosceaf,
gefreode ond gefreoðade   facnes clæne,
leahtra lease,   ond þone lig towearp,
heorogiferne,   þær seo halie stod ...

Dan. 335 b ff

                             Đa of roderum wæs
engel ælbeorht   ufan onsended,
wlitescyne wer   on his wuldorhaman,
se him cwom to frofre   and to feorhnere
mid lufan and mid lisse.   Se ðone lig tosceaf,
halig and heofonbeorht,   hatan fyres ...

(Jul. 564 — Dan. 340 noted by KAIL, p. 24.) It can hardly be denied that Cynewulf is here strongly influenced by the earlier epic. What is most worth noticing, however, is the fact that Cynewulf avoids bodily taking over words and phrases but rather models his verse on the pattern of the Daniel passage. This is most apparent in lines 565—67, which have only the alliterative pattern and the general tenor in common with ll. 338—40 in Daniel. Cynewulf, by the way, is in no wise indebted to Cædmon for the whole of his version of the torture. In Daniel, as in Juliana, the hostile heathens become the victims of the flames (in Juliana the lead) and not the holy persons for whom the fire was intended; but we need only read ll. 586 b in Juliana and 247 b ff and 343 b—45 in Daniel to see the essential difference of form:

Jul. 586 b ff

                             Hæleð wurdon acle
arasad for þy ræse.   Đær on rime forborn

>*þurh þæs fires fnæst   fif ond hundseofontig*
>*hæðnes herges.*

Dan. 247 b ff

>*... oðþæt up gewat*
>*lig ofer leofum   and þurh lust gesloh*
>*micle mare   þonne gemet wære.*
>*Ða se lig gewand   on laðe men,*
>*hæðne of halgum.*

" 343 b f

>*ac he on andan sloh*
>*fyr on feondas   for fyrendædum.*

(Cp., however, Juliana 589 b ff and Daniel 435 ff, p. 271.)

Between Cynewulf's unquestioned poems there are the following certain corresponding passages:

El. 976 ff

>*ond wæs Iudeum   gnornsorga mæst*
>*werum wansæligum,   wyrda laðost,*
>*þær hie hit for worulde   wendan meahton ...*

Jul. 569 f

>*Ðæt þam weligan wæs   weorc to þolianne,*
>*þær he hit for worulde   wendan meahte ...*

(KAIL, p. 31.) This correspondence, by the way, is of interest for textual criticism: as KRAPP-DOBBIE say, ... "the close similarity ... makes it reasonably certain that no emendation is necessary in either place". Earlier critics read *þæt* for *þær* and put in a *ne* before *meahte* and *meahton*. But the phrases probably mean: "if they only had been able to prevent it!", describing the grief and deception of the defeated enemies of the Christian party in the legends.

El. 479 b f

>*þeah he sume hwile*
>*on galgan his   gast onsende*

Jul. 310

>*þæt he of galgan his   gæst onsende.*

(BUTTENWIESER, p. 37.) The same phrase occurs also in Andreas 1327.

El. 574 f

>*Ic eow to soðe   secgan wille,*
>*ond þæs in life   lige ne wyrðeð ...*

Jul. 132 f

>*Ic þe to soðe   secgan wille,*
>*bi me lifgendre   nelle ic lyge fremman.*

El. 816 ff   *... þæt ðu ma ne sie   minra gylta,*
                    þara þe ic gefremede   nalles feam siðum,
                    metud, gemyndig.

Jul. 354   *(yfla gehwylces) þara þe ic gefremede   nalæs feam siðum*
The passage is met with in Andreas 605 (KRAPP A, p. 112).

El. 250 b ff   *Ceolas leton,*
           æt sæfearoðe,   sunde bewrecene,
           ald yðliodu,   oncrum fæste ...

Chr. 862 f   *hwær we sælan sceolon   sundhengestas,*
           ealde yðmearas,   ancrum fæste.

El. 1004 f   *(gif hie) ...gesundne sið   settan mosten,*
           hæleð hwætmode,   to þære halgan byrig.

Chr. 460 b f   *Sona wæron gearwe,*
          hæleð mid hlaford,   to þære halgan byrg.

(KAIL, p. 31.)

But the most important correspondence between the four poems of the Cynewulf canon are the acrostics:

El. 1256 b ff   *A wæs secg oð ðæt*
              cnyssed cearwelmum,   ᚻ drusende,
              þeah he in medohealle   maðmas þege,
              æplede gold.   ᛗ gnornode
              ᚾ gefera,   nearusorge dreah,
              enge rune,   þær him ᛗ fore
              milpaðas mæt,   modig þrægde
              wirum gewlenced.   ᚹ is geswiðrad,
              gomen æfter gearum,   geogoð is gecyrred,
              ald onmedla.   ᚢ wæs geara
              geogoðhades glæm.   Nu synt geardagas
              æfter fyrstmearce   forð gewitene,
              lifwynne geliden,   swa ᛚ toglideð,
              flodas gefysde.   ᚠ æghwam bið
              læne under lyfte.

Jul. 703 b ff   *Geomor hweorfeð*
              ·ᚻ·ᛗ· *ond* ·ᚾ·   *Cyning biþ reþe,*

sigora syllend,   þonne synnum fah

·ᛗ·ᛈ· ond ·ᚢ·   acle bidað

hwæt him æfter dædum   deman wille

lifes to leane.   ·ᚱ·ᚣ· beofað,

seomað sorgcearig.

Chr. 797 ff

Đonne ·ᚻ· cwacað,   gehyreð cyning mæðlan,

rodera ryhtend,   sprecan reþe word

þam þe him ær in worulde   wace hyrdon,

þendan ·ᚺ· ond ᚾ.   yþast meahtan

frofre findan.   Đær sceal forht monig

on þam wongstede   werig bidan

hwæt him æfter dædum   deman wille

wraþra wita.   Biþ se ·ᛈ· scæcen

eorþan frætwa.   ·ᚢ· wæs longe

·ᚱ· flodum bilocen,   lifwynna dæl,

·ᚣ· on foldan.

Fates 98 b ff

    ᚣ þær on ende standeþ,

eorlas þæs on eorðan brucaþ.   Ne moton hie awa

               ætsomne,

woruldwunigende;   ᚹ sceal gedreosan,

ᚢ on eðle,   æfter tohreosan

læne lices frætewa,   efne swa ᚱ toglideð.

⟨Đonne ᚻ ond ᚺ⟩   cræftes neosað

nihtes nearowe,   on him ⟨ᚾ ligeð,

cy⟩ninges þeodom.

We will not here discuss the interpretation of the runes or of the autobiographical problem of the passages. The corruption in the Fates is generally restored as above. These passages, it will be seen, can be divided into two groups. One group is formed by the section in Christ and Juliana and treats of the Day of Judgment. The similarity between these passages is obvious though it is restricted to certain verbal correspondences: Jul. *cyning biþ reþe* — Chr. *cyning ... sprecan reþe word*; Jul. *acle bidað hwæt him æfter dædum deman wille lifes to leane* — Chr. *sceal werig bidan hwæt him æfter dædum deman wille wraþra wita*; Jul. ·ᚱ·ᚣ· *beofað* — Chr. *Đonne* ·ᚻ· *cwacað*. (ᚱᚣ = *licfæt* (Trautmann K p. 49); ᚻ = *cene* (Gollancz C).) But if there is nothing clumsy or inconsistent about Cynewulf's manner of repeating himself here, the same can hardly be said of the repetitions in the second group, the acrostics in Elene and

Fata, which deal, chiefly, with the transitoriness of youth and wordly joy, cp. BROWN, Engl. Stud. XXXVIII, p. 201. The details in the Fates are of a quality below the corresponding ones in Elene; in fact, they are fairly surprising in a poem signed by Cynewulf. Elene has *Nu synt geardagas ... forð gewitene, lifwynne geliden ... swa* ᚱ *(lagu,* ZUPITZA) *toglideð* — Fata ᚹ *(wyn,* SIEVERS, Anglia XIII, p. 3) *sceal gedreosan,* ᚢ *(ur,* COSIJN, CR, p. 57) *on eðle, æfter tohreosan læne lices frætewa, efne swa* ᚱ *toglideð.* We notice the great difference of style: the passage in the Fates is written in the Gnomic manner otherwise alien to Cynewulf. *Sceal* has a general sense quite different from the sense in Christ 801 ff. *Ðær sceal forht monig ... bidan,* where it means "on that occasion shall ...". We further notice the doubtful metaphor in the Fates: "joy decays just as water glides away", a metaphor that only fits in with the conception of the lapse of time, not with the idea of decay and deterioration. Such a mixture of ideas is not to be found in the passage in Elene; here the *geardagas gewitene, lifwynne geliden* fit in quite well with *lagu toglideð.* The text which follows is not so corrupt that we are unable to draw conclusions as to its meaning, and it seems as if it contains some rather doubtful ideas: *cræftes neosað nihtes nearowe, on him* ᚾ *(nyd,* TRAUTMANN K, p. 54) *ligeð, cy)ninges þeodom* seems to imply some conception of distress and servitude under God. If these lines are intended to describe the Judgment Day, which is probable, their vagueness and obscurity is obvious, not least when they are compared with the sections on the same theme in Elene. 104 a is not very well adapted to the context, unlike Elene 1239 a *(geþanc reodode nihtes nearwe).* The beginning of the section, again, is not of a kind that we are used to in Cynewulf. In ᚠ *þær on ende standeþ* the poet expressly states the function of the acrostic as being that of revealing his name, a statement repeated at l. 105 b ff. *Nu ðu cunnon miht hwa on þam wordum wæs werum oncyðig.* The acrostics in the other poems, however, are woven into extensive descriptions of the Doom and the decay of life, the author's name appears to the reader in an indirect way and is never, in the blunt manner of the Fates, directly demonstrated by the poet.

There is yet another parallel between the Fates and one of Cynewulf's poems to be noticed in this connection. The end of the Fates, as is well known, contains two requests to the reader to pray for the soul of the author of the poem; one ll. 88 ff

> *Nu ic þonne bidde   beorn se ðe lufige*
> *þysses giddes begang   þæt he geomrum me*
> *þone halgan heap   helpe bidde,*
> *friðes ond fultomes   Hu, ic freonda beþearf*
> *liðra on lade,   þonne ic sceal langne ham,*
> *eardwic uncuð,   ana gesecan,*
> *lætan me on laste   lic, eorðan dæl,*
> *wælreaf wunigean   weormum to hroðre.*

And one ll. 107 ff:

> *Sie þæs gemyndig,   mann se ðe lufige*
> *þisses galdres begang,   þæt he geoce me*
> *ond frofre fricle.   Ic sceall feor heonan,*
> *an elles forð,   eardes neosan,*
> *sið asettan,   nat ic sylfa hwær,*
> *of þisse worulde.   Wic sindon uncuð,*
> *eard ond eðel,   swa bið ælcum menn*
> *nemþe he godcundes   gastes bruce.*

We will not here discuss or decide whether this double epilogue is "inartistic" (SIEVERS, Anglia XIII, 24, TRAUTMANN, Anglia Beibl. VI. 21, KRAPP A p. XLV) or "in no structural sense inartistic" (KENNEDY p. 232) — this is a matter of taste. But two facts must be considered: first, that Cynewulf is not in the habit of repeating himself in this insistent manner (ll. 696 and 722 in Juliana are not comparable to the extensive repetition in the Fates); secondly, that the repetition is all the more remarkable as there are two close parallels, as SIEVERS noticed (ibid. p. 23 f), in

Juliana: 699 b ff

> *Min sceal of lice*
> *sawul on siðfæt,   nat ic sylfa hwider,*
> *eardes uncyðþu;   of sceal ic þissum,*
> *secan operne   ærgewyrhtum,*
> *gongan iudædum;*

and 718 b ff

> *Bidde ic monna gehwone*
> *gumena cynnes,   þe þis gied wræce,*
> *þæt he mec neodful   bi noman minum*
> *gemyne modig,   ond meotud bidde*
> *þæt me heofona helm   helpe gefremme.*

The question is, how shall we interpret the existence of all these puzzling passages, the correspondences between the Fates on the one hand and Elene and Juliana on the other, and the double epilogue? They must, it seems, be indicative of the chronological relations of the Fates to Elene and Juliana. It is probable that the Fates was written after the two longer poems and that the author, feeling a certain lack of inspiration, reverted to some ideas in these earlier poems and made use of them a second time. But he had no longer the power of reshaping his ideas and making something new out of them; hence the lack of consistency l. 102 (*efne swa lagu toglideð*) and the repetition of the double epilogue. As for this repetition, it seems as if the poet has fused the two Juliana passages ll. 699 b ff and 718 b ff together, made alterations and expansions, and used his "borrowing" in two places.

An analysis of the parallels referred to in the Fates, then, tends to confirm SIEVER's theory (Anglia XIII, 11—15) that Elene and Juliana are the earliest poems. KENNEDY's objection (p. 200) that "Elene ... should be one of the earlier poems, whereas it is in this signature that the poet specifically dwells upon his age and describes himself near to death" is not relevant; we do not know how far this is merely subjective or perhaps poetically conventional. But there is an obvious lack of inspiration in the Fates, this short catalogue almost wholly founded on the old heroic tradition; perhaps the author was a very old man when the poem was written.

Between Cynewulf's poems and Andreas the following parallels exist:

Andreas and Elene.

Andr. 37 ff (*Syððan him geblendan ... dryas ... drync*)
            þæt hie ne murndan   æfter mandreame,
            hælep heorogrædige,   ac hie hig ond gærs
            for meteleaste   meðe gedrehte.

"Was soll dies heissen" exclaims BUTTENWIESER, p. 75, in commenting upon this passage; and we must admit that it does not give much sense. But one can disregard the objection that "der Satz passt nicht als Antithese zu dem vorhergehenden", although this may be true enough. What the poet wants to say here is that the human beings, transformed by the Mermedonians' magic potion into animals, had to change their food as well, eating hay and grass like cattle. What is disturbing here is *for meteleaste meðe*: the victims of the man-eaters cannot be weary for want of food when it is said, at the same time, that they get grass and hay to eat, the less so as they are changed to animals and have the needs of animals. In order to get some effective expression for the miserable condition of the Mermedonians' prisoners the author of Andreas has apparently borrowed from El. 611 ff:

<blockquote>

Hu mæg þæm geweorðan   þe on westenne
meðe ond meteleas   morland trydeð;
or 698   *(cleopigan ongan)   meðe ond meteleas,*
</blockquote>

where the words make perfect sense. Another absurd point in the Andreas passage is the combination *hæleþ heorogrædige*, which seems to refer to the prisoners but only would make sense referring to the man-eaters.

Another curious passage where the expression *meðe — meteleast* occurs is 1156 b ff:

<blockquote>

Hreopon friccan,
mændon meteleaste,   meðe stodon,
hungre gehæfte.   Hornsalu wunedon . . .
</blockquote>

Here the *meteleaste-meðe* is more suitable, but *Hreopon friccan* is loosely tacked on to the passage. In Elene 54 b it occurs in a natural context, the heralds summoning the warriors to battle, and 550 b, the queen's heralds summoning the Jews to a meeting.

Andr. 203 f   *Eala, Andreas,   þæt ðu a woldest*
þæs siðfætes   sæne weorþan!
"   211   *Ne meaht ðu þæs siðfætes   sæne weorðan . . .*
El. 219 b f   *Elene ne wolde*
þæs siðfætes   sæne weorðan . . .

(Buttenwieser, p. 32.)

Andr. 561 b ff   *Hæleð unsælige*
no ðær gelyfdon   in hira liffruman . . .
. . . þeah ðe he wundra feala   weorodum gecyðde;

El. 864 b ff   *. . . ond gebidan þær*
oððæt him gecyðde   cyning ælmihtig
wundor for weorodum . . .

(Buttenwieser, p. 33.)

Andr. 573 ff   *Hu mihte þæt gewyrðan   in werþeode,*
                      þæt ðu ne gehyrde   hælendes miht . . .

El. 643 ff   *Hu is þæt geworden   on þysse werþeode,*
                     þæt ge swa monigfeald   on gemynd witon . . .

(KRAPP A, p. 111.) In Elene *on þysse werþeode* has a distinct
meaning: How does it happen among this people that you know so
much, i. e. why does this people know so much (viz. about the Troian
war, while they do not know anything about the Cross of Christ).
In Andreas l. 573 is obviously an awkward borrowing of the Elene
passage, used as a sort of ingression to the following question but
almost meaningless: *on þysse werþeode* has no function whatever.

Andr. 577 ff   *Sealde he dumbum gesprec,   deafe gehyrdon,*
                    healtum ond hreofum   hyge blissode,
                    ða þe limseoce   lange wæron,
                    werige, wanhale,   witum gebundene,
                    æfter burhstedum   blinde gesegon.

El. 1212 b ff   *Oft him feorran to*
            laman, limseoce,   lefe cwomon,
            healte, heorudreorige,   hreofe ond blinde,
            heane, hygegeomre . . .

(BUTTENWIESER, p. 33.) Andreas 577 ff is an accumulation of in-
firmities in the manner favoured by this poet; in Elene, as one would
expect, there is more concentration. If the passage in Andreas is a
borrowing, which is probable, he took the *limseoce, healte, hreofe*
and *blinde* and made them the kernel of his miserable troop.

Andr. 595 f   *Nu ðu miht gehyran,   hyse leofesta,*
                   hu us wuldres weard   wordum ond dædum
                                           (lufode) . . .

  "   811 f   *Nu ðu miht gehyran,   hyse leofesta,*
                   hu he wundra worn   wordum cyðde . . .

El. 511 f   *Nu ðu meaht gehyran,   hæleð min se leofa.*
                   hu arfæst is   ealles wealdend . . .

(BUTTENWIESER, p. 34.)

Andr. 609 b ff   *Me þæt þinceð,*
            ðæt hie for æfstum   inwit syredon
            þurh deopne gedwolan.   Deofles larum

hæleð hynfuse   hyrdon to georne,
wraðum wærlogan.   Hie seo wyrd beswac,
forleolc ond forlærde.   Nu hie lungre sceolon,
werige mid werigum,   wræce þrowian,
biterne bryne   on banan fæðme.

El. 205 ff (se æðeling fand) hwær ahangen wæs   heriges beorhtme
on rode treo   rodora waldend
æfstum þurh inwit,   swa se ealda feond
forlærde ligesearwum,   leode fortyhte,
Iudea cyn,   þæt hie god sylfne
ahengon, herga fruman.   Ðæs hie in hynðum sculon
to widan feore   wergðu dreogan!

(BUTTENWIESER, p. 34.) The similarity between the latter passages is difficult to deny. Earlier on, ll. 557—571, Christ has asked for the reason why the Jews in general did not believe in Christ though He performed miracles before them, and also asked whether He really did perform any miracles (cp. p. 54). Now the lines here quoted make up a digression which does not at all cohere with what precedes and follows: they form the end of a speech in which Christ — the helmsman has just asked whether the miracles, perhaps, were performed only before the people and not before the priests and the chiefs (cp. p. 55). Andrew then answers that Christ did work them also before the chiefs. Ll. 609 b ff in Andreas are therefore illogical and unnecessary since there is no reason for the helmsman to enlarge upon the black sin and eternal death of the chiefs before he has heard that they did not believe in Christ although He worked miracles before them. Such a deviation is neither to be found in the Πράξεις nor in the Casanatensis. Besides, it is the apostle, not Jesus, who generally condemns the hostility and scepticism of the enemies of Christ. There can hardly be any doubt, therefore, that the poet took the passage over from Elene, and slightly changed its form, in order to get a bit of drastic description and emphatic language of the kind he is so fond of. In Elene, it will be observed, the lines fit perfectly well into the context: the recently converted emperor studies the Gospel and learns where the Cross can be found on which the perverted Jews, seduced by the devil, crucified the Lord, for which deed eternal damnation is the righteous punishment.

Andr. 693 b f   (Swa hleoðrodon ræswan),   dyrnan þohton
meotudes mihte.

El. 583 b f   *ne magon ge þa wyrd bemiðan,*
          bedyrnan þa deopan mihte.

(BUTTENWIESER, p. 35.)

Andr. 709 b ff   *Haliges lare*
          synnige ne swulgon,   þeah he soðra swa feala
          tacna gecyðde,   þær hie to segon.

El. 1104   *Leort ða tacen forð,   þær hie to sægon ...*

(BUTTENWIESER, p. 35.) The Andreas poet here gives up his habit
of using the word *wundor* for "miracle" (so ll. 564, 569, 584, 604, 620
twice, 699, 730, 736, 812). The use of *tacen*, here, seems due to influence from the line in Elene, where *tacen* is employed in the sense
"sign": the *lacende lig* reveals the spot where the holy nails lie
hidden.

Andr. 746 b ff   *Ge mon cigað*
          godes ece bearn,   þone þe grund ond sund,
          heofon ond eorðan   ond hreo wægas,
          salte sæstreamas   ond swegl uppe
          amearcode   mundum sinum.

El. 726 ff   *... ond þu geworhtest   þurh þines wuldres miht*
          heofon ond eorðan   ond holmþræce,
          sæs sidne fæðm,   samod ealle gesceaft,
          ond þu amæte   mundum þinum
          ealne ymbhwyrft   ond uprador.

(Andr. 750b—El. 729: KRAPP A, p. 118.) In Elene 726 ff we have
the order: Heaven — earth — sea — sea — summary — earth —
Heaven (cp. p. 190); in Andreas 746 ff this order is changed into the
monotonous: earth — sea — Heaven — earth — sea — sea —
Heaven. The passage in Andreas is probably a borrowing from the
other poem, and in trying to put it into its new context the poet has
lost the elaborate chiasmus in Elene.

Andr. 892 f   *Ða wæs modsefa   myclum geblissod*
          haliges on hreðre ...

El. 874 b f   *Ða ðær Iudas wæs*
          on modsefan   miclum geblissod.

(BUTTENWIESER, p. 35.)

Andr. 1201 ff
   Ða wæs beacen boden   burhsittendum,
   Ahleopon hildfrome   heriges brehtme
   ond to weallgeatum   wigend þrungon,
   cene under cumblum,   corðre mycle
   to ðam orlege,   ordum ond bordum.

This passage does not, as one might think, describe the doings of warriors preparing to defend their city against a siege. It corresponds to passages in P and B, telling us that after the devil had heard the voice of the invisible apostle, and when he had told the Mermedonians to search for Andrew, t h e y s h u t t h e g a t e s o f t h e c i t y and went looking for him. The man-eaters, then, went to the gates to prevent the apostle from escaping. But if this is so, what is the meaning and function of l. 1205? KRAPP A (p. 137) remarks that these passages in Andreas are ... "a confused reflection ... of its source"; but the confusion here seems due to special circumstances. I suspect that the unexpected hint at a battle, as in so many similar cases, is really an awkward borrowing. In Elene l. 18 b ff we read:

              Him wæs hild boden,
   wiges woma.   Werod samnodan
   Huna leode   ond Hreðgotan,
   foron fyrdhwate   Francan ond Hugas.
   Wæron hwate weras,
   gearwe to guðe.   Garas lixtan,
   wriðene wælhlencan.   Wordum ond bordum
   hofon herecombol.

This passage seems to have inspired the Andreas poet. To some extent he is successful: l. 1201 is no unfortunate rendering of the devil's command; the Mermedonians, further, are a warlike tribe, so *ahleopon hildfrome ... wigend þrungon, cene under cumblum* is as appropriate as Cynewulf's *werod samnodan ... foron fyrdhwate ... hofon herecombol.* But then the poet forgets the context. When he continues: *to ðam orlege, ordum ond bordum,* he is imitating Cynewulf's *gearwe to guðe ... Wordum ond bordum,* without considering that while the latter is speaking of the heathens' preparations for war, he himself was going to say that the man-eaters went out to bolt the gates.

Andr. 1311 f
   Ða com seofona sum   to sele geongan
   atol æglæca   yfela gemyndig ...

El. 900 f   *Ongan þa hleoðrian helledeofol,*
      eatol æclæca, yfela gemyndig.

(BUTTENWIESER, p. 36.)

Andr. 1632 b ff   *Ða se modiga het,*
    cyninges cræftiga, ciricean getimbran,
    gerwan godes tempel

El. 1006 ff *Heht hire þa aras eac gebeodan*
           ... þæt hio cirican þær
    ... getimbrede, tempel dryhtnes ...

(BUTTENWIESER, p. 37.)

Andr. 1687 f *Swylce se halga herigeas þreade,*
      deofulgild todraf ond gedwolan fylde.

El. 1041 b f *(He þæt betere geceas) ... ond þam wyrsan wiðsoc,*
      deofulgildum, ond gedwolan fylde ...

(BUTTENWIESER, p. 38.)

Andr. 1698   *Ongan hine þa fysan ond to flote gyrwan ...*
El. 225 f   *Ongan þa ofstlice eorla mengu*
      to flote fysan.

(BUTTENWIESER, p. 38.)

Andreas and Juliana have several passages in common:

Andr. 51 b f   *Hwæðre he in breostum þa git*
    herede in heortan heofonrices weard ...

Jul. 238 b f   *Symle heo wuldorcyning*
    herede æt heortan, heofonrices god ...

(BUTTENWIESER, p. 27.)

Andr. 54 ff *Eadig ond onmod, he mid elne forð*
     wyrðode wordum wuldres aldor,
     heofonrices weard, halgan stefne,
     of carcerne. Him wæs Cristes lof
     on fyrðlocan fæste bewunden.

Jul. 231 ff

ond he œdre het   eft asettan,
laðgeniðla,   ond gelœdan bibead
to carcerne.   Hyre wœs Cristes lof
in ferðlocan   fœste biwunden,
milde modsefan,   mœgen unbrice.

BUTTENWIESER draws attention to the similarity of the two latter passages, saying that "in der Jul. ein Vers mit Variation folgt, wodurch der Stil ein ganz anderes Gepräge erhält" (p. 64). It might be added that the style in Juliana is carefully elaborated so that the clause *Hyre wœs* etc. balances the preceding clauses and makes up a full conclusion. In Andreas, on the contrary, the sentence is shortened and loosely attached to the preceding periods; *of carcerne* stirring up reminiscences of the passage in Juliana. Further the antithesis in Juliana gets lost through the borrowing: while in Cynewulf's poem there is an important concessive relation between the clauses (though they threw her in prison yet she was steadfast in her belief), the lines 57b—58 in Andreas are only a cumbersome repetition of the idea in the preceding passage.

Andr. 1074 b ff

Him seo wen gelah,
syððan mid corðre   carcernes duru
eorre œscberend   opene fundon,
onhliden hamera geweorc,   hyrdas deade.

Jul. 236 f

Ða wœs mid clustre   carcernes duru
behliden, homra geweorc.

(BUTTENWIESER, p. 29.) The Andreas passage 1074 b ff has been mentioned as an instance of unessential variation (cp. p. 203), and in comparing it with the sentence in Juliana we apparently get the reason why the Andreas poet dwells with so much interest on the door of the prison that he forgets to emphasize the important *hyrdas deade*. In Juliana, of course, there can be no objection to *behliden homra geweorc.*

Andr. 1179 ff

Nu ge magon eaðe   oncyðdœda
wrecan on gewyrhtum.   Lœtað wœpnes spor,
iren ecgheard,   ealdorgeard sceoran,
fœges feorhhord.

Jul. 622 f

Lœtað hy lapra   leana hleotan
þurh wœpnes spor,   wrecað ealdne nið ...

(BUTTENWIESER, p. 30.) In Andreas *wæpnes spor* etc. has not much to do with what ensues: the apostle is not tortured by swords and spears. Apparently *wrecan* and *wæpnes spor* are inspired by the passage in Juliana, and then the latter words have been further expounded with *iren ecgheard*. In Cynewulf's legend the passage is on the contrary the introduction to the ensuing episode, since the saint is shortly afterwords executed by the sword.

Andr. 1288 ff   *swa ic þæt gefremme,   þenden feorh leofað,*
                   min on moldan,   þæt ic, meotud, þinum
                   larum leofwendum   lyt geswice.

Jul. 119 ff   *Ic þæt gefremme,   gif min feorh leofað,*
                   gif þu unrædes   ær ne geswicest ...
                   ... (þæt þu ... þurh deora gripe   deaþe sweltest).

(BUTTENWIESER, p. 30.) Here also, as in some preceding cases, the author of the longer epic has made some fairly forced and doubtful poetry out of lines which possess the vigour and clarity of the original. The passage in Juliana means, roughly: "as sure as I live, I shall see to it that you shall die ... if you do not abandon this folly". The expressive *gif min feorh leofað* in Juliana does not give much sense as it stands in Andreas, and *gefremman*, in the latter epic, is employed in a pressed and artificial manner, being followed by the blank litotes *þæt ic þinum larum ... lyt geswice*, which has the effect of an anticlimax. One may compare other instances of *þæt*-clauses after *gefremman* in Old English poetry, which always have a "positive" character.

The whole passage in Andreas is a weakened and diluted borrowing from Cynewulf.

Andr. 1317 b ff   *Hwær is wuldor þin,*
            þe ðu oferhigdum   upp arærdest,
            þa ðu goda ussa   gild gehnægdest?

Jul. 145 f   *... þe þu unsnyttrum   ær gespræce,*
                þa þu goda ussa   gield forhogdest.

(BUTTENWIESER, p. 30.) The emendation *gild* for *gilp* in Andreas (GREIN), in itself reasonable, is supported by the parallel passage in Juliana. Now the clause l. 1319 in Andreas scarcely gives any sense; apart from the queer logic of the passage it is hard to understand how the devil can reprove the apostle for breaking "the worship of our gods".. The words sound strange in the devil's mouth, and the apostle has as yet done nothing to prevent idolatry. But in Juliana the saint is persecuted partly just because she refuses to worship the heathen idols, and it is round this refusal that the plot, concluded by her martyrdom, is built up.

Andr. 1326 b f   (Ðone Herodes ealdre besnyðede,)   ... ond hine
                                                              rode befealg,
                   þæt he on gealgan   his gast onsende.

Jul. 481 b ff   Sume ic rode bifealh,
                   þæt hi hyra dreorge   on hean galgan
                   lif aletan.

"   310   (Andreas het ahon ...)   þæt he of galgan his
                                                       gæst onsende.
       (BUTTENWIESER, p. 30.)

Andr. 1429 f   Him þa stefn oncwæð,   stiðhycgendum,
                   wuldorcyninges   word hloðrode.

"   92 f   ... ða wearð gehyred   heofoncyninges stefn
                   wrætlic under wolcnum,   wordhleoðres sweg ...

Jul. 282 b f   Hyre stefn oncwæð
                   wlitig of wolcnum,   word hleoþrade.

(BUTTENWIESER, p. 27.) I have previously drawn attention to ll. 88—96 in Andreas, of which the second passage quoted above forms part (cp. p. 132). The unnecessary prolongation of the lines describing how the voice of God was heard seems partly due to a borrowing from Juliana; in the latter poem the corresponding passage has a shortness which suits its secondary importance.

Andr. 1462 b f   Ða com dryhten god
                   in þæt hlinræced,   hæleða wuldor ...

Jul. 242 b f   Ða cwom semninga
                   in þæt hlinræced   hæleða gewinna ...

       (BUTTENWIESER, p. 31.)

Andr. 1471 ff   Næs him gewemmed wlite,   ne wloh of hrægle
                   lungre alysed,   ne loc of heafde,

ne ban gebrocen,   ne blodig wund
lice gelenge,   ne laðes dœl
þurh dolgslege   dreore bestemed ...

Jul. 589 b ff

Ða gen sio halge stod
ungewemde wlite.   Nœs hyre wloh ne hrœgl,
ne feax ne fel   fyre gemœled,
ne lic ne leoþu.

(Buttenwieser, p. 31.) The relation between the latter two passages is somewhat complicated, in so far as some similar lines are to be found in Daniel 434 ff, where it is described how the three men are preserved by God in the fiery furnace:

wœron þa bende forburnene .... and hyra lice geborgen.
Nœs hyra wlite gewemmed   ne nœnig wroht on hrœgle,
ne feax fyre beswœled ...

Now the original of these passages, or at least of the last of them, is Dan. 3, 94: ... *capillus capitis eorum non esset adustus, et sarabala eorum non fuissent immutata, et odor ignis non transisset per eos.* Here we have the unharmed hair and the intact clothes. As for the different shapes of this passage in the Old English poems they may be adduced, if I am not mistaken, as instances of different stages of stylistic technique in this poetry. The Daniel passage can safely be taken as the earliest, and it comes closest to the Bible, though the unharmed parts of the body are enumerated in the inverse order. The language of this passage is the simplest; the adversative *and* brings out a laconic antithesis, and in spite of the full verses the passage has a certain inartistic moderation which is a feature characteristic of the poem. In Juliana there is more organized elaboration. We get the *ungewemmed wlite* as a general statement, then come the details, arranged from the external to the internal, as in Daniel, combined with a sequence from the smaller to the bigger, which order is inverted in the last half-line as a kind of chiasmus: fringe — garment; hair — skin; body — limbs. In Andreas the order is partly preserved and partly dissolved, and new details are added so that we get such a heap of injured parts of the body that the effect achieved by the enumeration ll. 1471—1475 is the very opposite of the purpose intended, viz. to emphasize the fact that the body was not injured. The language is doubtful: that a fringe is not *lungre alysed* from the garments is far from good since *lungre alysed* here describes a condition, not a process. Perhaps we have here an influence from Beowulf 1629 f

> Ða wæs of þæm hroran   helm ond byrne
> lungre alysed,

where the phrase fits in quite naturally, denoting a swift action. Ll. 1472 b—75 are obscure and overloaded. Even if we cannot exactly trace the affinities between the passages it seems very probable that the author of Andreas knew at least some of the other two; but between them and his own exuberant lines there is a great distance.

Andr. 1558 f   *Nu ge magon sylfe   soð gecnawan,*
                  þæt we mid unrihte ...

Jul. 341 b f   *Nu þu sylfa meaht*
        on sefan þinum   soð gecnawan ...

Parallels in Andreas and Christ II:

Andr. 130   *þa þe on carcerne   clommum fæste ...*

Chr. 734 b f   *þær he gen ligeð*
        in carcerne   clommum gefæstnad ...

(BUTTENWIESER, p. 39.)

Andr. 250 ff   *Wæron hie on gescirplan   scipferendum,*
            eorlas onlice   ealiðendum,
            þonne hie on flodes fæðm   ofer feorne wæg
            on cald wæter   ceolum lacað.

Chr. 850 f   *Nu is þon gelicost   swa we on laguflode*
        ofer cald wæter   ceolum liðan ...

(BUTTENWIESER, p. 39.) In Cynewulf's poem the passage plays an important part, symbolizing as it does the perilous course of life; in Andreas the corresponding lines are a mere digression, the main point being l. 250 *Wæron hie on gescirplan scipferendum* and the variational line 251.

Andr. 313 b ff   *Is se drohtað strang*
        þam þe lagolade   lange cunnaþ

Chr. 856   *(windge holmas) ofer deop gelad.   Wæs se*
                                      drohtað strong ...

(BUTTENWIESER, p. 39.)

Andr. 332 ff   *Farað nu geond ealle   eorðan sceatas,*
                emne swa wide   swa wæter bebugeð,
                oððe stedewangas   stræte gelicgaþ.
                Bodiað æfter burgum   beorhtne geleafan
                ofer foldan fæðm.   Ic eow freoðo healde.
                Ne ðurfan ge on þa fore   frætwe lædan,
                gold ne seolfor.

Chr. 481 ff   *Farað nu geond ealne   yrmenne grund,*
                geond widwegas,   weoredum cyðað,
                bodiað ond bremað   beorhtne geleafan
                ond fulwiað   folc under roderum.
                      ... Ic eow mid wunige,
                forð on frofre,   ond eow friðe healde.

(BUTTENWIESER, p. 40.) The passage in Andreas is put in to explain why the apostle and his disciples have no money with them: the Lord had ordered them not to bring any possessions with them when preaching to the people. This prohibition, then, is the main point, the preaching the secondary point, as is the case in the other versions: P: "When you go out preaching, do not bring money with you nor bread nor scrip" etc. C: *quando pergeremus ad predicandum evangelium eius, ne portaremus nobiscum nec pecuniam neque peram neque panem* etc. We shall soon point out the dependence of the Andreas passage on Beowulf, involving a digression on the question where the apostles will lead their mission; the dependence on Christ, apart from the introductory *Farað* etc., entails a second digression: *bodiað* etc., and *ic eow freoðo healde*, couched in main clauses so as to get the same importance as the fundamental *Ne ðurfan ge* etc. This passage almost disappears after the preceding irrelevant lines since its volume is far too small. We here see the same quality as is indicated by the poet's use of parataxis and hypotaxis: his inability to distinguish between principal and accessory.

Andr. 562   *no ðær gelyfdon   in hira liffruman ...*

Chr. 656   *ond þæt ne gelyfdon,   þætte liffruma ...*

(BUTTENWIESER, p. 41.)

Andr. 566 b ff   *... se ðe acenned wearð*
                to hleo ond to hroðre   hæleða cynne,
                eallum eorðwarum.

Chr. 722 b f   ... *þæt to frofre gewearð*
              eallum eorðwarum.

(BUTTENWIESER, p. 41.)

Andr. 1291   *Ðu eart gescyldend*   *wið sceaðan wæpnum*

Chr. 775   ... *þæt he us gescilde*   *wið sceaþan wæpnum*

(BUTTENWIESER, p. 44.)

Andr. 1602 f   *Nu is gesyne*   *ðæt þe soð meotud,*
                  cyning eallwihta,   *cræftum wealdeð* ...

Chr. 686 f   *Ðus god meahtig*   *geofum unhneawum,*
                  cyning alwihta,   *cræftum weorðaþ* ...

(BUTTENWIESER, p. 44.)

We have had reason to comment only on some of the parallel passages enumerated above. Yet it is obvious that if, for instance, three passages in Andreas clearly point to dependence on Elene, all the other parallels between these poems point in the same direction since we cannot reasonably hold that some passages were taken over by Cynewulf from Andreas and some by the Andreas poet from Cynewulf's works. Thus all the parallels add to the sum-total of the evidence.

There are also parallels between the Cynewulf canon and the other poems belonging to the Cynewulf group except Andreas. But although some of these parallels are so close that we must assume that in these cases one passage is imitated from the other, I am unable to make out which is the original and which the borrowing. Since we are here concerned with the effect of borrowings on the style of the poems, such cases are irrelevant, and I shall only refer to some of the most noticeable: Jul. 376b—78a : Gu. 84b—86a; Chr. II 761—62a : Gu. 404—05; Jul. 697—98 : Gu. 967b—69a; Chr. II 499b—500 : Gu. 1208 —09a, 1335b—36a; El. 280—81 : Gu. 1121—22; Chr. 491 : Gu. 1315b —16a; Jul. 389b—90a : Gu. 1378b—79a. These parallels have been pointed out by CHARITIUS and LEFÈVRE. Further Jul. 35b—36 : Gu. 167b—69; Chr. II 487—88 : Ph. 640b—41; Juliana 504 : Ph. 405, cp. p. 303. Similar selected instances will be discussed on pp. 296, 298 f.

Passages from Beowulf are used in quite a different manner in Andreas as compared with the Cynewulf canon. The very beginning of Andreas is apparently inspired by Beowulf:

1 ff
> *Hwæt! We gefrunan   on fyrndagum*
> *twelfe under tunglum   tireadige hæleð,*
> *peodnes pegnas.   No hira prym alæg ...*

Beow. 1 ff
> *Hwæt, we Gar-Dena   in geardagum*
> *peodcyninga   prym gefrunon,*
> *hu ða æpelingas   ellen fremedon!*

(SARRAZIN, Engl. Stud. XXIII, p. 259.) It is not difficult to recognize the different elements of the Andreas passage in Beowulf; what is remarkable here is that the heathen formulary opening, as in the Fates, is used to introduce the twelve apostles in the shape of glorious retainers and famous warriors.

Andr. 122 ff
> *Ða wæs Matheus   miclum onbryrded*
> *niwan stefne.   Nihthelm toglad,*
> *lungre leorde.   Leoht æfter com,*
> *dægredwoma.   Duguð samnade,*
> *hæðne hildfrecan ...*
> *... Woldon cunnian   hwæðer cwice lifdon ...*

Beow. 1787 ff
> *Ða wæs eft swa ær   ellenrofum,*
> *fletsittendum   fægere gereorded*
> *niowan stefne.   Nihthelm geswearc*
> *deorc ofer dryhtgumum.   Duguð eal aras;*
> *wolde blondenfeax   beddes neosan ...*

(Andr. 123 — Beow. 1790: SARRAZIN, Engl. Stud. XXIII, p. 260.) The order of the details is identical, and the verbal correspondences — especially *niwan stefne.   Nihthelm toglad*, which is no natural or formulary combination — makes the influence from Beowulf fairly certain. The borrowing, on the whole, is well adapted to the context; one might observe, perhaps, that *niwan stefne* in Andreas is not so natural as the corresponding phrase in Beowulf: in the latter epic *niowan stefne* and *swa ær* refer back to the happy times before Heorot was haunted by the monster. In Andreas *niwan stefne* does not refer to anything; it is a rather unnecessary appendix to the description of the Lord inspiring his apostle with courage.

Andr. 150 ff ... *þæt hie banhringas   abrecan þohton,*
lungre tolysan   lic ond sawle,
ond þonne todælan   duguðe ond geogoðe,
werum to wiste   ond to wilþege,
fæges flæschoman.   Feorh ne bemurndan ...

Beow. 71 ff ... *ond þær on innan   eall gedælan*
geongum ond ealdum,   swylc him God sealde,
buton folcscare   ond feorum gumena.

(BUTTENWIESER, p. 23.) The same structure and similar details:
ond þonne (þær) to(ge)dælan   duguðe on geogoðe (geongum ond
ealdum) + f-alliterative line.

The distribution of gifts in Hroðgar's hall, described with a pious
colouring, has been perverted in Andreas into a grotesque caricature:
a division among the cannibals of the remnants of their slaughtered
victims.

Andr. 177 b ff   *Swa is þære menigo þeaw*
þæt hie uncuðra   ængum ne willað
on þam folcstede   feores geunnan
syþþan manfulle   on Mermedonia
onfindaþ feasceaftne.

Beow. 4 ff *Oft Scyld Scefing   sceaþena þreatum,*
monegum mægþum   meodosetla ofteah,
egsode eorlas,   syððan ærest wearð
feasceaft funden.

(BUTTENWIESER, p. 23, KRAPP A, p. 90.) The sub-clause in Beowulf
makes up a contrast to the main clause, the real significance of which
is brought out by the subordinate addition; *syððan* here almost
carries the meaning of *þeah*. In the Andreas parallel, on the contrary,
the *syððan*-clause has no function other than that of expanding what
has already been said; it is an unnecessary addition not only on
account of the *uncuðra* l. 178 but also because of ll. 25 ff:

Swelc wæs þeaw hira
þæt hie æghwylcne   ellðeodigra
dydan him to mose   meteþearfendum ...

One notices the endeavour, so frequent in Andreas, to render the
description as protracted as possible.

Andr. 256 ff   *Hwanon comon ge   ceolum liðan,*
macræftige menn,   on mereþissan,
ane ægflotan?   Hwanon eagorstream
ofer yða gewealc   eowic brohte?

If, for instance, the passage in Andreas had run instead *Hwider willað ge of waroðe liðan*, it would have been a great deal more comprehensible. As it now stands, if not quite meaningless, it is nevertheless extremely far-fetched: a man comes to the shore, sees a boat, and asks "from where do you come; take me with you" (l. 271 ff)?? All other versions of the legend have the necessary "whither do you go", and that the Andreas text is not corrupt is apparent from the *hwanon*-idea running throughout the passage as well as from the helmsman's answer *We of Marmedonia mægðe syndon feorran geferede* etc., a necessary consequence of the apostle's question. The odd phrases in Andreas are explained as being a mixture of two passages in Beowulf:

333 ff   *Hwanon ferigeað ge   fætte scyldas,*
græge syrcan,   ond grimhelmas,
heresceafta heap?

237 ff   *Hwæt syndon ge   searohæbbendra,*
byrnum werede,   þe þus brontne ceol
ofer lagustræte   lædan cwomon,
hider ofer holmas?

(BUTTENWIESER, p. 23.) In Beowulf, of course, the coast-guard's *hwanon*-question is quite justified since the hero and his men arrive as strangers in a foreign country. The borrowing by the author of Andreas is a very instructive example of the tendency in this poet to take over material which seems to him poetical or otherwise attractive without asking whether it fits into the context or not.

Andr. 301 ff   *Næbbe ic fæted gold   ne feohgestreon,*
welan ne wiste   ne wira gespann,
landes ne locenra beaga,   þæt ic þe mæge lust
ahwettan . . .

Beow. 2991 ff   *Geald þone guðræs   Geata dryhten,*
Hreðles eafora,   þa he to ham becom,
Iofore ond Wulfe   mid ofermaðmum,
sealde hiora gehwæðrum   hund þusenda,
landes ond locenra beaga . . .

(Sarrazin, Anglia XIV, p. 404, Engl. Stud. XXIII, p. 260; Krapp A, p. 97.) It is of no small interest to compare the different comments on this parallel, which is one of the few undisputable influences on Andreas that have really been discussed. Sarrazin (Engl. Stud. XXIII, 264) makes the following reflection, characteristic of earlier attribution research: "Wer nicht ganz stumpfsinnig oder absichtlich blind ist, wird zugeben müssen, dass solche parallelstellen wie z. B. bei And. 303 etc. ... gegeben sind, unmöglich alle auf zufall beruhen oder dem epischen formelschatz entnommen sein können". This scholar, then, looks upon single authorship as the only alternative except the less probable "Zufall". Buttenwieser, however, observes: "Der falsche Gebrauch des Genetivs, *landes ne locenra beaga*' im And. statt des Acc. tritt sofort frappant zu Tage, während im B. der Genetiv am Platze ist. Die Parallelstelle wird nun in ein ganz anderes Licht gerückt" (p. 63). Inspired, obviously, by the latter critic Krapp remarks: "Apparently taken over bodily from Beow. 2995, *landes ond locenra beaga*, and perhaps never completely assimilated to the context in Andreas". Krapp might have spared himself the hesitating "perhaps": it is obvious that the genitival phrase has nothing whatever to do after *nœbbe*, and Buttenwieser is perfectly right in her analysis. It need hardly be pointed out that an isolated instance of the partitive genitive after *habban* such as Gen. 678 *Nu hœbbe ic his her on handa* (cp. Grein-Köhler p. 288) is in no way comparable to the passage in Andreas, with its accumulation of genitives after a series of normal accusatives. Monroe, defending l. 303 a, tries to persuade us that the genitives depend on an implied noun and compares Jud. 158, 330. But it is impossible to imagine any one implied noun here, and we may content ourselves by stating not only that the genitives are unthinkable in correct Old English but also that the answer *nœbbe landes ne locenra beaga*, after a demand to pay the *gafulrœdenn*, is not too appropriate. But in Beowulf, of course, the phrase is not only in formal but also in material harmony with the context.

Andr. 332 ff   *Farað nu geond ealle   eorðan sceatas,*
                  emne swa wide   swa wœter bebugeð,
                  oððe stedewangas   strœte gelicgaþ.

Beow. 1221 ff   *Hafast þu gefered,   þœt ðe feor ond neah*
                  ealne wideferhþ   weras ehtigað,

> *efne swa side swa sæ bebugeð*
> *windgeard, weallas.*

(KRAPP A, p. 99.) The influence on Andreas is unmistakable; even
if the rhetorical overstatement is more becoming in the praise of
Beowulf than in Christ's order, yet it is no inferior poetical expansion
of *Et misit illos prædicare regnum Dei* of Luke 9, 1. Christ II has
a version more independent of Beowulf and less emphatic: *Farað nu
geond ealne yrmenne grund, geond widwegas.* The idea, however,
is not taken over from Cynewulf's poem, a similar section being found
in the P and C texts. We notice the different use of *bebugan*: transitive
in Beowulf, intransitive in Andreas.

Andr. 377 b ff
> *   Ænig ne wende*
> *þæt he lifgende land begete,*
> *þara þe mid Andreas on eagorstream*
> *ceol gesohte.*

Beow. 1595 ff
> *gomele ymb godne ongeador spræcon,*
> *þæt hig þæs æðelinges eft ne wendon,*
> *þæt he sigehreðig secean come*
> *mærne þeoden*

691 f
> *Nænig heora þohte, þæt he þanon scolde*
> *eft eardlufan æfre gesecean*

BUTTENWIESER (p. 24) connects these passages, and no doubt rightly:
as in some other cases, the Andreas sentence is apparently a mixture
of two passages in Beowulf.

Andr. 429 f
> *Ge þæt gehogodon, þa ge on holm stigon,*
> *þæt ge on fara folc feorh gelæddon . . .*

Beow. 632
> *Ic þæt hogode, þa ic on holm gestah . . .*

(SARRAZIN, Anglia XIV, p. 406). The passage is no alliterative
formula. The Andreas lines, which have been taken over bodily from
Beowulf, give good context.

Andr. 471 ff
> *Næfre ic sælidan selran mette,*
> *macræftigan, þæs ðe me þynceð,*
> *rowend rofran, rædsnotterran,*
> *wordes wisran.*

493 f   *swa ic æfre ne geseah*   *ænigne mann,*
                   þryðbearn hæleða,   *þe gelicne . . .*

(Sarrazin, Anglia IX, p. 519, BS p. 115, Eng. Stud. XXIII, p. 261.)
The setting of the periods seems to be taken over from Beow. 247 f.

                             Næfre ic maran geseah
           eorla ofer eorþan,   *ðonne is eower sum* etc.

The author's imitation here forms a contrast to Cynewulf in respect
of the two poets' different ways of further elaborating a borrowed
idea. Beow. 625 ff was developed by Cynewulf (El. 961 ff) into a
well balanced and skilfully varied pattern; the *Næfre ic* etc. in
Beowulf is enlarged by the Andreas poet into an accumulation of
comparatives representing different qualities, general and special:
*selran — macræftigan — rofran — rædsnotterran — wisran. Ræd-
snotteran, wordes wisran* are not so well adapted to the context,
cp. Andr. 505 ff, Beow. 1841 ff, p. 281.

Andr. 474 b ff   *Ic wille þe,*
              eorl unforcuð,   *anre nu gena*
              bene biddan: *þeah ic þe beaga lyt,*
              sincweorðunga,   *syllan mihte,*
              fætedsinces,   *wolde ic freondscipe*
              þeoden þrymfæst,   *þinne, gif ic mehte,*
              begitan godne.

Beow. 426 b ff   *Ic þe nu ða,*
              brego Beorht-Dena,   *biddan wille,*
              eodor Scyldinga,   *anre bene,*
              þæt ðu me ne forwyrne,   *wigendra hleo*
              (. . . þæt ic mote . . . Heorot fælsian).

(Sarrazin, Anglia IX, p. 520, BS, p. 115.) There can be no doubt as
to the borrowing in Andreas, but here *Ic wille* etc. is as fitting in
the context of this poem as it is in Beowulf.

Andr. 505 b ff   *Ðu eart seolfa geong,*
              wigendra hleo,   *nalas wintrum frod,*
              hafast þe on fyrhðe,   *faroðlacende,*
              eorles ondsware.   *Æghwylces canst*
              worda for worulde   *wislic andgit.*

(KRAPP A, p. 109.) Andrew's praise of the helmsman is somewhat strange and unexpected. The unknown seafarer, from the apostle's point of view, can be worthy of praise in only two respects; 1) he has shown kindness to the travellers by generously taking them on board without payment; 2) he has proved a master sailor. It is, consequently, quite logical that Andrew should ask for his friendship (ll. 478 b ff) and for some insight into his art of sailing (ll. 483 b ff). But there is certainly no reason why he should extol the mariner's ready wit. KRAPP remarks: "That the Lord should be described as wise in wit and in words is not strange"; but Andrew does not know that the sailor is the Lord. There is, in fact, nothing corresponding to this passage in the Greek and Latin versions. But when, in Beowulf 1841 ff, the aged Hroðgar addresses the young hero after the latter's farewell speech, full of promises and wisdom, he begins with the following words:

> Ðe þa wordcwydas   wigtig Drihten
> on sefan sende;   ne hyrde ic snotorlicor
> on swa geongum feore   guman þingian.
> Ðu eart mægenes strang   ond on mode frod,
> wis wordcwida!

The author of Andreas, apparently, thought that something of this kind might be a dignified close of Andrew's speech to the young sailor, but he did not quite consider the demands of the context.

Andr. 667 f   *þær getimbred wæs   tempel dryhtnes,*
                heah ond horngeap ...

Beow. 81 b f   *Sele hlifade*
                heah ond horngeap.

(SARRAZIN, Engl. Stud. XXIII, 261, BS, p. 115.) The description of the building fits Hroðgar's meadhall better than the *tempel dryhtnes.*

Andr. 736 b ff   *... ac of wealle ahleop,*
        frod fyrngeweorc,   þæt he on foldan stod,
        stan fram stane.   Stefn æfter cwom,
        hlud þurh heardne,   hleoðor dynede ...

Beow. 2552 b f   *stefn in becom*
        headotorht hlynnan   under harne stan

(BUTTENWIESER, p. 24.) The borrowing here seems to be a vague reminiscence, and there is nothing left of the original context. The strange use of *stan* in Andreas seems dependent on the natural use in Beowulf.

Andr. 767 b ff

Man wridode
geond beorna breost,   brandhata nið
weoll on gewitte,   weorm blædum fag,
attor ælfæle.

It may be that the incredulous priests were *synfulle*, but one is taken aback at this, to say the least, effective picture of horrible wickedness, as well as at the odd. *weorm*. The suspicion that here, as in many other instances, we have to do with deficiency of taste and judgment on the part of the poet is supported by the parallel Beow. 2713 b ff:

he þæt sona onfand,
þæt him on breostum   bealoniðe weoll
attor on innan.

(BUTTENWIESER, pp. 24, 64.) The terminology, it must be admitted, is more suitable in a description of the frightful effect of a dragon's bite than of the hostility of Christ's enemies, and in all probability an Anglo-Saxon audience was also capable of feeling its greater suitability in Beowulf.

Andr. 984 f

maga mode rof,   meotude getreowe,
stop on stræte,   (stig wisode)

"   1232 ff

Drogon deormodne   æfter dunscræfum ...
efne swa wide swa   wegas to lagon,
... stræte stanfage.

Beow. 320 f

Stræt wæs stanfah,   stig wisode
gumum ætgædere.

(SARRAZIN, Engl. Stud. XXIII, p. 262.) *Stræte stanfage* has been quoted as an instance of unessential variation (p. 203); there is also a contrast between the phrase and the context in Andreas which is not to be found in Beowulf: *stræte stanfage* has a solemn ring that is hardly in keeping with the torture in the city of the cannibals. But the lines in Beowulf are part of a magnificent and stately passage describing the march of the *Geatas* to Heorot.

Andr. 999 b ff

Duru sona onarn

þurh handhrine   *haliges gastes,*
ond þær in eode,   *elnes gemyndig,*
hæle hildedeor.   *Hæðene swæfon,*
dreore druncne,   *deaðwang rudon.*
Geseh he Matheus   *im þam morðorcofan,*
hæleð higerofne   *under heolstorlocan,*
secgan dryhtne lof ...

Beow. 721 b f

Duru sona onarn

fyrbendum fæst,   *syþðan he hire folmum*
⟨*æthr*⟩*an* ...

"   703 b

Sceotend swæfon ...

"   728 ff

Geseah he in recede   *rinca manige,*
swefan sibbegedriht   *samod ætgædere,*
magorinca heap ...

SARRAZIN (Anglia IX, p. 520), and BRANDL (p. 1010) call attention to this parallel, which is fairly striking. But the latter's criticism hardly seems to do the Andreas poet justice. BRANDL is of opinion that the passage in Andreas has suffered from the borrowings; only monsters, he says, open doors in the manner described here, whereas in the Greek legend the door opens after the apostle has touched it making the sign of the Cross. It is hard to see the point of this remark. He further thinks that *swæfon* in the Andreas legend destroys the consistency since it has already been said (l. 994 b) that the guards are dead. But surely we must not take *swæfon* too literally here: when the poet took it over from Beowulf, he used it symbolically, associating it with *dreore druncne*. This is far more likely than that he should have forgotten the death of the guards. The borrowing, far from being awkward, is rather one of the better instances of the boldness and vigour of the Andreas poet's style.

Andr. 1011 ff   *Aras þa togenes,*   *gode þancade*
þæs ðe hie onsunde   *æfre moston*
geseon under sunnan.

Beow. 1397 ff   *Ahleop ða se gomela,*   *Gode þancode,*
mihtigan Drihtne,   *þæs se man gespræc.*

(SARRAZIN, Engl. Stud. XXIII, p. 262, KRAPP A, p. 128.)

Andr. 1093 f   *Đa ic lungre gefrægn   leode tosomne*
               burgwaru bannan.

Beow. 74   *Đa ic wide gefrægn   weorc gebannan ...*

(SARRAZIN, Anglia XIV, p. 406.)
Both passages fit into the context.

Andr. 1158 b ff   *Hornsalu wunedon,*
               weste winræced,   welan ne benohton
               beornas to brucanne   on þa bitran tid,
               gesæton searupancle   sundor to rune
               ermðu eahtigan.

Beow. 144 ff   *Swa rixode   ond wið rihte wan*
               ana wið eallum,   oð þæt idel stod
               husa selest.

"   171 b f   *Monig oft gesæt*
               rice to rune;   ræd eahtedon ...

"   2455 ff *Gesyhð sorhcearig   on his suna bure*
               winsele westne ...   ... nis þær hearpan sweg,
               gomen in geardum ...

In Andr. 1158 b ff it is partly the wording and structure but
chiefly the idea that have been taken over from Beowulf; but whereas
in the latter poem the derelict hall is accounted for by the monster's
raids in one case and the king's sorrow in the other, it is hardly
justified in the context in Andreas, where it is boldly taken over
as an adornment (cp. p. 160). The passage about the council is far
better adapted to the situation. The deserted halls as symbols of
vanished joy and wealth decayed occur also in the Wanderer 78 ff

               Woriað þa winsalo,   waldend licgað
               dreame bidrorene,   duguþ eal gecrong ...
               ... Yþde swa þisne eardgeard   ælda scyppend
               opþæt burgwara   breahtma lease
               eald enta geweorc   idlu stodon.

This passage, however, is less similar to the section in Andreas.

Andr. 1275 b ff   *Swat yðum weoll*
               þurh bancofan,   blodlifrum swealg,
               hatan heolfre.

KRAPP's remark (A) that "the passage means that the fresh blood breaking out from Andrew's wounds flowed over, or swallowed up, the clotted blood" no doubt solves the difficulty of these lines. Nevertheless they are a bit too extravagant even for a poet of the Andreas author's boldness, and it seems rather unlikely that this passage should be entirely his own invention. I think that he was influenced by the description of Grendel's attack on the sleeping warrior in Beowulf 741 b ff (cp. SARRAZIN, Engl. Stud. XXIII, p. 263):

> slat unwearnum,
> bat banlocan,   blod edrum dranc,
> synsnædum swealh.

Andr. 1278 b f   Ða cwom wopes hring
          þurh þæs beornes breost,   blat ut faran ...
Beow. 2550 f   Let ða of breostum,   ða he gebolgen wæs,
          Weder-Geata leod   word ut faran ...

(BUTTENWIESER, p. 25.) Both passages are suitable as expressions of emotion: complaint of pain in one case, wrath in the other.

Andr. 1349 ff   Ðær þu gegninga   guðe findest,
          frecne feohtan,   gif ðu furður dearst
          to þam anhagan   aldre geneðan.
Beow. 525 ff   Ðonne wene ic to þe   wyrsan geþingea,
          ..... grimre guðe,   gif þu Grendles dearst
          nihtlongne fyrst   nean bidan.

(BUTTENWIESER, p. 25.) Unferð's sarcastic words to Beowulf are picked up by the Andreas poet and employed with no small degree of inventiveness. When the devil's retainers ironically exhort their master, who does his best to encourage them to the battle, to go himself and fight with Andrew, this is consistent with the version of the P and C legends.

Andr. 1492 ff   He be wealle geseah   wundrum fæste
          under sælwage   sweras unlytle,
          stapulas standan,   storme bedrifene,
          eald enta geweorc.
Beow. 2715 b ff   Ða se æðeling giong,
          þæt he bi wealle   wishycgende
          gesæt on sesse;   seah on enta geweorc,
          hu ða stanbogan   stapulum fæste ...

(SARRAZIN, Engl. Stud. XXIII, p. 264, BUTTENWIESER, p. 25.) The general setting of the passage in Andreas is obviously borrowed from Beowulf, but what can be traced to the latter epic fits much better into the context of Andreas than the *storme bedrifene*, which is not taken from Beowulf. KRAPP says that the strange *storme bedrifene*, to which KOCK objects (Anglia XLVI, 73), is "a bit of emotional, not realistic, description". I do not know what an "emotional description" is, but I think it is highly probable that the *storme bedrifene* existed in some poem now lost, and was taken over from it by the author of the legend. SCHÜCKING's remark (Dichtersprache p. 80) that the *stapulas*, being *storme bedrifene*, "draussen sind", does not explain the phrase. It is not improbable that the context of which it originally formed part was a description of a deserted mead-hall since a similar line occurs in the Wanderer 76 in connection with such a description:

> *winde biwaune*   *weallas stondaþ.*

(KRAPP A, p. 150.) However, such a context is not to be found in Andreas, and that the line does not make much sense in the imitation there is obvious.

Andr. 1526 b ff   *Meoduscerwen wearð*
         æfter symbeldæge,   *slæpe tobrugdon*
         searuhæbbende ...   *... Ðæt wæs sorgbyrþen,*
         biter beorþegu.   *Byrlas ne gældon,*
         ombehtþegnas.

Beow. 767 b ff   *Denum eallum wearð,*
         ceasterbuendum,   *cenra gehwylcum,*
         eorlum ealuscerwen.

(SARRAZIN, Engl. Stud. XXIII, p. 264, KRAPP A, p. 151 ff.)
KLAEBER, Engl. Stud. LXXIII, p. 185 ff, gives the best analysis, I think, of these passages, which have often been discussed. According to him, *meoduscerwen* in Andreas means "Metbescherung", and *ealuscerwen* in Beowulf "Bierberaubung". The word was used by the Andreas poet, slightly changed, and fitted into a new context. Here, it must be said, the poet is in a way successful in his borrowing: the devastating deluge is a ghastly *meoduscerwen*, but the idea is grotesquely perverted in the continuation *Byrlas ne gældon, ombeht-þegnas*, which, apparently, is a blending of El. 692b *scealcas ne*

gældon, and Beow. 1161 b f *byrelas sealdon wīn* etc., which two cases are quite in harmony with their context. The bizarre extravagance of the passage is as far from Cynewulf's manner as possible.

Andreas and the Cædmon group have the following passages in common:

Andr. 1269 b ff

                Ða com hæleða þreat
to ðære dimman ding,   *duguð unlytel,*
wadan wælgifre   *weorodes brehtme.*
Heton ut hræðe   *æðeling lædan*
in wraðra geweald,   *wærfæstne hæleð.*

„   1388 ff   *Com þa on uhtan*   *mid ærdæge*
hæðenra hloð   *haliges neosan*
leoda weorude.   *Heton lædan ut*
þrohtheardne þegn   *þriddan siðe ...*

It seems as if the poet had modelled these passages on some lines in the Loth episode in Genesis:

2450 b ff

                Ða com æfter niht
on last dæge ...   *Comon Sodomware,*
geonge and ealde,   *gode unleofe*
corðrum miclum ...   *Heton lædan ut*
of þam hean hofe   *halige aras,*
weras to gewealde ...

(Andr. 1272, 1390 b — Gen. 2457 b: BUTTENWIESER, p. 56.) The coming of night, the arrival of the hostile crowd, the command about the prisoner, are described in almost the same terms as the scene outside Loth's door in Genesis. It will be observed that a somewhat puzzling detail in the Andreas passage is explained when compared with Genesis. It is surprising that the Andreas poet should prefer the phrase *heton lædan ut* instead of the simpler and, in this context, more consistent *lædon ut*. Why should the Mermedonians order anyone to lead out the apostle? He is already in their power; they are all intent on tormenting him. The Casanatensis (ch. 28) has *miserunt ad carcerem, et eduxerunt beatum andream* etc.; the Greek version gives only ἐξήνεγκαν αὐτὸν (ch. 26) and ἐξήνεγκαν τὸν Ἀνδρέαν (ch. 28); cp. BLATT pp. 80, 84, 85. The poet must have followed the Genesis version on this point; there, of course, *heton lædan ut* is quite logical: the crowd gathers outside Loth's door, ordering him to bring out to them the two men who have come to him during the night.

Other similarities which suggest that the Andreas poet was well acquainted with Genesis are the following:

Andr. 174 ff   *Đu scealt feran   ond frið lædan,*
                  siðe gesecan,   þær sylfætan
                  eard weardigað,   eðel healdaþ ...
Gen. 1746 ff   *Gewit þu nu feran   and þine fare lædan,*
                  ceapas to cnosle.   Carran ofgif,
                  fæder eðelstol ...

Andr. 526 ff   *Forþan is gesyne,   soð orgete,*
                  cuð, oncnawen,   þæt ðu cyninges eart
                  þegen geþungen,   þrymsittendes,
                  forþan þe sona   sæholm oncneow ...
Gen. 2807 ff   *Sweotol is and gesene   þæt þe soð metod*
                  on gesiðõe is,   swegles aldor ...
                        ... Forðon ðe giena speow ...

Andr. 633 ff   *Ne frine ic ðe for tæle   ne ðurh teoncwide*
                  on hranrade,   ac min hige blissað,
                  wynnum wridað,   þurh þine wordlæðe ...
Gen. 2692 ff   *Ne dyde ic for facne   ne for feondscipe*
                  ne for wihte þæs   ic þe wean uðe.
                  Ac ic me, gumena baldor,   ... (lare gebearh etc.).

Andr. 914 ff   *Wes ðu, Andreas, hal,   mid þas willgedryht,*
                  ferðgefeonde!   Ic þe friðe healde,
                  þæt þe ne moton   mangeniðlan
                  grame grynsmiðas,   gaste gesceððan.
Gen. 2529 b ff   *Teng recene nu*
                  þam fæstenne;   wit þe friðe healdað
                  and mundbyrde.   Ne moton wyt
                  on wærlogum   wrecan torn godes ...

All of these parallels are of the same kind: a general similarity of context and a similarity of certain details, but nowhere very striking correspondences. They suggest that the Andreas poet, perhaps unconsciously, associates his motifs with similar ones in Genesis, but hardly that he deliberately borrows from this poem.

Andreas and Exodus.

Andr. 1528 b ff		*Sund grunde onfeng,*	
	deope gedrefed.	*Duguð wearð afyrhted*	
	þurh þæs flodes fær.	*Fæge swulton,*	
	geonge on geofene	*guðræs fornam*	
	þurh sealtne weg.		
" 1536 f	*Weox wæteres þrym.*	*Weras cwanedon,*	
	ealde æscberend.		
" 1542 b ff		*Hreoh wæs þær inne*	
	beatende brim.	*Ne mihte beorna hloð*	
	of þam fæstenne	*fleame spowan.*	
	Wægas weoxon,	*wadu hlynsodon,*	
	flugon fyrgnastas,	*flod yðum weoll.*	
" 1572 b f		*Wæter fæðmedon,*	
	fleow firgendstream,	*flod wæs on luste* etc.	
Ex. 447 f	*Folc wæs afæred,*	*flodegsa becwom*	
	gastas geomre,	*geofon deaðe hweop.*	
" 452 ff	*Wæron Egypte*	*eft oncyrde,*	
	flugon forhtigende,	*fær ongeton,*	
	woldon herebleaðe	*hamas findan* etc.	
" 482 ff	*Flod famgode,*	*fæge crungon,*	
	lagu land gefeol,	*lyft wæs onhrered,*	
	wicon weallfæsten,	*wægas burston* etc.	
" 490 b ff		*Garsecg wedde,*	
	up ateah, on sleap.	*Egesan stodon,*	
	weollon wælbenna.		

The description of the ravages of the water that gushes forth from the mouth of the sphinx in Andreas is highly suggestive of the incident in Exodus when Pharao's army is swallowed up by the Red Sea. In fact, if we did not know the context, we should believe that it was the sea that drowned the sinful inhabitants of Mermedonia: *Sund grunde onfeng, deope gedrefed — on geofone — þurh sealtne weg — beatende brim — wægas weoxon, wadu hlynsodon — fleow firgendstream.* The whole setting, with its short compound units, is similar to the Exodus passage, and if we look at the details we find fairly close reminiscences: Andr. *Duguð wearð afyrhted þurh þæs flodes fær. Fæge swulton, geonge on geofone guðræs fornam*; Exod. *Folc wæs afæred, flodegsa becwom gastas geomre, geofon deaðe hweop.* Andr. *Wægas weoxon, wadu hlynsodon, flugon fyrgnastas, flod yðum weoll ... Wæter fæðmedon ... flod wæs on luste*; Exod. *flugon forhtigende, fær ongeton ... Flod famgode ... Garsecg wedde ... Egesan stodon, weollon wælbenna.* The Andreas poet seems, in other words, to be inspired by the passage in Exodus; quite naturally since the motifs in the two poems are very much alike. But it is better to say that the episode in Andreas has been modelled on Exodus than that it is an actual borrowing from the Cædmon epic. If we compare the episodes in Andreas and Exodus with the story about the Deluge in Genesis we see at once the difference in style between this poem and the two others:

1375 b ff

Sæs up stigon
ofer stæðweallas.   Strang wæs and reðe
se ðe wætrum weold;   wreah and þeahte
manfæhðu bearn   middangeardes
wonnan wæge,   wera eðelland;
hof hergode,   hygeteonan wræc
metod on monnum.   Mere swiðe grap
on fæge folc   feowertig daga,
nihta oðer swilc.   Nið wæs reðe
wællgrim werum;   wuldorcyninges
yða wræcon   arleasra feorh
of flæschoman.   Flod ealle wreah,
hreoh under heofonum   hea beorgas
geond sidne grund ...

The pattern is different with longer units, enlarged by variations; the vocabulary is different; the description does not dwell on the terror of the victims but is more matter-of-fact and descriptive of outward events.

Andreas and Daniel.

The Mermedonians give their victims a fatal drink:

Andr. 35 ff   *se onwende gewit,   wera ingeþanc,*
                heortan on hreðre,   (hyge wæs oncyrred),

þæt hie ne murndan   æfter mandreame ...
... (ac hie hig ond gærs ...   meðe gedrehte.)
Dan. 569 ff   *... and þonne onhweorfeð   heortan þine*
þæt þu ne gemyndgast   æfter mandreame,
ne gewittes wast   butan wildeora þeaw,
ac þu lifgende ...   ... geond holt wunast.

(KAIL, p. 24; and also BUTTENWIESER, p. 47.) The relation between these passages seems fairly clear. Apart from the verbal correspondences one may observe the similarity between the ideas here: the expression *ne murnan æfter mandreame* is not, as might seem natural in Anglo-Saxon poetry, linked up with the longing for the heavenly bliss of holy souls — cp. for instance Gu. A 319 *ne ic me eorðwelan owiht sinne* etc. — but with the conception of animal existence.

Parallels between Andreas and Guthlac are:

Andr. 915 b ff   *Ic þe friðe healde,*
               þæt þe ne moton   mangeniðlan,
               grame grynsmiðas,   gaste gesceððan.
"   954 b f   *Hie þin feorh ne magon*
               deaðe gedælan,   þeh ðu drype ðolie ...
Gu. 226 ff   *Ne mostun hy Guþlaces   gæste sceþþan,*
               ne þurh sarslege   sawle gedælan
               wið lichoman ...

Andr. 1072 f   *Wendan ond woldon   wiðerhycgende*
               þæt hie on elþeodigum   æt geworhton ...
Gu. 663 f   *Wendun ge ond woldun,   wiþerhycgende,*
               þæt ge scyppende   sceoldun gelice (wesan.)

Andr. 1210 b ff   *Nis seo stund latu*
               þæt þe wælreowe   witum belecgaþ,
               cealdan clommum.
Gu. 903 b ff   *Næs seo stund latu*
               earmra gæsta,   ne þæt onbid long,
               þæt þa wrohtsmiðas   wop ahofun ...

Andr. 1481 b ff   *Mycel is to secganne,*
               langsum leornung,   þæt he in life adreag,
               eall æfter orde.

Gu. 531 b f   *Micel is to secgan*
                eall æfter orde,   *þæt he on elne adreag.*

(BUTTENWIESER, pp. 54—57.) These parallels are all consistent in meaning.

Andr. 1241 b ff   *Hæfde him on innan*
                ellen untweonde,   *wæs þæt æðele mod*
                asyndrad fram synnum,   *þeah he sares swa feala*
                deopum dolgslegum   *dreogan sceolde.*

Part of the passage is comprehensible: that the apostle could have an *ellen untweonde* though he had to suffer so much pain is clear. But how can his *mod* be *asyndrad fram synnum þeah he sares swa feala dreogan sceolde*? Only the contrary would make sense: that he had to suffer the pain although he was free from sin. But the text does not call for any emendation here. The sentence in Andreas is a distorted version of a passage in Guthlac 514 ff:

                Wæs se martyre   *from moncynnes*
                synnum asundrad.   *Sceolde he sares þa gen*
                dæl adreogan,   *ðeah þe dryhten his*
                witum weolde.

(BUTTENWIESER, p. 55.) The context in Guthlac is clear: The martyr was free from sin; nevertheless he had to suffer pain though God controlled this pain. Now the author of Andreas, to all appearances, remembered some phrases in the Guthlac passage and had a vague reminiscence of its structure. Thus remembering that there was a *þeah*-clause as well as the series *sceolde—sares—dreogan* after *synnum asundrad* he mixed the two elements up and put them together with the awkward result.

Andr. 1284 ff   *Ic gelyfe to ðe,*   *min liffruma,*
                þæt ðu mildheort me   *for þinum mægenspedum,*
                nerigend fira,   *næfre wille,*
                ece ælmihtig,   *anforlætan ...*
Gu. 637 ff   *Ond ic þæt gelyfe*   *in liffruman,*
                ecne onwealdan   *ealra gesceafta,*
                þæt he mec for miltsum   *ond mægenspedum,*
                niðða nergend,   *næfre wille*
                þurh ellenweorc   *anforlætan ...*

(KRAPP A, p. 143.) The Andreas passage is an instance of the complex series, which is otherwise rare in the poem.

Andr. 1330 b ff

                     "Lætað gares ord,
     earh ættre gemæl,   in gedufan
     in fæges ferð.   Gað fromlice,
     ðæt ge guðfrecan   gylp forbegan."
     Hie wæron reowe,   ræsdon on sona
     gifrum grapum.

Is the passage consistent in meaning? The devil orders his retainers to attack the apostle with spears — and they set about carrying out his orders as if they had been told to tear him to pieces with their bare hands. The lines 1334—35 a are more easily explained if we remember the Guthlac A passage 404 ff

     He hine scilde   wið sceðpendra
     eglum onfengum   earma gæsta;
     wæron hy reowe   to ræsanne
     gifrum grapum.

The phrase also occurs ll. 995 b ff in Guthlac B: man cannot protect himself against death, the terrible adversary,

                       ac hine ræseð on
     gifrum grapum.

(BUTTENWIESER, p. 56.) The latter instance is not objectionable, and as to the former, *eglum onfengum* fits in well with *gifrum grapum.* Now *grap* is a favourite word in Beowulf, used about Beowulf's struggle with the monsters (ll. 438, 765, 1542), the murderous assault of the *merefixas* (555), and Grendel's arm torn loose from his body (836). It is interesting to note how Beowulf, in his solemn vow to kill the monster, makes distinction between an attack with weapons — *sweord* and *scyld* (l. 437) — and one carried out *mid grape* alone. This distinction rules out any possibility of vagueness in the use of *grap*, and we may safely assume that the distinction made in Beowulf was maintained in the language as a whole. The use of the word in Guthlac A and B is probably inspired by Beowulf, but the Andreas poet evidently borrowed from Guthlac A 406 ff without considering the situation in his own narrative.

Andr. 1392 f   *woldon aninga   ellenrofes*
                  mod gemyltan.   Hit ne mihte swa!

Gu. 574 ff   *Woldun hy geteon   mid torncwidum*
                  earme aglœcan   in orwennysse,
                  meotudes cempan.   Hit ne meahte swa!

Verbal correspondences. The Guthlac passage 574 ff is in perfect harmony with the context: the devils can do no harm to the saint nor can they dishearten him; to their threatenings the steadfast anchorite replies by a very long and crushing speech in which unshaken belief in the Lord is combined with contempt for his adversaries: *niðða nergend næfre wille þurh ellenweorc anforlœtan* etc. (640); *ne þurfun ge wenan ... þæt ge mec synfulle ... under scœd sconde scufan motan* (673 ff) etc. But in Andreas, after the cocksure declaration l. 1393 b, there follows the final torture and the apostle's dispirited lament full of doubts as to the power of the Lord, so the cannibals certainly succeeded in their attempt to *ellenrofes mod gemyltan*. The conclusion seems to be that the author of the latter legend took the passage over and put it into his description, as usual without considering its appropriateness in the context.

Andr. 1443 b ff   *No þe laðes ma*
            þurh daroða gedrep   gedon motan
            þa þe heardra mœst   hearma gefremedan.

   "   1473 ff   *(Næs him) ... ne ban gebrocen,   ne blodig wund,*
                    lice gelenge,   ne laðes dœl ...

Gu. 698 ff   *Ne sy him banes bryce   ne blodig wund,*
                  lices lœla   ne laþes wiht,
                  þœs þe ge him to dare   gedon motan ...

(Buttenwieser, p. 57.) The similarity between the passages is obvious. Now in the Andreas passage *þurh daroða gedrep* is surprising: never before in the narrative has there been any question of torture with spears. Andrew has only been tormented by being dragged on the ground in the city of the man-eaters, and for this torture various expressions have been used: *ðragmœlum teon*; *lic* is *sarbennum soden, swate bestemed, banhus* is *abrocen*; he must *dreogan dolgslegum*, he is *swungen sarslegum* etc. Only 1330 b ff the devil speaks of an attack with spears, but this is never carried out. The strange *No þe laðes ma þurh daroða gedrep gedon motan* is explained by the parallel passage in Guthlac: *to dare gedon motan*

l. 700 seems to be vaguely remembered by the Andreas poet and made into *daroða gedrep gedon motan*, an association which is easily explained in an author with an interest in warlike vocabulary, but which does not fit the context. The other elements in the Guthlac passage are more suitable in Andreas.

Andr. 1581 f   *Smeolt wæs se sigewang,   symble wæs dryge*
                 folde fram flode,   swa his fot gestop.
Gu. 742 f   *Smolt wæs se sigewong   ond sele niwe,*
                 fæger fugla reord,   folde geblowen.

(BUTTENWIESER, p. 58.) The combination *smylte is se sigewang* occurs also in the Phoenix 33 a, but the form *smolt* as well as the continuation with *folde* seems to connect the Andreas passage more closely with Guthlac than with the other poem. Anyhow the dissimilarity between the passages in Guthlac and Phoenix on the one hand and in Andreas on the other is striking: *smolt wæs se sigewang*, in the two former poems, is used in the description of a serene and paradisical landscape; in Guthlac *se grena wong* where the anchorite is brought by the angels after he has withstood the devils' attacks, in the Phoenix the wonderful land where suffering and rough weather are unknown. But in Andreas — what is the *smolt sigewang*? The ground which has just been flooded by a terrible deluge, from which all the water has not yet receded and which is still covered with corpses: they are later swept by the waves into an abyss which opens in the rock. The obvious exaggeration testifies to the same lack of taste and logic that is so often perceptible in Andreas.

There are yet other correspondences between Andreas and Guthlac, but the ones instanced here should suffice to demonstrate the frequent similarities between the poems. It is difficult not to infer that the author of Andreas, to a great extent, borrows material from the other poem since passages in Guthlac are often found in a distorted syntactical and stylistic condition in Andreas, or, torn from their natural environment, are forced into an unnatural context. We see, then, one and the same treatment of the poetical matter taken from Guthlac and from Beowulf.

We shall now proceed to examine how far the other unsigned poems are dependent on Beowulf, on the Cædmon group, and on the poems of the Cynewulf group.

In the Dream of the Rood I am unable to discover anything that might point to influence from the Cædmon poetry and Beowulf. It is especially natural that we should look for some similarity between the descriptions of the dream visions here and in Daniel, but there is much less resemblance between these passages than between the dreams in Daniel and Elene; cp. p. 251 f. As has already been pointed out, the bloodstained Cross ll. 22—23 and 48 has a parallel in Christ III: l. 1085, but it is impossible to say anything about dependence here.

The Christ I poet does not seem dependent on the earlier epics. There may be a correspondence between ll. 59 ff.

> *Sioh nu sylfa þe   geond þas sidan gesceaft,*
> *swylce rodores hrof   rume geondwlite*
> *ymb healfa gehwone,   hu þec heofones cyning*
> *siðe geseceð ...*

and Gen. 673 ff

> *Gehyran mæg ic rume*
> *and swa wide geseon   on woruld ealle*
> *ofer þas sidan gesceaft,   ic mæg swegles gamen*
> *gehyran on heofnum* etc.,

The final lines, 437—439, are very similar to the end of Guthlac A, ll. 816—818, (cp. Cook C p. 114):

Chr. 437 ff

> *(þær he ær ne cwom),*
> *in lifgendra   londes wynne,*
> *þær he gesælig   siþþan eardað,*
> *ealne widan feorh   wunað butan ende. Amen.*

Gu. A 816 b ff

> *... þær heo soð wunað,*
> *wlitig, wuldorfæst,   ealne widan ferh*
> *on lifgendra   londes wynne.*

But it is impossible to say which passage is imitated from the other; one of them is no doubt a borrowing. Otherwise there are no clear indications of borrowings.

Perhaps the similar passages 152 b f

> *Is seo bot gelong*
> *eal æt þe anum*

and 365 b f

> *Is seo bot gelong*
> *eall æt þe anum*

are imitations of Beow. 1376 b ff

Nu is se ræd gelang

eft æt þe anum;

but they may rather be considered formulary turns of expression
(another instance is Hy. 4, 109 (cp. Cook C p. 95)). There is another
parallel of such a formulary character between Chr. 403 ff and Andr.
540 ff.

Christ III, likewise, is a poem almost uninfluenced by the Cædmon
group and Beowulf. The only passage which, as far as I can see,
may have been inspired by one of the old poems, is the description
of the apocalyptic conflagration and its horrors (ll. 964 ff):

> ... *ðonne eall þreo*   *on efen nimeð*
> *won fyres wælm*   *wide tosomne,*
> *se swearta lig* ...

> ... *Teonleg somod*
> *þryþum bærneð*   *þreo eal on an*
> *grimme togædre.*   *Grornað gesargad*
> *eal middangeard*   *on þa mæran tid.*
> *Swa se gifra gæst*   *grundas geondseceð;*
> *hiþende leg*   *heahgetimbro* .
> *fylleð on foldwong*   *fyres egsan,*
> *widmære blæst*   *woruld mid ealle,*
> *hat, heorogifre.*   *Hreosað geneahhe*
> *tobrocene burgweallas.*   *Beorgas gemeltað*
> *ond heàhcleofu* ...

The fate of Sodom and Gomorrha is described, Gen. 2542 ff, as
follows:

> ... *þa ic sendan gefrægn*   *swegles aldor*
> *swefl of heofnum*   *and sweartne lig*
> *werum to wite,*   *weallende fyr* ...
> *Hlynn wearð on ceastrum,*
> *cirm arleasra*   *cwealmes on ore,*
> *laðan cynnes.*   *Lig eall fornam* ...
> *(unlytel dæl) sidre foldan*   *geondsended wæs*
> *bryne and brogan.*   *Bearwas wurdon*
> *to axan and to yslan* ...

> *Strudende fyr   steapes and geapes,*
> *swogende leg,   forswealh eall geador*
> *þæt on Sodoma byrig   secgas ahton* ...

The general style of the passages, the order of the different episodes, and some of the details may suggest a connexion here. Further l. 1234 f,

> *þær bið on eadgum   eðgesyne*
> *þreo tacen somod* ...,

suggests Beow. 1243 b ff
> *ʃær on bence wæs*
> *ofer æþelinge   yþgesene*
> *heaþosteapa helm* ...

and El. 256 f   *Ðær wæs on eorle   eðgesyne*
> *brogden byrne   ond bill gecost* etc.

(Sarrazin, Anglia IX, p. 526.) An influence from the latter passages would explain the somewhat puzzling use of *on* in Chr. III: only one of the *þreo tacen* can really be seen o n the blessed (*þæt hy fore leodum leohte blicaþ* l. 1238); the other two are signs f o r them and would demand a pure instrumental (as in Beow. 3158 *wægliðendum wide gesyne*). Otherwise, as Cook has shown (ibid., notes), the poem contains turns of expressions, phrases, and whole lines which are also found in other texts but which, like the end of Christ I, are irrelevant in a discussion of borrowings. Thus, to mention some of them, the phrase *Wel is þam þe motun on þa grimman tid gode lician* ll. 1079b—1080 is also found in the Phoenix 516b—517 and in a somewhat different form Beow. 186b—187; the blood-stained Cross 1085 ff is described in a similar way in the Dream of the Rood ll. 22 ff, 48 ff. Ll. 1111—1112, Christ bleeding on the Cross, remind us of Andr. 968 and Juliana 292:

Chr.   *... ond of his sidan swa some   swat forletan,*
> *þær blod ond wæter   bu tu ætsomne*
> *ut bicwoman   fore eagna gesyhð* ...

Andr.   *of minre sidan   swat ut forlet,*
> *dreor to foldan.*

Jul.   *... þæt þær blod ond wæter   bu tu ætgædre*
> *eorþan sohtun.*

The passages in Christ III and Juliana are almost identical; it would hardly be a just estimation of the possibilities of Anglo-Saxon poetical language to believe that the idea here must necessarily be expressed in this form; everything points to imitation in one of the passages (perhaps two) — but who shall decide which the imitation is? The lines are all equally well adapted to the context, there is nothing strange about vocabulary or syntax. Riddles of this kind are common in the religious poetry. Another instance in Christ III is 1437—38:

> Swylce hi me geblendon   bittre tosomne
> unswetne drync   ecedes ond geallan

Andr. 33—34   Syððan him geblendan   bitere tosomne,
              dryas þurh dwolcræft,   drync unheorne ...,

the passage in Christ is closer to the original: *Et dederunt ei vinum bibere cum felle mixtum* (Mt. 27, 34), but that is all we can say about this parallel. Theories concerning the relation between the passages would be mere guesswork. The delights of Paradise l. 1660 b ff, further, have much in common with those in the Phoenix l. 50—59, but it is equally difficult to know whether one of the poems has influenced the other.

In Guthlac A we see the same lack of correspondences with the early poetry. Possibly there may be some connexion between l. 344 f

> Swa sceal oretta   a in his mode
> gode compian,   ond his gæst beran ...

and Beow. 20 f   Swa sceal ⟨geong g⟩uma   gode gewyrcean,
              fromum feohgiftum   on fæder bearme ...

But the similarity is not so very striking. Sarrazin KK, p. 139, quotes several passages in Beowulf and Guthlac A which he regards as parallels: "Diese Anklänge gehen über das gewöhnliche Mass formelhafter Übereinstimmungen ... erheblich hinaus". However, only two of these can really be looked upon in this way:

48 f	þæt he us fægran gefean bringe
	ofer þa niþas þe we nu dreogað,
Beow. 1858	inwitniþas, þe hie ær drugon;
Gu. A 436	hæfde feonda feng feore gedyged,
Beow. 578	hwæþere ic fara feng feore gedigde.

The lines fit in quite well with the context in Guthlac A. The parallels Andreas — Guthlac A have already been referred to and interpreted, and similarly the parallels Cynewulf — Guthlac A. "Irrelevant" correspondences in other poems are not numerous.

Guthlac B appears to contain more reminiscences from Beowulf. It seems, for instance, highly probable that behind the assault of the illness (ll. 1139 b ff):

> Dead nealæcte,
> stop stalgongum, strong ond hreðe
> sohte sawelhus,

looms the menacing shadow of Grendel:

Beow. 702 b f   Com on wanre niht
scriðan sceadugenga.
"   710 f   Ða com of more   under misthleoþum
Grendel gongan ...
"   714   Wod under wolcnum ...
"   720   Com þa to recede   rinc siðian ...

The details are not identical, and yet, on reading one passage, one immediately associates it with the other: The mood and atmosphere of the scenes are unmistakably the same. Gu. B 1221 b ff: Guthlac's servant besets his master with questions as to the origin of the mysterious messenger:

> Huru, ic giet ne wat,
> ær þu me, frea min, furþor cyðe
> þurh cwide þinne, hwonan his cyme sindon.

We should have expected the singular in 1223 b as in Juliana's question l. 259 (Frægn þa fromlice) ... hwonan his cyme wære. But the surprising sindon is explained if we compare Beow. 256 b ff:

> ofost is selest
> to gecyðanne, hwanan eowre cyme syndon.

(Sarrazin, Anglia IX, p. 517.) The inconsistency in Guthlac B is a slip of the pen rather than an awkward adaptation of the kind we have seen instanced, many times, in Andreas. According to Sarrazin, Anglia IX, 518, BS, p. 113, there is a connection between Gu. 1171 b ff

> Læst ealle well
> wære ond winescype, word þa wit spræcon,
> leofast manna;

and Beow. 2663 *Leofa Biowulf,   læst eall tela,*
swa ðu on geoguðfeore   geara gecwæde,

and, in fact, this seems highly probable; but it is more doubtful whether SARRAZIN is right in establishing a connection between Gu. 1359

se selesta   bi sæm tweonum
and Beow. 1685 *ðæm selestan   be sæm tweonum;*

both lines are followed by a *þara þe*-clause (Gu. *þara þe we on Engle æfre gefrunen* ..., Beow. *ðara þe on Scedenigge sceattas dælde*). The connection here is only a possibility since, of course, the line in question may be an alliterative formula of a traditional character. It is more probable, as SARRAZIN thinks (Anglia IX, p. 547), that there is a connexion between the lines on Guthlac's death, 1057 b ff

Wyrd ne meahte
in fægum leng   feorg gehealdan,
deore frætwe,   þonne him gedemed wæs;
and Beow. 2855 ff *Ne meahte he on eorðan,   ðeah he uðe wel,*
on ðam frumgare   feorh gehealdan,
ne ðæs Wealdendes   wiht oncirran;

but the Guthlac passage seems to be a reminiscence rather than a conscious borrowing. We may have an influence from one of the Cædmon poems at work ll. 935 ff

siþþan he on westenne   wiceard geceas,
fiftynu gear,   þa wæs frofre gæst
eadgum æbodan   ufan onsended,
halig of heahþu.   Hreþer innan born,
afysed on forðsið.   Him færinga
adl in gewod ... (*Wæs þam bancofan* ... *neah geþrungen* ...)

In Felix there is no mention of an angel; the message from God is described in the following way: *statimque cum se subita infirmitate diri languoris vir Dei arreptum persensisset, confestim manum Domini ad se missam cognovit* (XI, p. 48). The Guthlac B poet, after the episode with the messenger from God and the sudden attack of illness, returns to the version of his original, ll. 950 b ff:

Ða se ælmihtiga
let his hond cuman   þær se halga þeow,
deormod on degle   domeadig bad,

heard ond hygerof.   Hyht wæs geniwad,
blis in breostum.   Wæs se bancofa
adle onæled,   in bendum fæst ...

We have, then, in the poem, two different accounts of the onset of
Guthlac's illness, and only the second agrees with Felix's version.
There is, therefore, some probability that the first of these accounts
was derived from some other source and "interpolated" by the poet
into his narrative. It seems as if the digression in the passage is due
to influence from

Dan. 335 b ff   *Đa of roderum wæs*
                   engel ælbeorht   ufan onsended,
                   wlitescyne wer   on his wuldorhaman,
                   se him cwom to frofre   and to feorhnere ...

Guthlac B, like the other poems here discussed, contains some
"irrelevant" passages; the most remarkable one being 819—855,
which, according to ABBETMEYER (p. 28), has a source in common
with the Phoenix 393—423. This is possible; on the other hand there
are some verbal correspondences which seem difficult to account for
unless we assume that one poet borrowed from another:

Gu. 819 ff   *Đæt is wide cuð   wera cneorissum,*
               folcum gefræge,   þætte frymþa god
               þone ærestan   ælda cynnes
               of þære clænestan,   cyning ælmihtig,
               foldan geworhte.
Ph. 393 ff   *Habbaþ we geascad   þæt se ælmihtiga*
               worhte wer ond wif   þurh his wundra sped,
               ond hi þa gesette   on þone selestan
               foldan sceata ...
Gu. 827 b f   *... þær him nænges wæs*
               willan onsyn,
Ph. 397 b f   *... þær him nænges wæs*
               eades onsyn;
Gu. 852 ff   *Siþþan se eþel   uðgenge wearð*
               Adame ond Euan,   eardwica cyst
               beorht oðbroden,   ond hyra bearnum swa,
               eaferum æfter,   þa hy on uncyððu,
               scomum scudende,   scofene wurdon ...

Ph. 404 b ff

> Ðær him bitter wearð
> yrmþu æfter æte   ond hyra eaferum swa:
> sarlic symbel   sunum ond dohtrum
> (wurdon teonlice   toþas idge)
> ageald æfter gylte. ... Forþon hy eðles wyn
> geomormode   ofgiefan sceoldon ...

Gu. 854b—855a and Ph. 405 have also a close parallel in Juliana 504: *yrmþu to ealdre ond hyra eaferum swa*. SHEARIN, who does not seem to be acquainted with ABBETMEYER's work, thinks that "the author of the Phoenix had before him the more detailed and expanded statement in the Guthlac"; but we might equally well hold that the author of Guthlac had before him, and expanded, the less detailed section in the Phoenix. It is, however, impossible to say anything about priority here since there is nothing to indicate originality or imitation.

As far as I can see, the Phoenix does not betray any clear influence from Beowulf or the Cædmon poetry. Perhaps in Ph. 516 b ff:

> Wel biþ þam þe mot
> in þa geomran tid   gode lician,

we have a reminiscence from Beowulf 186 b ff:

> Wel bið þæm þe mot
> æfter deaðdæge   Drihten secean etc.

(SARRAZIN, Anglia IX, p. 517.) But this may be an instance of conventional phrasing. SARRAZIN's suggestion (Anglia IX, pp. 546, 47) that there is a relation between Ph. 117 — Beow. 2072, Ph. 469 — Beow. 882, Ph. 573 — Beow. 2770, is very doubtful — these passages are not real correspondences. However, if the poem has no connection with the early poetry, it abounds in suggestions of relationship with other poems. It is natural that we should find correspondences with the Physiologus, as for example the lines about the sweet odours and flowers (206, 652, 659), which remind us strongly of the Panther 44 ff (*stenc-swettra ond swiþra swæcca gehwylcum, wyrta blostmum ond wudubledum*). We also find a parallel in Christ and Satan 355 ff (cp. p. 90 f). Less similar are the passages in Gu. 1271 ff, Riddle 40, 29. Another correspondence with the Panther is the description of the bird's beauty (ll. 291 ff), which is suggestive of ll. 23 ff in the

Panther. The extensive parallel Ph. 393—423 — Gu. B 819—855 has already been referred to. The Phoenix 409 b—411 a is very similar to Guthlac 985 b—87 a, but it is impossible to say whether we have a borrowing here. We also find numerous phrases suggestive of the Christ trilogy.

In Guthlac A, The Dream of the Rood, Christ I and III, and the Phoenix, we are, then, unable to discover any certain borrowings from the other poems of the Cynewulf group, and the influence from Beowulf and the Cædmon poems is very inconsiderable.

We have chiefly, hitherto, been concerned with such parallels as seem due to borrowing on the part of one of the poets quoted. We shall now examine a group of parallels which does not, in the first place, consist of originals and borrowings, but of traditional phrases. As we shall see, the distribution of these phrases is different in the different poems.

The theological þœr-clause.

El. 818 b ff

                          Lœt mec, mihta god,
on rimtale   rices þines
mid haligra   hlyte wunigan
in þœre beorhtan byrig,   þœr is broðor min
geweorðod in wuldre ...

Andr. 102 b ff

                           Ðe is neorxnawang,
blœda beorhtost,   boldwela fœgrost,
hama hyhtlicost,   halegum mihtum
torht ontyned.   Ðœr ðu tyres most
to widan feore   willan brucan.

"   225 ff   *Gewat him þa se halga   healdend ond wealdend,*
upengla fruma,   eðel secan,
middangeardes weard,   þone mœran ham,
þœr soðfœstra   sawla moton
œfter lices hryre   lifes brucan.

"   597 b ff   *... ond þurh lare speon*
to þam fœgeran gefean,   þœr freo moton,
eadige mid englum,   eard weardigan ...

"   977 ff   *Gewat him þa se halga   heofonas secan,*
eallra cyninga cining,   þone clœnan ham,
eaðmedum upp,   þœr is ar gelang
fira gehwylcum,   þam þe hie findan cann.

Andr. 1682 ff ... *wenede to wuldre*   *weorod unmæte,*
to þam halgan ham   *heofona rices,*
þær fæder ond sunu   *ond frofre gast*
in þrinnesse   *þrymme wealdeð* ...

" 1689 ff *Ðæt wæs Satane*   *sar to geþolienne,*
mycel modes sorg,   *þæt he ða menigeo geseah*
hweorfan higeblíðe   *fram helltrafum*
þurh Andreas   *este lare*
to fægeran gefean,   *þær næfre feondes ne bið,*
gastes gramhydiges,   *gang on lande.*

Fata 117 ff ... *þæt we þæs botles*   *brucan motan,*
hames in hehðo,   *þær is hihta mæst,*
þær cyning engla   *clænum gildeð*
lean unhwilen.

Dream 139 ff ... *ond me þonne gebringe*   *þær is blis mycel,*
dream on heofonum,   *þær is dryhtnes folc*
geseted to symle,   *þær is singal blis* ...

Chr. 345 ff ... *ac þæt he usic geferge*   *in fæder rice,*
þær we sorglease   *siþþan motan*
wunigan in wuldre   *mid weoroda god.*

" 437 ff ... *in lifgendra*   *londes wynne,*
þær he gesælig   *siþþan eardað,*
ealne widan feorh   *wunað butan ende.*

" 749 f ... *þæt we to þam hyhstan*   *hrofe gestigan*
halgum weorcum,   *þær is hyht ond blis* ...

" 1639 *Ðæt is se eþel*   *þe no geendad weorþeð* ...

" 1649 ff ... *Ðær is engla song,*   *eadigra blis,*
þær is seo dyre   *dryhtnes onsien* ...
... *Ðær is leofra lufu,*   *lif butan endedeaðe* ... etc.

Gu. 9 b ff   *Eart nu tidfara*
to þam halgan ham.   *Ðær næfre hreow cymeð,*
edergong fore yrmþum ...

" 15 b ff   *He him ece lean*
healdeð on heofonum,   *þær se hyhsta*
ealra cyninga cyning   *ceastrum wealdeð*

— 306 —

Gu. 120 b ff
.... on þa longan god
herede on heofonum,   þær haligra
sawla gesittað   in sigorwuldre ...

" 655 ff
... leomum inlyhted   to þam leofestan
ecan earde,   þær is eþellond
fæger ond gefealic   in fæder wuldre ...

" 681 f
... agan mid englum   in þam uplican
rodera rice,   þær is ryht cyning ...

" 784 b ff
   Him wæs lean geseald,
setl on swegle,   þær he symle mot
awo to ealdre   eardfæst wesan ...

" 813 ff
... gongað gegnunga   to Hierusalem,
þær hi to worulde   wynnum motum
godes onsyne   georne bihealdan ...

" 827 f
... on neorxnawong,   þær him nænges wæs
willan onsyn ...

" 1081 f
Nis me wracu ne gewin,   þæt ic wuldres god
sece, swegelcyning,   þær is sib ond blis ...

" 1186 ff
... þæt wit unc eft   in þam ecan gefean
on sweglwuldre   geseon mostun ...
   ... Ðær sceal lufu uncer
wærfæst wunian ...

Ph. 395 ff
... ond hi þa gesette   on þone selestan
foldan sceata,   þone fira bearn
nemnað neorxnawong,   þær him nænges wæs
eades onsyn ...

" 560 f
... dreamas mid dryhten,   þær seo deore scolu
leofne lofiað.

" 586 ff
... in eadwelum   æþelum stencum,
þær seo soþfæste   sunne lihteð
wlitig ofer weoredum   in wuldres byrig.

" 593 ff
... in þam gladan ham,   gæstas gecorene,
ece to ealdre.   Ðær him yfle ne mæg
fah feond gemah   facne sceþþan ...

" 600 ff
... fore onsyne   ecan dryhtnes,
symle in sibbe,   sunnan gelice.
Ðær se beorhta beag ... (eadigra gehwam ...
hlifað ofer heafde.)

Ph. 615 b f   (... *on þam wicum* ...)   *Ðær gæsta gedryht*
                hælend hergað ...

"   658 ff   ... *in dreama dream,*   *þær hi dryhtne to giefe*
                worda ond weorca   *wynsumne stenc*
                in þa mæran gesceaft   *meotude bringað* ...

"   668 ff   ... *þæt we motun her*   *mereri,*
                goddædum begietan   *gaudia in celo,*
                þær we motun   *maxima regna*
                secan ond gesittan   *sedibus altis* ...

Jul. 643 ff   *He is þæs wyrðe,*   *þæt hine werþeode*
                ond eal engla cynn   *up on roderum*
                hergen, heahmægen,   *þær is help gelong*
                ece to ealdre ...

Ðær-clauses of the kind here quoted, introduced into a religious context to describe the joys of Paradise and Heaven, are of a formulary character and found in a great many religious Anglo-Saxon poems, except for the Cædmon poems, where they are extremely rare. Apart from the instances enumerated above, we find such clauses in the Seafarer 121 ff, the Riming Poem 82 b ff, Exodus 546; above all Christ and Satan: 142 b ff, 153 ff, 213 ff, 232 ff, 287 b, 308 b ff, 311 ff, 328 ff, 353 ff, 360 b ff, 552 b ff, 589 ff, 591 ff, 617 b ff, 647 ff, 653 ff, 660 b ff. They are also to be found in the Judgment Day II 284 ff, 287 ff, 289 and 290 ff, Gloria I 46 b, Summons to Prayer 30 ff, the Lord's Prayer II 30 ff, 32 ff, 41 b ff. The interesting thing with these stereotyped *þær*-clauses is their scantiness in the Cynewulf canon, the Dream, Christ I and III, the only instances being Elene 818 b, Juliana 645 b ff, Christ II 750 b ff, Fata 119 ff, the Dream 139 ff, Chr. I 345 ff, 437 ff, Chr. III 1639 ff — one in each poem except Chr. I — and their great frequency in other poems of the Cynewulf group: Andreas, Guthlac A, Guthlac B, and the Phoenix. In these four poems the "theological *þær*" is a characteristic stylistic feature to the same extent as it is in Christ and Satan, and we may say that in Old English poetry these texts form a group of their own, marked by this particular usage, and distinguished from the Cædmon group, the Cynewulf canon, the Dream and Chr. III, where the use is very rare. This fact, it should be pointed out, is not due to difference of subject-matter — there is quite as much reason for this type of clauses in the Cædmon group and the Cynewulf canon as in the other poems. It seems very often, in the latter class of texts, as if the mere mention of Paradise called forth, in the poets' minds, associations about the bliss of the holy, which are then expressed in this partic-ular way. In most cases, in the poems concerned, the *pær*-clause fits in quite well; but sometimes, when Heaven is mentioned only incident-ally, it deteriorates into a sort of tag, being loosely connected with the general context. This is the case especially in Andreas 228 ff, where the main point is God's return to Heaven after having de-livered his message; similarly 979 b with an identical situation, and 1693 b ff, where the essential point is Satan's anger at the success of Andrew's mission as the apostle of the Lord.

We may, then, as a result of our analysis of parallels in the Cyne-wulf group, divide the poems of this group into two main classes, apart from the class with the "paradisic" *pær*-clause, which does not comprise the Cynewulf canon, the Dream, and Chr. III. The first main class comprises the Cynewulf canon and Andreas. This class is characterized by the remarkable influence exerted by Beowulf and the Cædmon poems. It is obvious that both Cynewulf and the Andreas poet were widely read in this early epic literature, and their acquaintance with it appears in clearly deliberate borrowings as well as in slight and unconscious reminiscences. But the similarity between Andreas and the Cynewulf canon does not extend further than this. The poets' ways of using their borrowings are highly different. While Cynewulf, nearly always, succeeds in arranging the foreign poetic material so that it accords with his preconceived ideas of composition, while he sometimes even is capable of trans-forming meagre and monotonous poetry into rich and elaborate art (as in his utilization of the dream episode in Daniel), the Andreas poet lacks this organizing quality. His borrowings are often out of place because they have been torn out of their natural context and employed in a forced or fantastic manner. We are, in his poem, concerned not only with lack of harmony in the æsthetic sense, but still more often, with violation of narrative logic. This is also true of the borrowings in Andreas from other poems of the Cynewulf group. In one of Cynewulf's poems, however, his usual organizing talent is obviously lacking — in the Fata Apostolorum he seems to have borrowed from his earlier poetry in a way that is not elsewhere to be instanced.

The second main class is formed by the remaining poems of the

Cynewulf group, which were composed almost independent of the
our early epics, except for Guthlac B, where the parallels, however,
are neither numerous nor striking. The old heroic tradition is no
longer at work here, the poets only rarely resort to their earliest
predecessors for support in moulding their ideas, and when they do,
only faint echoes, mostly, reach us from Beowulf and Cædmon through
their works. It is important for us to realize that this is in no way
due to the fact that the authors of the Dream, Christ I and III, the
Guthlac poems, and the Phoenix are occupied with religious subjects
different from the old tales of valour and brave deeds. The themes of
Cynewulf and the Andreas poet are also religious, and nothing, a
priori, need have prevented the authors of Guthlac A and B from
describing the saint's struggle with the devils and the disease in the
same way as similar situations are described by the Andreas poet, in
terms culled from Beowulf; or the authors of the Dream and of
Christ I and III from dwelling on the Lord as the heroic chieftain in
the manner of Cædmon; or the Phoenix poet from echoing, for instance, phrases from the lines on Beowulf's funeral in his account
of the death of the holy bird, or from adding a heroic martial note
to his version of the fight of the good powers against sin and evil.
But this is not so, and the reason may be that these "independent"
poems form part of a special movement in Anglo-Saxon poetry, a
movement trying to create new poetical ideas, free from the influence
of the heroic age.

8 Heroic vocabulary

We now know a great deal more about the use of poetical words
than was known in BODE's and MEYER's days. The works of RANKIN,
MOHR, V. D. MERWE-SCHOLTZ, and, above all, of KEISER and MARQUARDT,
have revealed to us important facts concerning the poetical conceptions of the Anglo-Saxons. In this short excursus on the vocabulary of our poems we shall not attempt a complete examination
of the choice of words. We shall only consider the vocabulary from
some special points of view by asking how far our poets are dependent on heroic vocabulary. We shall, in other words, continue the
line of thought that made us examine the frequency, in the Cynewulf
group, of borrowings from the earliest poetry. In the first place we
mean, by the term "heroic vocabulary", words used for notions which

belong to the "martial" sphere. There are sometimes more instances of the words than those listed below; in these cases the meaning of the instances not listed is irrelevant to our purpose.

1. Battle, fight.

Andr. *beadu* 982, 1186; *beadulac* 1118; *billhete* 78; *camp* 234, 1325; *campræden* 4; *feohte* 1023, 1350; *gargewinn* 958; *gefeoht* 1188, 1196; *gewinn* 197, 932 (the battle of waves; *gewinn* l. 888 means apparently "sorrow", as SIMONS thinks); *guþ* 234, 951, 1330, 1349, 1354, 1487; *guðgeðingu* 1022, 1043; *guðgewinn* 217; *guðplega* 1369; *guðræs* 1531; *guðweorc* 1066; *handgewinn* 186; *hild* 412, 1420, 1491; *niðplega* 414; *orlege* 47, 1146, 1205, 1302; *sæcc* 1132; *secgplega* 1353; *wig* 839, 1183, 1226, 1355.

El. *beadu* 34, 45; *ceas* 56; *ealdgewin* 647; *fær* 93; *fyrngeflit* 903; *garþracu* 1185; *gefeoht* 646, 1183; *geflit* 443, 953; *guþ* 23; *handgeswing* 115; *hereweorc* 656; *hild* 18, 32, 49, 52, 65, 83, 149; *nið* 837, 904; *sacu* 905, 940, 1177, 1182; *tohte* 1179; *þracu* 45, 185; *wæpenþracu* 106; *wig* 19, 48, 112, 131, 150, 824, 1181, 1188, 1195; *wigþracu* 430, 658.

Jul. *beadu* 385; *cumbolhete* 637; *flanþracu* 384; *geflit* 484; *gewin* 190, 421; *guþ* 393, 397; *hondgewinn* 526; *sacu* 200, 230; *þracu* 12, 333; *wig* 576.

Chr. *guþ* 674; *guðplega* 573; *hild* 566; *þracu* 593; *wig* 564, 673.

Fa. *guðplega* 22, *sweordræs* 59, *wig* 74, *lindgelac* 76; *sacu* 59; *tohte* 75; *wæpenhete* 80.

Gu. A *gewin* 115, 134; *orlege* 196, 455, 564; *sacu* 300, 678.

Gu. B *lac* 1034.

What is striking in this comparison is the fact that in Cynewulf's poems there is more question of real battles (fights between armies, between man and devil, between the devil and God) than in Andreas; nevertheless words for this conception are more frequent in the latter poem. On the other hand there are, in Cynewulf, many opportunities of using the words in the same sense as in Andreas, but this is seldom done. Apart from the instances with *beadu* 1186 and *gefeoht* 1196, the words for "battle", "slaughter" are used, in Andreas, either in the sense ("violence in) persecution" — speaking of the torture of the apostle — or in order to describe the apostles, and particularly of course the hero of the poem, as warriors performing their martial duty in the service of their Lord. In Cynewulf a similar use is to be found with *wig* in El. 824 *He hafað wigges lean* (which phrase represents Stephen as a militant Christian); *wigþracu* 430, the persecution of Christ. Further Jul. *cumbolhete* 637, Juliana's execution; *sacu* 230, the torture. It is interesting that Cynewulf elsewhere, when speaking about Elene's mission, or about Judas as a servant of God, about the life of Juliana or about the passion of Christ, avoids these heroic "battle words".

It is further striking that in the unsigned poems, apart from Andreas, words for "battle" are almost completely lacking although, especially in Guthlac A, there are occasions to use them, and there are no kennings.

2. Warrior.

The same tendency is met with in the use of words expressing this conception.

Andr. *æscberend* 47, 1076, 1537; *cempa* 230, 324, 461, 538, 991, 1055, 1446; *freca* 1163; *guðfreca* 1333; *guðgelæca* 1600; *guðrinc* 155, 392; *hildfreca* 126, 1070; *hildstapa* 1258; *oretta* 463, 879, 983; *orettmæcg* 664; *rinc* 9, 967, 1116, 1343; *særohæbbend* 1468, 1528; *wælwulf* 149; *wiga* 1711; *wigend* 506, 850, 887, 896, 1053, 1095, 1203, 1297, 1450, 1572, 1608, 1672.

El. *æscwiga* 259; *burgwigend* 34; *byrnwigend* 224, 235; *daroðlacende* 37, 651; *fyrdrinc* 261; *guðgelæca* 43; *hilderinc* 263; *lindwigend* 270; *rinc* 46; *wiga* 63, 150, 153, 217, 246, 344, 937, 1089; *wigend* 106, 983.

Jul. *cempa* 17, 290, 383, 395; *daroðhæbbende* 68; *hererinc* 189; *hildeþremma* 64; *wiga* 641, 680.

Chr. *cempa* 563.

Fata *rinc* 11.

Dream *hilderinc* 61, 72.

Chr. III *rinc* 1114; *wiga* 984.

Gu. A *oretta* 176, 344, 401, 569; *cempa* 91, 153, 180, 324, 402, 438, 513, 558, 576, 580, 688, 727, 797.

Gu. B *cempa* 889, 901; *wiga* 999, 1033.

Ph. *cempa* 452, 471; *wiga* 486.

It is remarkable, first, that the Andreas poet has a greater varitey of words for "warrior" than Cynewulf. It is further to be observed that along with natural expressions such as *manfulra hloð, fordenera gedræg, deofles þegnas,* speaking of the Mermedonians, the Andreas author more frequently uses words for "warrior", i. e. the above instances ll. 47, 1076, 1537, 1600, 155, 126, 1163, 1116,

1468, 1528, 149, 1203, 1572, 1608, 1095. It should be pointed out that these heroic words are employed in descriptions of a tribe that is depicted as the loathsome and horrible enemies of God, Andrew, and mankind, the perpetrators of crimes and the servants of the devil. The heathen tribe, apparently, become "warriors" when confronted with the intruding apostle. Andrew himself and in some instances his disciples and Matthew are said to be warriors ll. 230, 324, 461, 538, 991, 1055, 1446, 1333, 392, 983, 463, 1711, 850, 1053. The twelve apostles are described in such terms ll. 664 and 9. *Wigend* occurs mostly in the combination *wigendra hleo*, used three times for Andrew (896, 1450, 1672), and once for Christ (506). *Wigendra þrym* 887 means the blessed in Paradise. The *oretta* l. 879 is king David, *hildstapa* 1258 is an image for winter. Strictly speaking it is only the *rinc* l. 976 who is a warrior in the narrower sense of the word; it has here the meaning of the Bible: *sed unus militum lancea latus eius aperuit* St. John 19, 34.

In Cynewulf words of this kind are partly restricted in use, partly otherwise employed. In El. ll. 259, 235, 261, 263, 217, 246 the words are used, quite naturally, for the members of Elene's expedition; ll. 224, 46, 63, 150, 153, 106 for Constantine's warriors and 34, 43, 37, likewise naturally, for their heathen adversaries; l. 651 with reference to the Troian war. It is not surprising, either, that Constantine and Judas should be called warriors ll. 937, 938 (cp. p. 68). Instances in Elene of a use of these words similar to the common use in Andreas are rare: l. 270 *lindwigendra* refers to the Jews, but this is the only instance of a term of this kind applied to a tribe which is inimical from the point of view of the Roman expedition, even if it cannot, of course, be compared to the Mermedonians.

In Juliana a use similar to that in Andreas is a little more frequent. Along with a more normal use of words for "warrior" (ll. 290, the same use as A. 967; 383, 395 the fight man — devil) such words are employed to designate the Christians (l. 17), Juliana's heathen father and the prefect (64, 68, 189), Heliseus' retainers (680). *Wigena wyn* l. 641 is used for God.

The instance Chr. 563 means the devils. But otherwise, in Cynewulf, words for "warrior" are avoided in referring to the enemies of Christ and the Christians as well as to apostles and servants of God.

In the unsigned poems, except for Andreas, words for warrior are rare and used with much less variety than in Andreas and the Cynewulf canon, *oretta* and *cempa* being the main alternatives. In the Dream, the *hilderincas* are simply the people (Anglosaxonism); *oretta* and *cempa* in Guthlac A refer to the hero of the legend (l. 153, 176, 569, 324, 438, 513, 558, 576, 580, 688, 727); to God's servants in general (l. 91, 344, 401, 402, 797); to Christ l. 180. In Guthlac B *cempa* is the hermit (l. 889, 901); the severe illness is called *wiga* l. 999, 1033. *rinc* in Chr. III 1114 has the same sense as *hilderinc* in the Dream; *wiga* 984 is the flame. In the Phoenix *cempa* is the holy bird l. 452 and *cempan* 471 are the righteous; *wiga* l. 486 is death. The use of these words in Guthlac A, then, reminds us of Andreas but is more restricted; in Chr. III, Guthlac B, and the Phoenix words of this kind are very rare. Christ I does not at all use the words for the sinners and the righteous, for the angels and the Lord.

3. Enemy, enmity, inimical.

Andr. *æfest* 610; *ealdgeniðla* 1048, 1341; *fæhðo* 1386, 284; *fah* 430, 769, 1023, 1060, 1188, 1346, 1593, 1599, 1705; *feond* 20, 49, 1196, 1294, 1619, 1693 (the devil); *folcsceaða* 1593; *fyrnsceaða* 1346; *gewinna* 1197, 1249, 1301; *gram* 217, 563, 917, 951, 1059; *gramhydig* 1694; *grynsmið* 917; *hete* 944; *hetegrim* 1395, 1562; *heterof* 1420; *hettend* 31; *lað* 80, 944 (the instances 408, 1249 mean "odious"); *leodhete* 112, 1138, 1149; *leodsceaða* 80; *mangeniðla* 916; *nið* 768, 1037, 1303, 1394; *niðhete* 834; *ondsaca* 1148, 1459; *sceaða* 1133, 1291; *scyldhata* 85, 1047, 1147; *torngeniðla* 1230; *ðeodsceaða* 1115; *wiðerfeohtend* 1183; *wiðerhycgende* 1072, 1172; *wiðerhydig* 675; *wiðermeda* 1195; *wrað* 613, 1273, 1297, 1317; *ondsaca* 1148, 1459.

El. *æfest* 207, 308, 496, 524; *ealdfeond* 493; *fah* 768, 924; *feond* 68, 93, 108, 207, 721, 899, 953; *feondscipe* 356, 498; *geniðla* 610; *gram* 43, 118; *hellesceaða* 956; *hete* 424; *hettend* 18, 119; *lað* 30, 94, 142 (other instances = odious); *leodhæta* 1300; *sceaða* 761; *sweordgeniðla* 1180; *torngeniðla* 568, 1306; *wiðerhycgende* 951; *wrað* 165, 459, 1181, (*wraðe* 294).

Ju. *feond* 159, 317, 348, 350, 523, 545, 573, 630; *feondlice* 118; *feondscype* 14; *gæstgeniðla* 245; *geniðla* 151; *gewinna* 243, 345, 555; *gram* 215, 628; *hæstlice* 136; *hellsceapa* 157; *hettend* 663; *laðgeniðla* 232; *nið* 56, 623; *sceapa* 672; *synscapa* 671; *wiþerbreca* 269; *wiðerfeohtend* 664; *wiðerhycgende* 196; *womsceaða* 211.

Chr. *ealdfeond* 567; *fæhðo* 617; *feond* 569, 623, 639, 733, 770; *feondscype* 486; *gram* 781; *gramhydig* 734; *lað* 776, 846; *sceapa* 775; *wiþerbroga* 564; *wrað* 595.

Fa. *æfest* 73; *wæpenhete* 80.

Dream *feond* 30, 33, 38.

Chr. I *helsceaþa* 364, *wraд* 16, 185; *niд* 69.

Chr. III *æfest* 1658; *feond* 1394, 1404, 1415, 1439, 1485, 1529, 1614, 1625; *geniдla* 1439; *niд* 1659; *sceaдa* 870, 1395; *þeodsceaþa* 1595, 1609.

Gu. A *æfst* 187, 712; *bealoniþ* 809; *feond* 136, 152, 186, 201, 265, 326, 421, 436, 442, 566, 691, 748, 773, 803; *ealdfeond* 141, 203, 218, 365, 390, 475; *ealdorgewinna* 534; *mansceaþa* 650; *ondsaca* 210, 233; *nyдgist* 540; *fæhд* 186; *orlege* 196, 564; *wracu* 199; *niд* 49, 141, 241, 290, 390, 525, 553, 648; *wroht* 391; *onda* 346, 565, 773; *gromhydig* 375; *wraд* 666; *wiþerbreca* 294.

Gu. B *feond* 864, 902, 915, 961, 982; *mansceaþa* 909.

Ph. *laдgeniдla* 50; *wracu* 51; *niд* 400, 413, 451, 469; *æfest* 401; *ealdfeond* 401, 449; *hettend* 441; *feond* 419, 595; *wroht* 612.

Here also we see a very great variety of words for these kindred conceptions in Andreas as compared with Cynewulf's poems, even if the greater length of the former epic is taken into account. It should be observed, further, that the words are often otherwise used in Cynewulf's poems than in Andreas. In the latter text the words ll. 80, 1048, 284, 430, 1023, 1593, 20, 49, 217, 917, 951, 1059, 917, 944, 1395, 31, 80, 944, 916, 834, 1072, 1148, 1459, 1133, 1273, 1317, 1148, 1459, 85, 1047, 1147, 1599, 1593, are used about or in immediate connexion with the Mermedonians. Ll. 1341, 1386, 1346, 1705, 1196, 1294, 1619, 1693, 1346, 1694, 1172, 1195, 613, 1297, they refer to the devil or devils and their activity; ll. 610, 768, 769, 1188, 1291, 563, 675 to the enemies of Christ. Andrew himself is called an enemy ll. 1197, 1249, 1301, 1230, 1183. Fate is inimical (1562), and hunger is an enemy (1115). In Elene, however, the Jews, who in this poem play the same part as the Mermedonians in Andreas, are only once (l. 568) referred to as enemies. It is true, as has been pointed out above, that the Jews are not quite comparable to the cannibal heathen tribe; but both are described as hostile to the Christian religion, until missions set out from Christian centres and oblige them to accept it. So it would have been possible, from this point of view, for Cynewulf to refer to them in the same way as the Andreas poet refers to the heathens. The fact that Cynewulf avoids these words when speaking about the Jews is apparently due to his tendency to restrict the use of heroic vocabulary as much as possible. It is characteristic that words of the kind referred to here are more often used about the attack of the heathens, the enemies of Rome (ll. 43, 68, 93, 108, 118,

18, 119, 30, 94, 165), in which case they are, of course, indispensable. Otherwise words for "enmity", "enemy", "inimical" refer, in Elene, to the enemies of the Christians (493, 356, 498), to the devils (207, 721, 761, 768, 924, 899, 951, 953, 956), to the enemie of Jesus (207 a, 308, 424, 496, 459, 524), to the damned (1306, 1300), to the queen 610, or are found in a more general sense ll. 1180, 1181.

In Juliana we see the same scarcity in employing the words in connexion with the anti-Christian groups or individuals of the legend. Speaking about the heathens in the opening lines Cynewulf says that they raised enmity l. 14; Heliseus is called an enemy ll. 159, 211, 232 and 671, and acts in a hostile manner l. 136. L. 672 Heliseus' followers are "enemies". Otherwise "inimical" words are mostly employed in connexion with the devil (ll. 245, 243, 317, 345, 348, 350, 523, 545, 555, 573, 628, 630, 663, 269, 664). The heathen idols are called enemies ll. 151, 157, 215; and Juliana herself is an enemy from the heathen point of view l. 196.

Christ, in conformity with the subject-matter of this poem, makes little use of words of our category; ll. 569, 623, 733, 781, 734, 770, 775, 776 they refer to the devil; ll. 846, 595 to the damned, and ll. 567, 617, 639 to the enemies of Christ. Ll. 486 "enmity" is used in a general sense. The scantiness of the words in the Fates should be noted.

About the use of words for "inimical" etc. one may say, then, that Cynewulf, unlike the author of Andreas, tends to restrict them to cases where they indicate "enmity" in the sense it has in earlier poetry (hostility between fighting armies and men), and, in so far as he uses them in other connections, does so chiefly in speaking of the devil (who, to the Christian mind, is the chief adversary of man). It is remarkable, too, that Cynewulf, except for two instances, avoids making the heathens speak of his Christian heroines as enemies — as we have seen, the author of Andreas is not so troubled by his apostle being referred to in this way. The extension, in Andreas, of the "inimical" words fits in with the poet's general tendency, demonstrated also in his use of words for "battle" and "warrior", to make his descriptions as martial as possible — in the old heroic style.

There is, in the unsigned poems except for Andreas, as much enmity and hatred as in the other poems, though of a spiritual kind. But it is only in Guthlac A that the conception of enmity plays any considerable part. There we frequently find the words in the account of the struggle between the devil and the saint or the devil and the righteous, much more extensively than in any of the Cynewulf poems. In the Dream the *feondas* are the enemies of Christ. In Guthlac B *feond* and *mansceapa* refer to the evil powers. All instances in Chr. I refer to the devil; in l. 185 *wrapum* are Joseph's adversaries; *nið* is the enmity of the devil. The *feondas* in Christ III are the devils ll. 1394, 1395, 1404, 1415, 1485, 1614, 1625; the sinners 1439, 1529, 1595, and 1609; ll. 1658 and 1659 the poet means enmity in a general sense. L. 870: the enemy of mankind. The Phoenix poet refers to the devil on ll. 400, 413, 401, 441, 419, 595; the words ll. 50, 51, 451, 469, 449, and 612 are used in a general sense.

We may say, as a summing-up, that these poems use words of this class in a way different from Cynewulf's: in Guthlac A they are more frequent than in Cynewulf's poems; in the other texts, with the exception of the Phoenix, they are used with much less variety: kennings, so frequent in Cynewulf's poetry, are very rare and occur only in the Phoenix ll. 50, 449.

We are now passing on to a set of synonyms representing yet another aspect of heroic style.

4. Sea, waves, ship.

Andr. *argeblond* 383; *arwela* 853; *aryð* 532; *fisces bæð* 293; *bæð-weg* 223, 513; *bat* 444, 496; *brim* 242, 442, 444, 504, 519, 1543, 1574, 1710; *brimhengest* 513; *brimrad* 1262, 1587; *brimstream* 239, 348, 903; *brimpisa* 1657, 1699; *ceol* 222, 253, 256, 273, 310, 349, 361, 380, 450, 555, 854, 899; *ea* 1504; *eagorstream* 258, 379, 441, 492; *ealad* 441; *eastream* 1261; *faroð* 236, 255, 1658; *faroðstræt* 311, 898; *flod* 252, 265, 367, 421, 906, 1530, 1546, 1573, 1582, 1589, 1616, 1629, 1635; *flodwylm* 516; *flot* 1698; *flota* 397; *garsecg* 238, 371, 392, 530; *gelad* 190; *geofon* 393, 498, 852, 1508, 1531, 1585, 1615, 1624; *grund* 393, 425; *hærn* 531; *holm* 195, 429; *holmpracu* 467; *holmweg* 382; *hornscip* 274; *hranrad* 266, 634, 821; *hwælmere* 370; *hwæles eðel* 274; *lagu* 437; *lagufæsten* 398, 825; *laguflod* 244; *lagustream* 423; *lid* 398, 403, 1707; *mere* 221, 283, 465, 491; *merebat* 246; *merefaroð* 289, 351; *mereflod* 1526; *merestream* 309, 454; *merepissa* 257, 446; *naca* 266, 291; *sæ* 236, 247, 453, 515, 1658; *sæbat* 438, 490; *sæflota* 381; *sæhengest* 488; *sæholm* 529; *sæmearh* 267; *sæstream* 196, 749; *scip* 240, 512; *seolhpæð* 1714; *stream* 374, 852, 1280, 1503, 1523, 1538; *streamfaru* 1576; *streamracu* 1580; *streamwelm* 495; *sund* 267, 381, 424, 488, 747, 1528; *swanrad* 196; *wæd* 439, 533, 1457, 1545; *wæg* 373, 456, 533, 601, 632, 748, 932, 1532, 1545, 1589, 1594; *wægfaru*

923; *wægflota* 487; *wægþel* 1711; *wær* 269, 487; *wæter*. 201, 222, 253, 333, 1260, 1507, 1536, 1553, 1572; *wæterbroga* 197, 456; *wæteregesa* 375, 435; *wæterflod* 503; *walca* 1524; *waroðfaruð* 197; *waruðgewinn* 439; *waðuma* 1280; *wudubat* 905; *flodes wylm* 367; *wæteres wælm* 452; *wylm* 863; *yð* 259, 352, 368, 443, 451, 466, 514, 519, 823, 863, 1546, 1591, 1713; *yðbord* 298; *yðfaru* 900; *yðlad* 499; *yðlid* 278, 445.

El. *bæðweg* 244; *brim* 253, 971, 1003; *brimþisa* 238; *brimwudu* 244; *ceol* 250; *earhgeblond* 239; *egstream* 241; *faroðhengest* 226; *fifelwæg* 237; *flod* 1269; *flot* 226; *geofon* 227, 1200; *holm* 982; *holmþracu* 727; *hringedstefna* 248; *lagu* 1268 almost certain (the rune ⟨ᚱ⟩); *lagufæsten* 249, 1016; *lagustream* 137; *merestræt* 242; *sæ* 240, 728; *sæmearh* 228, 245; *stream* 1200; *sund* 228, 251; *swanrad* 996; *wæg* 230; *wægflota* 246; *wæghengest* 236; *yð* 239; *yðlid* 252.

Jul. *ehstream* 673; *holm* 112; *laguflod* 674; *mereflod* 480; *scip* 672; *stream* 481; *swanrad* 675; *wæg* 479, 680; *wæter* 479; *yðfaru* 478.

Chr. II *ceol* 852, 862; *flod* 806; *flodwudu* 853; *gelad* 856; *holm* 855; *holmþracu* 678; *laguflod* 850; *sæ* 677, 852; *stream* 853; *sundhengest* 852; *sundwudu* 677; *wæter* 851; *yð* 854; *yðmearh* 863.

Chr. III *sund* 986; *wæter* 981, 984, 988; *sæ* 966, 1144, 1163; *holm* 978; *flod* 979, 985, 1168; *wæg* 980; *yð* 1167; *eahstream* 1167.

Gu. B *bat* 1328; *wæghengest, wæterþisa* 1329; *brimwudu* 1331; *lagumearg* 1332; *hærnflota* 1333.

Ph. *wætres þrym* 41; *mereflod* 42; *wæg* 45; *yðfaru* 44; *yðmere* 94; *firgendstream* 100; *sæ* 103, *lagu* 101; *holmþræce* 115; *geofon* 118; *stream* 120; *wæter* 184; *garsecg* 289; *waðuma* 97.

Even if one takes into account the fact that there is more question of sea and water in Andreas — an episode like the deluge having no counterpart in Cynewulf's poems — yet it is impossible to avoid the conclusion that the author of Andreas seizes any opportunity, in his description of the voyage, to demonstrate his command of a maritime vocabulary, in the manner of the Beowulf poet, which does not at all conform with Cynewulf's artistry and style. The author of Andreas not only imitates the use of maritime terms in Beowulf but develops and exaggerates it: Beowulf, with 1460 verses more than Andreas, has at most 52 instances of synonyms for "sea", "water", "ship", as compared with 84 in Andreas.

Christ III, Guthlac B, and the Phoenix all give their authors occasion to use words for 'sea' and 'ship'. But only in the Phoenix do such words occur to an extent that is suggestive of Cynewulf;

in the other two poems the authors seem little interested in the poetical effect produced by descriptions of the sea. The Guthlac B poet, curiously enough, has only the servant's ship in mind; the poetical charm of the sea leaves him quite indifferent. We may, then, distinguish three groups of poems according to the relative frequency of words belonging to this class: first Andreas, a poem of marine Marinism, whose author almost carries to excess a feature of heroic poetry, the description of sea and ships, which is much less overloaded with kennings in Beowulf. Secondly the Cynewulf canon and the Phoenix, where the use of these words is more restricted, and thirdly Christ III and Guthlac B, where they play a very inconsiderable part. These three stages, in fact, may characterize the decay of the heroic ideal in Old English poetry.

This classification, in the main, may also hold good applied to the other sets of synonyms here listed and belonging to a special warlike and heroic character. Andreas is richest in these synonyms, the Cynewulf canon is less rich, the remaining poems have few, if any, instances (except for the relatively frequent "inimical" words in Guthlac A).

9. Narrative looseness

Looseness of narrative and gaps in the story are to be found, more or less, in nearly all Old English poems. Now the former feature (digressions, the insertion of irrelevant episodes etc.) can hardly be censured as a mere defect of narrative technique, as is sometimes held by critics lacking in historical sense: the Old English standards of literary judgment had not much in common with ours. But the second quality referred to, i. e. the omission of such parts or details of the story as are essential for a tolerable comprehension of the course and development of the narrative, can hardly have been looked upon as desirable or good since the interest of the listener or reader must have been much absorbed by the plot itself. Differences in this respect between the Old English poems, therefore, probably tell us something about their various literary merits, so it is of special interest to compare the frequency of such inconsistencies of narrative in the Cynewulf group. We shall also examine some obscure points which seem due to a certain laxity of composition.

Cynewulf's poems do not display many inconsistencies, apart from such gaps as are due to damage to the text (as for instance in Juliana and the small gap in Elene 1043 ff). Thus in Elene we get a perfectly clear idea of what happens, and problems of context such as ll. 436 ff, 924 ff, and others, are elucidated by textual criticism (cp. p. 60 ff).

Neither is there anything strange about the progress of the narrative in Juliana. Except for the gaps 268 ff, 558 ff, one is surprised only at 29 b ff *hogde georne þæt hire mægðhad mana gehwylces ... clæne geheolde*, followed, after a few lines, by the offer to marry Heliseus under certain conditions. But as has been pointed out p. 29, this logical licence existed in Cynewulf's source. Christ, finally, being of a type demanding less rigour of structure than an epic, is less prone to dangers of obscurity of plot. All we can say about this poem is that all the important paragraphs of Gregory are found in it and that the ideas are developed in perfect order and coherence, although somewhat lengthily, but this is explained as an influence from Gregory himself (cp. p. 32 f). The obscurity in the Fates ll. 100 may, as has been pointed out above (p. 259), be explained as an unsuccessful borrowing from Cynewulf's earlier poems.

As we turn from Cynewulf's poetry to Andreas, we find no small difference in respect of narrative coherence. Our attention is drawn to certain points in the narrative where, in a modern reader's opinion, some link in the chain of events is either omitted or only vaguely hinted at. There is also an inconsistency (no. 2) that reminds us of the cases analysed in the chapter on the parallels. In a critical revision of the text, however, we get rid of some inconsistencies due to scribal errors, just as we can free the poem from obscurities imputed to it by awkward interpreters (cp. p. 49 ff), but even after such revision there remain the following instances of narrative looseness which must be put down to the poet himself, apart from the awkward cases due to borrowed passages badly assimilated:

1. Matthew is blinded by the Mermedonians and prays ll. 76 ff to get his sight back. But when later, ll. 1033 ff, Matthew leads his fellow-prisoners out of the city this implies that he is no longer blind. Yet there has not been any question of his blindness being cured (cp. KRAPP A p. 84). This, on the contrary, is the case in P and C, where Matthew is able to see again after his prayer for the recovery of his sight. The light ll. 88 ff occurs in all the versions and does not refer to the curing of Matthew's blindness; it is a sign that accompanies the sound of God's voice.

2. When God commands Andrew to go to the land of the Mermedonians and release Matthew, the apostle makes several objections
of a fairly timorous kind. One is then surprised at reading,

ll. 231 b ff:

	ne wæs him bleað hyge,
ah he wæs anræd	*ellenweorces,*
heard ond higerof,	*nalas hildlata,*
gearo, guðe fram,	*to godes campe.*

These lines would probably have been denounced by earlier
criticism as an interpolation, but they are no doubt original and an
instance of the poet's general tendency to quicken the narrative with
heroic matter.

3. We are never told when the vessel puts off. In P and C this
happens after the Lord has promised Andrew's disciples that they
may go ashore if they fear the storm which suddenly breaks out.

4. For the casting of lots ll. 1099 ff there is no reason. Since the
Mermedonians ate the bodies of the guards one does not see why,
compelled by hunger, they should have to summon the citizens and
decide which one of them to eat to compensate for the food that has
been lost. In P and C the context is clear since in these versions the
hands of the man-eaters, on the point of cutting up the dead bodies
of the guardians, were turned to stone. However, the episode in
Andreas may have formed part of the source. Cp. also KRAPP A p. 132.

KRAPP A (p. 137) is wrong in saying that "the poet has omitted
to mention that Andrew has made himself invisible to the Mermedonians", a fact mentioned in the other versions; this is stated as
early as l. 986: ... *swa him nænig gumena ongitan ne mihte.*

The Dream of the Rood does not contain any inconsistencies or
obscure points, and those that are to be found in Christ I can easily
be emended, being due to a copyist's error (l. 60), to gaps in the MS
(ll. 24, 153), or to wrong punctuation (l. 208; cp. p. 71 ff). Christ
III, however, contains some obscure passages and only some of these
are due to errors of scribes and editors (ll. 1312 ff, 1562; cp. p. 76 ff).
Thus 921 ff

Ðæt mæg wites to wearninga	*þam þe hafað wisne geþoht,*
þæt se him eallunga	*owiht ne ondrædeð,*
se for ðære onsyne	*egsan ne weorþeð,*
forht on ferðe,	*þonne he frean gesihð,*
ealra gesceafta	*ondweardne faran (... to þinge)*

etc. no doubt refers to the sinner who does not fear God: *wites* must be < *wite*, and *wearninga* must be 'warning' and can hardly mean 'sign', as GOLLANCZ thinks. But if this is so, the passage is unsuccessfully fitted into the context, for in the preceding lines (910—920) the poet tells us that on Judgment Day, Christ turns a mild and beautiful countenance to the just but a terrible and grim one to the sinful. Consequently, we should have thought that *se him eallunga owiht ne ondrædeð* belongs to the former category, but we have here, to all appearances, quite a different idea: there are, generally speaking, people who do not fear God. The transition between the two ideas is so abrupt as to cause inevitable confusion. Another doubtful point is 1095 ff:

> *þær he leoflice   lifes ceapode,*
> *þeoden moncynne,   on þam dæge,*
> *mid þy weorðe,   þe no wom dyde*
> *his lichoma   leahtra firena,*
> *mid þy usic alysde.*

I do not believe, with COOK (C), that the passage is corrupt; on the other hand interpretations such as BRIGHT's (COOK's quotation): "with this price, (namely) because (that) his body was sinless, with this he released us", or KRAPP-DOBBIE's "with a ransom of such sort, that his body wrought no evil" are not very tempting. And yet, something of the kind is probably what the passage means, and I should think that the poet has misunderstood his original here. It would seem that the ransom with which Christ released mankind was his death on the Cross, not his freedom from sin, and it is probable that the poet mixed up these two ideas.

Guthlac A, at first sight, seems to contain several enigmatical points, but on closer inspection these do not seem due to the poet but prove to be repaired and rendered intelligible by slight critical operations. Copyist's errors and unsatifactory interpretation are responsible for the obscurities dealt with on p. 78 ff.

The story of Guthlac B is told in a straightforward way without obscure points or instances of narrative looseness.

In the Phoenix there are some doubtful points, but these are cleared up in a critical revision. The symbolism of the poem is complicated, the Phoenix bird representing different things, but it is not confused.

We may say, as a summing-up, that there is a certain laxity of composition in Andreas and some obscure points in Christ III. The Cynewulf canon, the Dream of the Rood, Christ I, Guthlac A and B, and the Phoenix, on the other hand, do not present any difficulties of this kind.

Before we sum up our results, we must ask ourselves an important question: is it possible that the differences of style and manner described in these chapters, to some extent, at least, are due to corresponding differences in the sources of the poems? Now, as we have seen, we only know the exact sources of Christ I and II, Guthlac B, and the first half of the Phoenix. However, we know fairly well what the other sources must have been like. As far as I can see, there are traces of the style of the sources only in the repetitions in the opening section of Christ II (cp. p. 32 f; the *sum*-series is a vernacular feature, cp. pp. 33, 125); further in the Latinisms analysed on pp. 59, 85, 91; again, in the loose variation, as is explained on p. 233 f. We may notice that the cases of combinations with *ne*-series + *ac* in the Phoenix (cp. p. 228 ff) are not necessarily imitations of the constructions with *nec*-series + *sed* in the beginning of *De Ave Phoenice*: such series are traditional in Anglo-Saxon poetical style and found in nearly all poems. It seems that apart from these cases, of which only the loose variation has been of importance in our stylistic analysis, all the features of style may be looked upon as wholly vernacular and uninfluenced by foreign models.

Retrospect

We are back where we started. Let us begin with the influence of tradition on our poems.

All of them are strongly dependent on Latin hagiographic or homiletic tradition, all, in other words, contain the pious theme. Elaborations in the vernacular manner, which do not seem due to borrowing, are common in Andreas, the Cynewulf canon, and Guthlac B; and the martial theme is especially striking in Andreas, Elene, Juliana, and the Fates. In two cases, further, we have found the vernacular tradition of style identical with the martial theme: in the borrowings and in the vocabulary. The Andreas poet is strongly dependent on the early heroic poetry: with borrowings from Beowulf and Exodus we see him quicken his narrative, in itself effective enough, by some rather pungent seasoning. These borrowings are often forced into a strange context, and we have seen that the poet is notable for a not very strict logical consistency and for a rather eccentric taste. His liking for the vigorous and the emphatic is also apparent from certain details of vocabulary that we have examined: an exuberance of heroic and warlike elements is manifest here. Cynewulf's poetry also contains borrowings and an heroic vocabulary; however, the borrowings do not testify to imitation only, but also to creative talent since the poet, as we have seen, is capable of inspiring the borrowed material with new poetic life and of making it accord with his design and with his style. As for the vocabulary, we clearly see that the author was not dominated by traditional heroic conceptions to the same extent as the Andreas poet. The latter has further a strong inclination for the violent, the revolting, and the fantastic — no wonder that he chose for his theme a story which originally contained elements of this kind exclusively. The other poems are not indebted to the early poetry except for Guthlac B: here we can perceive a certain influence from Beowulf and probably from Daniel, and, on the whole, the poet is skilful and able in his use of the borrowings. These other poems also have few traces of heroic vocabulary.

Now let us pass on to consider the influence of those parts of the vernacular tradition which are not identical with the martial theme. A study of the use of compound and complex clause-series gave us ample occasion to consider the selective capacity of our poets, their different ability to distinguish between vital and subordinate epic matter, and at the same time their different dependence on traditional epic style. We found that the Cynewulf canon, the Dream of the Rood, and Christ III are poems constructed along traditional lines and that the authors of these texts show the finest sense of arranging and organizing the language so as to accord with the varying character of the subject-matter. This discriminative talent is not noticeable in the authors of the other poems, though the Andreas and the Guthlac A poets are more radical in expressing different matter by the same stylistic means than the authors of Christ I, Guthlac B, and the Phoenix.

While we are dealing with different methods of expressing and developing ideas, methods that are supported by traditional influence, we have to pay attention to the results of our study of the variations. A certain concentration in the way of reconsidering a conception, as we have seen, is characteristic of the poets making extensive use of the close variation: the thought is not allowed to stray too far away from the object contemplated, far-fetched associations are not allowed, and the close formal relation between correlative and variation produces a certain symmetry. The use of chiasmus prevents monotony, little frequency of unessential variation gives prominence to elements of weight, and a moderate use of accumulation prevents excessive emphasis. The poetry distinguished by these features, as we remember, is, above all, the Cynewulf canon. Also Guthlac B and the Dream of the Rood may be characterized in this way. A contrast to them is formed by the group of poets who make extensive use of the loose variation: their way of reconsidering an idea is less coherent and less concentrated. They are attracted, we may say, by certain aspects of an idea; while, in the relation between correlative and close variation, there is a very high degree of congruence, the loose variation stresses the significance, the contrast, the different parts of the correlative, or the reverse. The poets who prefer the close variation, in other words, have a somewhat different manner of associating ideas as compared with the poets who more often employ the loose variation, and are also subject to different traditional influence: whereas the former poets, in their use of variation,

re chiefly indebted to vernacular tradition, the latter authors seem
o owe their habits of association to Latin influence. But do not let
s exaggerate the difference: the former poets know the loose varia-
ion and make use of it, the latter know and employ the close
ariation. And close variation in general, not only regarded from
ur special points of view, is used with almost the same frequency
n all the poems, as PAETZEL has shown, except for Guthlac A. The
nain tendencies, though, are obvious.

We pass on to features which are of psychological interest but
vhich do not seem to be supported by tradition.

An examination of causal parataxis demonstrates various degrees
f logical sensitivity in the poets, the lowest degree being represented
y the authors of Andreas and Guthlac A. Between the other poets
he differences are not considerable. Our study of essential hypotaxis
eveals another symptom of this logical laxity of the Andreas poet.
The result of our analysis of adversative asyndeton testifies to some
nability to differentiate divergent matter on the part of the Andreas
nd the Guthlac A poets. This epic stiffness is also perceptible in the
Cynewulf canon, but there it seems to be a conscious device used to
mphasize certain situations (cp. p. 175). The other poets are careful
o establish relations between different matter by means of syndetic
combinations. Further, as regards consistency and precision, we have
seen that Andreas and Christ III present a certain laxity of composition which is indicative of some carelessness on the part of the
authors. Several obscure points in all the texts, however, are due to
the ravages of time, scribes, and editors, as was apparent from our
critical revision of the texts.

As for the poems which, to some extent, are independent of their
sources, we may notice that Andreas and Guthlac B contain descriptions of scenery, which are not met with in their originals, and that
such descriptions are not, to the same degree, met with in the Cynewulf canon.

If we are to classify the poems belonging to the Cynewulf group,
we may take the Cynewulf canon as the basis. Cynewulf's style, as
we have described it, is distinguished by elaborateness combined
with moderation and variety. He is dependent on vernacular tradition,
but he is not overwhelmed by it. In Elene the poet is at his ripest
and richest, and this epic, it seems to me, contains much of the best
poetry in Old English poetical literature on the whole. There is much
excellent poetry in Juliana and Christ II as well, but the former

poem is less mature and has a certain epic meagreness. In Christ II the poet is somewhat overwhelmed by the rhetoric of Gregory. The Fata Apostolorum is inferior in quality to the other poems. As for the other texts, the Dream of the Rood and Guthlac B seem to me to be most closely related to the Cynewulf canon. These poems have a smooth and supple style which is not far from the signed poems. Christ I is also fairly close to Cynewulf's poetry. But Christ III and the Phoenix, in spite of the Cynewulfian use of compound series in the former poem, are clearly distinguished from the signed poems by their extensive use of the loose variation, which points to different manner of thinking and different tradition. This use in Christ III, by the way, markedly different from that of the other two Christ texts, seems difficult to explain for those who believe in the unity of the Christ trilogy. In this connexion I should like to stress a point in the palæographic analysis made by BROTHER AUGUSTINE PHILIP: it seems that the s c r i b e arranged the three poems according to their motifs, just as he arranged the Guthlac texts according to theirs, and that he was, consequently, aware of the coherence between the Nativity, the Ascension, and the Judgment Day motifs which has been pointed out by MOORE and MILDENBERGER.

Andreas and Guthlac A, finally, are least similar to Cynewulf: not so much on account of different traditional influence, which, in the former poem, is quite as strong as it is in Cynewulf, but on account of mannerisms and lack of discriminative talent which are as foreign as possible to the characteristics of Cynewulf's work. The loose variation is also frequent in these poems.

The result of our examination tends, then, to confirm S. K. DAS's and earlier scholars' view that Christ III, Guthlac A, Andreas, and the Phoenix, cannot be the work of Cynewulf. Even if we accept the conclusion that the Dream of the Rood, Christ I, and Guthlac B were also written by other authors, they must have been composed by poets whose style and manner had much in common with Cynewulf's.

To sum up: behind the outward uniformity of style and manner of the Cynewulf group we are able to discern considerable divergencies, which have their cause in individual and traditional differences. The poets, about whose lives and destinies we know nothing, give us, unconsciously, some important characteristics of their poetic personalities, even though the ancient vernacular and the new Latin traditions abundantly supplied them with matter as well as with form.

Bibliography

Texts

Some of the abbreviations used in the book are explained in the bibliography, the others are so generally used that no explanation is necessary.)

Acta Sanctorum edd. lo. BOLLANDUS, G. HENSCHENIUS, lo. CARNANDET. Parisiis 1863—75. (Acta Sanctorum).

D'ARDENNE, S. T. R. O., An Edition of þe Liflade ant te Passiun of Seinte Iuliene. Liège, 1936. (Bibl. de la Fac. de Philos. et Lettres de l'Univ. de Liège, Fasc. LXIV). (Liflade).

BASKERVILL, W. M., Andreas, a Legend of St. Andrew. Boston, 1885.

BLACKBURN, F. A., Exodus and Daniel. Boston and London, 1907. (BLACKBURN ED).

BLATT, F., Die lateinischen Bearbeitungen der Acta Andreæ et Matthiæ apud anthropophagos. Giessen-Kopenhagen, 1930. (BLATT).

BOUTERWEK, K. W., Cædmon's des Angelsachsen biblische Dichtungen, I. Gütersloh, 1854.

BRIGHT, J. W., An Anglo-Saxon Reader, New York, 1892.

BÜTOW, H., Das altenglische „Traumgesicht vom Kreuz". Heidelberg, 1935. In *Anglistische Forschungen* 78. (BÜTOW).

R. W. CHAMBERS, M. FÖRSTER, R. FLOWER, The Exeter Book of Old English Poetry. London, 1933 (facsimile). (CHAMBERS).

CLUBB, M. D., Christ and Satan, an Old English Poem. New Haven, 1925. In *Yale Studies in English* LXX, I ff. (CLUBB).

COCKAYNE, O., Ðe Liflade of St. Juliana. London, 1872. In *Early English Text Society* 51, p. 81 ff. (Ashmole).

COOK, A. S., A First Book in Old English. Boston, 1900. (COOK, First Book).

— The Christ of Cynewulf. Boston, 1900. (COOK C).

— The Dream of the Rood. Oxford, 1905.

— The Old English Elene, Phoenix, and Physiologus. New Haven, 1919. (COOK EPh).

CRAIGIE, W. A., Specimens of Anglo-Saxon Poetry, I—III. Edinburgh, 1923—31. (CRAIGIE).

B. DICKINS and A. S. C. ROSS, The Dream of the Rood. London, 1934. (DICKINS-ROSS).

DOBBIE, E., The Anglo-Saxon Minor Poems. New York, 1942. (DOBBIE).

ETTMÜLLER, L., Engla and Seaxna Scôpas and Bôceras. Quedlinburg and Leipzig, 1850. (ETTMÜLLER).

v. FEILITZEN, H., Li Ver del Juïse, en fornfransk predikan. Appendices. Upsala 1883. (OF Juliana).

FOERSTER, M., Il Codice Vercellese con Omelie e Poesie in Lingua Anglosasson Roma, 1913. (FOERSTER).

GOLLANCZ, I., Cynewulf's Christ. London, 1892. (GOLLANCZ C).

— The Exeter Book I. In *Early English Text Society* 104. London, 189 (GOLLANCZ).

GREIN, C. W. M., Bibliothek der angelsächsischen Poesie I—II. Göttinge 1857—58. (GREIN).

GRIMM, J., Andreas und Elene. Cassel, 1840. (GRIMM).

GRUNDTVIG, N. F. S., Phenix-Fuglen, et Angelsachsisk Kvad. Kjöbenhavn, 184 (GRUNDTVIG).

GRÄSSE, TH., Jacobi a Voragine Legenda Aurea, editio tertia. Vratislaviae, 189 (Legenda Aurea).

HETZENAVER, M., Biblia Sacra Vulgatæ Editionis. Oeniponte, 1906.

HOLDER, A., Inventio Sanctæ Crvcis. Lipsiæ, 1889.

HOLTHAUSEN, F., Cynewulf's Elene, 4th ed. Heidelberg, 1936. (HOLTHAUSEN).

JAFFÉ, PH., Monumenta Alcuiniana. Berolini, 1873. In *Bibliotheca Rerum Ge manicarum* VI. (JAFFÉ).

KEMBLE, J., The Poetry of the Codex Vercellensis, I—II. London, 1843—4 (KEMBLE).

KENT, CH. W., Elene, An Old English Poem. Boston, 1889. (KENT).

KLAEBER, FR., Beowulf and the Fight at Finnsburg, 3rd ed. New York, 194 (KLAEBER).

KLIPSTEIN, L. F., Analecta Anglo-Saxonica II. New York, 1849. (KLIPSTEIN).

KLUGE, FR., Angelsächsisches Lesebuch. Halle, 1888.

KRAPP, G. P., Andreas and the Fates of the Apostles. Boston, 1906. (KRAPP A

— The Junius Manuscript. London and New York, 1931.

— The Vercelli Book. London and New York, 1932. (KRAPP).

KRAPP, G. P. and DOBBIE, E., The Exeter Book. London and New York, 193 (KRAPP-DOBBIE).

LAUCHERT, FR., Geschichte des Physiologus, p. 229 ff. Strassburg, 1889. (LAUCHERT

LIPSIUS, R. A. and BONNET, M., Acta Apostolorum Apocrypha post Constantinu Tischendorf, I—II. Lipsiæ 1891—1903.

METCALFE, W. M., Legends of the Saints, vol. II, p. 424 ff. Edinburgh an London, 1896 (Scottish Juliana).

MIGNE, J. P., Patrologiæ cursus completus. Patres Græci. 1—161. Parisiis, 185 —87. (MIGNE P. G.).

— Patrologiæ cursus completus. Patres Latini. 1—221. Parisiis, 1844—64 (MIGNE P. L.).

MOMBRITIUS, B., Sanctuarium seu Vitæ Sanctorum I—II. Mediolani 1479, ed. nov Parisiis 1910.

NESTLE, E., De Sancta Cruce. Berlin, 1889. (NESTLE).

PACIUS, A., Das heilige Kreuz. Gera, 1873.

PLUMMER, G., Baedae Opera Historica I—II. Oxonii, 1896. (PLUMMER).

RICCI, A., Il Sogno della Croce. Firenze, 1926.

RYSSEL, V., Syrische Quellen abendländischer Erzählungsstoffe, I. In *Archi für das Studium der neueren Sprachen* XCIII, p. 1 ff. (RYSSEL).

SCHIRMER, G., Die Kreuzeslegenden im Leabhar Breac. St. Gallen, 1886. (Leabhar Breac).

SCHLOTTEROSE, O., Die altenglische Dichtung Phoenix herausgegeben und erläutert. Bonn, 1908. In *Bonner Beiträge zur Anglistik* XXV. (SCHLOTTEROSE).

SCHÖNBACH, A., Mittheilungen aus altdeutschen Handschriften V: Priester Arnolts Legende von St. Juliana. In *Sitzungsberichte der Kaiserl. Akademie der Wissenschaften, Philos.-Hist. Classe* 101, p. 445 ff. Wien, 1882. (Arnolt).

SEDGEFIELD, W. J., An Anglo-Saxon Verse Book. Manchester, 1922. (SEDGEFFIELD, Verse Book).

STEPHENS, G., The Old-Northern Runic Monuments of Scandinavia and England, I. London and Köbenhavn, 1866—67.

STRUNK, W., The Juliana of Cynewulf. Boston and London, 1904. (STRUNK).

SWEET, H., An Anglo-Saxon Reader, 9th ed. Oxford, 1922. (SWEET).

THORPE, B., Codex Exoniensis. London, 1842. (THORPE).

TISCHENDORF, C., Acta Apostolorum Apocrypha. Leipzig, 1851.

WALKER, A., Apocryphal Gospels, Acts, and Revelations, translated by ALEXANDER WALKER. In *Ante-Nicene Christian Library* XVI, p. 348 ff. Edinburgh, 1870.

WILLIAMS, O. T., Short Extracts from Old English Poetry. Bangor, 1909. (WILLIAMS).

WÜLKER, R., Bibliothek der angelsächsischen Poesie I—II. Kassel-Leipzig, 1883—94. (WÜLKER); III ed. ASSMANN, Leipzig, 1898. (ASSMANN).

— Codex Vercellensis. Die angelsæchsische Handschrift zu Vercelli in getreuer Nachbildung. Leipzig, 1894.

ZUPITZA, J., Cynewulfs Elene. Berlin, 1877. (ZUPITZA).

Other works consulted

ABBETMEYER, CH., Old English Poetical Motives derived from the Doctrine of Sin. Minneapolis, 1903. (ABBETMEYER).

AHRENS, J., Darstellung der Syntax im angelsächsischen Gedicht Phönix. Rostock, 1904. (AHRENS).

ARNGART, O., The Seafarer. Lund, 1938. In *K. Hum. Vet. Samf. Lund Årsber.* 1937—38. 21. (ARNGART).

— Some Notes on Cynewulf's Elene. In *English Studies* XXVII, p. 19 ff, 1946. (ARNGART, English Studies XXVII).

BACKHAUS, O., Über die Quelle der mittelenglischen Legende von der heiligen Juliana und ihr Verhältnis zu Cynewulfs Juliana. Halle, 1899. (BACKHAUS).

BARNOUW, A. J., Textkritische Untersuchungen nach dem Gebrauch des bestimmten Artikels und des schwachen Adjectivs in der altenglischen Poesie. Leiden, 1902. (BARNOUW).

BARTLETT, A. C., The Larger Rhetorical Patterns in Anglo-Saxon Poetry. New York, 1935. (BARTLETT).

BEHRE, F., The Subjunctive in Old English Poetry. In *Göteborgs Högskolas Årsskrift* XL, 1934: 2. Göteborg, 1934. (BEHRE).

BLACKBURN, F. A., Is the Christ of Cynewulf a Single Poem? In *Anglia* XIX, p. 89 ff, 1897. (BLACKBURN, Anglia XIX).

BODE, W., Die Kenningar in der angelsächsischen Poesie. Darmstadt, 1886. (BODE).

BOSWORTH, J. and TOLLER, T. N., An Anglo-Saxon Dictionary. Oxford, 1882—1921. (BOSWORTH-TOLLER).

BOURAUEL, J., Zur Quellen- und Verfasserfragen von Andreas Crist und Fata. In *Bonner Beiträge zur Anglistik* XI, 65 ff, 1901. (BOURAUEL).

BRANDL, A., Englische Literatur. In *Paul's Grundriss der Germanischen Philologie*, 2d ed., II, p. 941 ff, 1908. (BRANDL).

BRETT, C., Notes on Old and Middle English. In *Modern Language Review* XXII, p. 257 ff, 1927. (BRETT, MLR XXII).

BROOKE, S. A., The History of Early English Literature I—II. New York, 1892. (BROOKE).

BROTHER AUGUSTINE PHILIP, The Exeter Scribe and the Unity of the *Christ*. In *Publications of the Modern Language Association of America* LV, p. 903 ff, 1940. (BROTHER AUGUSTINE PHILIP).

BROWN, CARLETON F., The Autobiographical Element in the Cynewulfian Rune Passages. In *Englische Studien* XXXVIII, p. 196 ff, 1907. (BROWN, Engl. Stud. XXXVIII).

— Irish-Latin Influence in Cynewulfian Texts. In *Englische Studien* XL, p. 1 ff, 1908. (BROWN, Engl. Stud. XL).

BRUNÖHLER, E., Über einige lateinische, englische, französische und deutsche Fassungen der Julianenlegende. Bonn, 1912. (BRUNÖHLER).

BURGERT, E., The Dependence of Part I of Cynewulf's Christ upon the Antiphonary. Washington, 1921. (BURGERT).

BUTTENWIESER, E. C., Studien über die Verfasserschaft des Andreas. Heidelberg, 1899. (BUTTENWIESER).

CHARITIUS, F., Über die angelsächsischen Gedichte vom hl. Guthlac. In *Anglia* II, p. 265ff, 1879. (CHARITIUS).

CONRADI, B., Darstellung der Syntax in Cynewulf's Gedicht Juliana. Halle, 1886. (CONRADI).

COOK, A. S., A Remote Analogue to the Miracle Play. In *Journal of Germanic Philology* IV, 421 ff, 1902. (COOK JEGPh IV).

— Cynewulf's Part in our Beowulf. In *Transactions of the Connecticut Academy of Arts and Sciences*, XXVII, p. 385 ff, 1925. (COOK, Trans. Con. Ac. XXVII).

COSIJN, P. J., Cynewulf's Runenverzen. In *Verslagen en Mededeelingen der koninklijke Akademie van Wetenschappen. Afdeeling Letterkunde. 3. Reeks, 7. Deel*, p. 54 ff, 1890. (COSIJN CR).

— Aanteekeningen op den Beowulf. Leiden, 1892. (COSIJN, Anteekeningen).

— Anglosaxonica. III. In *Beiträge zur Geschichte der deutschen Sprache und Literatur*, hrsg. von Paul und Braune, XXI, p. 8 ff, 1896. (COSIJN, Btr. XXI).

— Anglosaxonica. IV. In *Beiträge zur Geschichte der deutschen Sprache und Literatur*, hrsg. von Paul und Braune, XXIII, p. 109 ff, 1898. (COSIJN, Btr. XXIII).

CREMER, M., Metrische und sprachliche Untersuchung der altenglischen Gedichte Andreas, Guðlac, Phoenix (Elene, Juliana, Crist). Bonn, 1888. (CREMER).

DAS, S. K., Cynewulf and the Cynewulf Canon. Calcutta, 1942. (S. K. DAS).

DEERING, W., The Anglosaxon Poets on the Judgment Day. Halle, 1890. (DEERING).

DIETRICH, F., Cynevulfs Christ. In *Zeitschrift für deutsches Altertum* IX, p. 193 ff, 1853. (DIETRICH).

DUBOIS, M.-M., Les Elements Latins dans la Poésie Religieuse de Cynewulf. Paris, 1943. (DUBOIS).

EBERT, A., Über das angelsächsische Gedicht: Der Traum vom heiligen Kreuze. In *Berichte über die Verhandlungen der königlich sächsischen Gesellschaft der Wissenschaften, Phil.-Hist. Classe*, XXXVI, p. 81 ff, 1884. (EBERT).

EKWALL, E., [Review of COOK, The Old English Elene, Phoenix, and Physiologus.] In *Beiblatt zur Anglia* XXXIII, p. 61 ff, 1922. (EKWALL, Anglia Beibl. XXXIII).

EMERSON, O. F., Originality in Old English Poetry. In *Review of English Studies* II, p. 18 ff, 1926. (EMERSON).

FICK, A., Vergleichendes Wörterbuch der Indogermanischen Sprachen. 4. Aufl. III. Wortschatz der germanischen Spracheinheit ... umgearb. von A. TORP. Göttingen, 1909. (FICK-TORP).

FORSTMANN, H., Untersuchungen zur Guthlac-Legende. In *Bonner Beiträge zur Anglistik* XII, p. 1 ff, 1902. (FORSTMANN).

FRITZSCHE, A., Das angelsächsische Gedicht Andreas und Cynewulf. Halle, 1879. (FRITZSCHE).

FULTON, E., On the Authorship of the Anglo-Saxon Poem Phoenix. In *Modern Language Notes* XI, p. 73 ff, 1896. (FULTON).

GAEBLER, H., Ueber die Autorschaft des angelsächsischen Gedichtes vom Phoenix. In *Anglia* III, p. 488 ff, 1880. (GAEBLER).

GARNETT, J. M., The Latin and the Anglo-Saxon Juliana. In *Publications of the Modern Language Association of America* XIV, p. 279 ff, 1899. (GARNETT).

GEROULD, G. H., Studies in the Christ. In *Englische Studien* XLI, p. 1 ff, 1909 (GEROULD, Engl. Stud. XLI).

— Cynewulf's Christ 678—679. In *Modern Language Notes* XXXI, p. 403 f, 1916. (GEROULD, MLN XXXI).

— The Old English Poems on St. Guthlac and their Latin Source. In *Modern Language Notes* XXXII, p. 77 ff, 1917. (GEROULD, MLN XXXII).

GLOGAUER, E., Die Bedeutungsübergänge der Konjunktionen in der angelsächsischen Dichtersprache. In *Neue Anglistische Arbeiten*, no. 6, 1922. (GLOGAUER).

GLÖDE, O., Untersuchungen über die Quelle von Cynewulf's Elene. In *Anglia* IX, p. 271 ff, 1886. (GLÖDE, Anglia IX).

— Cynewulfs Juliana und ihre Quelle. In *Anglia* XI, p. 146 ff, 1889. (GLÖDE, Anglia XI).

GRAU, G., Quellen und Verwandtschaften der älteren germanischen Darstellungen des Jüngsten Gerichtes. In *Studien zur Englischen Philologie* XXXI, 1908. (GRAU).

GREIN, C. W. M., Zur Textkritik der angelsächsischen Dichter. In *Germania* X, p. 416 ff, 1865. (GREIN, Germania X).

— Sprachschatz der angelsächsischen Dichter. Neu hrsg. v. J. J. KÖHLER. Heidelberg, 1912—14. (GREIN-KÖHLER).

GROTH, E. J., Composition und Alter der altenglischen (angelsächsischen) Exodus. Göttingen, 1883. (GROTH).

HAMILTON, G. L., The Sources of the Fates of the Apostles and Andreas. In Modern Language Notes XXXV, p. 385 ff, 1920. (HAMILTON).

HEINZEL, R., Über den Stil der altgermanischen Poesie. In Quellen und Forschungen zur Sprach- und Culturgeschichte der germanischen Völker X, p. 1 ff, 1875. (HEINZEL).

HEUSLER, A., Heliand, Liedstil und Epenstil. In Zeitschrift für deutsches Altertum LVII, p. 1 ff, 1920. (HEUSLER, ZfdA LVII).

— Die altgermanische Dichtung. Berlin-Neubabelsberg, 1923. (HEUSLER).

HODGKIN, R. H., A History of the Anglo-Saxons I—II. Oxford, 1935. (HODGKIN)

HOLTBUER, F., Der syntaktische Gebrauch des Genitives in Andreas, Guðlac, Phönix, dem heiligen Kreuz und der Höllenfahrt. In Anglia VIII, p. 1 ff, 1884. (HOLTBUER).

HOLTHAUSEN, F., Beiträge zur Erklärung und Textkritik altenglischer Dichter. In Indogermanische Forschungen IV, p. 379 ff, 1894. (HOLTHAUSEN, IF IV).

— [Review of GREIN-WÜLKER-ASSMANN]. In Beiblatt zur Anglia IX, p. 353 ff, 1899. (HOLTHAUSEN, Anglia Beibl. IX).

— [Review of COOK, The Christ of Cynewulf]. In Literaturblatt XXI, p. 369 ff, 1900. (HOLTHAUSEN, Literaturblatt XXI).

— Zum Schluss des altengl. Phönix. In Archiv für das Studium der neueren Sprachen CXII, p. 132 ff, 1904. (HOLTHAUSEN, Archiv CXII).

— Die Quelle von Cynewulfs Elene. In Zeitschrift für deutsche Philologie XXXVII, p. 1 ff, 1905. (HOLTHAUSEN, ZfdPh XXXVII).

— [Review of STRUNK's Juliana]. In Literaturblatt XXVIII, p. 10 ff, 1907. (HOLTHAUSEN, Literaturblatt XXVIII).

— Zur Quelle von Cynewulfs Elene. In Archiv für das Studium der neueren Sprachen CXXV, p. 83 ff, 1910. (HOLTHAUSEN, Archiv CXXV).

— Zu altenglischen Dichtungen. In Beiblatt zur Anglia XXXI, p. 25 ff, 1920. (HOLTHAUSEN, Anglia Beibl. XXXI).

— Zu altenglischen Dichtungen. In Beiblatt zur Anglia XXXV, p. 276 ff, 1924. (HOLTHAUSEN, Anglia Beibl. XXXV).

— Die Quelle der altenglischen Andreas-Legenden. In Beiblatt zur Anglia XLIV, p. 90 f, 1933. (HOLTHAUSEN, Anglia Beibl. XLIV).

— Altenglisches Etymologisches Wörterbuch. Heidelberg, 1932—34. (HOLTHAUSEN, Et. W.).

— Eine neue lateinische Fassung der Andreaslegende. In Anglia LXII, p. 190 f, 1938. (HOLTHAUSEN, Anglia LXII).

— Zur Elene (v. 629). In Beiblatt zur Anglia XLIX, p. 348 f, 1938. (HOLTHAUSEN, Anglia Beibl. XLIX).

— Zum ae. Crist I. In Beiblatt zur Anglia LIV, p. 31 f, 1943. (HOLTHAUSEN, Anglia Beibl. LIV).

HUCHON, R., Histoire de la Langue Anglaise I, 2d ed. Paris, 1942. (HUCHON I).

HUNT, W., A History of the English Church 597—1066. London, 1901. (HUNT).

JANSEN, G., Beiträge zur Synonymik und Poetik der allgemein als ächt anerkannten Dichtungen Cynewulfs. Münster, 1883. (G. JANSEN).

JÓNSSON, F., Lexicon Poeticum Antiquæ Linguæ Septentrionalis. 2d ed. Kjøbenhavn, 1931. (FINNUR JÓNSSON, Lex. Poet.).

JOST, K., Crist 558—585. In English Studies XXVII, p. 175 ff, 1946. (JOST, English Studies XXVII).

Jost, K., [Review of Kennedy, The Earliest English Poetry]. In *English Studies* XXVIII, p. 116 f, 1947.

Kail, J., Über die Parallelstellen in der angelsächsischen Poesie. In *Anglia* XII, p. 21 ff, 1889. (Kail).

Kaluza, M., Der altenglische Vers: eine metrische Untersuchung I—II. Berlin, 1894.

Keiser, A., The Influence of Christianity on the Vocabulary of Old English Poetry I—II. In *University of Illinois Studies in Language and Literature* V, p. 1 ff, 1919. (Keiser).

Kellner, L., Historical Outlines of English Syntax. London, 1905. (Kellner).

Kennedy, Ch. W., The Earliest English Poetry. Oxford, 1943. (Kennedy).

Klaeber, Fr., [Review of Cook, The Christ of Cynewulf]. In *Journal of Germanic Philology* IV, p. 101 ff, 1902. (Klaeber, JEGPh IV).

— Guðlac 1252 ff. In *Beiblatt zur Anglia* XV, p. 345 ff, 1904. (Klaeber, Anglia Beibl. XV).

— Notizen zu Cynewulfs Elene. In *Anglia* XXIX, p. 271 f, 1906. (Klaeber, Anglia XXIX).

— Jottings on the Andreas. In *Archiv für das Studium der neueren Sprachen* CXX, p. 153 ff, 1908. (Klaeber, Archiv CXX).

— Notes on Old English Poems. In *Journal of English and Germanic Philology* XII, p. 252 ff, 1913. (Klaeber, JEGPh XII).

— Concerning the Relations between *Exodus* and *Beowulf*. In *Modern Language Notes* XXXIII, p. 218 ff, 1918. (Klaeber, MLN XXXIII).

— Beowulfiana. In *Anglia* L, p. 195 ff, 1926. (Klaeber, Anglia L).

— Beowulf 769 und Andreas 1526 ff. In *Englische Studien* LXXIII, p. 185 ff, 1939. (Klaeber, Engl. Stud. LXXIII).

Kock, E. A., [Review of Holthausen, Cynewulfs Elene, 2d ed.]. In *Englische Studien* XLIV, p. 392 ff, 1912. (Kock, Engl. Stud. XLIV).

— Jubilee Jaunts and Jottings. In *Lunds Universitets Arsskrift*, N. F., Avd. 1, Bd 14, Nr. 26, 1918. (Kock, JJJ).

— Interpretations and Emendations of Early English Texts V. In *Anglia* XLIII, p. 298 ff, 1919. (Kock, Anglia XLIII).

— Interpretations and Emendations of Early English Texts VI. In *Anglia* XLIV, p. 97 ff, 1920. (Kock, Anglia XLIV).

— Interpretations and Emendations of Early English Texts IX. In *Anglia* XLVI, p. 63 ff, 1922. (Kock, Anglia XLVI).

— Interpretations and Emendations of Early English Texts XI. In *Anglia* XLVII, p. 264 ff, 1923. (Kock, Anglia XLVII).

— Notationes Norrœnæ. In *Lunds Universitets Arsskrift*, 1923—44. (Kock, NN).

Kopas, W., Die Grundzüge der Satzverknüpfung in Cynewulfs Schriften. Breslau, 1910. (Kopas).

Körner, K., [Review of Zupitza, Cynewulfs Elene]. In *Englische Studien* II, p. 252 ff, 1879. (Körner, Engl. Stud. II).

Körting, G., Grundriss der Geschichte der Englischen Litteratur. Münster, 1887. (Körting).

Laistner, M. L. W., Thought and Letters in Western Europe A. D. 500 to 900. London, 1931. (Laistner).

LAWRENCE, W. W., Beowulf and Epic Tradition. Cambridge, 1928. (LAWRENCE).

LEFÈVRE, P., Das altenglische Gedicht vom heiligen Guthlac. In *Anglia* VI, p. 181 ff, 1883. (LEFÈVRE).

LEO, H., Quæ de se ipso Cynevulfus (sive Cenevulfus sive Coenevulfus) poeta Anglosaxonicus tradiderit. Halle, 1857. (LEO).

LIEBERMANN, F., Ueber Ostenglische Geschichtsquellen des 12., 13., 14. Jahrhunderts, besonders den falschen Ingulf. In *Neues Archiv der Gesellschaft für ältere deutsche Geschichtskunde* XVIII, p. 225 ff, 1893. (LIEBERMANN).

LIPSIUS, R. A., Die apokryphen Apostelgeschichten und Apostellegenden I—II. Braunschweig, 1883—90. (LIPSIUS).

MANITIUS, M., Geschichte der lateinischen Literatur des Mittelalters I—III. München 1911—31. (MANITIUS).

MARQUARDT, H., Die altenglischen Kenningar. In *Schriften der Königsberger Gelehrten Gesellschaft* XIV, Heft III, p. I ff, 1938. (MARQUARDT).

MATHER, F. J., The Cynewulf Question from a Metrical Point of View. In *Modern Language Notes* VII, p. 193 ff, 1892. (MATHER).

V. D. MERWE SCHOLTZ, H., The Kenning in Anglo-Saxon and Old Norse Poetry. Utrecht, 1927. (V. D. MERWE SCHOLTZ).

MEYER, R. M., Die altgermanische Poesie. Berlin, 1889. (MEYER).

MILDENBERGER, K., Unity of Cynewulf's *Christ* in the Light of Iconography. In *Speculum* XXIII, p. 426 ff, 1948. (MILDENBERGER).

MOHR, W., Kenningstudien. Stuttgart, 1933. (MOHR).

MONROE, B. S., Notes on the Anglo-Saxon Andreas. In *Modern Language Notes* XXXI, p. 374 ff, 1916. (MONROE).

MOORE, S., Notes on the Old English Christ. In *Archiv für das Studium der neueren Sprachen* CXXXI, p. 311 ff, 1913. (MOORE, Archiv CXXXI)

— The Source of Christ 416 ff. In *Modern Language Notes* XXIX, p. 226 f, 1914. (MOORE, MLN XXIX).

— The Old English Christ: Is It a Unit? In *Journal of English and Germanic Philology* XIV, p. 550 ff, 1915. (MOORE, JEGPh XIV).

MÄTZNER, E., Englische Grammatik I—III. Berlin 1880—85. (MÄTZNER).

NAPIER, A. S., The Old English Poem The Fates of the Apostles. In *Academy* XXXIV, p. 153, 1888.

PAETZEL, W., Die Variationen in der altgermanischen Allitterationspoesie. In *Palaestra* XLVIII, 1913. (PAETZEL).

POGATSCHER, A., Unausgedrücktes subject im altenglischen. In *Anglia* XXIII, p. 261 ff, 1901. (POGATSCHER).

PONS, E., Le Thème et le Sentiment de la Nature dans la Poésie Anglo-Saxonne. In *Publications de la faculté des lettres de l'univ. de Strasbourg. Fasc.* 25, 1925. (PONS).

PROLLIUS, M., Ueber den syntactischen Gebrauch des Conjunctivs in den Cynewulfschen Dichtungen Elene, Juliana und Crist. Marburg, 1888.

RAMHORST, FR., Das altenglische Gedicht vom heiligen Andreas und der Dichter Cynewulf. Berlin, 1885. (RAMHORST).

RANKIN, J. W., A Study of the Kennings in Anglo-Saxon Poetry. In *Journal of English and Germanic Philology* VIII, p. 357 ff, 1909, IX, p. 49 ff, 1910. (RANKIN).

REINACH, S., Cultes, Mythes et Religions. Paris, 1905.

REUSSNER, H. A., Untersuchungen über die Syntax in dem angelsächsischen Gedichte vom heiligen Andreas. Halle, 1889.

RICCI, A., The Chronology of Anglo-Saxon Poetry. In *Review of English Studies*
V, p. 257 ff, 1929. (RICCI, RES V).

RICHTER, C., Chronologische Studien zur angelsächsischen Literatur auf Grund
sprachlich-metrischer Kriterien. Halle, 1910. (RICHTER).

RIEGER, M., Über Cynewulf. In *Zeitschrift für deutsche Philologie* I, pp. 215 ff,
313 ff, 1869. (RIEGER).

ROSE, A., Darstellung der Syntax in Cynewulfs Crist. Halle, 1890.

RÖSSGER, R., Über den syntaktischen Gebrauch des Genitivs in Cynewulfs Crist,
Elene und Juliana. Halle, 1885.

SARRAZIN, G., Beowulf und Kynewulf. In *Anglia* IX, p. 515 ff, 1886. (SARRAZIN,
Anglia IX).

— Beowulf-Studien. Berlin, 1888. (SARRAZIN, BS).

— Die Abfassungszeit des Beowulfliedes. In *Anglia* XIV, p. 399 ff, 1892. (SAR-
RAZIN, Anglia XIV).

— Paralellstellen in altenglischer Dichtung. Ibid. p. 186 ff.

— Neue Beowulf-Studien. In *Englische Studien* XXIII, p. 221 ff, 1897. (SAR-
RAZIN, Engl. Stud. XXIII).

— [Review of SIMONS, Cynewulfs Wortschatz]. In *Zeitschrift für deutsche
Philologie* XXXII, p. 547 ff, 1900. (SARRAZIN, ZfdPh XXXII).

— Zur Chronologie und Verfasserfrage angelsächsischer Dichtungen. In *Englische Studien* XXXVIII, p. 145 ff, 1907. (SARRAZIN, Engl. Stud. XXXVIII).

— Von Kädmon bis Kynewulf. Berlin, 1913. (SARRAZIN, KK).

SCHIPPER, J., Zum Codex Exoniensis. In *Germania* XIX, p. 327 ff, 1874. (SCHIPPER,
Germania XIX).

SCHÜCKING, L., Die Grundzüge der Satzverknüpfung im Beowulf. Halle, 1904.
(SCHÜCKING, Satzverknüpfung).

— Untersuchungen zur Bedeutungslehre der angelsächsischen Dichtersprache.
Heidelberg, 1915. (SCHÜCKING, Dichtersprache).

— Die angelsächsische und frühmittelenglische Dichtung. In HECHT-SCHÜCKING,
Die englische Literatur im Mittelalter, p. 1 ff, 1927. (SCHÜCKING).

— Noch einmal "enge anpaðas, uncuð gelad". In *Studies in English Philology,
A Miscellany in honor of* FREDERICK KLAEBER, p. 213 ff, 1929. (SCHÜCKING,
St. E. Ph. Kl.).

SCHÜRMANN, J., Darstellung der Syntax in Cynewulfs Elene. In *Neuphiloloqische
Studien* No. 4, p. 287 ff, 1884. (SCHÜRMANN).

SCHWARZ, F., Cynewulfs Anteil am Christ. Königsberg, 1905. (SCHWARZ).

SCHÖLL, FR., Vom Vogel Phönix. Heidelberg, 1890. (SCHÖLL).

SHEARIN, H. G., The Phoenix and the Guthlac. In *Modern Language Notes*
XXII, p. 263, 1907. (SHEARIN).

SIEVERS, E., [Review of ZUPITZA, Cynewulfs Elene]. In *Anglia* I, p. 573 ff, 1878.
(SIEVERS, Anglia I).

— Zum Beowulf. In *Beiträge zur Geschichte der deutschen Sprache und Literatur, hrsg von Paul und Braune* IX, p. 135 ff, 1884. (SIEVERS, Btr. IX).

— Miscellen zur angelsächsischen Grammatik, ibid. p. 197 ff.

— Zur Rhythmik des germanischen Alliterationsverses. II. In *Beiträge zur*

Geschichte der deutschen Sprache und Literatur, hrsg von Paul und Braune X, p. 451 ff, 1885. (Sievers, Btr. X).

Sievers, E., Zur Rhythmik des germanischen Alliterationsverses. III. In *Beiträge zur Geschichte der deutschen Sprache und Literatur, hrsg. von Paul und Braune* XII, pp. 454 ff, 1887. (Sievers, Btr. XII).

— Zu Cynewulf. In *Anglia* XIII, p. 1 ff, 1891. (Sievers, Anglia XIII).

— Notes on Holthausen, Zur Textkritik altenglischer Dichtungen. In *Beiträge zur Geschichte der deutschen Sprache und Literatur, hrsg. von Paul und Braune* XVI, p. 549 ff, 1892. (Sievers, Btr. XVI).

Simons, R., Cynewulfs Wortschatz. In *Bonner Beiträge zur Anglistik* III, 1899. (Simons).

Sisam, K., Cynewulf and his Poetry. In *Proceedings of the British Academy* XVIII, p. 303 ff, 1932. (Sisam).

Skeat, W. W., Andreas and Fata Apostolorum. In *An English Miscellany presented to Dr.* Furnivall, p. 408 ff, 1901. (Skeat).

Smithson, G. A., The Old English Christian Epic. In *University of California Publications in Modern Philology* I, p. 303 ff, 1910. (Smithson).

Stenton, F. M., Anglo-Saxon England. Oxford, 1943. (Stenton).

Sweet, H., The Student's Dictionary of Anglo-Saxon. Oxford, 1928. (Sweet, Student's Dictionary).

Ten Brink, B., [Review of Zupitza, Cynewulfs Elene]. In *Anzeiger für deutsches Altertum* V, p. 53 ff, 1879. (Ten Brink, Anz. f. d. A. V).

— Geschichte der englischen Litteratur I. Berlin, 1877. (Ten Brink).

Thomas, P. G., 'Beowulf' and 'Daniel A'. In *Modern Language Review* VIII, p. 537 ff, 1913. (Thomas).

Timmer, B. J., Wyrd in Anglo-Saxon Prose and Poetry. In *Neophilologus* XXVI, I p. 24, II p. 27, III p. 213 ff, 1940—41. (Timmer).

Trautmann, M., Zur Kenntnis des altgermanischen Verses. In *Beiblatt zur Anglia* V, p. 87 ff, 1894. (Trautmann, Anglia Beibl. V).

— Der Andreas doch von Cynewulf. In *Beiblatt zur Anglia* VI, p. 17 ff, 1895. (Trautmann, Anglia Beibl. VI).

— Kynewulf der Bischof und Dichter. In *Bonner Beiträge zur Anglistik* I, 1898. (Trautmann, K).

— Berichtigungen, Erklärungen und Vermutungen zu Cynewulfs werken. In *Bonner Beiträge zur Anglistik* XXIII, p. 85 ff, 1907. (Trautmann, BEV).

— Der sogenannte Crist. In *Anglia* XVIII, p. 382 ff, 1896. (Trautmann, Anglia XVIII).

Tupper, Fr. Jr., Textual Criticism as a Pseudo-science. In *Publications of the Modern Language Association of America* XXV, p. 164 ff, 1910. (Tupper, PMLA XXV).

Voges, F., Der reflexive Dativ im Englischen. In *Anglia* VI, p. 317 ff, 1883. (Voges).

Wack, G., Artikel und Demonstrativpronomen in Andreas und Elene. In *Anglia* XV, p. 209 ff, 1893. (Wack).

Walde, A. and Pokorny, J., Vergleichendes Wörterbuch der indogermanischen Sprachen. I—III, Berlin—Leipzig, 1926—32. (Walde-Pokorny).

v. d. Warth, J. J., Metrisch-sprachliches und Textkritisches zu Cynewulfs Werken. Halle, 1908. (v. d. Warth).

WILLARD, R., Vercelli Homily VIII and the Christ. In *Publications of the Modern Language Association of America* XLII, p. 314 ff, 1927. (WILLARD).

WÜLKER, R., Die Bedeutung einer neuen Entdeckung für die angelsächsische Literaturgeschichte. In *Berichte über die Verhandlungen der königlich sächsischen Gesellschaft der Wissenschaften, Philol.-Hist. Classe*, XL, p. 209 ff, 1888.

WÜLKER, R., Geschichte der Englischen Literatur I, 2d ed. Leipzig—Wien, 1906.

ZIEGLER, H., Der Poetische Sprachgebrauch in den sogen. Cædmonschen Dichtungen. Münster, 1883. (ZIEGLER).

ZUPITZA, J., Zur Frage nach der Quelle von Cynewulfs Andreas. In *Zeitschrift für deutsches Altertum* XXX, p. 175 ff, 1886. (ZUPITZA, ZfdA XXX).

Corrigenda

. 39 middle of the page: KÖRTING (p. 51); read KÖRTING (p. 49).
. 193: Fata Apostolorum 91 b *freondu* read *freonda*.